Mini Mickey

THE POCKET-SIZED *unofficial* GUIDE®
TO Walt Disney World®

10TH EDITION

sunscreen
bandaids
✓ check-in
rain gear ?
food p. 116

luggage
ND ignite
Epcot - La Hacienda ?

OTHER UNOFFICIAL GUIDES

Mini Mickey

THE POCKET-SIZED *unofficial* GUIDE® TO Walt Disney World®*

10TH EDITION

BOB SEHLINGER,
RITCHEY HALPHEN, *and* LEN TESTA

*Walt Disney World is officially known as the
Walt Disney World Resort®.

keen
communications

For Beverly Brown Halphen (1936–2013) —R. H.

Please note that prices fluctuate in the course of time and that travel information changes under the impact of many factors that influence the travel industry. We therefore suggest that you write or call ahead for confirmation when making your travel plans. Every effort has been made to ensure the accuracy of information throughout this book, and the contents of this publication are believed to be correct at the time of printing. Nevertheless, the publishers cannot accept responsibility for errors or omissions, for changes in details given in this guide, or for the consequences of any reliance on the information provided by the same. Assessments of attractions and so forth are based upon the authors' own experiences; therefore, descriptions given in this guide necessarily contain an element of subjective opinion, which may not reflect the publisher's opinion or dictate a reader's own experience on another occasion. Readers are invited to write the publisher with ideas, comments, and suggestions for future editions.

Published by:
Keen Communications, LLC
PO Box 43673
Birmingham, AL 35243

Cover design by Scott McGrew

Text design by Vertigo Design and Annie Long

For information on our other products and services or to obtain technical support, please contact us from within the United States at 888-604-4537 or by fax at 205-326-1012.

Keen Communications, LLC, also publishes its books in a variety of electronic formats. Some content that appears in print may not be available electronically.

ISBN: 978-1-628-09008-6

Distributed by Publishers Group West

Manufactured in the United States of America

5 4 3 2 1

CONTENTS

PART ELEVEN   Disney's Animal Kingdom   206

PART TWELVE   Disney's Hollywood Studios   230

LIST *of* MAPS

SPECIAL THANKS

A BIG SALUTE TO OUR WHOLE *UNOFFICIAL* TEAM, who rendered a Herculean effort in what must have seemed like a fantasy version of Sartre's *No Exit* to the tune of "It's a Small World." We hope you all recover to tour another day.

Kudos to cartoonist Tami Knight; child psychologist Karen Turnbow, PhD; *Unofficial Guide* statistician Fred Hazleton; and a horde of contributors and friends too numerous to list here.

Much appreciation also to editorial and production manager Molly Merkle, text designer Annie Long, cartographers Steve Jones and Scott McGrew, and indexer Ann Cassar.

—*Bob, Ritchey, and Len*

ABOUT THE AUTHORS

BOB SEHLINGER, a Lowell Thomas Award–winning journalist, is the creator and producer of the *Unofficial Guides*. Three titles in the series—*The Unofficial Guide to Walt Disney World, The Unofficial Guide to Disneyland,* and *The Unofficial Guide to Las Vegas*—are the best-selling travel guidebooks in the world on their respective subjects. Bob is also the founder and co-owner of Keen Communications, which publishes the *Unofficial Guides* as well as outdoors and trade-nonfiction books under the Clerisy Press, Menasha Ridge Press, and Wilderness Press imprints.

RITCHEY HALPHEN is a project editor at Keen Communications. He started his publishing career as a copy editor at *Cooking Light* magazine, later serving as senior copy editor at *Southern Living* and copy chief at *Health*.

LEN TESTA is the coauthor of *The Unofficial Guide to Walt Disney World, The Unofficial Guide to Disneyland, The Unofficial Guide to Walt Disney World with Kids, The Unofficial Guide Color Companion to Walt Disney World,* and *The Unofficial Guide to Britain's Best Days Out: Theme Parks and Attractions.* A computer scientist, Len created both the *Unofficial Guides* touring plan software and the **touringplans.com** website.

Mini Mickey

THE POCKET-SIZED *unofficial* GUIDE®

TO Walt Disney World®

10TH EDITION

INTRODUCTION

◨ WHY *This* POCKET GUIDE?

THE OPTIMUM STAY AT WALT DISNEY WORLD is seven days, but many visitors don't have nearly that long to devote to all that this massive destination affords. Some folks are in town on business, with only a day or two available for Disney's enticements. Others are en route elsewhere, or they want to sample additional attractions in Orlando and Central Florida. For these visitors, efficient, time-effective touring is a must. They can't afford long waits in line for rides, shows, or meals. It's imperative that they determine as far in advance as possible what they really want to see.

This guide distills essential information from our comprehensive *Unofficial Guide to Walt Disney World* to help short-stay or last-minute visitors decide quickly how best to spend their limited hours. It aids these guests in answering questions vital to their enjoyment: "What are the rides and attractions that appeal to me most? Which additional rides and attractions would I like to experience if I have any time left? What am I willing to skip?"

DECLARATION OF INDEPENDENCE

THE AUTHORS AND RESEARCHERS OF THIS guide are totally independent of Walt Disney Co., Inc.; Disneyland, Inc.; Walt Disney World, Inc.; and all other members of the Disney corporate family. We represent and serve the consumer. The material in this guide originated with the authors and researchers and hasn't been reviewed or edited by the Walt Disney Co., Disneyland, or Walt Disney World. Ours is the first comprehensive *critical* appraisal of Walt Disney World. It aims to provide the information necessary to tour Walt Disney World with the greatest efficiency and economy.

WALT DISNEY WORLD:
An Overview

THERE'S NOTHING ON EARTH LIKE WALT DISNEY WORLD. Incredible in its scope, genius, beauty, and imagination, it's a joy and wonder for all ages. Disney attractions are a quantum leap beyond most man-made entertainment we know. We can't understand how anyone could visit Florida and bypass Walt Disney World.

WHAT WALT DISNEY WORLD ENCOMPASSES

WALT DISNEY WORLD COMPRISES 43 square miles, an area twice as large as Manhattan. Within this expanse lie the **Magic Kingdom, Epcot, Disney's Animal Kingdom,** and **Disney's Hollywood Studios** theme parks; 2 swimming theme parks; a sports complex; 5 golf courses; 36 hotels and a campground; more than 100 restaurants; 4 interconnected lakes; a shopping complex; 8 convention venues; a nature preserve; and a transportation system.

Walt Disney World has around 62,000 employees, or "cast members," making it the largest single-site employer in the United States. Keeping the costumes of those cast members clean requires the equivalent of 16,000 loads of laundry a day and the dry cleaning of 30,000 garments daily. (Mickey Mouse alone has 290 different sets of duds, ranging from a scuba wet suit to a tux; Minnie boasts more than 200 outfits.) Each year, Disney restaurants serve 10 million burgers, 6 million hot dogs, 75 million Cokes, 9 million pounds of French fries, and 150 tons of popcorn. In the state of Florida, only Miami and Jacksonville have bus systems larger than Disney World's. The Disney monorail trains have logged mileage equal to more than 30 round-trips to the moon.

THE MAJOR THEME PARKS
The Magic Kingdom

When people think of Walt Disney World, most think of the Magic Kingdom, opened in 1971. It consists of the adventures, rides, and shows featuring the Disney cartoon characters, and Cinderella Castle. It's only one element of Disney World, but it remains the heart.

The Magic Kingdom is divided into six "lands," five of which are arranged around a central hub. First you come to **Main Street, U.S.A.,** which connects the Magic Kingdom entrance with the hub. Clockwise around the hub are **Adventureland, Frontierland, Liberty Square, Fantasyland,** and **Tomorrowland.** An ambitious expansion of Fantasyland was begun in 2010 and largely completed in 2012, more than doubling its size at an estimated cost of more than

$600 million. Five hotels (**Bay Lake Tower; the Contemporary, Polynesian,** and **Grand Floridian Resorts;** and **The Villas at the Grand Floridian**) are connected to the park by monorail and boat; two other hotels, **Shades of Green** and **Wilderness Lodge & Villas,** are nearby but aren't served by the monorail.

Epcot

Opened in October 1982 as EPCOT Center, Epcot is twice as big as the Magic Kingdom and comparable in scope. It has two major areas: **Future World** consists of pavilions concerning human creativity and technological advancement; **World Showcase,** arranged around a 40-acre lagoon, presents the architectural, social, and cultural heritages of almost a dozen nations, each country represented by replicas of famous landmarks and settings familiar to world travelers.

The Epcot resort hotels—the **BoardWalk Inn & Villas, Caribbean Beach Resort, Dolphin, Swan,** and **Yacht & Beach Club Resorts and Beach Club Villas**—are within a 5- to 15-minute walk of the International Gateway, the World Showcase entrance to the theme park. The hotels are also linked to Epcot and Disney's Hollywood Studios by canal and walkway. Epcot is connected to the Magic Kingdom and its hotels by monorail.

Disney's Animal Kingdom

About five times the size of the Magic Kingdom, Disney's Animal Kingdom combines zoological exhibits with rides, shows, and live entertainment. The park is arranged in a hub-and-spoke configuration somewhat like the Magic Kingdom. A lush tropical rainforest serves as Main Street, funneling visitors to **Discovery Island,** the park's hub. Dominated by the park's central icon, the 14-story-tall, hand-carved **Tree of Life,** Discovery Island offers services, shopping, and dining. From there, guests can access the themed areas: **Africa, Asia, DinoLand U.S.A.,** and **Camp Minnie-Mickey.** Africa, the largest themed area, at 100 acres, features free-roaming herds in a re-creation of the Serengeti Plain. Camp Minnie-Mickey is likely to be the site of the park's next expansion phase, with construction taking place from late 2013 to around 2017.

Animal Kingdom has its own parking lot and is connected to other Walt Disney World destinations by the Disney bus system. Although no hotels lie within the park proper, the **All-Star Resorts, Animal Kingdom Lodge & Villas,** and **Coronado Springs Resort** are all nearby.

Disney's Hollywood Studios

Opened in 1989 as Disney-MGM Studios and a little larger than the Magic Kingdom, Disney's Hollywood Studios has two areas.

One area, occupying about 75% of the Studios, is a theme park focused on the motion picture, music, and television industries. Park highlights include a re-creation of Hollywood and Sunset Boulevards from Hollywood's Golden Age, four high-tech rides, several musical shows, and a movie stunt show.

The second area consists of soundstages, a backlot of streets and sets, and an outdoor theater for an auto stunt show. Public access to the soundstages is limited to a tour that takes visitors behind the scenes of Disney animation and moviemaking.

Disney's Hollywood Studios is connected to other Walt Disney World areas by highway and canal but not by monorail. You can park in the Studios' pay parking lot or commute by bus. Guests at Epcot resort hotels can reach the Studios by boat or on foot.

THE WATER PARKS

DISNEY WORLD HAS TWO WATER THEME PARKS: **Typhoon Lagoon** and **Blizzard Beach.** Typhoon Lagoon has a wave pool capable of producing 6-foot waves; Blizzard Beach features more slides. Typhoon Lagoon and Blizzard Beach have their own parking lots and can be reached by bus.

OTHER DISNEY WORLD VENUES
Downtown Disney (Disney Springs)

This shopping, dining, and entertainment complex currently encompasses **Downtown Disney Marketplace** on the east, **Downtown Disney West Side** on the west, and the area formerly known as **Pleasure Island** in the middle. The Marketplace contains the world's largest store that sells Disney-character merchandise, along with upscale specialty shops and several restaurants. The West Side combines nightlife, shopping, dining, and entertainment, including a permanent showplace for the extraordinary 70-person cast of **Cirque du Soleil La Nouba; DisneyQuest,** an interactive virtual-reality and electronic-games venue; and a 24-screen movie theater. Downtown Disney is accessible by bus from the Disney resorts.

For several years after the nighttime-entertainment venues at Pleasure Island were shuttered in 2008, The Big Mouse was stuck in a quandary regarding Downtown Disney's overall vision. After several false starts, Disney has embarked on an expansion with a Florida-waterfront-town theme. Called **Disney Springs,** it will take in the current three areas and add a fourth. Pleasure Island will become **Town Center** and be built out toward the parking lot. Adjacent to the waterfront will be **The Landing,** with shops, restaurants, docks, and a promenade. Construction began in April 2013 and will be completed in 2016.

Disney's BoardWalk

Near Epcot, the BoardWalk is an idealized replication of an East Coast 1930s waterfront resort. Open all day, the BoardWalk features upscale restaurants, shops and galleries, a brewpub, and an ESPN sports bar. In the evening, a nightclub with dueling pianos and a DJ dance club join the lineup. Both are for guests age 21 and up only. There's no admission fee for the BoardWalk, but the piano bar levies a cover charge at night. This area is anchored by the BoardWalk Inn and Villas, plus its adjacent convention center.

The BoardWalk is within walking distance of the Epcot resorts, Epcot's International Gateway, and Disney's Hollywood Studios. Boat transportation is available to and from Epcot and Disney's Hollywood Studios; buses serve other Disney World locations.

ESPN Wide World of Sports Complex

The 220-acre Wide World of Sports is a state-of-the-art competition and training facility consisting of a 9,500-seat ballpark, two field houses, and venues for baseball, softball, tennis, track and field, beach volleyball, and 27 other sports. The spring-training home of the Atlanta Braves, the complex also hosts a mind-boggling calendar of professional and amateur competitions. Walt Disney World guests not participating in events may pay admission to use the PlayStation Pavilion or watch any of the scheduled competitions.

HOW TO CONTACT
the AUTHORS

YOU CAN WRITE OR E-MAIL US at the following addresses:

Bob, Ritchey, and Len
Mini Mickey: The Pocket-Sized Unofficial Guide to
 Walt Disney World
P.O. Box 43673
Birmingham, AL 35243
unofficialguides@menasharidge.com

READER SURVEY

In the back of this guide is a questionnaire you can use to express opinions about your Walt Disney World visit. The questionnaire lets every member of your party, regardless of age, tell us what he or she thinks about attractions, hotels, restaurants, and more. Clip out the survey and mail it to the address above, or fill out the electronic version at **touringplans.com/walt-disney-world/survey**.

Walt Disney World

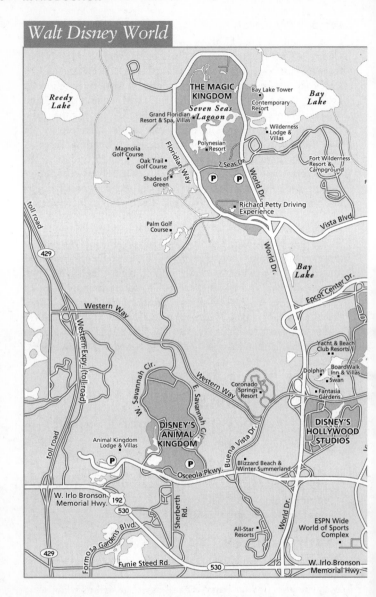

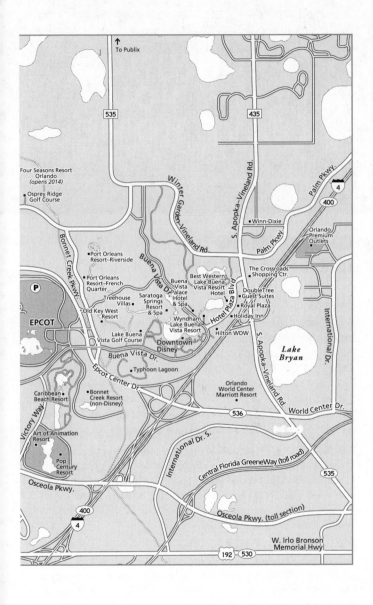

PART ONE

PLANNING *before* YOU LEAVE HOME

GATHERING INFORMATION

IN ADDITION TO THIS GUIDE, we recommend the following resources:

1. THE WALT DISNEY TRAVEL COMPANY FLORIDA VACATIONS BROCHURE AND DVD These cover Walt Disney World in its entirety, list rates for all Disney resort hotels and campgrounds, and describe Disney World package vacations. They're available from most travel agents, by calling the Walt Disney Travel Company at ☎ 407-828-8101 or 407-934-7639, or by visiting **disneyworld .com.** Be prepared to hold if you inquire by phone (ask the representative for the DVD vacation planner).

2. THE DISNEY CRUISE LINE BROCHURE AND DVD This brochure provides details on vacation packages that combine a cruise on the Disney Cruise Line with a stay at Disney World. Disney Cruise Line also offers a free DVD that tells all you need to know about Disney cruises and then some. To obtain a copy, call ☎ 800-951-3532 or order online at **disneycruise.com.**

3. TOURINGPLANS.COM Our website offers more than 140 different touring plans and updates on changes at Walt Disney World, along with photos and videos of Disney hotel rooms and complete menus for every dining venue in the World. Our most popular feature for site subscribers is **Lines,** a mobile app that provides continuous real-time updates on wait times at Walt Disney World and Disneyland, plus touring plans that you can update while you're in the parks. Lines is free to subscribers for the Apple iPhone and iPad at the iTunes Store (search for "TouringPlans"; requires iOS 4.3 or later) and for Android-based devices at the Google Play Store (requires Android 2.1 Eclair or later). Owners of BlackBerries, Windows Phones, and other Internet-capable phones can use the web-based version at **m.touringplans.com**.

4. ORLANDO MAGICARD If you're considering lodging, dining, or visiting other attractions outside of Walt Disney World, it's worth-while to obtain an Orlando Magicard, a Vacation Planner, and the *Orlando Official Vacation Guide* (all free) from the Orlando Official Visitor Center. The card can be conveniently downloaded from **orlandoinfo.com/magicard**. To order the accommodations guide, call ☎ 800-643-9492. For more information and materials, call ☎ 407-363-5872 or go to **visitorlando.com**. Phones are staffed during week-day business hours and 9 a.m.–3 p.m. EST weekends.

5. *HOTELCOUPONS.COM FLORIDA GUIDE* This is another good source of discounts on lodging, restaurants, and attractions. You can sign up at **hotelcoupons.com** to have a free monthly guide sent to you by e-mail, or you can view the guide online. To request a hard copy, call ☎ 800-222-3948 Monday–Friday, 8 a.m.–5 p.m. Eastern time. The guide is free, but you pay $3 for handling ($5 if shipped to Canada).

6. *KISSIMMEE VISITOR'S GUIDE* This full-color guide is one of the most complete available and is of particular interest to those who intend to book lodging outside of Disney World. It features ads for rental houses, time-shares, and condominiums, as well as a direc-tory of attractions, restaurants, and other useful info. To receive a copy, call ☎ 800-327-9159 or 407-944-2400, or view it online at **floridakiss.com**.

7. *GUIDEBOOK FOR GUESTS WITH DISABILITIES* Available at Guest Relations when entering the theme and water parks, at Disney resort front desks, and wheelchair-rental areas (listed in each theme park chapter). Printable PDF versions are available at **tinyurl.com /wdwguestswithdisabilities**.

DISNEY ONLINE: OFFICIAL AND OTHERWISE

AT WALT DISNEY WORLD'S OFFICIAL WEBSITE (**disney world.com**), you can make hotel, dining, and recreation reserva-tions; buy admission; and get park hours, attraction information, and much more. To use some of the site's features, you'll (1) need to register by providing your e-mail address and choosing a pass-word and (2) need to have reserved a room at a Disney-owned hotel or have in your possession a valid theme park ticket.

IMPORTANT WALT DISNEY WORLD ADDRESSES

Compliments, Complaints, and Suggestions
Walt Disney World Guest Communications
P. O. Box 10040
Lake Buena Vista, FL 32830-1000

Convention and Banquet Information
Walt Disney World Resort South
P.O. Box 10000
Lake Buena Vista, FL 32830-1000

Merchandise Mail Order (Guest Service Mail Order)
P.O. Box 10070
Lake Buena Vista, FL 32830-0070

Walt Disney World Central Reservations
P.O. Box 10100
Lake Buena Vista, FL 32830-0100

Walt Disney World Educational Programs
P.O. Box 10000
Lake Buena Vista, FL 32830-1000

Walt Disney World Info/Guest Letters/Letters to Mickey Mouse
P.O. Box 10040
Lake Buena Vista, FL 32830-0040

Walt Disney World Ticket Mail Order
P.O. Box 10140
Lake Buena Vista, FL 32830-0140

IMPORTANT WALT DISNEY WORLD PHONE NUMBERS

General Information	☎ 407-824-4321 or 407-824-2222
Accommodations/Reservations	☎ 407-934-7639
Convention Information	☎ 407-828-3200
Dining Advance Reservations	☎ 407-939-3463
Disabled Guests Special Requests	☎ 407-939-7807
Lost and Found	☎ 407-824-4245
Merchandise Guest Services	☎ 407-363-6200
Walt Disney World Travel Company	☎ 407-939-6244

GETTING STARTED First, click "My Disney Experience" in the upper-right corner of the home page. The site will then display a list of your existing hotel and dining reservations. Click the "My Family" link and enter the names and ages of everyone traveling with you. You'll need this information when you make your dining and Fastpass+ attraction reservations.

From the "My Disney Experience" page, click "My Itinerary" in the lower-right corner of the page (use your browser's "find" feature to locate it, if needed). If you haven't already created an account, you'll be asked to do that now; otherwise, a calendar will appear. If you've got a Disney-hotel reservation, the calendar should display those dates of travel. If not, you'll need to select your travel dates using the calendar.

For each day of your trip, the website will display operating hours for the theme and water parks. Select the theme park you'll be visiting on a particular day; if you're visiting more than one, select the one at which you want to make reservations now.

MAKING FASTPASS+ RESERVATIONS A list of the park's attractions will appear as a series of rows going down the page. One attraction per row is listed. In each row is a description of the attraction, including operating hours, height requirements, and whether it supports Fastpass+ (see page 26). You can adjust the list of attractions shown by using the filtering criteria at the top of the page.

Clicking an attraction's name brings up another page dedicated to that attraction, including available Fastpass+ ride times for a given day. If all the attraction's Fastpass+ opportunities have been exhausted, you'll get a message informing you so. If Fastpass+ times are still available, select one and indicate which members of your group will be riding. You'll need to repeat these steps for every attraction for which you want Fastpass reservations, for every day you're in the theme parks.

Depending on when you arrive and what you want to see, you may not need Fastpasses for most attractions. If you're unsure of the attractions or times of day for which you should use Fastpass+, our touring plan software can make recommendations that will minimize your overall time in line.

MAKING DINING RESERVATIONS From the "My Itinerary" page, click the "Book Dining" link. (You may have to reenter your travel dates.) A list of every Disney World eatery will be displayed. Use the filtering criteria at the top of the page to narrow the list.

Once you've settled on a restaurant, click the restaurant's name to check availability for your dining time and number of people. If space is available and you want to make a reservation, you'll need to indicate which members of your party will be joining you. If you want to make other dining reservations, you'll need to repeat this process for every reservation.

Our Recommended Websites

Searching online for Disney information is like navigating an immense maze for a very small piece of cheese: There's a lot of stuff out there, but you may find a lot of dead-ends before getting what you want. Our picks follow.

BEST Q&A SITE Who knew? Walt Disney World has a **Mom's Panel** all chosen from among 10,000-plus applicants. The panelists have a website, **disneyworldmoms.com,** where they offer tips and discuss how to plan a Disney World vacation. Several moms have specialized experience in areas such as the Disney Cruise Line, runDisney, and traveling with sports groups; some speak Spanish, too. The parents are unpaid and are free to speak their minds.

BEST GENERAL UNOFFICIAL WALT DISNEY WORLD WEBSITE
Besides touringplans.com, Deb Wills's **allears.net** is the first website we recommend to friends who want to make a trip to Disney World. Updated several times a week, the site includes breaking news, tons of photos, Disney restaurant menus, resort and ticket information, tips for guests with special needs, and more. We also check **wdw magic.com** for news and happenings around Walt Disney World.

BEST MONEY-SAVING SITE Mary Waring's **MouseSavers** (**mouse savers.com**) keeps an updated list of discounts and reservation codes for use at Disney resorts. Codes are separated into categories such as "For the general public" and "For residents of certain states." Anyone who calls or books online can use a current code and get the discounted rate. Savings can be considerable—up to 40% in many cases. MouseSavers also has discount codes for rental cars and non-Disney hotels in the area, along with a calendar showing when Disney sales typically launch.

BEST WALT DISNEY WORLD PREVIEW SITE If you want to see what a particular attraction is like, visit **YouTube** (**youtube.com**). Enter the name of the desired attraction in the search bar at the top of the page, and multiple videos should come up. Even the videos of indoor ("dark") rides generally provide a good sense of what the attraction is about. YouTube is great for gauging whether your child will find a particular attraction too scary or intimidating.

SOCIAL MEDIA Facebook, Twitter, and Instagram are popular places for Disney fans to gather online and share comments, tips, and photos. Following fellow Disneyphiles as they share their in-park experiences can make you feel like you're there, even as you're stuck in a cubicle at work.

BEST INTERNET RADIO STATION MouseWorld Radio (**mouseworld radio.com**) plays everything from attraction themes and hotel background music to sound clips from old TV ads for Disney resorts. What makes MouseWorld Radio special is that the tracks match what the Disney parks are playing at the time of day you're listening. Also try the **Walt Disney World Today Podcast,** cohosted by the *Unofficial Guide*'s Len Testa, on iTunes and at **wdwtoday.com.**

BEST THEME-PARK-INSIDER SITE It's been said that people who eat sausage should never watch it being made. If you have the stomach to learn how theme parks get built, take a look around **jimhillmedia.com.** Jim's got insider accounts of the politics, frantic project management, and pipe dreams that somehow combine into the attractions that Disney creates.

BEST DISNEY DISCUSSION BOARDS There are tons of these; among the most active are **disboards.com, forums.wdwmagic.com, micechat.com,** and for Brits, **thedibb.co.uk** (*DIBB* stands for "Disney Information Bulletin Board").

BEST SITE FOR GUESTS WITH FOOD ALLERGIES At **allergyeats .com/disney,** you put in your allergies and your park, and it shows you where and what you can eat.

BEST SITES FOR TRAFFIC, ROADWORK, CONSTRUCTION, AND SAFETY INFORMATION Visit **expresswayauthority.com** for the latest information on roadwork in the Orlando and Orange County areas. The site also contains detailed maps, directions, and toll-rate information for the most popular tourist destinations. Check **flhsmv .gov/fhp/cps** to learn about state child-restraint requirements. Finally, we like **mapquest.com** for driving directions.

WHEN *to* GO *to* WALT DISNEY WORLD

SELECTING THE TIME OF YEAR FOR YOUR VISIT

WALT DISNEY WORLD IS BUSIEST Christmas Day through the first few days of January. Next busiest is the spring-break period from mid-March through the week of Easter, then Thanksgiving week. Following those are the first few weeks of June, when summer vacation starts, and the week of Presidents Day.

The least busy time is from Labor Day in September through the beginning of October. Next slowest are the weeks in mid-January after the Martin Luther King Jr. holiday weekend up to Presidents Day in February (except when the Walk Disney World Marathon runs after MLK Day). The weeks after Thanksgiving and before Christmas are less crowded than average, as is mid-April–mid-May, after spring break and before Memorial Day.

Late February, March, and early April are dicey. Crowds ebb and flow according to spring-break schedules and the timing of Presidents Day weekend. Besides being asphalt-melting hot, July brings throngs of South American tourists on their winter holiday.

Though crowds have grown somewhat during September and October as a result of promotions aimed at locals and the international market, these months continue to be good for week-day touring at the Magic Kingdom, Disney's Hollywood Studios, and Disney's Animal Kingdom, and for weekend visits to Epcot.

THE PROS AND CONS OF OFF-SEASON TOURING Though we strongly recommend going to Disney World in the fall, winter, or spring, there are a few trade-offs. The parks often close early during the off-season, either because of low crowds or special events such as the Halloween and Christmas parties at the Magic Kingdom. This drastically reduces touring hours. Even when crowds are small, it's difficult to see big parks such as the Magic Kingdom between 9 a.m. and 7 p.m. Early closing also usually means no evening parades or fireworks. And because these are slow times, some rides and attractions may be closed. Finally, Central Florida temperatures fluctuate wildly during late fall, winter, and early spring; daytime highs in the 40s and 50s aren't uncommon.

Given the choice, however, smaller crowds, bargain prices, and stress-free touring are worth risking cold weather or closed attractions. Touring in fall and other "off" periods is so much easier that our research team, at the risk of being blasphemous, advises taking children out of school for a Disney World visit.

CROWD CONDITIONS AND THE BEST AND WORST PARKS TO VISIT FOR EACH DAY OF THE YEAR We receive thousands of e-mails and letters inquiring about crowd conditions on specific dates throughout the year. Readers also want to know which park is best to visit on each day of their stay. To make things easier for you (and us!), we provide at **touringplans.com** a calendar covering the next year (click "Crowd Calendar" on the home page). For each date, we offer a crowd-level index based on a scale of 1–10, with 1 being least crowded and 10 being most crowded. Our calendar takes into account all holidays, special events, and more The same calendar lists the best and worst park(s) to visit in terms of crowd conditions on any given day.

Collecting data for the Crowd Calendar requires us to have researchers in the parks year-round. To keep the calendar current on a daily basis, we charge a modest subscription fee, which also provides access to additional touring plans and other features. Owners of the current edition of *The Unofficial Guide to Walt Disney World,* as well as owners of the previous year's "Big Book," are eligible for a substantial discount on the subscription.

EXTRA MAGIC HOURS

EXTRA MAGIC HOURS (EMHs) are a perk for families staying at a Walt Disney World resort, including the Swan, Dolphin, and Shades of Green, and the Hilton in the Downtown Disney Resort Area. On selected days of the week, Disney resort guests will be able to enter a Disney theme park 1 hour earlier or stay in a selected theme park about 2 hours later than the official park-operating hours. Theme park visitors not staying at a Disney resort may stay in the park for Extra Magic Hour evenings, but they can't experience any rides, attractions, or shows. In other words, they can shop and eat. The swimming theme parks, Typhoon Lagoon and Blizzard Beach, rarely offer EMHs. If they do, it's usually during the summer.

WHAT'S REQUIRED? A valid admission ticket or MagicBand RFID wristband is required to enter the park, and you must show your Disney resort ID or have your MagicBand scanned when entering. For evening EMHs, you may be asked to show your Disney resort ID or MagicBand to experience rides or attractions.

WHEN ARE EMHs OFFERED? Check the Crowd Calendar at **touringplans.com** for the dates of your visit, check the parks calendar at **disneyworld.com,** or call Disney at ☎ 407-824-4321 or 407-939-6244 (press 0 for a live representative).

Morning Extra Magic Hours (a.k.a. Early Entry)

Morning Extra Magic Hours are offered at all four theme parks throughout the year, and rarely (during summer) at Blizzard Beach and Typhoon Lagoon water parks. Several days of the week, Disney resort guests are invited to enter a designated theme park 1 hour before the general public. During this hour, guests can enjoy selected attractions opened early just for them.

Morning EMHs strongly affect attendance at Disney's Hollywood Studios and Epcot, especially during busier times of the year. Magic Kingdom crowds are about average when it has morning EMHs (usually Thursday). Because Disney's Animal Kingdom typically has two morning EMHs but none at night, crowds are spread out, resulting in lower-than-average waits on both days.

During holiday periods and summer, when Disney hotels are full, getting in early makes a tremendous difference in crowds at the designated park. The EMH program funnels so many people into that park that it fills by about 10 a.m. and is practically gridlocked by noon.

Evening Extra Magic Hours

The evening EMH program lets Disney resort guests enjoy a different theme park on specified nights for about 2 hours after it closes to the general public. Guests pay no additional charge to participate but must show their resort IDs at each ride or attraction they wish to experience. You can also show up at the turnstiles at any point after evening Extra Magic Hours have started. Note that if you've been in another park that day, you'll need the Park Hopper feature on your admission ticket to enter (see Part Two).

Evening sessions are usually more crowded at the Magic Kingdom and the Studios than at Epcot. Those evening EMH crowds can be just as large as those throughout the day. During summer, when the Magic Kingdom's evening EMH session runs until 1 a.m., lines at headliner attractions can still be long at midnight.

SUMMER AND HOLIDAYS

IF YOU VISIT ON A NONHOLIDAY MIDSUMMER DAY, arrive at the turnstile 30–40 minutes before the stated opening on a non-morning-EMH day. If you visit during a major holiday period, arrive 1 hour before. To save time in the morning, buy your admission in advance. Also, consider bringing your own stroller or wheelchair instead of renting one of Disney's.

Hit your favorite rides early using one of our touring plans, then go back to your hotel for lunch, a swim, and perhaps a nap. If you're interested in the special parades and shows, return to the park in late afternoon or early evening. Assume that unless you use Fastpass+, early morning will be the only time you can experience the attractions without long waits. Finally, don't wait until the last minute in the evening to leave the park—the exodus at closing is truly mind-boggling. Above all, bring your sense of humor, and pay attention to your group's morale.

PART TWO

MAKING *the* MOST *of* YOUR TIME *and* MONEY

█▌ ALLOCATING MONEY

HOW MUCH YOU SPEND AT DISNEY WORLD depends on how long you stay. But even if you visit for only an afternoon, be prepared to drop a bundle. In Part Three we'll show you how to save money on lodging, and in Part Eight you'll find tips for economizing on meals. This section will give you some sense of what you can expect to pay for admission, as well as which admission options will best meet your needs.

WALT DISNEY WORLD ADMISSION OPTIONS

DISNEY OFFERS A NUMBER OF different admission options in order to accommodate various vacation needs. These range from the humble **1-Day Base Ticket,** good for a single day's entry into one Disney theme park, to the blinged-out **Premium Annual Pass,** good for 365 days of admission into every Disney theme or water park, plus DisneyQuest.

The sheer number of ticket options available makes it difficult and, yes, daunting to sort out which option represents the least expensive way to see and do everything you want. Finding the optimum admission, or combination of admissions, however, could save you a nice chunk of change.

THIS IS A JOB FOR . . . A COMPUTER!

IT'S COMPLICATED ENOUGH that we wrote a computer program to solve it. Visit **touringplans.com** and try our **Park Ticket Calculator,** on the home page. It aggregates ticket prices from Disney and a number of online ticket vendors. Just answer a few simple questions about the size of your party and the theme parks you intend to visit—the calculator will identify your four least expensive ticket options and will show you how much money you'll save.

MAGIC YOUR WAY

WALT DISNEY WORLD OFFERS AN ARRAY of theme park ticket options, grouped into a program called Magic Your Way. The simplest option—visiting one theme park for one day—is called a **1-Day Base Ticket.** Other features, such as the ability to visit more than one park per day ("park-hopping"), or the inclusion of admission to Disney's minor venues (Typhoon Lagoon, Blizzard Beach, DisneyQuest, mini-golf, and the like), are available as individual add-ons to the Base Ticket.

In 2013 Disney not only raised ticket prices across the board but also introduced separate pricing for a single day's admission to the Magic Kingdom versus the other theme parks. An adult 1-Day Base Ticket for the Magic Kingdom costs $101.18, while one day's admission to any other theme park is $95.85 (including tax)—not exactly a good value if you have only a day to spend in the World. Blessedly, multiday pricing is still uniform across the parks, and the more days of admission you buy, the lower the cost per day. For example, if you buy an adult 4-Day Base Ticket for $297.14 (taxes included), each day will cost $74.28, regardless of which theme park you want to see. Tickets can be purchased from 1 up to 10 days and admit you to exactly one theme park per day; you may reenter your chosen park as many times as you like on that day.

Disney says its tickets expire within 14 days of the first day of use. In practice, they really mean 13 days after the first day of use. If, say, you purchase a 4-Day Base Ticket on June 1 and use it that day for admission to the Magic Kingdom, you'll be able to visit a single Disney theme park on any of your three remaining days from June 2 through June 14. After that, the ticket expires and any unused days will be lost. Through another add-on, however, you can avoid the 14-day expiration (see facing page).

BASE TICKET ADD-ON OPTIONS

THREE ADD-ON OPTIONS ARE OFFERED with the Base Ticket, each at an additional cost:

PARK HOPPER Adding this feature to your ticket allows you to visit more than one theme park per day. The cost is about $36–$42 (including tax) on top of the price of adult and child 1-Day Base Tickets and $62.84 added to the price of adult and child multiday tickets—exorbitant for one or two days, but more affordable the longer your stay. As an add-on to a 7-Day Base Ticket, the flat fee

MAGIC YOUR WAY 2013–14 TICKET PRICES

TICKET TYPE						
7-Day	**6-Day**	**5-Day**	**4-Day**	**3-Day**	**2-Day**	**1-Day**
Base Ticket Adults						
$329 $47/day	$318 $53/day	$308 $62/day	$297 $74/day	$279 $93/day	$196 $98/day	$96/$101* —
Base Ticket Children (ages 3–9)						
$309 $44/day	$298 $50/day	$288 $56/day	$277 $69/day	$260 $87/day	$196 $98/day	$89/$95* —
Park Hopper Add-On						
$63 $9/day	$63 $10/day	$63 $13/day	$63 $16/day	$63 $21/day	$63 $31/day	$131/$137** —
Water Park Fun and More Add-On						
$89 for 7 visits $13/visit	$89 for 6 visits $15/visit	$89 for 5 visits $18/visit	$89 for 4 visits $22/visit	$89 for 3 visits $30/visit	$89 for 2 visits $45/visit	$152/$159** for 2 visits $76–$80/visit
No Expiration Add-On						
$234	$202	$154	$101	$48	$37	—

* 1-Day Base Tickets cost more for the Magic Kingdom than for the other three parks.
** 1-Day Park Hopper and WPFAM cost more for guests age 10 and up. Prices shown include the cost of a 1-Day Base Ticket.
All prices include tax and are rounded to the nearest dollar.

would work out to $8.98 per day for park-hopping privileges. If you want to visit the Magic Kingdom in the morning and eat at Epcot in the evening, this is the feature to request.

NO EXPIRATION Adding this option to your ticket means that unused admissions to the major theme parks and the swimming parks, as well as other minor venues, never expire. If you added this option to a 10-Day Base Ticket and used only 4 days this year, the remaining 6 days could be used for admission at any date in the future. No Expiration ranges from $37.28 with tax for a 2-Day Base Ticket to $346.13 for a 10-Day Base Ticket. Unavailable for single-day tickets, this option must be purchased in person before the ticket expires—you can't buy it online.

WATER PARK FUN AND MORE (WPFAM) This option gives you a single admission to one of Disney's water parks (Blizzard Beach and Typhoon Lagoon), DisneyQuest, Oak Trail Golf Course, Fantasia Gardens or Winter Summerland mini-golf, or the ESPN Wide World of Sports Complex. The cost is a flat $62.84 (including tax). Except for the single-day WPFAM ticket, which gives you two admissions, the number of admissions equals the number of days on your ticket. If you buy an 8-Day Base Ticket, for example, and add the WPFAM option, you get eight WPFAM admissions. What you *can't* do is, say, buy a 10-Day Base Ticket with only three WPFAM admissions or a 3-Day Base Ticket with four WPFAM admissions. You can, however, skip WPFAM entirely and buy an individual admission to any of these minor parks—that's almost always the best deal if you want to visit only one of the venues on the previous page.

Annual Passes

An **Annual Pass** provides unlimited use of the major theme parks for one year; a **Premium Annual Pass** also provides unlimited use of the minor parks. Annual Pass holders also get perks, including free parking and seasonal offers such as room-rate discounts at Disney resorts. The Annual Pass is not valid for special events, such as admission to Mickey's Very Merry Christmas Party. Tax included, Annual Passes run $648.59 for both adults and kids age 3 and up. A Premium Annual Pass, at $776.39 for adults and kids age 3 and up, provides unlimited admission to Blizzard Beach, Typhoon Lagoon, DisneyQuest, and Oak Trail Golf Course, in addition to the four major theme parks, plus minigolf discounts and 30 minutes of game access at ESPN Wide World of Sports' PlayStation Pavilion (when the pavilion is open).

HOW TO GET THE MOST FROM MAGIC YOUR WAY

FIRST, HAVE A REALISTIC IDEA of what you want out of your vacation. Don't waste money on options you're unlikely to use. A 7-Day Base Ticket plus Water Park Fun and More, for instance, might seem delightful in theory, but actually trying to visit all those destinations in a week in July could end up feeling more like Navy SEAL training.

Next, think carefully about paying for No Expiration. An inside source reports that fewer than 1 in 10 admission tickets with rollover days are ever reused at a Disney theme park. The rest are misplaced, discarded, or forgotten. Unless you're absolutely certain you'll be returning to Walt Disney World within the next year or two and you've identified a safe place to keep those unused tickets, we don't think the additional cost is worth the risk.

WHERE TO PURCHASE MAGIC YOUR WAY TICKETS

YOU CAN BUY YOUR ADMISSION PASSES on arrival at Walt Disney World or purchase them in advance. Admission passes are available at Walt Disney World resorts and theme parks. Passes are also available at some non-Disney hotels and certain Walt Disney World–area grocery stores, and from independent ticket brokers.

Offers of free or heavily discounted tickets abound, but there's nearly always a catch: You have to sit through a high-pressure time-share sales pitch, or the seller is offering partially used passes that may or may not be expired. At worst, the tickets could be stolen or could have been purchased fraudulently.

Magic Your Way tickets are available at Disney Stores and at **disneyworld.com** for the same prices listed in the chart on page 19.

unofficial **TIP**
Never buy tickets from an unauthorized reseller—chances are good they'll be worthless if you try to use them. Likewise, don't buy tickets off eBay or Craigslist.

If you're trying to keep costs to an absolute minimum, consider an online ticket wholesaler, such as **mapleleaftickets.com, theofficialticketcenter.com,** or **undercovertourist.com,** especially for trips with five or more days in the theme parks. All tickets sold are brand-new, and the savings can range from $2 to more than $65, depending on the ticket and options you choose.

The Official Ticket Center, Maple Leaf Tickets, and Undercover Tourist offer discounts on tickets for almost all Central Florida attractions, including Disney World, Universal Orlando, SeaWorld, and Cirque du Soleil. Discounts for the major theme parks are about 6–8.5%. Tickets for other attractions are more deeply discounted.

Finally, if all this is too confusing, our website will help you navigate all of the choices and find you the least-expensive ticket options for your vacation. Visit **touringplans.com** for more details.

For Additional Information on Passes

If you have a question or concern regarding admissions that can be addressed only by talking to a living, breathing human being, call **Disney Ticket Inquiries** at ☎ 407-566-4985, or e-mail **ticket.inquiries@disneyworld.com**. If you need current prices or routine information, you're better off calling ☎ 407-824-4321 for recorded admission details, or visiting **disneyworld.com**.

Special Passes

Walt Disney World offers a number of special and situational passes that are not known to the general public and are not sold at any Disney World ticket booth. The best information we've found on these passes is available at **tinyurl.com/wdwdiscounttix**.

ALLOCATING TIME

WHICH PARK TO SEE FIRST?

THIS QUESTION IS LESS ACADEMIC than it appears, especially if there are children or teenagers in your party. Children who see the Magic Kingdom first expect more of the same type of entertainment at the other parks. At Epcot, they're often disappointed by the educational orientation and more serious tone (many adults react the same way). Disney's Hollywood Studios offers some pretty wild action, but the general presentation is educational and more adult. Though most children enjoy zoos, animals can't be programmed to entertain. Thus, children may not find Disney's Animal Kingdom as exciting as the Magic Kingdom or Disney's Hollywood Studios.

First-time visitors should see Epcot first; you'll be able to enjoy it fully without having been preconditioned to think of Disney entertainment as solely fantasy or adventure.

See Disney's Animal Kingdom second. Like Epcot, it's educational, but its live animals provide a change of pace.

Next, see Disney's Hollywood Studios, which helps all ages make a fluid transition from the educational Epcot and Animal Kingdom to the fanciful Magic Kingdom. Also, because Disney's Hollywood Studios is smaller, you won't walk as much or stay as long. Save the Magic Kingdom for last.

OPERATING HOURS

THE DISNEY WORLD WEBSITE publishes preliminary park hours 180 days in advance, but schedule adjustments can happen at any time, including the day of your visit. Check **disneyworld.com** or call ☎ 407-824-4321 for exact hours before you arrive. Off-season, parks may be open as few as 8 hours (9 a.m.–5 p.m.). At busy times (particularly holidays), they may operate 8 a.m.–2 a.m.

Official Opening vs. Real Opening

Operating hours you're quoted when you call are "official hours." Sometimes, the parks actually open earlier. If the official hours are 9 a.m.–9 p.m., for example, Main Street in the Magic Kingdom might open at 8:30 a.m. and the remainder of the park will open at 9 a.m.

Disney surveys local hotel reservations, estimates how many visitors to expect on a given day, and opens the theme parks early to avoid bottlenecks at parking facilities and ticket windows and to absorb crowds as they arrive.

Rides and attractions shut down at approximately the official closing time. Main Street, U.S.A. in the Magic Kingdom remains open 30 minutes to an hour after the rest of the park has closed.

THE CARDINAL RULES
FOR SUCCESSFUL TOURING

EVEN THE MOST EFFICIENT TOURING PLAN won't allow you to cover two or more major theme parks in one day. Plan to allocate at least an entire day to each park. (An exception to this rule is when the parks close at different times, allowing you to tour one park until closing and then proceed to another.)

One-Day Touring

A comprehensive one-day tour of the Magic Kingdom, Disney's Animal Kingdom, Epcot, or Disney's Hollywood Studios is possible, but it requires knowledge of the park, good planning, and plenty of energy and endurance. It doesn't leave much time for sit-down meals, prolonged browsing in shops, or lengthy breaks. One-day touring can be fun and rewarding, but allocating two days per park, especially for the Magic Kingdom and Epcot, is always preferable.

Successful touring of the Magic Kingdom, Animal Kingdom, Epcot, or Disney's Hollywood Studios hinges on *three rules:*

1. Determine in Advance What You Really Want to See

To help you set your touring priorities, we describe the theme parks and every attraction in detail. In each description, we include the authors' evaluation of the attraction and the opinions of Walt Disney World guests expressed as star ratings. Five stars is the best possible rating.

*un*official **TIP**
If your schedule allows only one day of touring, concentrate on one park and save the rest for another visit.

Finally, because attractions range from midway-type rides and horse-drawn trolleys to colossal, high-tech extravaganzas, we've developed a hierarchy of categories to pinpoint an attraction's magnitude:

SUPER-HEADLINERS The best attractions that the theme park has to offer. Mind-boggling in size, scope, and imagination, they represent the cutting edge of modern attraction technology and design.

HEADLINERS Full-blown multimillion-dollar themed adventures and theater presentations. They are modern in technology and design and employ a full range of special effects.

MAJOR ATTRACTIONS Themed adventures on a more modest scale but which incorporate state-of-the-art technologies, or larger-scale attractions of older design.

MINOR ATTRACTIONS Midway-type rides, small "dark" rides (cars on a track, zigzagging through the dark), small theater presentations, transportation rides, and walk-through attractions.

DIVERSIONS Exhibits, both passive and interactive, such as playgrounds, video arcades, and street theater.

2. Arrive Early! Arrive Early! Arrive Early!

Have breakfast before you arrive so you won't waste prime touring time sitting in a restaurant. The earlier a park opens, the greater your potential advantage. This is because most vacationers won't make the sacrifice to rise early and get to a theme park before it opens. Fewer people are willing to be on hand for an 8 a.m. opening than for a 9 a.m. opening. On those rare occasions when a park opens at 10 a.m., almost everyone arrives at the same time, so it's almost impossible to get a jump on the crowd. If you are visiting during midsummer, arrive at the turnstile 30–40 minutes before official opening time. During holiday periods, get to the parks 45–60 minutes before official opening.

3. Avoid Bottlenecks

We provide touring plans for the Magic Kingdom, Disney's Animal Kingdom, Epcot, and Disney's Hollywood Studios to help you avoid bottlenecks. In addition, we provide detailed information on all rides and performances, enabling you to estimate how long you may have to wait in line and allowing you to compare rides for their capacity to accommodate large crowds. Touring plans for the Magic Kingdom begin on page 162; Epcot, on page 201; Disney's Animal Kingdom, on page 228; and Disney's Hollywood Studios, on page 252.

TOURING PLANS EXPLAINED

OUR TOURING PLANS ARE STEP-BY-STEP guides for seeing as much as possible with a minimum of standing in line. They're designed to help you avoid crowds and bottlenecks on days of moderate-to-heavy attendance. On days of lighter attendance (see "Selecting the Time of Year for Your Visit," page 13), the plans will still save time but won't be as critical to successful touring.

What You Can Expect from the Touring Plans

Though we present one-day touring plans for each of the theme parks, you should understand that the Magic Kingdom and Epcot have far more attractions than you can reasonably see in one day, even if you never wait in line. If you must cram your visit into a single day, the one-day touring plans will enable you to see as much as is humanly possible. Under certain circumstances, you may not complete the plan, and you definitely won't be able to see everything. For the Magic Kingdom and Epcot, the most comprehensive, efficient, and relaxing touring plans are the two-day plans. Although Disney's Hollywood Studios has grown considerably since its 1989 debut, you should have no problem seeing everything in one day. Likewise, Disney's Animal Kingdom is a one-day outing.

Customize Your Touring Plans

The attractions included in our touring plans are the most popular as determined by almost 50,000 reader surveys. Even so, your favorite attractions may be different. In that case, you can go create personalized versions at **touringplans.com.** Tell the software the date, time, and park you've chosen to visit, along with the attractions you want to see. The plan will tell you, for your specific travel date and time, the exact order in which to visit the attractions to minimize your waits in line. Our Lines app also supports "switching off" (see page 79) on thrill rides. Besides attractions, you can schedule meals, breaks, character greetings, and more. Plus, Lines can handle any Fastpass+ reservations you've already got and tell you which attractions would benefit most from your using them.

Alternatively, some changes are simple enough to make on your own. If a plan calls for an attraction you're not interested in, simply skip it. You can also substitute similar attractions in the same area of the park. If a plan calls for, say, riding Dumbo and you'd rather not, but you would enjoy the Mad Tea Party (which is not on the plan), then go ahead and substitute that for Dumbo. As long as the substitution is a similar attraction and is pretty close by the attraction called for in the touring plan, you won't compromise the plan's overall effectiveness.

Variables That Affect the Success of the Touring Plans

How quickly you move from one ride to another; when and how many refreshment and restroom breaks you take; when, where, and how you eat meals; and your ability to find your way around will all have an impact on the success of the plans. Smaller groups almost always move faster than larger groups, and parties of adults generally can cover more ground than families with young children. Switching off, among other things, inhibits families with little ones from moving expeditiously among attractions. Plus, some children simply cannot conform to the "early to rise" conditions of the touring plans.

If your kids collect character autographs, you need to anticipate these interruptions by including character greetings when creating your online touring plans, or else negotiate some understanding with your children about when you'll collect autographs. Note that queues for autographs, especially in the Magic Kingdom and Disney's Animal Kingdom, are sometimes as long as the queues for major attractions. The only time-efficient ways to collect autographs are to use Fastpass+ where available (such as for Mickey Mouse and the Disney princesses at the Town Square Theater) or to line up at the character-greeting areas first thing in the morning. Early morning is also the best

unofficial **TIP**
Meeting characters, posing for photos, and collecting autographs can burn hours of touring time.

time to experience popular attractions, so you may have some tough choices to make.

While we realize that following the touring plans isn't always easy, we still recommend continuous, expeditious touring until around noon. After that, breaks and diversions won't affect the plans significantly. If unforeseen events arise, skip a step on the plan for every 20 minutes you're delayed. If you're following a plan in our Lines app, just press "Optimize" when you're ready to start touring again. Or simply ditch the plan and organize the remainder of your day according to the standby wait times in Lines.

FASTPASS AND FASTPASS+

DISNEY INTRODUCED THIS RIDE-RESERVATION SYSTEM in 1999 as a way to moderate high wait times at headliner attractions. A new version of the system, called **Fastpass+,** was in beta testing in 2013 and will eventually replace the old system entirely. Fastpass and Fastpass+ are available free to all park guests, even if you're not staying at a Disney resort.

LIVING with the LAND

FASTPASS®
FASTPASS®
Return Anytime Between

2:15 PM
AND
3:15 PM
SAT APR 28 2012

Not able to
accommodate
late arrivals.

Another FASTPASS® ticket
will be available
after 2:15pm

Here's how the original system works: Your park map and signage at attractions tell you which attractions are included. Participating attractions have a regular line and a Fastpass line. A sign at the entrance tells how long the wait is in the regular line. If you don't mind the wait, hop in line. If it seems too long, insert your admission ticket into a Fastpass machine; it'll give you an appointment time to return and ride later in the day. When you return at the designated time, enter the Fastpass line and proceed with minimal waiting to the attraction's preshow or boarding area.

Fastpass doesn't eliminate the need to arrive early at a theme park. Because each park offers a limited number of Fastpass attractions, you still need an early start to avoid long lines at non-Fastpass attractions. Plus, there's a limited supply of Fastpasses available for each attraction on any day. If you don't arrive at a given theme park until midafternoon, you might find that all Fastpasses are gone. When it's available, though, it's great for those who like to sleep late or who choose an afternoon or evening at the parks on their arrival day. It also allows you to postpone wet rides, such as Kali River Rapids at Disney's Animal Kingdom or Splash Mountain at the Magic Kingdom, until a warmer time of day.

UNDERSTANDING THE FASTPASS SYSTEM When you insert your admission pass into a Fastpass machine, it spits out a small slip of paper, about two-thirds the size of a credit card (see previous page for an example). Printed on the paper is the name of the attraction and a specific 1-hour time window—for example, 2:15–3:15 p.m.—during which you can return to enjoy the ride. The interval before your return window can be as short as 30 minutes or as long as 3–7 hours, depending on park attendance and the attraction's popularity and hourly capacity. Generally, the earlier in the day you obtain a Fastpass, the shorter the interval. You can obtain a Fastpass anytime after a park opens, but the Fastpass return lines don't begin operating until 35–90 minutes after opening.

When you report back to the attraction during your 1-hour window, you'll enter a line marked FASTPASS RETURN that will route you more or less directly to the boarding or preshow area. Each person in your party must have his or her own Fastpass and be ready to show it to the Disney cast member at the entrance of the Fastpass return line. Before you enter the boarding area or theater, another cast member will collect your Fastpass.

Fastpass Attractions at WDW

MAGIC KINGDOM

• The Barnstormer • Big Thunder Mountain • Buzz Lightyear's Space Ranger Spin • Dumbo • Jungle Cruise	• Peter Pan's Flight • Seven Dwarfs Mine Train** • Space Mountain • Splash Mountain	• Town Square Theater (Mickey, Princesses Meet-and-Greets) • Under the Sea: Journey of the Little Mermaid • Winnie the Pooh

EPCOT

• *Captain EO** • Living with the Land*	• Maelstrom • Mission: SPACE	• Soarin' • Test Track

ANIMAL KINGDOM

• DINOSAUR • Expedition Everest	• Kali River Rapids • Kilimanjaro Safaris	• Primeval Whirl

DHS

• Rock 'n' Roller Coaster • Star Tours—The Adventures Continue	• Toy Story Mania! • Twilight Zone Tower of Terror	• *Voyage of the Little Mermaid**

25 - 30 min forget or less fastpass

* Available seasonally; ** opens 2014

WHEN TO USE FASTPASS Except as discussed on the next page, there's no reason to use Fastpass during the first 30–40 minutes a park is open. Lines for most attractions are quite manageable during this period, and this is the only time of day when Fastpass attractions exclusively serve those in the regular line. Regardless of the time of day, however, if the wait in the regular line at a Fastpass attraction is 25–30 minutes or less, we recommend joining the regular line.

FASTPASS RULES Disney allows you to obtain a second Fastpass at a time printed on the bottom of your most recent pass, usually 2 hours or less from the time the first was issued. Rules aside, the real lesson here is to check out the posted return time before obtaining a Fastpass. If the return time is hours away, forgo the Fastpass. Especially in the Magic Kingdom, there will be a number of other Fastpass attractions where the return time is only an hour or so away.

unofficial **TIP**
Obtain Fastpasses for all members of your party, including those who are too short, too young, or simply not interested in riding. This is a convenient way for parents and kids alike to work in extra rides on attractions they really enjoy.

Disney officially enforces the expiration time on the return window but will usually allow you to show up 5 minutes early or up to 15 minutes late and still use the pass. If you arrive late to the Fastpass line because of an unforeseen circumstance, explain the issue to the cast member working the line, and he or she will make the call on whether you can still use your pass.

Fastpass Guidelines

- Don't mess with Fastpass unless it can save you 30 minutes or more.

- Do not obtain a Fastpass for a theater attraction until you have experienced all the Fastpass rides on your itinerary (using Fastpass at theater attractions usually requires more time than using the standby line).

- Always check the Fastpass return period before obtaining your Fastpass.

- Obtain Fastpasses for Soarin' and Test Track at Epcot; Expedition Everest and Kilimanjaro Safaris at Disney's Animal Kingdom; Space Mountain, Splash Mountain, Peter Pan's Flight, Seven Dwarfs Mine Train, and Winnie the Pooh at the Magic Kingdom; and Rock 'n' Roller Coaster, Toy Story Mania!, and The Twilight Zone Tower of Terror at Disney's Hollywood Studios as early in the day as possible.

- Try to obtain Fastpasses for rides not mentioned in the preceding tip by 11 a.m., or 1 p.m. at the latest. Don't depend on Fastpasses being available after 2 p.m. during busy times of year.

- Make sure everyone in your party has a Fastpass of his or her own.

- Use our mobile app, **Lines,** to find out which Fastpass attractions still have passes available and when we estimate they'll run out. See Lines in action before you go at **touringplans.com/lines.**

Fastpass+

Disney's next-gen version of Fastpass hadn't officially launched before this guide was published, but it had gone through enough rounds of small-scale guest testing for us to form a general sense of how it's supposed to work.

One major change to the existing system is that Fastpass+ users will be able to select their own return-time windows for attractions. For example, Big Thunder Mountain Railroad may display a list of 1-hour time windows (1–2 p.m., 2–3 p.m., etc.) for you to choose from.

unofficial **TIP**
You won't be able to use Fastpass and Fastpass+ at the same time.

Another new feature of the Fastpass+ initiative is the ability to make Fastpass reservations in advance through the Disney World website and **My Disney Experience,** the official Disney mobile app; you'll need an existing Disney resort reservation or a theme park ticket in hand to do this. If you buy your admission the day you arrive at the parks or you want to change your Fastpass selections when you're in the park, you'll (eventually) be able to use the app or new in-park computer terminals to make reservations.

On the downside, we're told there will be a hard limit on the number of daily Fastpass+ reservations you can have. In addition, Disney seems ready to limit the combinations of Fastpasses you can have and the types of rides for which you can have them (read: fewer passes for headliner attractions). We also hear that Disney may start allocating Fastpasses according to whether guests are staying on- or off-property, whether they're staying in a Deluxe resort versus a Moderate or Value one, or whether they've booked a vacation months in advance versus at the last minute. Clearly, these strategies are designed to do three things: increase Disney's revenue, decrease its operating expenses, and induce guests to spend more time at Disney World than, say, Universal Orlando.

If such policies are indeed implemented, the end result, except for a privileged few, is that it will take more time to see less with Fastpass+. And if that's the case, we expect Disney to endure backlash eclipsing that which it's received regarding its ever-escalating ticket, dining, and hotel prices.

PART THREE

ACCOMMODATIONS

The BASIC CONSIDERATIONS

BENEFITS OF STAYING IN THE WORLD

WALT DISNEY WORLD RESORT HOTEL and campground guests have privileges and amenities unavailable to those staying outside the World. Though some of these perks are only advertising gimmicks, others are real and potentially valuable:

1. CONVENIENCE If you don't have a car, the commute to the theme parks is short via the Disney Transportation System. This is especially advantageous if you stay in one of the hotels connected by the monorail or boat service. If you have a car, however, there are dozens of hotels outside Disney World that are within 5–10 minutes of theme-park parking lots.

2. EXTRA MAGIC HOURS AT THE THEME PARKS Disney World lodging guests (excluding guests at the independent hotels of Downtown Disney Resort Area, except for the Hilton) are invited to enter a designated park 1 hour earlier than the general public each day or to enjoy a designated theme park for up to 2 hours after it closes to the general public in the evening. Extra Magic Hours can be valuable if you know how to use them. They can also land you in gridlock. (See our detailed discussion starting on page 14.)

3. BABYSITTING AND CHILD-CARE OPTIONS Disney hotel and campground guests have several options for babysitting, child care, and children's programs. The **Polynesian Resort** and **Animal Kingdom Lodge,** along with several other Disney hotels, offer "clubs"—themed child-care centers where potty-trained children ages 3–12 can stay while the adults go out.

4. PRIORITY THEME PARK ADMISSIONS On days of unusually heavy attendance, Disney may restrict admission into the theme parks for all customers. When deciding whom to admit into the parks, priority is given to guests staying at Disney resorts. In practice, no guest is turned away until a park's parking lot is full. When this happens, that park will be packed to gridlock. Under such conditions, you would exhibit the common sense of an amoeba to exercise your priority-admission privilege.

5. CHILDREN SHARING A ROOM WITH THEIR PARENTS There is no extra charge per night for children younger than age 18 sharing a room with their parents. Many hotels outside Disney World also offer this benefit.

6. FREE PARKING Disney resort guests with cars don't have to pay for parking in the theme park lots. This privilege saves $15 per day.

7. RECREATIONAL PRIVILEGES Disney resort guests get preferential treatment for tee times at the golf courses.

STAYING IN OR OUT OF THE WORLD: WEIGHING THE PROS AND CONS

1. COST If cost is a primary consideration, you'll lodge much less expensively outside Disney World. Our ratings of hotel quality and cost (see pages 63–69) compare specific hotels both in and out of the World.

2. EASE OF ACCESS Even if you stay in Disney World, you're dependent on some mode of transportation. It may be less stressful to use the Disney transportation system, but with the single exception of commuting to the Magic Kingdom, the fastest, most efficient, and most flexible way to get around is usually a car. Walt Disney World is so large that some destinations within the World can be reached more quickly from off-property hotels than from Disney hotels. For example, guests at hotels and motels on US 192 (near the so-called Walt Disney World Maingate) are closer to Disney's Hollywood Studios, Disney's Animal Kingdom, and Blizzard Beach water park than guests at many hotels inside Disney World.

3. YOUNG CHILDREN Although the hassle of commuting to most non-World hotels is only slightly (if at all) greater than that of commuting to Disney hotels, a definite peace of mind results from staying in Walt Disney World. The salient point, regardless of where you stay, is to make sure you get your young children back to the hotel for a nap each day.

4. SPLITTING UP If you're in a party that probably will split up to tour (as frequently happens in families with children of varying ages), staying in the World offers more transportation options and, thus, more independence. Mom and Dad can take the car and return to the hotel for a relaxed dinner and early bedtime while the teens remain in the park for evening parades and fireworks.

5. FEEDING THE ARMY OF THE POTOMAC If you have a large crew that chows down like cattle on a finishing lot, you may do better staying outside the World, where food is far less expensive.

6. VISITING OTHER ORLANDO-AREA ATTRACTIONS If you'll be visiting SeaWorld, Kennedy Space Center Visitor Complex, Universal Orlando, or other area attractions, it may be more convenient to stay outside the World.

HOW TO GET DISCOUNTS ON LODGING AT WALT DISNEY WORLD

THERE ARE SO MANY GUEST ROOMS in and around Disney World that competition is brisk, and everyone, including Disney, wheels and deals to fill them. Disney, however, has its own atypical way of managing its room inventory. To uphold the brand integrity of its hotels, Disney prefers to use "sweeteners" rather than discounts per se. (For example, Disney might include free dining if you reserve a certain number of nights at rack rate, or offer special deals only by e-mail to returning guests.) Consequently, many of the strategies for obtaining discounted rates in most cities and destinations don't work well for Disney hotels. Nonetheless, there are good deals to be found—check out our tips below.

1. SEASONAL SAVINGS You can save 15–35% per night or more on a Disney hotel room by visiting during slower times of year. However, Disney uses so many adjectives ("Regular," "Holiday," "Peak," "Value," and the like) to describe its seasonal calendar that it's hard to keep up. Plus, the dates for each "season" vary among resorts. If you're set on staying at a Disney resort, order a copy of the **Walt Disney Travel Company Florida Vacations Brochure and DVD** (see page 8).

2. ASK ABOUT SPECIALS When you talk to Disney reservationists, inquire specifically about special deals. Ask, for example, "What special rates or discounts are available at Disney hotels during the time of our visit?"

3. "TRADE-UP" OR "UPSELL" RATES If you request a room at a Disney Value resort and none are available, you may be offered a room in the next category up (Moderate resorts, in this example) at a discounted price. Similarly, if you ask for a room in a Moderate resort and none are available, Disney will usually offer a good deal for Disney Deluxe Villa rooms or a Deluxe resort. You can angle for a trade-up rate by asking for a resort category that is more likely to be sold out.

4. KNOW THE SECRET CODE The folks at **MouseSavers** (**mouse savers.com**) maintain an updated list of discounts and reservation codes for Disney resorts. The codes are separated into categories such as "for anyone," "for residents of certain states," and "for Annual Pass holders." For example, the site recently listed code DGA, published in an ad in some Spanish-language newspapers and magazines, offering a rate of $72 per night for Disney's All-Star Resorts from August 15 through September 28. Anyone calling the Disney Reservation Center at ☎ 407-W-DISNEY can use a current code and get the discounted rate.

unofficial **TIP**
Dozens of discounts are usually listed at the MouseSavers site, covering almost all Disney resort hotels.

MouseSavers maintains a great historical list of when hotel discounts were released and what they encompassed at **mousesavers .com/historicalwdwdiscounts.html**. The MouseSavers newsletter features discount announcements, Disney news, and exclusive offers not available to the general public.

5. INTERNET SELLERS Online travel sellers **Expedia** (**expedia.com**), **Travelocity** (**travelocity.com**), and **OneTravel** (**onetravel.com**) discount Disney hotels. Most breaks are in the 7–25% range, but they can go as deep as 40%. Disney also places its hotel rooms on **Priceline** (**priceline.com**). While Disney abstains from the "Name Your Own Price" aspect of the site, its hotel rooms are now in Priceline's inventory and available through its conventional booking engine at a discounted rate.

6. WALT DISNEY WORLD WEBSITE Disney still offers deals when it sees lower-than-usual future demand. Go to **disneyworld.com** and look for "Explore Our Special Offers" on the home page. In the same place, also look for seasonal discounts, usually listed as "Summertime Savings" or "Fall Savings" or something similar. You can also go to "Places to Stay" at the top at the top right of the home page, where you'll find a link to Special Offers. You must click on the particular special to get the discounts: If you fill out the information on "Price Your Vacation," you'll be charged the full rack rate. Reservations booked online are subject to a $200 penalty if canceled less than 45 days before arrival. Before you book rooms on Disney's or any website, click on "Terms and Conditions" and read the fine print.

7. RENTING DISNEY VACATION CLUB POINTS The Disney Vacation Club (DVC) is Disney's time-share-condominium program. DVC resorts (a.k.a. Disney Deluxe Villa resorts) at Walt Disney World are **Animal Kingdom Villas, Bay Lake Tower** at the Contemporary Resort, the **Beach Club Villas, BoardWalk Villas, Old Key West Resort, Saratoga Springs Resort & Spa, Treehouse Villas at Saratoga Springs, Grand Floridian Villas,** and **Wilderness Lodge Villas.** Each resort offers studios and one- and two-bedroom villas (some resorts also have three-bedroom villas). Accommodations are roomy and luxurious. The studios are equipped with kitchenettes, wet bars, and fridges; the villas come with full kitchens. Most accommodations also have patios or balconies.

DVC members receive a number of "points" annually that they use to pay for their accommodations. Sometimes members elect to "rent" (sell) their points to others instead of using them in a given year. Though Disney is not involved in the transaction, it permits DVC members to make these points available to the general public. The going rental rate is usually in the range of $13–$14 per point.

You have two options when renting points: go through a company that specializes in DVC points rental, or locate and deal directly with the selling DVC member. For a fixed rate of around $14 per point, the folks at **David's Disney Vacation Club Rentals** (**dvc request.com**) will act as a points broker in your behalf, matching your request for a specific resort and dates to their available supply.

The DVC discussion site **MouseOwners** (**mouseowners.com**) has a specific forum for matching DVC sellers and renters.

8. TRAVEL AGENTS In our opinion, a Disney-savvy travel agent is the best friend a traveler can have. The best of the best include **Sue Pisaturo** of **Small World Vacations,** whom we've used many times (**sue@smallworldvacations.com**); **Kathy Atchue** (**kathy@smallworld vacations.com**); **Coleen Bolton** (**coleen@mei-travel.com**); **Deanna Carrigan** (**deanna@smallworldvacations.com**); **Michelle Cunningham** (**michelle@mei-travel.com**); **Stephanie Hudson** (**stephanie@mousefan travel.com**); and **Leigh McCarty** (**leigh@smallworldvacations.com**).

9. ORGANIZATIONS AND AUTO CLUBS Disney has developed time-limited programs with some auto clubs and organizations. AAA, for example, can often offer discounts on hotels and packages comparable to those Disney offers its Annual Pass holders. Such deals come and go, but the market suggests there will be more. If you're a member of AARP, AAA, or any travel or auto club, ask whether the group has a program before shopping elsewhere.

10. ROOM UPGRADES Sometimes a room upgrade is as good as a discount. If you're visiting Disney World during a slower time, book the least expensive room your discounts will allow. Checking in, ask very politely about being upgraded to a "water view" or "pool view" room. A fair percentage of the time, you'll get one at no additional charge. Hotels are under no obligation to upgrade you, so if your request is not met, accept the decision graciously. Also, note that suites (such as the Art of Animation Family Suites) are exempt from discount offers.

11. MILITARY DISCOUNTS The **Shades of Green Armed Forces Recreation Center,** near the Grand Floridian Resort & Spa, offers luxury accommodations at rates based on a serviceman's rank as well as attraction tickets to the theme parks. Call ☎ 888-593-2242 or see **shadesofgreen.org.**

12. YEAR-ROUND DISCOUNTS AT THE SWAN AND DOLPHIN RESORTS Government workers, teachers, nurses, military, and AAA and *Entertainment Coupon Book* members can save on their rooms at the Dolphin or the Swan resort (when space is available, of course). Call ☎ 800-227-1500.

CHOOSING A WALT DISNEY WORLD HOTEL

IF YOU WANT TO STAY IN WALT DISNEY WORLD but don't know which hotel to choose, consider the following:

1. COST Hotel rooms start at about $90 a night at the **All-Star** and **Pop Century Resorts** during Value season and top out near $900 at the **Grand Floridian Resort & Spa** during Holiday Season. Suites, of course, are more expensive than standard rooms.

Animal Kingdom Villas, Bay Lake Tower, Beach Club Villas, Board-Walk Villas, Grand Floridian Villas, Old Key West Resort, Saratoga Springs Resort & Spa, and **Wilderness Lodge Villas** offer condo-type accommodations with one-, two-, and (at Saratoga Springs, BoardWalk Villas, Old Key West, Animal Kingdom Villas, Grand Floridian Villas, and Bay Lake Tower) three-bedroom units with kitchens, living rooms, DVD players, and washers and dryers. Studios have a kitchenette (with microwave, mini-fridge, and sink) but no washer or dryer. Prices range from $313 per night for a studio suite at Animal Kingdom Villas to more than $2,600 per night for a three-bedroom villa at Bay Lake Tower. Fully equipped cabins (minus a washer and dryer) at **Fort Wilderness Resort & Campground** cost $289–$481 per night. Family Suites at All-Star Music and Art of Animation have kitchenettes, separate bedrooms, and two bathrooms. A few suites without kitchens are available at the more expensive Disney resorts.

Also at Disney World are the seven hotels of the **Downtown Disney Resort Area (DDRA).** Accommodations range from fairly luxurious to motel-like. While the DDRA is technically part of Disney World, staying there is like visiting a colony rather than the motherland. Free parking at theme parks isn't offered—nor is early entry, with one exception, the Hilton—and hotels operate

COSTS PER NIGHT OF DISNEY RESORT HOTEL ROOMS (rack rate)	
All-Star Resorts	$85–$192
All-Star Music Resort Family Suites	$202–$392
Animal Kingdom Lodge	$279–$3,088
Animal Kingdom Villas (Jambo House, Kidani Village)	$313–$2,380
Art of Animation Family Suites	$252–$433
Art of Animation Resort	$100–$191
Bay Lake Tower	$431–$2,640
Beach Club Resort	$350–$2,826
Beach Club Villas	$360–$1,284
BoardWalk Inn	$392–$2,949
BoardWalk Villas	$360–$2,380
Caribbean Beach Resort	$162–$322
Contemporary Resort	$330–$3,178
Coronado Springs Resort	$167–$1,364
Dolphin (Sheraton)	$189–$359
Fort Wilderness Resort & Campground (cabins)	$289–$481
Grand Floridian Resort & Spa	$480–$3,306
Grand Floridian Villas	$480–$3,345
Old Key West Resort	$327–$1,822
Polynesian Resort	$422–$3,187
Pop Century Resort	$95–$206
Port Orleans Resort (French Quarter, Riverside)	$162–$328
Saratoga Springs Resort & Spa	$327–$1,822
Swan (Westin)	$189–$359
Treehouse Villas	$709–$1,144
Wilderness Lodge	$284–$1,563
Wilderness Lodge Villas	$368–$1,279
Yacht Club Resort	$350–$3,002

their own buses rather than use Disney transportation. See our profiles of the Hilton in the Walt Disney World Resort and the Buena Vista Palace in the section beginning on page 47.

2. LOCATION If you intend to use your own car, the location of your Disney hotel isn't especially important unless you plan to spend most of your time at the Magic Kingdom. (Disney transportation is always more efficient than your car in this case because it

WHAT IT COSTS TO STAY IN THE DOWNTOWN DISNEY RESORT AREA	
Best Western Lake Buena Vista Resort Hotel	$76–$149
Buena Vista Palace Hotel & Spa	$119–$214
DoubleTree Guest Suites	$189–$239
Hilton in the WDW Resort	$89–$169
Holiday Inn in the WDW Resort	$108–$181
Royal Plaza	$129–$305
Wyndham Lake Buena Vista Resort	$76–$168

bypasses the Transportation and Ticket Center and deposits you at the theme park entrance.)

Most convenient to the Magic Kingdom are the three resorts linked by monorail: the **Grand Floridian** and its **Villas, Contemporary, Bay Lake Tower,** and **Polynesian.** Commuting to the Magic Kingdom via monorail is quick and simple.

Contemporary Resort and Bay Lake Tower, in addition to being on the monorail, are only a 10- to 15-minute walk to the Magic Kingdom. Guests reach Epcot by monorail but must transfer at the Transportation and Ticket Center. Buses connect the resorts to Disney's Hollywood Studios, Disney's Animal Kingdom, the water parks, and Downtown Disney. No transfer is required, but the bus makes several stops before reaching either destination.

The Polynesian Resort is served by the Magic Kingdom monorail and is an easy walk from the transportation center. At the center, you can catch an express monorail to Epcot. This makes the Polynesian the only Disney resort with direct monorail access to both Epcot and the Magic Kingdom. To minimize your walk to the transportation center, request a room in the Rapa Nui, Tahiti, or Tokelau guest buildings.

Wilderness Lodge & Villas, along with **Fort Wilderness Resort & Campground,** are linked to the Magic Kingdom by boat, and are linked to everywhere else in the World by somewhat convoluted bus service.

The most centrally located resorts in Walt Disney World are the Epcot hotels—the **BoardWalk Inn, BoardWalk Villas, Yacht & Beach Club Resorts, Beach Club Villas, Swan,** and **Dolphin**—and **Coronado Springs,** an Animal Kingdom hotel. The Epcot hotels are within easy walking distance of Disney's Hollywood Studios and Epcot's International Gateway. Except at Coronado Springs, boat service is also available at these resorts, with vessels connecting to DHS. Epcot hotels are best for guests planning to spend most of their time at Epcot or DHS.

Caribbean Beach Resort, Pop Century Resort, and **Art of Animation Resort** are just south and east of Epcot and DHS. Along Bonnet Creek, **Disney's Old Key West** and **Port Orleans Resorts** also offer quick access to those parks.

Though not centrally located, the **All-Star Resorts, Coronado Springs Resort,** and **Animal Kingdom Lodge & Villas** have very good bus service to all Disney World destinations and are closest to Animal Kingdom.

If you plan to play golf, book **Old Key West Resort** or **Saratoga Springs Resort & Spa,** both built around golf courses. The military-only **Shades of Green** resort is adjacent to two courses. Near but not on a golf course are the **Grand Floridian, Polynesian,** and **Port Orleans** resorts. For boating and water sports, try the **Polynesian, Contemporary,** or **Grand Floridian** resorts, **Fort Wilderness Resort & Campground,** or **Wilderness Lodge & Villas.** The lodge and campground are also great for hikers, bikers, and joggers.

3. ROOM QUALITY Few Disney guests spend much time in their hotel rooms, though these rooms are among the best designed and most well appointed anywhere. Plus, they're meticulously maintained. At the top of the line are the luxurious rooms of the **Contemporary, Grand Floridian,** and **Polynesian** resorts. Bringing up the rear are the small rooms of the **All-Star Resorts,** but even these economy rooms are sparkling-clean and quite livable. Check our hotel table on pages 63–69 for ratings of all Disney and non-Disney hotels.

4. THE SIZE OF YOUR GROUP Larger families and groups may be interested in how many persons a Disney resort room can accommodate, but only Lilliputians would be comfortable in a room filled to capacity. Groups requiring two or more guest rooms should consider condo or villa accommodations in or out of the World. The most cost-efficient Disney lodging for groups of five is the **Alligator Bayou** section of **Port Orleans Riverside.** The cheapest digs for six are the **All-Star Music Family Suites.** For detailed room schematics that show the maximum number of persons per room as well as the rooms' relative size and configuration, see *The Unofficial Guide to Walt Disney World.*

*un*official **TIP**
If there are more than six in your party, you will need either two hotel rooms, a suite, or a condo.

5. THEME All Disney hotels are themed. Each is designed to make you feel you're in a special place or period of history.

Some resorts carry off their themes better than others, and some themes are more exciting. **Wilderness Lodge & Villas,** for example, is extraordinary, reminiscent of a grand national-park lodge from the early 20th century. The lobby opens eight stories to a timbered ceiling supported by giant columns of bundled logs. One look eases you into the Northwest-wilderness theme. The lodge is a great choice for couples and seniors and is heaven for children.

Animal Kingdom Lodge & Villas replicates grand safari lodges of Kenya and Tanzania and overlooks its own African game preserve. By far the most exotic Disney resort, it's made to order for couples on romantic getaways and for families with children. The **Polynesian,** likewise dramatic, conveys the feeling of the Pacific Islands. It's great for romantics and families. Many waterfront rooms offer a perfect view of Cinderella Castle and the Magic Kingdom fireworks across Seven Seas Lagoon.

Grandeur, nostalgia, and privilege are central to the **Grand Floridian Resort & Spa, Grand Floridian Villas, Yacht & Beach Club Resorts, BoardWalk Inn,** and **BoardWalk Villas.** Although modeled after Eastern-seaboard seaside hotels of different eras, the resorts are similar. **Saratoga Springs Resort & Spa,** supposedly representative of an upstate New York country retreat, looks like what you'd get if you crossed the Beach Club with the Wilderness Lodge. For all the resorts inspired by northeastern resorts, thematic distinctions are subtle and lost on many guests.

Port Orleans French Quarter Resort lacks the mystery and sultriness of the real New Orleans French Quarter but captures enough of its architectural essence to carry off the theme. **Port Orleans Riverside Resort** likewise succeeds with its plantation and bayou setting. **Old Key West Resort** gets the architecture right, but cloning its inspiration on such a large scale totally glosses over the real Key West's idiosyncratic patchwork personality. The **Caribbean Beach Resort**'s theme is much more effective at night, thanks to creative lighting. By day, it looks like a Miami condo development.

The **All-Star Resorts** comprise 30 three-story, T-shaped buildings with almost 6,000 guest rooms. There are 15 themed areas: 5 celebrate sports (surfing, basketball, tennis, football, and baseball), 5 recall Hollywood movies, and 5 have musical motifs. The resort's design, with entrances shaped like giant Dalmatians, Coke cups, footballs, and the like, is pretty adolescent, sacrificing grace and beauty for energy and novelty. Guest rooms are small, with decor reminiscent of a teenage boy's bedroom. Despite the theme, there is no sports, music, or movies at All-Star Resorts. **Pop Century Resort** is pretty much a clone of All-Star Resorts, only this time the giant icons symbolize decades of the 20th century (Big Wheels, 45-rpm records, silhouettes of people doing period dances, and such), and period memorabilia decorate the rooms. Across the lake from Pop Century Resort is the **Art of Animation Resort,** with icons and decor based on four Disney animated features: *Cars, Finding Nemo, The Lion King,* and *The Little Mermaid.*

Pretense aside, the **Contemporary, Swan,** and **Dolphin** are essentially themeless though architecturally interesting. The original Contemporary Resort is a 15-story A-frame building with monorails running through the middle. Views from guest rooms here and in Bay Lake Tower are among the best at Disney World. Swan and Dolphin are massive yet whimsical. Designed by Michael Graves, they're excellent examples of "entertainment architecture."

6. DINING The best resorts for dining quality and selection are the Epcot resorts: the **Beach Club Villas, BoardWalk Inn & Villas, Dolphin, Swan,** and **Yacht & Beach Club Resorts.** Each has good restaurants and is within easy walking distance of the others and of the 14 restaurants in Epcot's World Showcase section. If you stay at an Epcot resort, you have a total of 31 restaurants within a 5- to 12-minute walk.

The only other place in Disney World where restaurants and hotels are similarly concentrated is in the **Downtown Disney Resort Area.** In addition to restaurants in the hotels themselves, the **Hilton, Holiday Inn at Walt Disney World, Wyndham Lake Buena Vista Resort,** and **Buena Vista Palace Hotel & Spa,** as well as **Saratoga Springs Resort & Spa,** are within walking distance of restaurants in Downtown Disney.

Guests at the **Contemporary, Polynesian,** and **Grand Floridian** can eat in their hotels, or they can commute to restaurants in the Magic Kingdom (not recommended) or in other monorail-linked hotels. Riding the monorail to another hotel or to the Magic Kingdom takes about 10 minutes each way, plus waiting for the train.

All the other Disney resorts are somewhat isolated. This means you're stuck dining at your hotel unless (1) you have a car or (2) you're content to eat at the theme parks or Downtown Disney.

7. AMENITIES AND RECREATION Disney resorts provide elaborate swimming pools, themed shops, restaurants or food courts, nightclubs or lounges, and access to five Disney golf courses. The more you pay for your lodging, the more amenities and opportunities are at your disposal. **Animal Kingdom Lodge & Villas, BoardWalk Inn, Wilderness Lodge,** and the **Contemporary, Grand Floridian, Polynesian,** and **Yacht & Beach Club** resorts, for example, all offer concierge floors.

For swimming and sunning, the **Contemporary, Bay Lake Tower,** the **Polynesian, Wilderness Lodge & Villas,** and the **Grand Floridian & Villas** offer both pools and white-sand nonswimming beaches on Bay Lake or Seven Seas Lagoon. **Caribbean Beach Resort,** the **Dolphin,** and the **Yacht & Beach Club** also provide both pools and nonswimming beaches. Though lacking a lakefront beach, **Saratoga Springs Resort & Spa, Animal Kingdom Lodge & Villas, Port Orleans** and **Coronado Springs** resorts, and **BoardWalk Inn & Villas** have exceptionally creative pools.

Bay Lake and Seven Seas Lagoon are the best venues for boating. Resorts fronting these lakes are the **Contemporary, Bay Lake Tower,** the **Polynesian, Wilderness Lodge & Villas,** the **Grand Floridian & Villas,** and **Fort Wilderness Resort & Campground.** Though on smaller bodies of water, **BoardWalk Inn & Villas, Caribbean Beach, Coronado Springs,** the **Dolphin, Old Key West, Port Orleans, Saratoga Springs,** and the **Yacht & Beach Club** also rent watercraft.

Most convenient for golf are **Shades of Green, Saratoga Springs, Old Key West, Contemporary–Bay Lake Tower,** the **Polynesian,** the **Grand Floridian & Villas,** and **Port Orleans.**

While there are many places to bike or jog at Disney World (including golf-cart paths), the best biking and jogging are at **Fort Wilderness Resort & Campground** and the adjacent **Wilderness Lodge & Villas. Caribbean Beach Resort** offers a lovely hiking, biking, and jogging trail around the lake. Also good for biking and jogging is the area along Bonnet Creek extending through **Port Orleans** and **Old Key West** toward Downtown Disney. Epcot resorts offer a lakefront promenade and bike path, as well as a roadside walkway suitable for jogging.

On-site child care programs are offered at **Animal Kingdom Lodge & Villas,** the **Dolphin,** the **Hilton in the Walt Disney World Resort,** the **Polynesian,** the **Swan, Wilderness Lodge & Villas,** and the **Yacht & Beach Club Resorts.** All other resorts offer in-room babysitting (see pages 87 and 88 for details).

8. NIGHTLIFE The boardwalk at **BoardWalk Inn & Villas** has an upscale dance club (albeit one that has never lived up to its potential), a club featuring dueling pianos and sing-alongs, a brewpub, and a sports bar. The BoardWalk clubs are within easy walking distance of all Epcot resorts. Most non-Disney hotels in the **Downtown Disney Resort Area,** as well as **Saratoga Springs Resort & Spa,** are within walking distance of Downtown Disney nightspots. Nightlife at other Disney resorts is limited to lounges that stay open late.

At the Contemporary Resort's **California Grill Lounge,** you can relax over dinner and watch the *Wishes* fireworks show at the nearby Magic Kingdom.

CAMPING AT WALT DISNEY WORLD

DISNEY'S **Fort Wilderness Resort & Campground** is a spacious area for tent and RV camping. Fully equipped, air-conditioned prefabricated log cabins are also available for rent.

Tent/Pop-Up campsites provide water, electricity, and cable TV and run from $46 to $93 depending on season. **Full Hook-Up** campsites have all of the previous amenities, accommodate large RVs, and run $61–$108 per night. **Preferred Hook-Up** campsites for tents and RVs add sewer connections and run from $66 to $115 per night. **Premium** campsites add an extra-large concrete parking pad and run $76–$125 a night. All sites are level and provide picnic tables, waste containers, grills, and free Wi-Fi. Sites are arranged on loops accessible from one of three main roads. There are 28 loops, with Loops 100–2000 for tent and RV campers, and Loops 2100–2800 offering cabins at $275–$450 per night. RV sites are roomy by eastern-U.S. standards, with the Premium and Full Hook-Up campsites able to accommodate RVs more than 45 feet long, but tent campers will probably feel a bit cramped.

Fort Wilderness Resort & Campground arguably offers the most recreational facilities and activities of any Disney resort. Among them are two video arcades; nightly campfire programs; Disney movies; a dinner theater; two swimming pools; a beach; walking paths; bike, boat, canoe, golf-cart, and water-ski rentals; a petting zoo; horseback riding; hayrides; fishing; and tennis, basketball, and volleyball courts.

Access to the Magic Kingdom is by boat from Fort Wilderness Landing and to Epcot by bus, with a transfer at the Transportation and Ticket Center (TTC) to the Epcot monorail. Boat service may be suspended during thunderstorms, so if it's raining or looks like it's about to, Disney will provide buses. An alternate route to the Magic Kingdom is by internal bus to the TTC, then by monorail or ferry to the park. Transportation to all other Disney destinations is by bus. Motor traffic within the campground is permitted only when entering or exiting. Get around within the campground by bus, golf cart, or bike, the latter two available for rent.

HOTELS *outside* WALT DISNEY WORLD

SELECTING AND BOOKING A HOTEL OUTSIDE WALT DISNEY WORLD

LODGING COSTS OUTSIDE DISNEY WORLD vary incredibly. If you shop around, you can find a clean motel with a pool within 5–20 minutes of the World for as low as $40 a night.

There are four primary out-of-the-World areas to consider:

1. INTERNATIONAL DRIVE AREA This area, about 15–25 minutes northeast of the World, parallels I-4 on its eastern side and offers

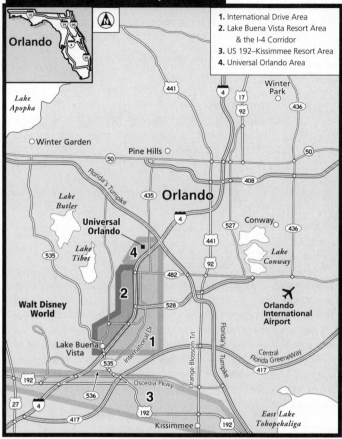

Hotel Concentrations Around Walt Disney World

Orlando

1. International Drive Area
2. Lake Buena Vista Resort Area & the I-4 Corridor
3. US 192–Kissimmee Resort Area
4. Universal Orlando Area

Lake Apopka

Winter Park

Winter Garden

Pine Hills

Orlando

Lake Butler

Universal Orlando

Conway

Lake Conway

Lake Tibet

Walt Disney World

Orlando International Airport

Lake Buena Vista

Central Florida GreeneWay

Osceola Pkwy.

Kissimmee

East Lake Tohopekaliga

a wide selection of hotels and restaurants. Prices range from $56 to $400 per night. The chief drawbacks of this area are its terribly congested roads, countless traffic signals, and inadequate access to westbound I-4. While International's biggest bottleneck is its intersection with Sand Lake Road, the mile between Kirkman and Sand Lake Roads is almost always gridlocked.

I-Drive hotels are listed in the *Official Vacation Guide,* published by the Orlando–Orange County Convention and Visitors Bureau. For a copy, call ☎ 800-972-3304 or 407-363-5872, or see **orlandoinfo.com**.

2. LAKE BUENA VISTA AND THE I-4 CORRIDOR A number of hotels are along FL 535 and west of I-4 between Disney World and I-4's intersection with Florida's Turnpike. They're easily reached from the interstate and are near many restaurants, including those on International Drive. The *Official Vacation Guide* (see previous page) lists most of them.

3. US 192 (IRLO BRONSON MEMORIAL HIGHWAY) This is the road to Kissimmee, to the south of Disney World. In addition to large, full-service hotels, there are many small, privately owned motels that are often a good value. Several dozen properties on US 192 are nearer Disney parks than are more expensive hotels inside the World. The number and variety of restaurants on US 192 have increased markedly, compensating for the area's primary short-coming. Locally, US 192 is called Irlo Bronson Memorial Highway. The section to the west of I-4 and the Disney World Maingate is designated Irlo Bronson Memorial Highway West, while the section from I-4 running southeast toward Kissimmee is Irlo Bronson Memorial Highway East.

Hotels along US 192 and in Kissimmee are listed in the *Kissimmee Visitor's Guide*. Order a copy by calling ☎ 800-327-9159, or view it online at **floridakiss.com**.

4. UNIVERSAL STUDIOS AREA In the triangular area bordered by I-4 on the southeast, Vineland Road on the north, and Turkey Lake Road on the west are Universal Orlando and the hotels most convenient to it. Running north–south through the middle of the triangle is Kirkman Road, which connects to I-4. On the east side of Kirkman are a number of independent hotels and restaurants. Traffic in this area isn't nearly as congested as on International Drive, and there are good interstate connections in both directions.

GETTING A GOOD DEAL ON A ROOM OUTSIDE WALT DISNEY WORLD

1. ORLANDO MAGICARD This discount program is sponsored by Visit Orlando. Cardholders are eligible for discounts of 12%–50% at about 50 hotels. The Magicard is also good for discounts at some area attractions, three dinner theaters, museums, performing-arts venues, restaurants, shops, and more. Valid for up to six persons, the card isn't available for larger groups or conventions.

To obtain a free Magicard and a list of participating hotels and attractions, call ☎ 800-643-9492 or 407-363-5872. On the web, go to **orlandoinfo.com/magicard;** the Magicard and accompanying brochure can be printed from your computer. If you miss getting one before you leave home, obtain one at the Convention and Visitors Bureau Information Center at 8723 International Dr.

When you call for your Magicard, also request the *Official Vacation Guide*.

2. *HOTELCOUPONS.COM FLORIDA GUIDE* This book of coupons for lodging statewide is free in many restaurants and motels on main highways leading to Florida. Because most travelers make reservations before leaving home, picking up the book en route doesn't help much. To view it online or sign up for a free monthly guide sent by e-mail, visit **hotelcoupons.com**. For a hard copy ($3 for handling, $5 if shipped to Canada), call ☎ 800-222-3948 Monday–Friday, 8 a.m.–5 p.m. Eastern time.

3. HOTEL SHOPPING ON THE INTERNET The Internet has become the primary tool for travelers seeking to shop for and book their own air travel, hotels, rental cars, entertainment, and travel packages. It's by far the best direct-to-consumer distribution channel in history.

Our advice: Shop the web for the lowest room price available, then call your travel agent or the hotel itself to ask if they can beat it. Any savvy reservationist knows that selling you the room directly will both cut the hotel's cost and improve gross margin. If the reservationist can't help you, ask to speak to his or her supervisor. (We've actually had to explain hotel economics to more than a few clueless reservation agents.)

When it comes to travel agents, they have clout based on the volume of business they send to a particular hotel or chain and can usually negotiate a rate even lower than what you've found online. Even if the agent can't beat the price, he or she can often obtain upgrades, preferred views, free breakfasts, and other deal sweeteners.

When we're really hungry for a deal, there are a number of sites that we always check out:

OUR FAVORITE ONLINE HOTEL RESOURCES
floridakiss.com   Primarily US 192–Kissimmee area hotels
mousesavers.com   Best for hotels inside Walt Disney World
hotelcoupons.com   Self-explanatory
orlandoinfo.com   Good info, though not user-friendly for booking
orlandovacation.com   Great rates for condos and home rentals

We scour these sites for unusually juicy hotel deals that meet our criteria: location, quality, price, and amenities. If we find a hotel that fills the bill, we check it out at other websites and comparative travel search engines such as **Kayak** (**kayak.com**) and **Mobissimo** (**mobissimo.com**) to see who has the best rate. Your initial shopping effort should take about 15–20 minutes, faster if you can zero in quickly on a particular hotel.

Now, armed with your insider knowledge of hotel economics, call the hotel or have your travel agent call. Start by asking about specials. If there are none, or if the hotel can't beat the best price you've found on the Internet, share your findings and ask if the hotel can do better. Sometimes you'll be asked for proof of the rate you've discovered online—to be prepared for this possibility, go to the site and enter the dates of your stay, plus the rate you've found to make sure it's available. If it is, print the page with this information and have it handy for your travel agent or for when you call the hotel.

unofficial TIP
Always call the hotel's local number, not its national toll-free number. Often, reservation agents at the toll-free number are unaware of local specials.

4. CONDOMINIUM AND VACATION-HOME DEALS The best deals in lodging in the Walt Disney World area are vacation homes and single-owner condos. Prices range from about $65 a night for two-bedroom condos and town homes to $200–$500 a night for three- to seven-bedroom vacation homes. Look for bargains, especially during off-peak periods.

Reservations and information can be obtained from the following online resources:

All Star Vacation Homes:	allstarvacationhomes.com
#1 Dream Homes	floridadreamhomes.com
Orlando's Finest Vacation Homes:	orlandosfinest.com
Last Minute Villas:	lastminutevillas.net
Vacation Rental by Owner:	vrbo.com
Vacation Rentals 411:	vacationrentals411.com
Visit Orlando:	visitorlando.com

Vacation homes are freestanding, while condominiums are essentially one- to three-bedroom accommodations in a larger building housing a number of similar units. Because condos tend to be part of large developments (frequently time-shares), amenities such as swimming pools, playgrounds, game arcades, and fitness centers often rival those found in the best hotels. Generally speaking, condo developments don't have restaurants, lounges, or spas. In a condo, if something goes wrong, there will be someone on hand to fix the problem. Vacation homes rented from a property-management company likewise will have someone to come to the rescue, though responsiveness tends to vary vastly from company to company. If you rent directly from an owner, correcting problems is often more difficult, particularly when the owner doesn't live in the same area as the rental home.

THE BEST HOTELS FOR FAMILIES OUTSIDE WALT DISNEY WORLD

WHAT MAKES A SUPER FAMILY HOTEL? Roomy accommodations, in-room fridge, great pool, complimentary breakfast, child-care options, and programs for kids are a few of the things the *Unofficial Guide* hotel team researched in selecting the top hotels for families from among hundreds of properties in the Disney World area. Some of our picks are expensive, others are more reasonable, and some are a bargain. Regardless of price, be assured that these hotels understand a family's needs.

Though all of the following hotels offer some type of shuttle to the theme parks, some offer very limited service, so call the hotel before you book and ask what the shuttle schedule will be when you visit. Because families, like individuals, have different wants and needs, we haven't ranked the following properties here; they're listed by zone and alphabetically.

International Drive & Universal Areas

CoCo Key Hotel and Water Resort–Orlando ★★★★

7400 International Dr., Orlando; ☎ 407-351-2626 or
877-875-4681; cocokeywaterresort.com

Rate per night $109–$279. **Pools** ★★★★. **Fridge in room** Yes. **Shuttle to parks** Yes (Aquatica, SeaWorld, Universal, Wet 'n Wild). **Maximum number of occupants per room** 4. **Special comments** Daily $19 room fee for use of the water park; day guests may use the water park for $22.95/person Monday–Friday ($24.95 on weekends and $17.95 for Florida residents).

DESCRIPTION AND COMMENTS CoCo Key is on International Drive, not far from the Universal Orlando theme parks. It combines a tropical-themed hotel with a canopied water park featuring 3 pools and 14 waterslides, as well as poolside food and arcade entertainment. A full-service restaurant serves breakfast and dinner; a food court offers family favorites such as burgers, chicken fingers, and pizza.

A unique feature of the resort is its cashless payment system, much like that on a cruise ship. At check-in, families receive bar-coded wristbands that allow purchased items to be easily charged to their room.

The unusually spacious guest rooms include 37-inch flat-panel TVs, free Wi-Fi, granite showers and countertops, and plenty of accessible outlets for guests' electronics.

DoubleTree by Hilton Orlando at SeaWorld ★★★★½

10100 International Dr., Orlando; ☎ 407-352-1100 or
800-327-0363; doubletreeorlandoidrive.com

Rate per night $89–$499. **Pools** ★★★½. **Fridge in room** Standard in some rooms; available in others for $10/day. **Shuttle to parks** Yes. **Maximum number of occupants per room** 4. **Special comments** A good option if you're visiting SeaWorld or Aquatica.

DESCRIPTION AND COMMENTS Formerly the International Plaza Resort & Spa, this hotel has undergone a comprehensive $35 million renovation. Situated on 28 lush, tropical acres with a Balinese feel, the Doubletree is adjacent to SeaWorld and Aquatica water park. All 1,094 rooms and suites—classified as "resort" or "tower"—have been completely refurbished and are equally suitable for business travelers or families. We recommend the tower rooms for good views and the resort rooms for maximum convenience. The Bamboo Grille serves steak and seafood along with breakfast; you can also get a quick bite at Bangli Lounge, the deli, or the pool bar. Relax and cool off at one of the three pools (there are three more just for kids), or indulge in a special spa treatment. A fitness center, minigolf course, children's day camp, and game area afford even more diversions. The resort is about a 15-minute drive to Walt Disney World, a 12-minute drive to Universal, or a short walk to SeaWorld.

Hard Rock Hotel ★★★★

5800 Universal Blvd., Orlando; ☎ 407-503-2000 or 888-464-3617; hardrockhotelorlando.com

Rate per night $200–$500. **Pool** ★★★★. **Fridge in room** $15/day. **Shuttle to parks** Yes (Universal, SeaWorld, Discovery Cove, Aquatica, and Wet 'n Wild). **Maximum number of occupants per room** 5 (double-queen) or 3 (king). **Special comments** Microwaves available for $15/day. Pets welcome ($50).

DESCRIPTION AND COMMENTS Opened in 2001, the Hard Rock is both Universal Orlando's least expensive on-site resort and the closest resort to Universal's theme parks. The exterior has a California Mission theme, with white stucco walls, arched entryways, and rust-colored roof tiles. Inside, the lobby is a tribute to rock-and-roll style, all marble, chrome, and stage lighting.

The eight floors hold 650 rooms and 29 suites, with the rooms categorized into standard, deluxe, and club-level tiers. Standard rooms are 375 square feet, slightly larger than rooms at Disney's Moderate resorts and a bit smaller than most Disney Deluxe rooms. Standard rooms are furnished with two queen beds, with smooth, plush, comfortable linens and more pillows than you'll know what to do with. Rooms also include a flat-panel LCD television, refrigerator, coffeemaker, and an alarm clock with a 30-pin iPhone docking port.

Each room's dressing area features a sink and hair dryer. The bathroom is probably large enough for most adults to get ready in the morning while another person gets ready in the dressing area.

Guests staying in standard rooms can choose from one of three views: "standard," which can include anything from walkways and parking lots to lawns and trees; "garden view," which includes the lawn, trees, and (in some rooms) the waterway around the resort; and "pool view," which includes the Hard Rock's expansive pool.

That pool is an attraction unto itself, and the place to see and be seen. Situated in the middle of the resort's C-shaped main building, the 12,000-square-foot pool includes a 250-foot water-slide, a sand beach, and underwater speakers so you can hear the music while you swim. Adjacent to the pool are a fountain play area for small children, a sand-volleyball court, hot tubs and a poolside bar. The Hard Rock also has a small, functional fitness center and a full-service Mandara Spa.

On-site dining includes The Kitchen, a casual full-service restaurant open for breakfast, lunch, and dinner, featuring American food such as burgers, steaks, and salads. The Palm Restaurant is an upscale steakhouse available for dinner only. And, of course, the Hard Rock Café is just a short distance away at Universal CityWalk.

Holiday Inn Resort Orlando–The Castle ★★★½

8629 International Dr., Orlando; ☎ 407-345-1511 or 800-952-2785; thecastleorlando.com

Rate per night $85–$250. **Pool** ★★★. **Fridge in room** Yes ($15/day). **Shuttle to parks** Yes (Universal, SeaWorld, and Wet 'n Wild). **Maximum number of occupants per room** 4. **Special comments** For an additional fee ($11.95 for adults, children age 12 and under free with paying adult), up to 4 people receive a full breakfast. Dogs up to 50 pounds welcome ($75).

DESCRIPTION AND COMMENTS You can't miss this one—it's the only castle on I-Drive. Inside you'll find royal colors (purple pre-dominates), opulent fixtures, European art, Renaissance music, and a mystic Castle Creature at the door. The 216 guest rooms also receive the royal treatment in decor, though some guests may find them gaudy. All, however, are fairly large and well equipped with TV, minibar (fridge is available at an extra charge), free Wi-Fi, coffeemaker, iron and board, hair dryer, and safe.

The Castle Café off the lobby serves full or Continental breakfast. For lunch or dinner, you might walk next door to Vito's Chop House (dinner only) or Café Tu Tu Tango (an *Unofficial* favorite). The heated circular pool is 5 feet deep and features a fountain in the center, a poolside bar, and a whirlpool. There's no separate kiddie pool.

Other amenities include fitness center, gift shop, lounge, valet laundry service and facilities, and guest-services desk with park passes for sale and babysitting recommendations. Security feature: Elevators require an electronic key card.

Loews Portofino Bay Hotel ★★★★½

5601 Universal Blvd., Orlando; ☎ 407-503-1000 or 888-464-3617; tinyurl.com/portofinobay

Rate per night $209–$559. **Pools** ★★★★. **Fridge in room** Minibar; fridge available for $15/day. **Shuttle to parks** Yes (Universal, SeaWorld, Discovery Cove, Aquatica, and Wet 'n Wild). **Maximum number of occupants per room** 4. **Special comments** Character dinner on Friday.

DESCRIPTION AND COMMENTS Universal's top-of-the-line hotel evokes the Italian seaside city of Portofino, complete with a man-made Portofino Bay. Inside, the lobby is decorated with pink marble floors, white-wood columns, and arches.

Most guest rooms are 450 square feet and have either one king bed or two queen beds. King rooms sleep up to three people with an optional rollaway bed; the same option allows queen rooms to sleep up to five. Two room-view options are available: "Garden" rooms look out over the landscaping and trees; "bay view" rooms face either west or south and overlook Portofino Bay, with a view of the piazza behind the lobby, too.

Rooms come furnished with a 32-inch LCD flat-panel TV, a refrigerator, a coffeemaker, and an alarm clock with a 30-pin iPhone docking port. Wi-Fi is $10 per day in guest rooms, free in the lobby. Beds are large and comfortable.

Guest bathrooms at Portofino Bay the best on Universal property. The shower has enough water pressure to strip paint from old furniture, not to mention an adjustable spray nozzle that varies the water pulses to simulate everything from monsoon season in the tropics to the rhythmic thumps of wildebeest hooves during migrating season. We love it.

Portofino Bay has three pools, the largest of which is the Beach Pool, on the west side of the resort. It has a zero-entry design and a waterslide themed after a Roman aqueduct, plus a children's play area, hot tubs, and a poolside bar and grill. The Villa Pool has private cabana rentals for that Italian Riviera feeling. Rounding out the luxuries are a full-service Mandara Spa and a complete fitness center with weight machines, treadmills, and more.

On-site dining includes three sit-down restaurants serving Italian cuisine; a deli; a pizzeria; and a café serving coffee and gelato. Perhaps because Universal figures that most guests have an expense account, some of the food prices go well beyond what we'd consider reasonable, even for a theme park hotel.

Loews Royal Pacific Resort ★★★★

6300 Hollywood Way, Orlando; ☎ 407-503-1000 or
888-464-3617; tinyurl.com/royal pacific

Rate per night $224–$369. **Pools** ★★★★. **Fridge in room** Minibar; fridge available for $15/day. **Shuttle to parks** Yes (Universal, SeaWorld, Discovery Cove, Aquatica, and Wet 'n Wild). **Maximum number of occupants per room** 5 (double queen) or 3 (king). **Special comments** Microwaves available for $15/day.

DESCRIPTION AND COMMENTS The Royal Pacific's South Seas–inspired theming is both relaxing and structured. You enter the lobby from a walkway two stories above an artificial stream that surrounds the resort. Once you're inside, the lobby's dark teakwood accents contrast nicely with the enormous amount of light coming in from the windows and three-story A-frame roof. Palms line the walkway through the lobby.

The 1,000 guest rooms are spread among three Y-shaped wings attached to the resort's main building. Standard rooms are 335 square feet and feature one king or two queen beds. King rooms sleep up to three people with an optional rollaway bed; queen rooms sleep five with that rollaway bed.

Rooms are decorated in neutral beige tones, with dark wood and paint accents and forest-colored carpet, and include a 32-inch flat-panel LCD TV, a refrigerator, a coffeemaker, and an alarm clock with a 30-pin iPhone docking port. Wi-Fi is $10 per day in guest rooms, free in the lobby.

Rooms have a dressing area with sink, separated from the rest of the room by a wall. Adjacent to the dressing area is the bathroom, with a tub, shower, and toilet.

Guests in north- and west-facing rooms in Tower 1 are closest to attractions at Islands of Adventure. East-facing rooms in Towers 1 and 2 are exposed to traffic noise from Universal Boulevard and, more distantly, I-4. Quietest are south-facing pool-view rooms in Tower 1 and south-facing rooms in Tower 3.

As at the Hard Rock, the Royal Pacific's zero-entry pool includes a sand beach, volleyball court, play area for kids, hot tub, and cabanas for rent, plus a poolside bar and grill.

The Royal Pacific includes a 5,000-square-foot fitness facility, two full-service restaurants, three bars, and a luau. The Islands Dining Room is open for breakfast. Emeril Lagasse's Tchoup Chop, the other table-service option, serves Asian-inspired food; it's open for lunch and dinner (reservations recommended).

Nickelodeon Suites Resort   ★★★½

14500 Continental Gateway, Orlando; ☎ 407-387-5437 or 877-NICK-111; nickhotel.com

Rate per night $129–$649. **Pools** ★★★★. **Fridge in room** Yes. **Shuttle to parks** Yes. **Maximum number of occupants per room** 8. **Special comments** Daily character breakfast; resort fee of $25/night.

DESCRIPTION AND COMMENTS This resort is as kid-friendly as they come and is sure to please any fan of TV shows the likes of and Nickelodeon characters hang out in the resort's lobby and mall area, greeting kids while parents check in. Guests can choose from among 777 suites—one-bedroom Family Suites and two- and three-bedroom KidSuites—executed in a number of different themes—all very brightly and creatively decorated. All suites include kitchenettes or full kitchens; also standard are a microwave, fridge, coffeemaker, TV, iron and board, hair dryer, and a safe. KidSuites feature a semiprivate kids' bedroom with bunk or twin beds, pull-out sleeper bed, 32-inch TV, CD player, and activity table. Additional amenities include a high-tech video arcade, Studio Nick—a game-show studio that hosts several game shows a night for the entertainment of a live studio audience, a buffet (kids 3 and younger eat free with a paying adult), a food court offering Subway and other choices, the full-service Nicktoons Cafe (offers character breakfasts), a convenience store, a lounge, a gift shop, a fitness center, a washer and dryer in each courtyard, and a guest-activities desk (buy Disney tickets and get recommendations on babysitting). Not to be missed—don't worry, your kids won't let you—are the resort's two pools, Oasis and Lagoon. Oasis features a water park complete with water cannons, rope ladders, geysers, and dump buckets, as well as a hot tub for adults (with a view of the rest of the pool to keep an eye on little ones) and a smaller play area for younger kids. Kids will love the huge, zero-depth-entry Lagoon Pool, replete with 400-gallon dump bucket, plus nearby basketball court and nine-hole minigolf course.

Rosen Shingle Creek ★★★★

9939 Universal Blvd., Orlando; ☎ 407-996-9939 or 866-996-6338; rosenshinglecreek.com

Rate per night $104–$294. **Pools** ★★★★. **Fridge in room** Yes. **Shuttle to parks** Yes (Universal, Wet 'n Wild, Discovery Cove, Aquatica, and SeaWorld only). **Maximum number of occupants per room** 4.

DESCRIPTION AND COMMENTS Beautiful rooms (east-facing ones have great views) and excellent restaurants distinguish this mostly meeting- and convention-oriented resort. The pools are large and lovely and include a lap pool, a family pool, and a kiddie wading pool. There's an 18-hole golf course on-site as well as a superior spa and an adequate fitness center. Child care is provided as well. Though a state-of-the-art video arcade will gobble up your kids' pocket change, the real kicker, especially for the 8-years-and-up crowd, is a natural area encompassing lily ponds, grassy wetlands, Shingle Creek, and an adjacent cypress swamp. Running through the area is a nature trail complete with signs to help you identify wildlife. Great blue herons, wood storks, coots, egrets, mallard ducks, anhingas, and ospreys are common, as are sliders (turtles), chameleons, and skinks (lizards). Oh yeah, there are alligators and snakes, too—real ones, but that's part of the fun. Hotel shuttle service is limited, departing and picking up at rather inconvenient times and stopping at three other hotels before delivering you to your destination.

Lake Buena Vista and I-4 Corridor

Buena Vista Palace Hotel & Spa ★★★½

1900 E. Buena Vista Dr., Lake Buena Vista; ☎ 407-827-2727 or 866-397-6516; buenavistapalace.com

Rate per night $99–$380. **Pools** ★★★½. **Fridge in room** Yes. **Shuttle to parks** Yes (Disney only). **Maximum number of occupants per room** 4. **Special comments** Sunday character brunch available.

DESCRIPTION AND COMMENTS In the Downtown Disney Resort Area, the Buena Vista Palace is upscale and convenient. Surrounded by an artificial lake and plenty of palms, the spacious pool area contains three heated pools, the largest of which is partially covered (nice for when you need a little shade); a whirlpool and sauna; a basketball court; and a sand-volleyball court. Plus, a pool concierge will fetch your favorite magazine or fruity drink. On Sunday, the Watercress Café hosts a Disney-character brunch ($22 for adults and $10 for children).

The 897 guest rooms are posh and spacious; each comes with a desk, coffeemaker, hair dryer, satellite TV with pay-per-view movies, iron and board, and minifridge. There are also 117 suites. In-room babysitting is available through All About Kids. One lighted tennis court, the sumptuous Kay Casperson Lifestyle Spa, a fitness center, an arcade, and a playground round out the amenities. Two restaurants and a mini-market are on-site. And if you aren't wiped out after time in the parks, drop by the Lobby Lounge or the full-menu sports bar for a nightcap. Be aware that all these amenities and services come at a price—a $17-per-night resort fee is added to your bill.

Hilton in the Walt Disney World Resort ★★★★

1751 Hotel Plaza Blvd., Lake Buena Vista; ☎ 407-827-4000; hilton-wdwv.com

Rate per night $99–$309. **Pools** ★★★½. **Fridge in room** Minibar; minifridge available free on request. **Shuttle to parks** Yes (Disney theme and water parks only). **Maximum number of occupants per room** 4. **Special comments** Sunday character breakfast and Disney Extra Magic Hours program.

DESCRIPTION AND COMMENTS The Hilton occupies 23 acres in the Downtown Disney Resort Area (DDRA). Its 814 guest rooms and suites are spacious, although the decor is a bit dated and the daily fees are outrageous ($45 plus tax). Standard rooms have a granite bath, iron and board, hair dryer, two phones, desk, mini-bar, coffeemaker, and cable TV with pay-per-view movies and video games. A character-breakfast buffet is served from 8:30 to 11 a.m. on Sunday (reservations recommended). Five characters attend; only two are present at a time.

Other important family amenities include babysitting, an arcade and pool table, and two landscaped heated swimming pools, plus a kiddie pool. Adults and older kids can relax in the fitness center after a long day touring. Seven restaurants, including Benihana, add to the hotel's convenience. This is the only hotel in the DDRA that participates in Disney's Extra Magic Hours program.

Holiday Inn Resort Lake Buena Vista ★★★½

13351 FL 535, Lake Buena Vista; ☎ 407-239-4500 or 866-808-8833; hisunspreelbv.com

Rate per night $71–$200. **Pool** ★★★. **Fridge in room** Yes. **Shuttle to parks** Yes (Disney only). **Maximum number of occupants per room** 4–6. **Special comments** Resort fee of $11.95/night entitles guests to numerous perks, including use of fitness center and daily fountain drinks for kids.

DESCRIPTION AND COMMENTS The big lure here is KidSuites—405-square-foot rooms, each with a separate children's area. Themes include a tree house, jail, space capsule, and fort, among others. The kids' area sleeps two to four children in one or two sets of bunk beds. The separate adult area has its own TV, safe, hair dryer, and mini-kitchenette with fridge, microwave, sink, and coffeemaker. Other kid-friendly amenities include the tiny Castle Movie Theater, which shows movies all day, every day; a playground; an arcade with video games and air hockey, among its many games; and a basketball court. Other amenities include a fitness center for the grown-ups and a large free-form pool complete with kiddie pool and two whirlpools. Applebee's serves breakfast and dinner and offers an à la carte menu for dinner. There's also a minimart. More perks: Kids age 12 and younger eat free from a special menu when dining with one paying adult (maximum four kids per adult), and "Dive-Inn" poolside movies are shown Saturday nights. Finally, pets weighing 30 pounds or less are welcome for an additional $40 nonrefundable fee.

Hyatt Regency Grand Cypress ★★★★½

1 Grand Cypress Blvd., Orlando; ☎ 407-239-1234; grandcypress.hyatt.com

Rate per night $144–$399. **Pool ★★★★★**. **Fridge in room** Yes, plus minibar. **Shuttle to parks** Yes (Disney, Universal, SeaWorld). **Maximum number of occupants per room** 4. **Special comments** Wow, what a pool!

DESCRIPTION AND COMMENTS There are myriad reasons to stay at this 1,500-acre resort, but the pool ranks as number one. The 800,000-gallon tropical paradise has two 45-foot water-slides, waterfalls, caves and grottoes, and a suspension bridge. The Hyatt also is a golfer's paradise. With 45 holes of Jack Nicklaus–designed championship golf, a 9-hole pitch-and-putt course, and a golf academy, there's something for golfers of all abilities. Other recreational perks include a racquet facility with hard and clay courts, a private lake with beach, a fitness center, and miles of trails for biking, walking, and jogging. (A daily $22 resort fee applies.) The 769 standard guest rooms are 360 square feet and have a Florida ambience, with green and reddish hues, touches of rattan, and private balconies. Amenities include minibar, iron and board, safe, hair dryer, ceiling fan, and cable/satellite TV with pay-per-view movies and video games. Camp Hyatt provides supervised programs for kids ages 3–12; in-room baby-sitting is available. Six restaurants offer dining options. Four lounges provide nighttime entertainment.

Marriott Village at Lake Buena Vista ★★★

8623 Vineland Ave., Orlando; ☎ 407-938-9001 or 800-761-7829; marriottvillage.com

Rate per night $79–$189. **Pools ★★★**. **Fridge in room** Yes. **Shuttle to parks** Disney only, $7. **Maximum number of occupants per room** 4 (Courtyard and

Fairfield) or 5 (SpringHill). **Special comments** Free Continental breakfast at Fairfield and SpringHill.

DESCRIPTION AND COMMENTS This gated hotel community includes a 388-room Fairfield Inn, a 400-suite SpringHill Suites, and a 312-room Courtyard. Amenities at all three properties include fridge, cable TV, iron and board, hair dryer, and microwave. Cribs and roll-away beds are available at no extra charge at all locations. Swimming pools at all three hotels are attractive and medium-sized, featuring children's interactive splash zones and whirlpools; in addition, each property has its own fitness center. The incredibly convenient Village Marketplace food court includes Pizza Hut, Village Grill, Village Coffee House, along with a 24-hour convenience store. Bahama Breeze and Golden Corral full-service restaurants are within walking distance. Other services and amenities include a Disney planning station and ticket sales, an arcade, and a Hertz car-rental desk. Shoppers will find the Orlando Premium Outlets adjacent.

Sheraton Lake Buena Vista Resort ★★★★

12205 S. Apopka–Vineland Rd., Lake Buena Vista; ☎ 407-239-0444 or 800-325-3535; sheratonlakebuenavistaresort.com

Rate per night $90–$351. **Pool ★★★★. Fridge in room** Yes. **Shuttle to parks** Yes (Disney only). **Maximum number of occupants per room** 4–6. **Special comments** Dogs 80 pounds and under welcome; $9.95/day resort fee.

DESCRIPTION AND COMMENTS Formerly the Sheraton Safari Hotel & Suites, this resort underwent a $25 million renovation in 2012. The entire property, including the 400 guest rooms and the 90 family junior suites, has gotten major upgrades that give it a sleek, modern feel. The family junior suites provide bunk beds for children, but gone are the kitchenettes. Amenities in each room include Sheraton Sweet Sleeper beds, free Wi-Fi, 42-inch HDTV, refrigerator, coffeemaker, hair dryer, safe, clock-radio, and iron and board. Microwaves are available at an extra charge. The relaxing pool area features cabanas with food service (for a fee), and youngsters can enjoy the cascading waterfall and waterslide. The Top of the Palms Spa offers massages, facials, manicures, and pedicures. Also on-site are two restaurants, a business center, a fitness center, an arcade, and a gift shop.

Sheraton Vistana Resort Villas ★★★★½

8800 Vistana Centre Dr., Lake Buena Vista; ☎ 407-239-3100 or 866-208-0003; sheraton.com

Rate per night $129–$209. **Pools ★★★½. Fridge in room** Yes. **Shuttle to parks** Yes (Disney free; other parks for a fee). **Maximum number of occupants per room** 4–8. **Special comments** Though time-shares, the villas are rented nightly as well.

DESCRIPTION AND COMMENTS The Vistana is one of Orlando's best off-Disney properties. If you want a serene retreat from your days in the theme parks, this is an excellent base. The spacious villas come in one-bedroom, two-bedroom, and two-bedroom-with-lock-off models (which can be reconfigured as one studio room and a one-bedroom suite). All are decorated in beachy pastels, but the emphasis is on the profusion of amenities. Each villa has a full kitchen (including fridge/freezer, microwave, oven/range, dishwasher, toaster, and coffeemaker, with an option to prestock with groceries and laundry products), clothes washer and dryer, TVs in the living room and each bedroom (one with DVD player), stereo with CD player in some villas, separate dining area, and private patio or balcony in most. Grounds offer seven swimming pools (three with bars), four playgrounds, two restaurants, game rooms, fitness centers, a minigolf course, sports equipment rental (including bikes), and courts for basketball, volleyball, tennis, and shuffleboard. A mind-boggling array of activities for kids (and adults) ranges from crafts to games and sports tournaments. Of special note: Vistana is highly secure, with locked gates bordering all guest areas, so children can have the run of the place without parents worrying about them wandering off.

Waldorf Astoria Orlando ★★★★½

14200 Bonnet Creek Resort Lane, Lake Buena Vista;
☎ 407-597-5500; waldorfastoriaorlando.com

Rate per night $309–$4,000+. **Pool** ★★★. **Fridge in room** Yes. **Shuttle to parks** Yes (Disney only) **Maximum number of occupants per room** 4, plus child in crib. **Special comments** Great alternative to Disney's Deluxe properties.

DESCRIPTION AND COMMENTS Opened in 2009, the Waldorf Astoria is between I-4 and Disney's Pop Century Resort, near the Hilton Orlando at the back of the Bonnet Creek Resort property. Getting here requires a GPS or good directions, so be prepared with those before you travel. Once you arrive, however, you'll know the trip was worth it. Beautifully decorated and well manicured, the Waldorf is more elegant than any Disney resort. Service is excellent, and the staff-to-guest ratio is far lower than at Disney properties.

At just under 450 square feet, standard rooms feature either two queen beds or one king. A full-size desk allows you to get work done if it's absolutely necessary, and rooms also have flat-screen televisions, high-speed Internet, and Wi-Fi. The bathrooms are spacious and gorgeous, with cool marble floors, glass-walled showers, separate tubs, and enough counter space for a Broadway makeup artist. This space is so nice that when we stayed here in 2009, we debated whether we'd rather stay at Pop Century with three others or sleep in a Waldorf bathroom by ourselves.

Amenities include a fitness center, a spa, a golf course, six restaurants, and two pools (including one zero-entry for kids). Pool-size cabanas are available for rent. The resort offers shuttle service to the Disney parks about every half-hour, but check with the front desk for the exact schedule when you arrive. Runners will enjoy the relative solitude—it's about a 1-mile round-trip to the nearest busy road.

Wyndham Bonnet Creek Resort ★★★★½

9560 Via Encinas, Lake Buena Vista; ☎ 407-238-3500 or 888-743-2687; wyndhambonnetcreek.com

Rate per night $179–$329. **Pool** ★★★★. **Fridge in room** Yes. **Shuttle to parks** Disney only. **Maximum number of occupants per room** 4–12 depending on room/suite. **Special comments** A non-Disney suite hotel within Walt Disney World.

DESCRIPTION AND COMMENTS This condo hotel lies on the south side of Buena Vista Drive, about a quarter-mile east of Disney's Caribbean Beach Resort. The property has an interesting history: When Walt Disney began secretly buying up real estate in the 1960s under the names of numerous front companies, the land on which this resort stands was the last holdout and was never sold to Disney, though the company tried repeatedly to acquire it through the years. (The owners reportedly took issue with the way Disney went about acquiring land and preferred to see the site languish undeveloped.) The 482-acre site was ultimately bought by Marriott, which put up a Fairfield Inn time-share development in 2004. The Wyndham is part of the Bonnet Creek Resort, a hotel, golf, and convention complex that also includes a 500-room Waldorf Astoria (see previous page) and a 1,000-room Hilton. The development is surrounded on three sides by Disney property and on one side by I-4.

The Wyndham Bonnet Creek offers upscale, family-friendly accommodations: one- and two-bedroom condos with fully equipped kitchens, washer-dryers, jetted tubs, and balconies. Activities and amenities on-site include two outdoor swimming pools, a "lazy river" float stream, a children's activities program, a game room, a playground, and miniature golf. Free scheduled transportation serves all the Disney parks. One-bedroom units are equipped with a king bed in the bedroom and a sleeper sofa in the living area; two-bedroom condos have two double beds in the second bedroom, a sleeper sofa in the living area, and an additional bath.

US 192

Clarion Suites Maingate ★★★½

7888 W. Irlo Bronson Memorial Hwy., Kissimmee; ☎ 407-390-9888 or 888-390-9888; clarionsuiteskissimmee.com

Rate per night $49–$149. **Pool** ★★★. **Fridge in room** Yes. **Shuttle to parks** Yes (Disney, Universal, and SeaWorld). **Maximum number of occupants per room** 6 for most suites. **Special comments** Free Continental breakfast served daily.

DESCRIPTION AND COMMENTS This property has 150 spacious one-room suites, each with double sofa bed, microwave, fridge, coffeemaker, TV, hair dryer, and safe. The suites are clean and contemporary, with muted deep-purple and beige tones. The large, heated pool has plenty of lounge chairs and moderate landscaping. A kiddie pool, whirlpool, and poolside bar complete the courtyard. Other amenities include an arcade and a gift shop. But Maingate's big plus is its location next door to a shopping center with about everything a family could need. There, you'll find 10 dining options, including Outback Steakhouse, Red Lobster, Subway, T.G.I. Friday's, and Chinese, Italian, and Japanese eateries; a Winn-Dixie Marketplace; a liquor store; a bank; a dry cleaner; and a tourist-information center with park passes for sale, among other services.

Gaylord Palms Hotel and Convention Center ★★★★½

6000 W. Osceola Pkwy., Kissimmee; ☎ 407-586-2000; gaylordpalms.com

Rate per night $144–$289. **Pool** ★★★★. **Fridge in room** Yes. **Shuttle to parks** Yes (Disney only). **Maximum number of occupants per room** 4. **Special comments** Probably the closest you'll get off-World to Disney-level extravagance. Resort fee of $15/day.

DESCRIPTION AND COMMENTS This decidedly upscale resort has a colossal convention facility and caters strongly to business clientele, but it's still a nice (if pricey) family resort. Hotel wings are defined by the three themed, glass-roofed atriums they overlook. Key West's design is reminiscent of island life in the Florida Keys; Everglades is an overgrown spectacle of shabby swamp chic, complete with piped-in cricket noise and a robotic alligator; and the immense, central St. Augustine harks back to Spanish Colonial Florida. Lagoons, streams, and waterfalls cut through and connect all three, and walkways and bridges abound. Rooms reflect the colors of their respective areas, though there's no particular connection in decor (St. Augustine atrium-view rooms are the most opulent, but they're not Spanish). A fourth wing, Emerald Bay Tower, overlooks the Emerald Plaza shopping and dining area of the St. Augustine atrium. These rooms are the nicest and the most expensive, and they're mostly used by convention-goers. Though rooms have fridges and alarm clocks with CD players (as well as other perks such as high-speed Internet access), the rooms themselves really work better as retreats for adults than for kids. However, children will enjoy wandering the themed areas, playing in the family pool (with water-squirting octopus); in-room child care is provided by Kid's Nite Out.

Orange Lake Resort ★★★★½

8505 W. Irlo Bronson Memorial Hwy., Kissimmee; ☎ 407-239-0000 or 800-877-6522; orangelake.com

Rate per night $69–$289. **Pools** ★★★★. **Fridge in room** Yes. **Shuttle to parks** Yes (fee varies depending on destination). **Maximum number of**

occupants per room Varies. **Special comments** This is a time-share property, but if you rent directly through the resort (as opposed to the sales office), you can avoid time-share sales pitches.

DESCRIPTION AND COMMENTS You could spend your entire vacation never leaving this property, about 6–10 minutes from the Disney theme parks. From its 10 pools and 2 mini–water parks to its golfing opportunities (36 holes of championship greens plus two 9-hole executive courses), Orange Lake offers an extensive menu of amenities and recreational opportunities. If you tire of lazing by the pool, try waterskiing, wakeboarding, tubing, fishing, or other activities on the 80-acre lake. There's also a live alligator show, exercise programs, organized competitive sports and games, arts-and-crafts sessions, and miniature golf. Activities don't end when the sun goes down. Karaoke, live music, a Hawaiian luau, and movies at the resort cinema are some of the evening options.

The 2,412 units are tastefully decorated and comfortably furnished, ranging from suites and studios to three-bedroom villas, all containing fully equipped kitchens. Seven restaurants are scattered across the resort: two cafes, three grills, one pizzeria, and a fast-food eatery. If you need help with (or a break from) the kids, babysitters are available.

Radisson Resort Orlando-Celebration ★★★★

2900 Parkway Blvd., Kissimmee; ☎ 407-396-7000 or 800-634-4774; radissonorlandoresort.com

Rate per night $70–$250. **Pool** ★★★★½. **Fridge in room** Yes. **Shuttle to parks** Yes (Disney only). **Maximum number of occupants per room** 5. **Special comments** $12.50/day resort fee; kids age 10 and younger eat free with a paying adult at Mandolin's restaurant.

DESCRIPTION AND COMMENTS The free-form swimming pool alone is worth a stay here, but the Radisson Resort gets high marks in all areas. The pool is huge, with a waterfall and waterslide surrounded by palms and flowering plants, plus a smaller heated pool, two whirlpools, and a kiddie pool. Other outdoor amenities include two lighted tennis courts, sand volleyball, a playground, and jogging areas. Kids can also blow off steam at the arcade, while adults might visit the fitness center. Rooms are elegant, featuring Italian furnishings and marble baths. They're of ample size and include a minibar (some rooms), coffeemaker, TV, iron and board, hair dryer, and safe. Dining options include Mandolin's for breakfast (buffet) and dinner, and a 1950s-style diner serving burgers, sandwiches, shakes, and Pizza Hut pizza, among other fare. A sports lounge with an 6 x 11–foot TV offers nighttime entertainment. Guest services can help with tours, park passes, car rental, and babysitting. While there are no children's programs per se, there are still plenty of activities for little ones to enjoy, such as face painting by a clown, juggling classes, bingo, and arts and crafts at the pool.

HOTELS *and* MOTELS:
Rated and Ranked

IN THIS SECTION, WE COMPARE HOTELS in four main areas outside Walt Disney World with those inside the World.

ROOM RATINGS

TO EVALUATE PROPERTIES FOR THEIR QUALITY, tastefulness, state of repair, cleanliness, and size of their standard rooms, we have grouped the hotels and motels into classifications denoted by stars—the overall star rating. Star ratings in this guide apply only to Orlando-area properties and don't necessarily correspond to ratings awarded by *Frommer's,* Mobil, AAA, or other travel critics. Because stars have little relevance when awarded in the absence of recognized standards of comparison, we have tied our ratings to expected levels of quality established by specific American hotel corporations.

Overall star ratings apply only to room quality and describe the property's standard accommodations. For most hotels, a standard accommodation is a room with one king bed or two queen beds. In an all-suite property, the standard accommodation is either a studio or one-bedroom suite. Star ratings for rooms are assigned without regard to whether a property has restaurant(s), recreational facilities, entertainment, or other extras.

In addition to stars (which delineate broad categories), we use a numerical rating system—the room-quality rating. Our scale is 0–100, with 100 being the best possible rating and zero (0) the worst. Numerical ratings show the difference we perceive between one property and another. For instance, rooms at both the Hawthorn Suites Universal and the Clarion Suites Maingate are rated 3½ stars (★★★½). In the supplemental numerical ratings, the former is an 82 and the latter a 76. This means that within the 3½-star category, Hawthorn Suites has slightly nicer rooms than Clarion Suites.

LODGING AREAS *(see map on page 43)*	
WDW	Walt Disney World
1	International Drive
2	Lake Buena Vista and I-4 Corridor
3	US 192 (Irlo Bronson Memorial Highway)
4	Universal Orlando Area

The location column identifies the area around Walt Disney World where you'll find a particular property. The designation

WDW means the property is inside Walt Disney World. A **1** means it's on or near International Drive. Properties on or near US 192 (a.k.a. Irlo Bronson Memorial Highway, Vine Street, and Space Coast Parkway) are indicated by a **3**, those in the vicinity of Universal Orlando as **4**. All others are marked with **2** and for the most part are along FL 535 and the I-4 corridor, though some are in nearby locations that don't meet any other criteria.

Names of properties along US 192 also designate location (for example, Holiday Inn Maingate West). The consensus in Orlando seems to be that the main entrance to Disney World is the broad interstate-type road that runs off US 192. This is called the **Maingate**. Properties along US 192 call themselves Maingate East or West to differentiate their positions along the highway. So, driving southeast from Clermont or Florida's Turnpike, the properties before you reach the Maingate turnoff are called Maingate West, while the properties after you pass the Maingate turnoff are called Maingate East.

OVERALL STAR RATINGS		
★★★★★	Superior rooms	Tasteful and luxurious by any standard
★★★★	Extremely nice rooms	What you'd expect at a Hyatt Regency or Marriott
★★★	Nice rooms	Holiday Inn or comparable quality
★★	Adequate rooms	Clean, comfortable, and functional without frills—like a Motel 6
★	Super-budget	These exist but are not included in our coverage

Cost estimates are based on the hotel's published rack rates for standard rooms. Each **$** represents $50. Thus a cost symbol of **$$$** means that a room (or suite) at that hotel will be about $150 a night; for space, rates of $250+ are indicated by **$ x 5** and so on.

We've focused on room quality and excluded consideration of location, services, recreation, or amenities. In some instances, a one- or two-room suite is available for the same price or less than that of a single standard hotel room.

If you've used an earlier edition of this guide, you'll notice that new properties have been added and many ratings and rankings have changed, some because of room renovation or improved maintenance or housekeeping. Failure to maintain rooms or lax housekeeping can bring down ratings.

The key to avoiding disappointment in a room is to snoop in advance. When you or your travel agent calls, ask how old the property is and when the guest room you're being assigned was last renovated. Note that some chains use the same guest-room

The Top 30 Best Deals

RANK	HOTEL	LODGING AREA	OVERALL QUALITY	ROOM QUALITY	($ = $50)
1.	Monumental Hotel	1	★★★★½	94	$+
2.	Extended Stay America Universal	4	★	87	$+
3.	Radisson Resort Orlando-Celebration	3	★★★★	86	$$−
4.	Claremont Hotel Kissimmee	3	★★½	63	$−
5.	Rodeway Inn Maingate	3	★★½	58	$−
6.	Grand Beach	1	★★★★½	90	$$
7.	DoubleTree by Hilton Orlando at SeaWorld *(resort)*	1	★★★★½	92	$$+
8.	DoubleTree by Hilton Orlando at SeaWorld *(tower)*	1	★★★★½	92	$$+
9.	Orlando Vista Hotel	2	★★★★	83	$$−
10.	Rosen Plaza Hotel	1	★★★★½	93	$$+
11.	Holiday Inn Main Gate East	3	★★★★½	90	$$+
12.	Orbit One Vacation Villas	3	★★★½	80	$$−
13.	Howard Johnson Enchanted Land Hotel	3	★★½	59	$−
14.	Extended Stay Deluxe Orlando Lake Buena Vista	2	★★★★	83	$$
15.	The Floridian Hotel & Suites	1	★★★	68	$+

photo in promotional literature for all their hotels and that the room in a specific property may not resemble the photo. If you're assigned a room inferior to expectations, demand to be moved.

THE 30 BEST HOTEL VALUES

LET'S LOOK AT THE BEST COMBINATIONS of quality and value in a room. Listed above are our top 30 buys for the money regardless of location or star rating, based on average rack rates. These rankings were made without consideration for the availability of restaurant(s), recreational facilities, entertainment, and/or other amenities.

A reader recently wrote to complain that he had booked one of our top-ranked rooms for value and had been very disappointed in it. The room had a quality rating of ★★½, but remember that the list of top deals is intended to give you some sense of value received *for dollars spent*. Regardless of whether it's a good deal, a ★★½ room is still a ★★½ room.

The Top 30 Best Deals (continued)

RANK	HOTEL	LODGING AREA	OVERALL QUALITY	ROOM QUALITY	($ = $50)
16.	Vacation Village at Parkway	3	★★★★½	91	$$–
17.	Country Inn & Suites Orlando Maingate at Calypso	3	★★★½	82	$$–
18.	Four Points by Sheraton Orlando Studio City	1	★★★★½	90	$$+
19.	Destiny Palms Maingate West	3	★★★	66	$+
20.	Rosen Centre Hotel	1	★★★★½	94	$$$–
21.	Westgate Town Center	2	★★★★½	94	$$$–
22.	DoubleTree Universal	4	★★★★	89	$$+
23.	Champions World Resort	3	★★★	66	$+
24.	Westgate Vacation Villas	2	★★★★½	93	$$$–
25.	Hilton Garden Inn Lake Buena Vista/Orlando	2	★★★★	88	$$+
26.	Shades of Green	WDW	★★★★½	91	$$$–
27.	CoCo Key Water Resort– Orlando	1	★★★★½	90	$$$–
28.	Wyndham Orlando Resort	1	★★★★½	90	$$$–
29.	Quality Suites Orlando	2	★★★	74	$+
30.	Super 8 Kissimmee	3	★★★	74	$+

For example, the Magic Castle Inn and Suites is clean and reasonably comfortable, has an exceptionally friendly staff, is within 15 minutes of every Disney theme park, and has great deals on rooms. The catch? They're right next door to a place that gives helicopter tours of Orlando . . . all day long.

How the Hotels Compare

HOTEL	LODGING AREA	OVERALL QUALITY	ROOM QUALITY	($ = $50)
Omni Orlando Resort at ChampionsGate	2	★★★★★	96	$$$$+
Animal Kingdom Villas (Kidani Village)	WDW	★★★★½	95	$ x 10–
Bay Lake Tower at Contemporary Resort	WDW	★★★★½	95	$ x 10+
Bohemian Celebration Hotel	2	★★★★½	95	$$$$+
Gaylord Palms Hotel & Convention Center	3	★★★★½	95	$ x 5

How the Hotels Compare (continued)

HOTEL	LODGING AREA	OVERALL QUALITY	ROOM QUALITY	($ = $50)
Hilton Grand Vacations Club at SeaWorld	1	★★★★½	95	$$$–
Marriott's Grande Vista	1	★★★★½	95	$ x 5
Sheraton Vistana Resort Villas	2	★★★★½	95	$$$
Contemporary Resort	WDW	★★★★½	94	$ x 9–
Hilton Grand Vacations Club on I-Drive	1	★★★★½	94	$$$+
Marriott's Sabal Palms	2	★★★★½	94	$ x 8+
Monumental Hotel	1	★★★★½	94	$+
Orange Lake Resort	3	★★★★½	94	$$$
Orlando World Center Marriott Resort	2	★★★★½	94	$ x 5+
The Ritz-Carlton Orlando, Grande Lakes	1	★★★★½	94	$ x 9+
Rosen Centre Hotel	1	★★★★½	94	$$$–
Westgate Town Center	2	★★★★½	94	$$$–
Floridays Resort Orlando	1	★★★★½	93	$$$$–
Grand Floridian Resort & Spa	WDW	★★★★½	93	$ x 17–
JW Marriott Orlando Grande Lakes	1	★★★★½	93	$$$$
Renaissance Orlando SeaWorld	1	★★★★½	93	$$$+
Rosen Plaza Hotel	1	★★★★½	93	$$+
Waldorf Astoria Orlando	2	★★★★½	93	$ x 7–
Westgate Vacation Villas	2	★★★★½	93	$$$–
DoubleTree by Hilton Orlando at SeaWorld (resort)	1	★★★★½	92	$$+
DoubleTree by Hilton Orlando at SeaWorld (tower)	1	★★★★½	92	$$+
Hilton Orlando	1	★★★★½	92	$$$+
Hyatt Regency Grand Cypress	2	★★★★½	92	$$$$+
Loews Portofino Bay Hotel	4	★★★★½	92	$ x 9–
Polynesian Resort	WDW	★★★★½	92	$ x 11
Westgate Lakes Resort & Spa	2	★★★★½	92	$$$–
Animal Kingdom Villas (Jambo House)	WDW	★★★★½	91	$ x 8+
Royal Plaza (tower)	WDW	★★★★½	91	$ x 6–
Shades of Green	WDW	★★★★½	91	$$$–
Vacation Village at Parkway	3	★★★★½	91	$$–
Beach Club Resort	WDW	★★★★½	90	$ x 9+
Beach Club Villas	WDW	★★★★½	90	$ x 10–
BoardWalk Villas	WDW	★★★★½	90	$ x 10–
CoCo Key Water Resort–Orlando	1	★★★★½	90	$$$–
Dolphin	WDW	★★★★½	90	$$$$+

How the Hotels Compare *(continued)*

HOTEL	LODGING AREA	OVERALL QUALITY	ROOM QUALITY	($ = $50)
Four Points by Sheraton Orlando Studio City	1	★★★★½	90	$$+
Grand Beach	1	★★★★½	90	$$
Holiday Inn Main Gate East	3	★★★★½	90	$$+
Lighthouse Key Resort & Spa	3	★★★★½	90	$ x 5–
Liki Tiki Village	3	★★★★½	90	$$$+
Marriott's Harbour Lake	2	★★★★½	90	$$$+
Old Key West Resort	WDW	★★★★½	90	$ x 8
Hyatt Regency Orlando Convention Center	1	★★★★½	90	$$$$
Polynesian Isles Resort (Diamond Resorts)	3	★★★★½	90	$$$$+
Saratoga Springs Resort & Spa	WDW	★★★★½	90	$ x 8
Swan	WDW	★★★★½	90	$ x 5–
Treehouse Villas at Saratoga Springs Resort & Spa	WDW	★★★★½	90	$ x 19–
Villas at Wilderness Lodge	WDW	★★★★½	90	$ x 9
Villas of Grand Cypress	2	★★★★½	90	$ x 10–
Wyndham Bonnet Creek Resort	2	★★★★½	90	$$$$+
Wyndham Orlando Resort	1	★★★★½	90	$$$–
Animal Kingdom Lodge	WDW	★★★★	89	$ x 8–
BoardWalk Inn	WDW	★★★★	89	$ x 10–
Courtyard Orlando Lake Buena Vista at Vista Centre	2	★★★★	89	$$$+
DoubleTree Universal	4	★★★★	89	$$+
Hilton Orlando Bonnet Creek	1	★★★★	89	$$$$
Caribe Royale All-Suite Hotel & Convention Center	1	★★★★	88	$ x 5–
Hilton Garden Inn Lake Buena Vista/Orlando	2	★★★★	88	$$+
Marriott's Royal Palms	1	★★★★	88	$ x 8+
Rosen Shingle Creek	1	★★★★	88	$$$
Sheraton Lake Buena Vista Resort	2	★★★★	88	$$$+
WorldQuest Orlando Resort	1	★★★★	88	$$$$+
Yacht Club Resort	WDW	★★★★	88	$ x 9+
Extended Stay America Orlando Convention Center	1	★★★★	87	$$$–
Extended Stay America Universal	4	★★★★	87	$+
Hawthorn Suites Lake Buena Vista	2	★★★★	87	$$$–
Hilton in the Walt Disney World Resort	WDW	★★★★	87	$$$–
Marriott Cypress Harbour Villas	1	★★★★	87	$ x 8–

How the Hotels Compare (continued)

HOTEL	LODGING AREA	OVERALL QUALITY	ROOM QUALITY	($ = $50)
Mystic Dunes Resort & Golf Club	3	★★★★	87	$$$$
Westin Imagine Orlando	1	★★★★	87	$$$$–
Wyndham Cypress Palms	3	★★★★	87	$$$–
Fort Wilderness Resort (cabins)	WDW	★★★★	86	$ x 8–
Marriott Imperial Palm Villas	1	★★★★	86	$ x 13–
Radisson Resort Orlando-Celebration	3	★★★★	86	$$–
Wilderness Lodge	WDW	★★★★	86	$ x 11
Barefoot'n Resort	3	★★★★	85	$$
Best Western Lake Buena Vista Resort Hotel	WDW	★★★★	85	$$$
Caribe Cove Resort Orlando	3	★★★★	85	$$$+
Homewood Suites by Hilton LBV-Orlando	2	★★★★	85	$$$+
Legacy Vacation Club Lake Buena Vista	2	★★★★	85	$$$–
Loews Royal Pacific Resort at Universal Orlando	4	★★★★	85	$ x 7+
Marriott Residence Inn Orlando SeaWorld/International Center	2	★★★★	85	$$+
Port Orleans Resort (French Quarter)	WDW	★★★★	85	$$$$+
Port Orleans Resort (Riverside)	WDW	★★★★	85	$$$$+
Extended Stay America Convention Center/Westwood	1	★★★★	84	$$$–
Hilton Garden Inn Orlando at SeaWorld	1	★★★★	84	$$$$–
Hyatt Place Orlando/Universal	4	★★★★	84	$$$+
Star Island Resort & Club	3	★★★★	84	$$+
Westgate Towers	2	★★★★	84	$$+
Buena Vista Suites	1	★★★★	83	$$$
Coronado Springs Resort	WDW	★★★★	83	$$$$+
Extended Stay Deluxe Orlando Lake Buena Vista	2	★★★★	83	$$
Hard Rock Hotel	4	★★★★	83	$ x 8
Hilton Garden Inn Orlando I-Drive North	1	★★★★	83	$$$–
Orlando Vista Hotel	2	★★★★	83	$$–
Country Inn & Suites Orlando Maingate at Calypso	3	★★★½	82	$$–
Courtyard Orlando LBV in Marriott Village	2	★★★½	82	$$$
Hawthorn Suites Universal	1	★★★½	82	$$$–
Holiday Inn Resort Lake Buena Vista	2	★★★½	82	$$$
Holiday Inn Resort Orlando–The Castle	1	★★★½	82	$$
Nickelodeon Suites Resort	1	★★★½	82	$ x 5–

How the Hotels Compare (continued)

HOTEL	LODGING AREA	OVERALL QUALITY	ROOM QUALITY	($ = $50)
Parkway International Resort	3	★★★½	82	$$+
The Point Orlando Resort	1	★★★½	82	$$$
Radisson Hotel Orlando Lake Buena Vista	2	★★★½	82	$$$$–
Embassy Suites Orlando–Lake Buena Vista	2	★★★½	81	$$$$+
Hawthorn Suites Orlando Convention Center	1	★★★½	81	$$$
Homewood Suites by Hilton I-Drive	1	★★★½	81	$$$$–
Residence Inn Orlando Convention Center	1	★★★½	81	$$$$–
Art of Animation Resort	WDW	★★★½	80	$$$
Buena Vista Palace Hotel & Spa	WDW	★★★½	80	$$$$–
Caribbean Beach Resort	WDW	★★★½	80	$$$$+
Courtyard Orlando I-Drive	1	★★★½	80	$$$–
Embassy Suites Orlando I-Drive/ Jamaican Court	1	★★★½	80	$$$$+
Fairfield Inn & Suites Near Universal Orlando Resort	4	★★★½	80	$$$–
Hampton Inn & Suites Orlando– South Lake Buena Vista	3	★★★½	80	$$+
Holiday Inn Express Lake Buena Vista	2	★★★½	80	$$+
Legacy Vacation Club Orlando	3	★★★½	80	$$$–
Lucaya Village Resort	3	★★★½	80	$$$–
Orbit One Vacation Villas	3	★★★½	80	$$–
SpringHill Suites Orlando Convention Center	1	★★★½	80	$$$$–
Holiday Inn & Suites Orlando Universal	4	★★★½	79	$$+
Holiday Inn in the Walt Disney World Resort	WDW	★★★½	79	$$$+
Fairfield Inn & Suites Orlando Lake Buena Vista (*rooms*)	2	★★★½	78	$$+
Fairfield Inn & Suites Orlando Lake Buena Vista (*suites*)	2	★★★½	78	$$$–
Ramada Plaza Resort and Suites Orlando I-Drive	1	★★★½	78	$$$
Extended Stay Deluxe Orlando Universal	4	★★★½	77	$$
WorldGate Resort	3	★★★½	77	$$+
Clarion Suites Maingate	3	★★★½	76	$$+
Grand Lake Resort	1	★★★½	76	$$+
Hampton Inn Orlando/Lake Buena Vista	2	★★★½	76	$$$–
Palms Hotel & Villas	3	★★★½	76	$$
Royal Plaza (*garden*)	WDW	★★★½	76	$ x 6–
Best Western Plus Universal Inn	4	★★★½	75	$$$–

How the Hotels Compare (continued)

HOTEL	LODGING AREA	OVERALL QUALITY	ROOM QUALITY	($ = $50)
Embassy Suites Orlando I-Drive	1	★★★½	75	$$$$–
Fairfield Inn & Suites Orlando LBV in Marriott Village	2	★★★½	75	$$$–
Hampton Inn I-Drive/Convention Center	1	★★★½	75	$$$–
Quality Suites Orlando Lake Buena Vista	2	★★★½	75	$$$
Quality Suites Royale Parc Suites	3	★★★½	75	$$+
Residence Inn Orlando I-Drive	1	★★★½	75	$$$–
Residence Inn Orlando Lake Buena Vista	2	★★★½	75	$$$$+
Rosen Inn at Pointe Orlando	1	★★★½	75	$$
Sonesta ES Suites Orlando	1	★★★½	75	$$$–
Wyndham Lake Buena Vista Resort	WDW	★★★½	75	$$$–
Fairfield Inn & Suites Orlando I-Drive/Convention Center	1	★★★	74	$$$–
Galleria Palms Kissimmee Hotel	3	★★★	74	$$
Quality Suites Orlando	2	★★★	74	$+
Super 8 Kissimmee	3	★★★	74	$+
All-Star Resorts	WDW	★★★	73	$$$–
Avanti Resort Orlando	1	★★★	73	$$$–
International Palms Resort & Conference Center	1	★★★	73	$$
La Quinta Inn Orlando I-Drive	1	★★★	73	$$–
Baymont Inn & Suites Celebration	3	★★★	72	$$–
Staybridge Suites Lake Buena Vista	2	★★★	72	$$$$–
Westgate Palace	1	★★★	72	$$$$
Crown Club Inn	3	★★★	71	$$
DoubleTree Guest Suites	WDW	★★★	71	$ x 5–
Pop Century Resort	WDW	★★★	71	$$$–
Ramada Gateway Kissimmee (tower)	3	★★★	71	$$–
SpringHill Suites Orlando LBV in Marriott Village	2	★★★	71	$$+
Best Western Orlando Gateway Hotel	1	★★★	70	$$+
Comfort Suites Universal	4	★★★	70	$$
Seralago Hotel & Suites Main Gate East	3	★★★	70	$$+
La Quinta Inn Orlando–Universal Studios	4	★★★	69	$$+
Silver Lake Resort	3	★★★	69	$$+
Comfort Inn I-Drive	1	★★★	68	$$$–
Days Inn Orlando/Universal Maingate	4	★★★	68	$$–
The Floridian Hotel & Suites	1	★★★	68	$+

How the Hotels Compare (continued)

HOTEL	LODGING AREA	OVERALL QUALITY	ROOM QUALITY	($ = $50)
Hampton Inn Universal	4	★★★	68	$$+
Monumental MovieLand Hotel	1	★★★	68	$$−
The Enclave Hotel & Suites	1	★★★	67	$$
Maingate Lakeside Resort	3	★★★	67	$+
Best Western I-Drive	1	★★★	66	$$$
Champions World Resort	3	★★★	66	$+
Comfort Inn Maingate	3	★★★	66	$$+
Destiny Palms Maingate West	3	★★★	66	$+
Quality Inn Universal Studios/I-Drive Area	1	★★★	66	$$
Rosen Inn International	1	★★★	65	$$−
Ramada Convention Center I-Drive	1	★★★	65	$$
Ramada Maingate West Kissimmee	3	★★★	65	$+
Rodeway Inn Universal Studios Area	1	★★★	65	$+
Celebration Suites	3	★★½	64	$$−
Clarion Inn & Suites at I-Drive	1	★★½	64	$$−
Clarion Inn Lake Buena Vista	2	★★½	64	$+
Country Inn & Suites Orlando Universal	1	★★½	64	$$+
Howard Johnson Inn Orlando I-Drive	1	★★½	64	$+
Ramada Gateway Kissimmee (garden)	3	★★½	64	$+
Claremont Hotel Kissimmee	3	★★½	63	$−
Hampton Inn South of Universal	1	★★½	63	$$+
Days Inn Orlando/I-Drive	1	★★½	61	$+
Knights Inn Maingate Kissimmee/Orlando	3	★★½	61	$
Motel 6 Orlando–I-Drive	1	★★½	61	$
Orlando Metropolitan Express	1	★★½	61	$+
Red Roof Inn Orlando Convention Center	1	★★½	61	$+
Continental Plaza Hotel Kissimmee	3	★★½	60	$+
Days Inn Orlando/Convention Center	1	★★½	60	$+
Royal Celebration Inn	3	★★½	60	$
Howard Johnson Enchanted Land Hotel	3	★★½	59	$−
Quality Inn & Suites Eastgate	3	★★½	59	$+
Extended Stay Deluxe Pointe Orlando	1	★★½	58	$$$
Rodeway Inn Maingate	3	★★½	58	$−
Super 8 Kissimmee/Maingate	3	★★½	58	$$−
Travelodge Suites East Gate Orange	3	★★½	58	$+

PART FOUR

WALT DISNEY WORLD *with* KIDS

RECOMMENDATIONS *for* MAKING *the* DREAM COME TRUE

WHEN PLANNING A DISNEY WORLD vacation with young children, consider the following:

AGE Although the color and festivity of Disney World will excite all children, and specific attractions delight toddlers and preschoolers, Disney entertainment is generally oriented to older children and adults. Children should be a fairly mature 7 years old to *appreciate* the Magic Kingdom and Disney's Animal Kingdom, and a year or two older to get much out of Epcot or Disney's Hollywood Studios.

TIME OF YEAR TO VISIT Avoid the hot, crowded summer months, especially if you have preschoolers. Go in October, November (except Thanksgiving), early December, January, February, or May. If you have children of varied ages and they're good students, take the older ones out of school and visit during the cooler, less congested off-season. Arrange special assignments relating to the educational aspects of Disney World. If your children can't afford to miss school, take your vacation as soon as the school year ends in late May or early June. Alternatively, try late August before school starts. But understand that you don't have to visit during one of the more ideal times of year to have a great vacation.

BUILD NAPS AND REST INTO YOUR ITINERARY The theme parks are huge; don't try to see everything in one day. Tour in early morning and return to your hotel around 11:30 a.m. for lunch, a swim, and a nap. Even during off-season when the crowds are smaller and the temperatures more pleasant, the size of the major theme parks will exhaust most children under age 8 by lunchtime. Return to the park in late afternoon or early evening and continue touring. If you plan to return to your hotel in midday and would like your room made up, let the housekeeping staff know.

unofficial **TIP**
Naps and relief from the frenetic pace of the theme parks, even during the off-season, are indispensable.

WHERE TO STAY The time and hassle involved in commuting to and from the theme parks will be lessened if you stay in a hotel close to the theme parks. We should point out that this doesn't necessarily mean you have to lodge at a hotel in Walt Disney World. Because Walt Disney World is so geographically dispersed, many off-property hotels are actually closer to the theme parks than some Disney resorts. Regardless of whether you stay in or out of the World, it's imperative that you take young children out of the parks each day for a few hours of rest. Neglecting to relax is the best way we know to get the whole family in a snit and ruin the day (or the vacation).

If you have young children, you must plan ahead. Make sure your hotel is within 20 minutes of the theme parks. It's true you can revive somewhat by retreating to a Disney hotel for lunch or by finding a quiet restaurant in the theme parks, but there's no substitute for returning to the familiarity and comfort of your own hotel. Regardless of what you have heard, children too large to sleep in a stroller won't relax unless you take them back to your hotel. If it takes renting a car to make returning to your hotel practicable, rent the car.

If you're traveling with children 12 years old and younger and you want to stay in the World, we recommend the Polynesian, Grand Floridian, or Wilderness Lodge & Villas (in that order), if they fit your budget. For less expensive rooms, try Port Orleans French Quarter. The least expensive on-site rooms are available at the All-Star Resorts. In addition to standard hotel rooms, the All-Star Music and Art of Animation Resorts offer two-room family suites that can sleep as many as six and provide kitchenettes. Log cabins at Fort Wilderness Resort & Campground and the DDV resorts are options for families who need a little more space. Outside the World, check our top hotels for families, starting on page 47.

BE IN TOUCH WITH YOUR FEELINGS When you or your children get tired and irritable, call time out and regroup. Trust your instincts. What would feel best—another ride, an ice-cream break, or going back to the room for a nap? The way to protect your considerable investment in your Disney vacation is to stay happy and have a good time. You don't have to meet a quota for experiencing attractions. *Do what you want.*

LEAST COMMON DENOMINATORS Somebody is going to run out of steam first, and when he or she does, the whole family will be affected. Sometimes a snack break will revive the flagging member. Sometimes, however, it's better to just return to your hotel. Pushing the tired or discontented beyond their capacity will spoil the day for them—and you. Accept that energy levels vary and be prepared to respond to members of your group who poop out.

BUILDING ENDURANCE Though most children are active, their normal play usually doesn't condition them for the exertion that's required to tour a Disney theme park. We recommend starting a program of family walks four to six weeks before your trip to get in shape.

SETTING LIMITS AND MAKING PLANS Avoid arguments and disappointment by establishing guidelines for each day, and get everybody committed.

BE FLEXIBLE Any day at Walt Disney World includes some surprises; be prepared to adjust your plan. Listen to your intuition.

OVERHEATING, SUNBURN, AND DEHYDRATION These are the most common problems of younger children at Disney World. Carry and use sunscreen. Be sure to put some on children in strollers, even if the stroller has a canopy. To avoid overheating, rest regularly in the shade or in an air-conditioned restaurant or show. Bottles with screw caps are sold in all major parks for about $3.

BLISTERS AND SORE FEET Everyone should wear comfortable, well-broken-in shoes. If you or your children are susceptible to blisters, bring along blister bandages, available at most drugstores (and at First Aid in the parks, if you didn't heed our warnings)—they offer excellent protection, stick well, and won't sweat off. When you feel a "hot spot" starting, stop, air out your foot, and place a bandage over the area before a blister forms. Young children may not tell their parents about a developing blister until it's too late, so inspect the feet of preschoolers two or more times a day.

FIRST AID Each major theme park has a First Aid Center. In the Magic Kingdom, it's at the end of Main Street to your left, between Casey's Corner and The Crystal Palace. At Epcot, it's on the World Showcase side of Odyssey Center. At Disney's Hollywood Studios, it's in the Guest Relations Building inside the main entrance. At Disney's Animal Kingdom, it's in Discovery Island, on your left just before you cross the bridge to Africa, behind Creature Comforts. And in all four parks, First Aid and the Baby Care Center are right next to each other. If you or your children have a medical problem, go to a first-aid center. They're friendlier than most doctor's offices and are accustomed to treating everything from paper cuts to allergic reactions.

CHILDREN ON MEDICATION Some parents of hyperactive children on medication discontinue or decrease the child's dosage at the end of the school year. If you have such a child, be aware that Disney World might overstimulate him or her. Consult your physician before altering your child's medication regimen.

SUNGLASSES If you want your younger children to wear sunglasses, put a strap or string on the frames so that the glasses will stay on during rides and can hang from the child's neck while you're indoors.

THINGS YOU FORGOT OR RAN OUT OF Rain gear, diapers, baby formula, sunburn treatments, memory cards, and other sundries are sold at all major theme parks and at Typhoon Lagoon, Blizzard Beach, and Downtown Disney. If you don't see something you need, ask if it's in stock. Basic over-the-counter meds are often available free in small quantities at the First Aid Centers in the parks.

INFANTS AND TODDLERS AT THE THEME PARKS The major parks have centralized facilities for infant and toddler care. Everything necessary for changing diapers, preparing formulas, and warming bottles and food is available. Supplies are for sale, and rockers and special chairs for nursing mothers are provided. At the Magic Kingdom, the Baby Care Center is next to The Crystal Palace at the end of Main Street. At Epcot, the Baby Care Center is in the Odyssey Center, between Test Track in Future World and Mexico in World Showcase. At Disney's Hollywood Studios, the Baby Care Center is in the Guest Relations Building left of the main entrance. At Disney's Animal Kingdom, the Baby Care Center is behind Creature Comforts. Dads are welcome at the centers and can use most services. In addition, many men's restrooms in the major parks have changing tables.

Babies and toddlers are allowed to experience any attraction that doesn't have minimum height or age restrictions. If you think you might try nursing during a theater attraction, be advised that most shows run about 17–20 minutes. Exceptions are *The Hall of Presidents* at the Magic Kingdom and *The American Adventure* at Epcot, which run 23 and 29 minutes, respectively.

Strollers are available for rent at all four theme parks and the Downtown Disney area (single stroller, $15 per day with no deposit, $13 per day for the entire stay; double stroller, $31 per day with no deposit, $27 per day for the entire stay; stroller rentals at Downtown Disney require a $100 credit card deposit; double strollers not available at Downtown Disney). Strollers are welcome at Blizzard Beach and Typhoon Lagoon, but no rentals are available. With multiday rentals, you can skip the rental line entirely after your first visit—just head over to the stroller-handout area, show your receipt, and you'll be wheeling out of there in no time. If you rent a stroller at the Magic Kingdom and you decide to go to Epcot, Disney's Animal Kingdom, or Disney's Hollywood Studios, turn in your Magic Kingdom stroller and present your receipt at the next park. You'll be issued another stroller at no extra charge.

You can pay in advance for stroller rentals—this allows you to bypass the "paying" line and head straight for the "pickup" line. Disney resort guests can pay in advance at their resort's gift shop. Save receipts! Obtain strollers at the Magic Kingdom entrance, to the left of Epcot's Entrance Plaza and at Epcot's International Gateway, and at Oscar's Super Service just inside the entrance of Disney's Hollywood Studios. At Disney's Animal Kingdom, they're at Garden Gate Gifts, to the right just inside the entrance. Returning the stroller is a breeze. You can ditch your rental stroller anywhere in the park when you're ready to leave. To see what the rental strollers look like, Google "rental strollers at Walt Disney World."

unofficial **TIP**

Baby Wheels Orlando (☎ 800-510-2480; **babywheelsorlando .com**) and **Orlando Stroller Rentals** (☎ 800-281-0884; **orlandostrollerrentals .com**) offer strollers of higher quality than Disney's. Both will also deliver to and pick up from your hotel.

Well-marked stroller parking is available in all the "lands" of every park. If you leave your stroller in front of an attraction instead of a designated parking area, it will be moved.

If you need to go to your hotel for a break and intend to return to the park, leave your rental stroller by an attraction near the park entrance, marking it with something personal like a bandanna. When you return, you'll know in an instant which one is yours.

Rental strollers are too large for all infants and many toddlers. If you plan to rent a stroller for your baby or toddler, bring pillows, cushions, or rolled towels to buttress her in.

It's OK to bring your own stroller. Note, however, that only collapsible strollers are allowed on monorails, parking-lot trams, and buses.

DISNEY, KIDS, AND SCARY STUFF

MONSTERS AND SPECIAL EFFECTS AT Disney's Hollywood Studios are more real and sinister than those in the other parks. If your child has difficulty coping with the ghouls of The Haunted Mansion, think twice about exposing him to machine-gun battles, earthquakes, and the creature from *Alien* on The Great Movie Ride.

Small-Child Fright-Potential Chart

This is a quick reference to identify attractions to be wary of, and why. The chart represents a generalization, and all kids are different. It relates specifically to kids ages 3–7. On average, children at the younger end of the range are more likely to be frightened than children in their sixth or seventh year.

THE MAGIC KINGDOM

Sorcerers of the Magic Kingdom Loud but not frightening.

MAIN STREET, U.S.A.

Main Street Vehicles Not frightening in any respect.

Walt Disney World Railroad Not frightening in any respect.

ADVENTURELAND

Jungle Cruise Moderately intense, some macabre sights. A good test attraction for little ones.

Pirates of the Caribbean Slightly intimidating queuing area; intense boat ride with gruesome (though humorously presented) sights and a short, unexpected slide down a flume.

The Magic Carpets of Aladdin Much like Dumbo. A favorite of young children.

Swiss Family Treehouse May not be suitable for kids who are afraid of heights.

Walt Disney's Enchanted Tiki Room A thunderstorm, loud volume level, and simulated explosions frighten some preschoolers.

FRONTIERLAND

Big Thunder Mountain Railroad Visually intimidating from outside, with moderately intense visual effects. The roller coaster is wild enough to frighten many adults, particularly seniors. Switching-off option provided (see page 79).

Country Bear Jamboree Not frightening in any respect.

Frontierland Shootin' Arcade Frightening to children who are scared of guns.

Splash Mountain Visually intimidating from outside, with moderately intense visual effects. The ride culminates in a 52-foot plunge down a steep chute. Switching-off option provided (see page 79).

Tom Sawyer Island and Fort Langhorn Some very young children are intimidated by dark walk-through tunnels that can be easily avoided.

LIBERTY SQUARE

The Hall of Presidents Not frightening, but boring for young ones.

The Haunted Mansion Name raises anxiety, as do sounds and sights of waiting area. Intense attraction with humorously presented macabre sights. The ride itself is gentle.

Liberty Belle Riverboat Not frightening in any respect.

FANTASYLAND

The Barnstormer May frighten some preschoolers.

Dumbo the Flying Elephant A tame midway ride; a great favorite of most young children.

Enchanted Tales with Belle Not frightening in any respect.

Small-Child Fright-Potential Chart (cont'd.)

THE MAGIC KINGDOM (cont'd.)

FANTASYLAND (continued)

It's a Small World Not frightening in any respect.

Mad Tea Party Midway-type ride can induce motion sickness in all ages.

The Many Adventures of Winnie the Pooh Frightens a small percentage of preschoolers.

Peter Pan's Flight Not frightening in any respect.

Prince Charming Regal Carrousel Not frightening in any respect.

Seven Dwarfs Mine Train Not open at press time.

Under the Sea: Journey of the Little Mermaid Animatronic octopus character frightens some preschoolers.

TOMORROWLAND

Astro Orbiter Visually intimidating from the waiting area, but the ride is relatively tame.

Buzz Lightyear's Space Ranger Spin Dark ride with cartoonlike aliens. May frighten some preschoolers.

Monsters, Inc. Laugh Floor May frighten a small percentage of preschoolers.

Space Mountain Very intense roller coaster in the dark; the Magic Kingdom's wildest ride and a scary roller coaster by any standard. Switching-off option provided (see page 79).

Stitch's Great Escape! Very intense. May frighten children age 9 and younger. Switching-off option provided (see page 79).

Tomorrowland Speedway Noise of waiting area slightly intimidates preschoolers; otherwise, not frightening.

Tomorrowland Transit Authority PeopleMover Not frightening in any respect.

Walt Disney's Carousel of Progress Not frightening in any respect.

EPCOT

FUTURE WORLD

Imagination!: Captain EO Extremely intense visual effects and loudness frighten many young children.

Innoventions East and West Not frightening in any respect.

Journey into Imagination with Figment Loud noises and unexpected flashing lights startle younger children.

The Land: The Circle of Life Not frightening in any respect.

The Land: Living with the Land Not frightening in any respect.

The Land: Soarin' May frighten kids age 7 and younger, or anyone with a fear of heights. Otherwise a very mellow ride.

Mission: SPACE Extremely intense space-simulation ride that has been known to frighten guests of all ages. Preshow may also frighten some children. Switching-off option provided (see page 79).

Small-Child Fright-Potential Chart (cont'd.)

The Seas: The Seas with Nemo & Friends Very sweet but may frighten some toddlers.

The Seas: Main Tank and Exhibits Not frightening in any respect.

The Seas: Turtle Talk with Crush Not frightening in any respect.

Spaceship Earth Dark, imposing presentation intimidates a few preschoolers.

Test Track Intense thrill ride may frighten guests of any age. Switching-off option provided (see page 79).

Universe of Energy: *Ellen's Energy Adventure* Dinosaur segment frightens some preschoolers; visually intense, with some intimidating effects.

WORLD SHOWCASE

Canada: *O Canada!* Not frightening, but audience must stand.

China: *Reflections of China* Not frightening in any respect.

France: *Impressions de France* Not frightening in any respect.

Germany Not frightening in any respect.

Italy Not frightening in any respect.

Japan Not frightening in any respect.

Mexico: Gran Fiesta Tour Not frightening in any respect.

Morocco Not frightening in any respect.

Norway: Maelstrom Visually intense in parts. Ride ends with a plunge down a 20-foot flume. A few preschoolers are frightened.

United Kingdom Not frightening in any respect.

United States: *The American Adventure* Not frightening in any respect.

DISNEY'S ANIMAL KINGDOM

The Oasis Not frightening in any respect.

Rafiki's Planet Watch Not frightening in any respect.

DISCOVERY ISLAND

The Tree of Life: *It's Tough to Be a Bug!* Very intense and loud, with special effects that startle viewers of all ages and potentially terrify little kids.

CAMP MINNIE-MICKEY

Festival of the Lion King A bit loud, but otherwise not frightening.

AFRICA

Kilimanjaro Safaris A "collapsing" bridge and the proximity of real animals make a few young children anxious.

Pangani Forest Exploration Trail Not frightening in any respect.

Wildlife Express Train Not frightening in any respect.

Small-Child Fright-Potential Chart (cont'd.)

DISNEY'S ANIMAL KINGDOM (cont'd.)

ASIA

Expedition Everest Can frighten guests of all ages. Switching-off option provided (see page 79).

Flights of Wonder Swooping birds alarm a few small children.

Kali River Rapids Potentially frightening and certainly wet for guests of all ages. Switching-off option provided (see page 79).

Maharajah Jungle Trek Some children may balk at the bat exhibit.

DINOLAND U.S.A.

The Boneyard Not frightening in any respect.

DINOSAUR High-tech thrill ride rattles riders of all ages. Switching-off option provided (see next page).

Primeval Whirl A beginner roller coaster. Most children age 7 and older will take it in stride. Switching-off option provided (see next page).

Theater in the Wild: *Finding Nemo—The Musical* Not frightening in any respect, albeit loud.

TriceraTop Spin A midway-type ride that will frighten only a small percentage of younger children.

DISNEY'S HOLLYWOOD STUDIOS

HOLLYWOOD BOULEVARD

The Great Movie Ride Intense in parts, with very realistic special effects and some visually intimidating sights. Frightens many preschoolers.

SUNSET BOULEVARD

Fantasmic! Terrifies some preschoolers.

Rock 'n' Roller Coaster The wildest coaster at Walt Disney World. May frighten guests of any age. Switching-off option provided (see next page).

Theater of the Stars: *Beauty and the Beast—Live on Stage* Not frightening in any respect.

The Twilight Zone Tower of Terror Visually intimidating to young children; contains intense and realistic special effects. The plummeting elevator at the ride's end frightens many adults as well as kids. Switching-off option provided (see next page).

ECHO LAKE

The American Idol Experience At times, the singing may frighten anyone.

Indiana Jones Epic Stunt Spectacular! An intense show with powerful special effects, including explosions, but young kids generally handle it well.

Star Tours—The Adventures Continue Extremely intense visually for all ages; too intense for children under age 8. Switching-off option provided (see next page).

STREETS OF AMERICA

Honey, I Shrunk the Kids Movie Set Adventure Not scary (though oversized).

Small-Child Fright-Potential Chart (cont'd.)

Jim Henson's Muppet-Vision 3-D Intense and loud, but not frightening.

Lights, Motors, Action! Extreme Stunt Show Super stunt spectacular; intense with loud noises and explosions, but not threatening in any way.

Studio Backlot Tour Sedate and not intimidating except for Catastrophe Canyon, where an earthquake and a flash flood are simulated. Prepare younger children for this part of the tour.

PIXAR PLACE

Toy Story Mania! Dark ride may frighten some preschoolers.

MICKEY AVENUE

The Legend of Captain Jack Sparrow Skeletons, monsters, and shooting can frighten small children.

Walt Disney: One Man's Dream Not frightening in any respect.

ANIMATION COURTYARD

Disney Junior—Live on Stage! Not frightening in any respect.

The Magic of Disney Animation Not frightening in any respect.

Voyage of the Little Mermaid Some kids are creeped out by Ursula.

Preschoolers should start with Dumbo and work up to the Jungle Cruise in late morning, after being revved up and before getting hungry, thirsty, or tired. Pirates of the Caribbean is out for preschoolers. You get the idea.

SWITCHING OFF (A.K.A. THE BABY SWAP)

SEVERAL ATTRACTIONS HAVE MINIMUM HEIGHT and/or age requirements. Some couples with children too small or too young forgo these attractions, while others take turns to ride. Missing some of Disney's best rides is an unnecessary sacrifice, and waiting in line twice for the same ride is a tremendous waste of time.

Instead, take advantage of "switching off," also known as "The Baby Swap" or "The Rider Swap" (or "The Baby/Rider Switch"). To switch off, there must be at least two adults. Adults and children wait in line together. When you reach a cast member, say you want to switch off. The cast member will allow everyone, including young children, to enter the attraction. When you reach the loading area, one adult rides while the other exits with the kids. Then the riding adult disembarks and takes charge of the children while the other adult rides. A third member of the party, either an adult or an older child, can ride twice, once with each switching-off adult, so that the switching-off adults don't have to ride alone.

On most Fastpass attractions, Disney handles switching off somewhat differently. When you tell the cast member that you want to switch off, he or she will issue you a special "rider exchange" Fastpass good for three people. One parent and the nonriding child (or children) will at that point be asked to leave the line. When those riding reunite with the waiting adult, the waiting adult and two other persons from the party can ride using the special Fastpass. This system eliminates confusion and congestion at the boarding area while sparing the nonriding adult and child the tedium and physical exertion of waiting in line.

ATTRACTIONS WHERE SWITCHING OFF IS COMMON	
THE MAGIC KINGDOM	**DISNEY'S ANIMAL KINGDOM**
Big Thunder Mountain Railroad	DINOSAUR
Seven Dwarfs Mine Train	Expedition Everest
Space Mountain	Kali River Rapids
Splash Mountain	Primeval Whirl
Stitch's Great Escape!	**DISNEY'S HOLLYWOOD STUDIOS**
EPCOT	Rock 'n' Roller Coaster
Mission: SPACE	Star Tours—The Adventures Continue
Test Track	The Twilight Zone Tower of Terror

If your young child gets cold feet just before boarding a ride where there's no age or height requirement, you usually can arrange a switch-off with the loading attendant. (This happens frequently in Pirates of the Caribbean's dungeon waiting area.)

No law says you have to ride. If you reach the boarding area and someone is unhappy, tell an attendant you've changed your mind and you'll be shown the way out.

The DISNEY CHARACTERS

WATCHING CHARACTERS HAS BECOME A PASTIME. Families once were content to meet a character occasionally. They now pursue them relentlessly, armed with autograph books and cameras. Because some characters are only rarely seen, character watching has become character collecting. (To cash in on character collecting, Disney sells autograph books throughout Disney World.) Mickey, Minnie, and Goofy are a snap to bag; they seem to be everywhere. But some characters, like the Queen of Hearts and Friar Tuck, seldom come out, and quite a few appear only in parades or stage shows. Other characters appear only in a location consistent with their starring role. The Fairy Godmother is often near Cinderella Castle in Fantasyland, while Buzz Lightyear appears close to his eponymous attraction in Tomorrowland.

WDW CHARACTER-GREETING VENUES

DISNEY HAS CREATED many permanent greeting locations intended to satisfy guests' inexhaustible desire to meet characters. The chart below and on the next page lists them by park and character.

THE MAGIC KINGDOM

MICKEY AND HIS POSSE

Chip 'n' Dale: Town Square, Tomorrowland

Daisy, Donald, Goofy, Minnie: Pete's Silly Sideshow (Fastpass/Fastpass+)

Mickey: Town Square Theater (Fastpass/Fastpass+)

Pluto: Town Square

DISNEY ROYALTY

Ariel: Ariel's Grotto

Aurora, Cinderella, Rapunzel, Snow White: Town Square Theater

Belle: *Enchanted Tales with Belle* (Fastpass/Fastpass+)

The Fairy Godmother, the Tremaines: Near Cinderella Castle

Gaston: Fountain outside Gaston's Tavern

Aladdin, Jasmine: Adventureland

Merida: Fairytale Garden

Naveen, Tiana: Liberty Square

FAIRIES

Tinker Bell and Friends: Adventureland

MISCELLANEOUS

ALICE IN WONDERLAND
Alice, the White Rabbit, Tweedledum and Tweedledee: Mad Tea Party
The Queen of Hearts: Mad Tea Party, Town Square

***THE ARISTOCATS* Marie:** Town Square

***LILO AND STITCH* Stitch:** Tomorrowland

PETER PAN Hook, Smee: Adventureland
Peter, Wendy: Between Adventureland and The Crystal Palace

***TOY STORY* Bullseye, Jessie, Woody:** Frontierland
Buzz Lightyear: Tomorrowland

EPCOT

MICKEY AND HIS POSSE

Chip 'n' Dale: Outside on the Land side of the Epcot Character Connection

Daisy: On the right as you enter Epcot through the main turnstiles

Donald, Goofy, Minnie, Mickey, Pluto: Epcot Character Connection

DISNEY ROYALTY

Aladdin, Jasmine: Morocco   **Aurora, The Beast, Belle:** France

Mulan: China   **Snow White:** Germany

EPCOT *(continued)*

FAIRIES

Tinker Bell and Friends: Future World between Mouse Gear and the Agent P World Showcase Adventure sign-up booth

MISCELLANEOUS

Alice, Mary Poppins and Bert: United Kingdom   **Geppetto, Pinocchio:** Italy

Marie (*The Aristocats*): France   **The Three Caballeros:** Mexico

DISNEY'S ANIMAL KINGDOM

MICKEY AND HIS POSSE

Mickey, Minnie: Adventurers Outpost on Discovery Island

MISCELLANEOUS

UP **Dug, Russell:** By *It's Tough to Be a Bug!*

DISNEY'S HOLLYWOOD STUDIOS

MICKEY AND HIS POSSE

Chip 'n' Dale: Sorcerer's Hat, The Magic of Disney Animation

Goofy, Minnie, Pluto, Sorcerer Mickey: The Magic of Disney Animation

CURRENT-MOVIE PALS

(Characters vary) Animation Courtyard

DISNEY CHANNEL STARS

Phineas and Ferb: Streets of America

PIRATES

Jack Sparrow: Near *The Legend of Captain Jack Sparrow*

MISCELLANEOUS

THE INCREDIBLES
Frozone, Mr. and Mrs. Incredible: The Magic of Disney Animation

***MONSTERS, INC.* Mike, Sully:** Backlot

***STAR WARS* Darth Maul, Darth Vader, Stormtroopers:** Near Star Tours

***TOY STORY* Buzz, Jessie, Woody:** Pixar Place

CHARACTER DINING

FRATERNIZING WITH CHARACTERS is so popular that Disney offers character breakfasts, brunches, and dinners where families can dine in the presence of Mickey, Minnie, Goofy, and assorted princesses. Besides grabbing customers from Denny's and Hardee's, character meals provide a familiar, controlled setting in which young children can warm gradually to characters. All meals are attended by several characters. Adult prices apply to persons ages 10 or older, children's prices to ages 3–9; little ones under age 3 eat free. For additional information on character dining, call ☎ 407-939-3463 (WDW-DINE).

Because of the incredible popularity of character dining, reservations can be hard to come by if you wait until a couple of months before your vacation to book your choices, so arrange Advance Reservations by calling WDW-DINE as far in advance as possible. To book a character meal, you must provide Disney with a credit-card number. Your card will be charged $10 per person if you no-show or cancel your reservation less than 24 hours in advance; you may, however, reschedule with no penalty.

*un**official*** **TIP**
Many children particularly enjoy meals with "face characters" such as Snow White, Belle, Jasmine, Cinderella, and Ariel, who speak and are thus able to engage children in a way not possible for the mute animal characters.

At very popular character meals like the breakfast at Cinderella's Royal Table, you're required to make a for-real reservation and guarantee it with a for-real deposit.

How to Choose a Character Meal

We receive a lot of mail asking for advice about character meals. Some *are* better than others, sometimes much better. Here's what we look for when we evaluate character meals:

1. THE CHARACTERS The various meals offer a diverse assortment of Disney characters. Selecting a meal that features your children's special favorites is a good first step. Check the Character-Meal Hit Parade chart on the following pages to see which characters are assigned to each meal.

2. ATTENTION FROM THE CHARACTERS In all character meals, the characters circulate among the guests hugging children, posing for pictures, and signing autographs. How much time a character spends with you and your children will depend primarily on the ratio of characters to guests. The more characters and fewer guests the better. Because many character meals never fill to capacity, the character–guest ratios found in our Character-Meal Hit Parade chart have been adjusted to reflect an average attendance as opposed to a sellout crowd. Even so, there's quite a range.

3. THE SETTING Some character meals are in exotic settings. For others, moving the event to an elementary-school cafeteria would be an improvement. Our chart rates each meal's setting with the familiar scale of zero (worst) to five (best) stars. Two restaurants, Cinderella's Royal Table in the Magic Kingdom and Garden Grill Restaurant in the Land Pavilion at Epcot, deserve special mention. Cinderella's Royal Table is on the first and second floors of Cinderella Castle in Fantasyland, offering guests a look inside the castle. Garden Grill is a revolving restaurant overlooking several scenes from the Living with the Land boat ride. Also at Epcot, the popular

Character-Meal Hit Parade

1. CINDERELLA'S ROYAL TABLE   MAGIC KINGDOM

MEALS SERVED DAILY Breakfast, lunch, and dinner

SETTING ★★★★

CHARACTERS Cinderella, Fairy Godmother, Aurora, Belle, Jasmine, Snow White

TYPE OF SERVICE Fixed menu

FOOD VARIETY & QUALITY ★★★

NOISE LEVEL Quiet   **CHARACTER–GUEST RATIO** 1:26

2. AKERSHUS ROYAL BANQUET HALL   EPCOT

MEALS SERVED Breakfast, lunch, and dinner

SETTING ★★★★

CHARACTERS 4–6 characters chosen from Alice, Ariel, Belle, Jasmine, Mary Poppins, Mulan, Sleeping Beauty, Snow White

TYPE OF SERVICE Family-style and menu (all you care to eat)

FOOD VARIETY & QUALITY ★★★½

NOISE LEVEL Quiet   **CHARACTER–GUEST RATIO** 1:54

3. CHEF MICKEY'S   CONTEMPORARY

MEALS SERVED Breakfast, dinner   **SETTING** ★★★

SETTING ★★★

CHARACTERS *Breakfast:* Mickey, Minnie, Donald, Goofy, Pluto (sometimes Chip 'n' Dale) *Dinner:* Mickey, Minnie, Donald, Goofy, Pluto (sometimes Chip 'n' Dale)

TYPE OF SERVICE Buffet

FOOD VARIETY & QUALITY Breakfast ★★★ Dinner ★★★½

NOISE LEVEL Loud   **CHARACTER–GUEST RATIO** 1:56

4. THE CRYSTAL PALACE   MAGIC KINGDOM

MEALS SERVED Breakfast, lunch, and dinner   **SETTING** ★★★

CHARACTERS Pooh, Eeyore, Piglet, Tigger

TYPE OF SERVICE Buffet

FOOD VARIETY & QUALITY Breakfast ★★½   Lunch and dinner ★★★

NOISE LEVEL Very loud

CHARACTER–GUEST RATIO Breakfast 1:67 Lunch and dinner 1:89

5. 1900 PARK FARE   GRAND FLORIDIAN

MEALS SERVED Breakfast, dinner   **SETTING** ★★★

CHARACTERS *Breakfast:* Mary Poppins, Alice, Mad Hatter, Pooh *Dinner:* Cinderella, Prince Charming, Lady Tremaine, the two stepsisters

TYPE OF SERVICE Buffet

FOOD VARIETY & QUALITY Breakfast ★★★ Dinner ★★★½

NOISE LEVEL Moderate

CHARACTER–GUEST RATIO Breakfast 1:54 Dinner 1:44

6. GARDEN GRILL RESTAURANT EPCOT

MEAL SERVED Dinner **SETTING** ★★★★½
CHARACTERS Mickey, Pluto, Chip 'n' Dale
TYPE OF SERVICE Family-style **FOOD VARIETY & QUALITY** ★★★½
NOISE LEVEL Very quiet **CHARACTER–GUEST RATIO** 1:46

7. TUSKER HOUSE RESTAURANT DISNEY'S ANIMAL KINGDOM

MEALS SERVED Breakfast, lunch **SETTING** ★★★
CHARACTERS Donald, Daisy, Mickey, Goofy
TYPE OF SERVICE Buffet **FOOD VARIETY & QUALITY** ★★★
NOISE LEVEL Very loud **CHARACTER–GUEST RATIO** 1:112

8. CAPE MAY CAFE BEACH CLUB

MEAL SERVED Breakfast **SETTING** ★★★
CHARACTERS Goofy, Donald, Minnie **TYPE OF SERVICE** Buffet
FOOD VARIETY & QUALITY ★★½ **NOISE LEVEL** Moderate
CHARACTER–GUEST RATIO 1:67

9. 'OHANA POLYNESIAN

MEAL SERVED Breakfast **SETTING** ★★
CHARACTERS Lilo and Stitch, Mickey, Pluto
TYPE OF SERVICE Family-style **FOOD VARIETY & QUALITY** ★★½
NOISE LEVEL Moderate **CHARACTER–GUEST RATIO** 1:57

10. HOLLYWOOD & VINE DISNEY'S HOLLYWOOD STUDIOS

MEALS SERVED Breakfast, lunch **SETTING** ★★½
CHARACTERS June, Leo, Handy Manny, Agent Oso
TYPE OF SERVICE Buffet **FOOD VARIETY & QUALITY** ★★★
NOISE LEVEL Moderate **CHARACTER–GUEST RATIO** 1:71

11. GARDEN GROVE SWAN

MEALS SERVED Breakfast (Sat & Sun only), dinner **SETTING** ★★★
CHARACTERS Rafiki, Timon, Goofy, Pluto **TYPE OF SERVICE** Buffet
FOOD VARIETY & QUALITY ★★★½ **NOISE LEVEL** Moderate
NOISE LEVEL Moderate
CHARACTER–GUEST RATIO 1:198, but often much better

Princess Storybook Meals are held in the castlelike Akershus Royal Banquet Hall. Though Chef Mickey's at the Contemporary Resort is rather sterile in appearance, it affords a great view of the monorail running through the hotel. Themes and settings of the remaining character-meal venues, while apparent to adults, will be lost on most children.

4. THE FOOD Although some food served at character meals is quite good, most is average—in other words, palatable but nothing to get excited about. In terms of variety, consistency, and quality, restaurants generally do a better job with breakfast than with lunch or dinner (if served). Some restaurants offer a buffet, while others opt for "one-skillet" family-style service, in which all the hot items on the bill of fare are served from the same pot or skillet. To help you sort it out, we rate the food at each character meal in our chart using the tried-and-true five-star scale.

5. THE PROGRAM Some larger restaurants stage modest performances where the characters dance, head a parade around the room, or lead songs and cheers. For some guests, these activities give the meal a celebratory air; for others, they turn what was already mayhem into absolute chaos. Either way, the antics consume time the characters could spend with families at their table.

6. NOISE If you want to eat in peace, character meals are a bad choice. That said, some are much noisier than others. Once again, our chart gives you some idea of what to expect.

7. WHICH MEAL? Although character breakfasts seem to be the most popular, character lunches and dinners are usually more practical because they do not interfere with your early-morning touring. During hot weather especially, a character lunch at midday can be heavenly.

8. COST Dinners cost more than lunches and lunches more than breakfasts. Prices for meals (except at Cinderella Castle) vary only about $10 from the least expensive to the most expensive restaurant. Breakfasts run $21–$53 for adults and $11–$34 for kids ages 3–9. For character lunches, expect to pay $26–$57 for adults and $15–$36 for kids. Dinners are $36–$67 for adults and $14–$41 for children. Little ones ages 2 years and younger eat free. The meals at the high end of the price range are at Cinderella's Royal Table in the Magic Kingdom and Akershus Royal Banquet Hall at Epcot. The reasons for the sky-high prices: (1) Cinderella's Royal Table is small but in great demand and (2) the prices at Cinderella's and Akershus include a set of photos of your group taken by a Disney photographer. Whereas photos at other venues are optional, at Cindy's and Akershus you don't have a say in the matter.

9. ADVANCE RESERVATIONS Disney makes Advance Reservations for character meals 180 days before you wish to dine (Disney resort guests can reserve 190 days out, or 10 additional days in advance); moreover, Disney resort guests can make Advance Reservations for all meals during their stay. Advance Reservations for most character meals are easy to obtain even if you call only a couple of weeks before you leave home. Meals at Cinderella's Royal

Table are another story; they are without doubt among the very hottest tickets at Disney World.

10. CHECKING IT TWICE Disney occasionally shuffles the characters and theme of a character meal. If your little one's heart is set on Pooh and Piglet, getting Hook and Mr. Smee is just a waste of time and money. Reconfirm all character-meal Advance Reservations three weeks or so before you leave home by calling ☎ 407-WDW-DINE.

11. "FRIENDS" For some venues, Disney has stopped specifying characters scheduled for a particular meal. Instead, they say it's a given character "and friends"—for example, "Pooh and friends," meaning Eeyore, Piglet, and Tigger, or some combination thereof, or "Mickey and friends" with some assortment chosen among Minnie, Goofy, Pluto, Donald, Daisy, Chip, and Dale.

12. THE BUM'S RUSH Most character meals are leisurely affairs, and you can usually stay as long as you want. An exception is Cinderella's Royal Table. Because Cindy's is in such high demand, the restaurant does everything short of pre-chewing your food to move you through.

▮ BABYSITTING

CHILD-CARE CENTERS Child care isn't available inside the theme parks, but two Magic Kingdom resorts connected by monorail or boat (Polynesian and Wilderness Lodge & Villas), four Epcot resorts (the Yacht & Beach Club Resorts, the Swan, and the Dolphin), and Animal Kingdom Lodge, along with the Hilton at Walt Disney World, have child-care centers for potty-trained children age 3 and older (see chart on the next page). Services vary, but children generally can be left between 4:30 p.m. and midnight. Milk and cookies and blankets and pillows are provided at all centers, and dinner is provided at most. Play is supervised but not organized, and toys, videos, and games are plentiful. Guests at any Disney resort or campground may use the services.

The most elaborate of the child-care centers (variously called "clubs" or "camps") is **Never Land Club** at the Polynesian. The rate for ages 3–12 is $12 per hour, per child (2-hour minimum).

All the clubs accept reservations (some six months in advance!) with a credit card guarantee. Call the club yourself, or reserve through Disney at ☎ 407-WDW-DINE. Most clubs require a 24-hour cancellation notice and levy a hefty penalty of 2 hours' time or $22.50 per call for no-shows. A limited number of walk-ins are usually accepted on a first-come, first-served basis.

WALT DISNEY WORLD CHILD-CARE CLUBS*			
HOTEL	NAME OF PROGRAM	AGES	PHONE
Animal Kingdom Lodge			
Simba's Cubhouse		3–12	☎ 407-938-4785
Dolphin and Swan			
Camp Dolphin		4–12	☎ 407-934-4241
Polynesian Resort			
Never Land Club		3–12	☎ 407-824-1639
Yacht & Beach Club Resorts			
Sandcastle Club		3–12	☎ 407-934-3750
Wilderness Lodge & Villas			
Cub's Den		3–12	☎ 407-824-1083

*Child-care clubs operate afternoons and evenings. Before 4 p.m., call the hotels rather than the numbers listed above. All programs require reservations; call ☎ 407-WDW-DINE (939-3463).

If you're staying in a Disney resort that doesn't offer a child-care club and you *don't* have a car, then you're better off using in-room babysitting. Trying to take your child to a club in another hotel by Disney bus requires a 50- to 90-minute trip each way. By the time you've deposited your little one, it will almost be time to pick him or her up again.

IN-ROOM BABYSITTING Three local companies provide in-room sitting in Walt Disney World and surrounding areas: **All About Kids** (☎ 407-812-9300 or 800-728-6506; **all-about-kids.com**), **Kid's Nite Out** (☎ 407-828-0920 or 800-696-8105; **kidsniteout.com**), and, yes, **Fairy Godmothers** (☎ 407-277-3724). Kid's Nite Out also serves hotels in the greater Orlando area, including downtown. All three provide sitters older than age 18 who are insured, bonded, screened, reference-checked, police-checked, and trained in CPR. In addition to caring for your kids in your room, the sitters will, if you direct (and pay), take your children to the theme parks or other venues. All three services offer bilingual sitters.

PART FIVE

SPECIAL TIPS *for* SPECIAL PEOPLE

WALT DISNEY WORLD *for* SINGLES

WALT DISNEY WORLD IS GREAT FOR SINGLES. It's safe, clean, and low-pressure. If you're looking for a place to relax without being hit on, Disney World is perfect. Bars, lounges, and nightclubs are the most laid-back and friendly you're likely to find anywhere. In many, you can hang out and not even be asked to buy a drink (or asked to let someone buy a drink for you). Parking lots are well lit and constantly patrolled. For women alone, safety and comfort are unsurpassed.

unofficial **TIP**
Virtually every type of entertainment performed fully clothed is available at amazingly reasonable prices at Disney nightspots.

There's also no need to while away the evening hours alone in your hotel room. Between the BoardWalk and Downtown Disney, nightlife options abound. If you drink more than you should and are a Disney resort guest, Disney buses will return you safely to your hotel.

WALT DISNEY WORLD *for* COUPLES

WEDDINGS AND HONEYMOONS

SO MANY COUPLES TIE THE KNOT or honeymoon in the World that Disney has a dedicated department to help them arrange the day of their dreams. **Disney's Fairy Tale Weddings & Honeymoons** (☎ 321-939-4610; **disneyweddings.com**) offers a range of ceremony venues and services, plus honeymoon planning and registries. Wedding packages start at $2,495.

Most packages include a bouquet, a cake and Champagne toast (not included in the basic Memories Collection package), live music, photography, limo service, a wedding-planning website, a wedding coordinator, and Annual Passes to Disney World for the happy couple (not part of the Memories Collection). The officiant and marriage certificate cost extra. Disney has a list of local officiants from which to choose, or the couple can bring their own.

ROMANTIC GETAWAYS

DISNEY WORLD IS A FAVORITE GETAWAY FOR COUPLES, but not all Disney hotels are equally romantic. Some are too family-oriented; others swarm with convention-goers. For romantic (though expensive) lodging, we recommend **Animal Kingdom Lodge & Villas, Bay Lake Tower** at the Contemporary, the **Polynesian, Wilderness Lodge & Villas,** the **Grand Floridian, BoardWalk Inn & Villas,** and the **Yacht & Beach Clubs.** The **Alligator Bayou** section at **Port Orleans Riverside,** a Moderate Disney resort, also has secluded rooms.

QUIET, ROMANTIC PLACES TO EAT

RESTAURANTS WITH GOOD FOOD *and* a couple-friendly ambience are rare in the parks. Only a handful of dining locales satisfy both requirements: **Coral Reef Restaurant,** an alfresco table at **Tutto Italia Ristorante,** the terrace at the **Rose & Crown Dining Room,** and the upstairs tables at the France Pavilion's **Monsieur Paul,** all in Epcot; and the corner booths at **The Hollywood Brown Derby** in Disney's Hollywood Studios. Waterfront (though not necessarily quiet or romantic) dining is available at **Fulton's Crab House, Paradiso 37,** and **Portobello** at Downtown Disney and **Narcoossee's** at the Grand Floridian.

Victoria & Albert's at the Grand Floridian is the World's showcase gourmet restaurant; expect to pay big bucks. Other good choices for couples include **Artist Point** at Wilderness Lodge, **Yachtsman Steakhouse** at the Yacht Club, **Shula's Steak House** at the Dolphin, **Jiko—The Cooking Place** at Animal Kingdom Lodge, and **Flying Fish Cafe** at the BoardWalk.

Eating later in the evening and choosing a restaurant we've mentioned will improve your chances for intimate dining; nevertheless, children—well behaved or otherwise—are everywhere at Walt Disney World, and there's no way to escape them.

WALT DISNEY WORLD *for* SENIORS

MOST SENIORS WE INTERVIEW ENJOY Disney World much more when they tour with folks their own age. If, however, you're considering going to Disney World with your grandchildren, we recommend an orientation visit without them first. If you know first-hand what to expect, it's much easier to establish limits, maintain control, and set a comfortable pace when you visit with the youngsters.

If you're determined to take the grandkids, read carefully those sections of this book that discuss family touring. Because seniors are a varied and willing lot, there aren't any attractions we would suggest they avoid. For seniors, as with other Disney visitors, personal taste is more important than age. We hate to see mature visitors pass up an exceptional attraction like Splash Mountain because younger visitors call it a "thrill ride." A full-blown adventure, Splash Mountain gets its appeal more from music and visual effects than from the thrill of the ride. Because you must choose among attractions that might interest you, we provide facts to help you make informed decisions.

GETTING AROUND

MANY SENIORS LIKE TO WALK, but a 7-hour visit to a theme park includes 4–10 miles on foot. If you're not up to that, let someone push you in a rented wheelchair (theme parks: $12 per day with no deposit, $10 per day for multiday rentals; Downtown Disney: $100 rental deposit required). The theme parks also offer fun-to-drive electric carts (electric convenience vehicles, or ECVs) for $50 per day, with a $20 refundable deposit. Don't let your pride keep you from having a good time. Sure, you could march 10 miles if you had to—*but you don't have to!*

Your rental deposit slip is good for a replacement wheelchair in any park during the same day. You can rent a chair at the Magic Kingdom in the morning, return it, go to Epcot, present your deposit slip, and get another chair at no additional charge.

LODGING

IF YOU CAN AFFORD IT, stay in Walt Disney World. If you're concerned about the quality of your accommodations or the availability of transportation, staying inside the Disney complex will ease your mind. The rooms are some of the nicest in the Orlando area and are always clean and well maintained. Plus, transportation is always available to any destination in Disney World at no additional cost.

Disney hotels reserve rooms closer to restaurants and transportation for guests of any age who can't tolerate much walking. They also provide golf carts to pick up from and deliver guests to their rooms. Cart service can vary dramatically depending on the time of day and the number of guests requesting service. At check-in time (around 3 p.m.), for example, the wait for a ride can be as long as 40 minutes.

Seniors intending to spend more time at Epcot and Disney's Hollywood Studios than at the Magic Kingdom or Disney's Animal Kingdom should consider the **Yacht & Beach Club Resorts,** the **Swan,** the **Dolphin,** or BoardWalk Inn & Villas.

The **Contemporary Resort** and the adjacent **Bay Lake Tower** are good choices for seniors who want to be on the monorail system. So are the **Grand Floridian** and the **Polynesian,** though they cover many acres, necessitating a lot of walking. For a restful, rustic feeling, choose **Wilderness Lodge & Villas.** If you want a kitchen and the comforts of home, book **Old Key West Resort,** the **Beach Club Villas, Animal Kingdom Villas,** or **BoardWalk Villas.** If you enjoy watching animals, try **Animal Kingdom Lodge & Villas.** Try **Saratoga Springs** for golf.

RV-ers will find pleasant surroundings at Disney's **Fort Wilderness Resort & Campground.** Several independent campgrounds are within 30 minutes of Disney World. None offers the wilderness setting or amenities that Disney does, but they cost less.

SENIOR DINING

EAT BREAKFAST AT YOUR HOTEL RESTAURANT, or save money by having juice and pastries in your room. Although you aren't allowed to bring food into the parks, fruit, juices, and soft drinks are sold throughout Disney World. Follow with an early dinner and be out of the restaurants, rested and ready for evening touring and fireworks, long before the main crowd begins to think about dinner. We recommend fitting dining and rest times into the day. Plan lunch as your break in the day. Sit back, relax, and enjoy. Then return to your hotel for a nap or a swim.

unofficial **TIP**
Make your dining Advance Reservations for before noon to avoid the lunch crowds.

WALT DISNEY WORLD *for* GUESTS *with* SPECIAL NEEDS

DISNEY WORLD IS SO ATTUNED TO GUESTS with physical challenges that unscrupulous people have been known to fake a disability in order to take unfair advantage. If you have a disability, even a restricted diet, Disney World is prepared to meet your needs.

Valuable trip-planning information is available at **disneyworld .com.** Each major theme park offers a free booklet that describes disabled services and facilities; get it when entering the theme and water parks, at resort front desks, and at wheelchair-rental locations in the theme parks. Printable PDF versions of the guides are available online at **tinyurl.com/wdwguestswithdisabilities**. For specific requests, such as those regarding special accommodations at hotels or on the Disney transportation system, call ☎ 407-939-7807 (voice) or 407-939-7670 (TTY). When the recorded menu comes up, press *1*.

VISITORS WITH DISABILITIES

WHOLLY OR PARTIALLY NONAMBULATORY guests may rent wheelchairs. Most rides, shows, attractions, restrooms, and restaurants accommodate the nonambulatory disabled. If you're in a park and need assistance, go to Guest Relations.

A limited number of electric carts, ECVs (electric convenience vehicles), and ESVs (electric standing vehicles) are available for rent. Easy to drive, they give nonambulatory guests tremendous freedom and mobility.

All Disney lots have close-in parking for disabled visitors; ask for directions when you pay your parking fee. All monorails and most rides, shows, restrooms, and restaurants accommodate wheelchairs.

Wheelchairs rent for $12 with no deposit required, $10 per day for multiday rentals; ECVs and ESVs are $50 per day, plus a $20 refundable deposit (prices do not include tax). Rentals are available at all Disney World theme parks (see Parts 9–12 for specific locations) and Downtown Disney; to reserve an ESV, call ☎ 407-824-5217. Wheelchairs are welcome at Blizzard Beach and Typhoon Lagoon water parks but are not available for rent. The rental deposit at Downtown Disney is $100. If you're looking to save money on an ECV, **Buena Vista Scooters** (**buenavistascooters.com**) rents them for $30 per day with delivery and pick up at your Disney resort.

Even if an attraction doesn't accommodate wheelchairs, nonambulatory guests still may ride if they can transfer from their wheelchair to the ride's vehicle. Disney staff, however, aren't trained or permitted to assist in transfers. Guests must be able to board the ride unassisted or have a member of their party assist them. Either way, members of the nonambulatory guest's party will be permitted to go along on the ride.

Because waiting areas of most attractions won't accommodate wheelchairs, nonambulatory guests and their party should request boarding instructions from a Disney attendant as soon as they arrive at an attraction. Almost always, the entire group will be allowed to board without a lengthy wait.

DIETARY RESTRICTIONS Disney works hard to accommodate guests with special dietary needs. When you make a dining reservation online or by phone, you'll be asked about food allergies and the like. The host or hostess and your server will also ask about this and send the chef out to discuss the menu; if you're not asked, just talk to your server when you're seated. For more information, e-mail **special.diets@disneyworld.com** or visit **tinyurl.com/wdwspecialdiets**.

SIGHT- AND/OR HEARING-IMPAIRED GUESTS Guest Relations at the parks provides free assistive-technology devices to visually and hearing-impaired guests ($25–$100 refundable deposit, depending on the device). Sight-impaired guests can customize the given information (such architectural details, restroom locations, and descriptions of attractions and restaurants) through an interactive audio menu that is guided by a GPS system in the device. Hearing-impaired guests can benefit from amplified audio and closed-captioning for attractions loaded into the same device.

Braille guidebooks are available from Guest Relations at all parks ($25 refundable deposit). Closed captioning is provided on some rides, while many theater attractions provide reflective captioning. A sign-language interpreter performs at some live-theater presentations; for show information, call ☎ 407-824-4321 (voice) or 407-939-8255 (TTY).

NONAPPARENT DISABILITIES We receive many letters from readers whose traveling companion or child requires special assistance, but who, unlike an individual on crutches or in a wheelchair, is not visibly disabled. Autism, for example, makes it very difficult or even impossible to wait in lines for more than a few minutes, or in queues surrounded by a large number of people.

Visitors with nonapparent disabilities should obtain a **Guest Assistance Card (GAC)**, a pass that explains to cast members any special accommodation a guest may need. To request the card, go to the Guest Relations area inside any Disney theme park or just outside the park's gates. If you're requesting the GAC for someone else (your child, for example), he or she must be with you when you make the request. You don't need a doctor's letter to request a GAC: The federal Americans with Disabilities Act states that you cannot be required to provide proof of a disability.

GACs are available at the theme parks but not at Downtown Disney or Disney resorts. A card issued at one park is good at all parks and is usually valid for your whole vacation, but theme park GACs are not valid at the water parks. If you obtained a GAC on a previous trip to Walt Disney World, you cannot reuse it. Also, a GAC cannot be obtained in advance of your visit.

PART SIX

ARRIVING *and* GETTING AROUND

◨ GETTING THERE

DIRECTIONS

YOU CAN DRIVE TO ANY Walt Disney World destination via World Drive off US 192; via Epcot Center Drive off Interstate 4, which connects Daytona and Tampa; via FL 536 and West Osceola Parkway from FL 417/Central Florida GreeneWay; or from the Hartzog Road/Walt Disney World interchange off FL 429, a.k.a. the Western Beltway (see the map on the next page).

FROM INTERSTATE 10 Take I-10 east across Florida to I-75 southbound at Exit 296A/Tampa; then take Florida's Turnpike (toll road) southbound at Exit 328 (on the left) toward Orlando. Take FL 429 (another toll road) to Exit 267A/Tampa southbound off the turnpike. Leave FL 429 at Exit 8, the Hartzog Road/Walt Disney World interchange, in the direction of Walt Disney World, and follow the signs to your Disney destination. Also use these directions to reach hotels along US 192, the Irlo Bronson Memorial Highway.

FROM INTERSTATE 75 SOUTHBOUND Take I-75 south onto Florida's Turnpike via Exit 328 (on the left) toward Orlando. Take FL 429 (toll) southbound off the turnpike. Leave FL 429 at Exit 8, the Hartzog Road/Walt Disney World interchange, in the direction of Walt Disney World, and follow the signs to your Disney destination. Also use these directions to reach hotels along US 192.

unofficial **TIP**
Warning! I-4 is an east–west highway but takes a north–south slant through the Orlando-Kissimmee area. This directional change complicates getting oriented in and around Disney World. Logic suggests that highways branching off I-4 should run north and south, but most run east and west here.

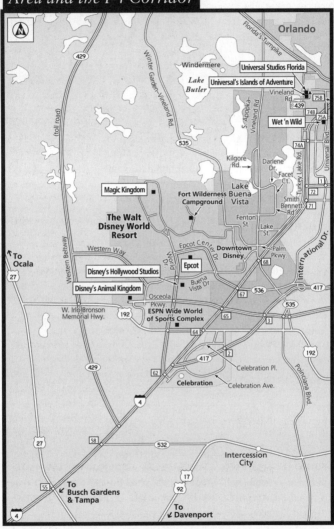

Lake Buena Vista Resort Area and the I-4 Corridor

FROM INTERSTATE 95 SOUTHBOUND Take Exit 67/FL 536, marked Epcot/Downtown Disney, and follow the signs. During rush hour, take FL 417/Central Florida GreeneWay; take Exit 6 to FL 536 West or Exit 3 to Osceola Parkway, and follow the signs. Take Exit 67/FL 536, marked Epcot/Downtown Disney (or take other appropriate exit—see below and following for the full list of I-4 exits), and follow the signs.

FROM ORLANDO INTERNATIONAL AIRPORT (MCO) There are two routes from here to Walt Disney World. Both take almost exactly the same time to drive, except during rush hour, when Route One is far less congested than Route Two. Also, Route One eliminates the need to drive on I-4, which is always congested.

Route One: Drive southwest on FL 417 (a.k.a. Central Florida GreeneWay), a toll road. Take Exit 6/International Drive toward FL 535. FL 536 will cross I-4 and become Epcot Center Drive. From here, follow the signs to your Walt Disney World destination. If you're going to a hotel on US 192 (Irlo Bronson Memorial Highway), follow the same route until you reach I-4. Take I-4 west toward Tampa. Take the first US 192 exit if your hotel is on West Irlo Bronson, the second exit if your hotel is on East Irlo Bronson. If your hotel is in Lake Buena Vista, take Exit 6 onto FL 536 as described previously, and then turn right on FL 535 to the Lake Buena Vista area. If you're headed to Animal Kingdom, Animal Kingdom Lodge, Pop Century, Art of Animation, All-Star Resorts, or ESPN Wide World of Sports, the quickest route is to take Exit 3/Osceola Parkway and follow the signs to your destination.

unofficial **TIP**
Both routes require money for tolls. Some exits are unmanned and require exact change, so be sure you have at least $2 in quarters. Also, note that while the manned toll booths take bills up to $20, they don't accept credit cards. For details, see **sunpass.com.**

Route Two: Take FL 528/Beachline Expressway, a toll road, west for about 12 miles to the intersection with I-4. Go west on I-4 to Exit 67/FL 536, marked Epcot/Downtown Disney, and then follow the signs to your Walt Disney World destination. This is also the route to take if your hotel is on International Drive or Universal Boulevard, near Universal Studios, near SeaWorld, or near the Orange County Convention Center. For these destinations, take I-4 east toward Orlando.

FROM MIAMI, FORT LAUDERDALE, AND SOUTHEAST FLORIDA Head north on Florida's Turnpike to I-4 westbound. Take Exit 67/FL 536, marked Epcot/Downtown Disney, and follow the signs.

FROM TAMPA AND SOUTHWESTERN FLORIDA Take I-75 northbound to I-4. Go east on I-4, take Exit 64 onto US 192 West, and follow the signs.

Walt Disney World Exits Off I-4

East to west (from Orlando to Tampa), five I-4 exits serve Walt Disney World.

EXIT 68 (MARKED FL 535/LAKE BUENA VISTA) primarily serves the Downtown Disney Resort Area and Downtown Disney, including Downtown Disney Marketplace and Downtown Disney West Side. It also serves non-Disney hotels with a Lake Buena Vista address. This exit puts you on a road with lots of traffic signals. Avoid it unless you're headed to one of the preceding destinations.

EXIT 67 (MARKED FL 536/EPCOT/DOWNTOWN DISNEY) delivers you to a four-lane expressway into the heart of Disney World. It's the fastest and most convenient way for westbound travelers to access almost all Disney destinations except Disney's Animal Kingdom and the ESPN Wide World of Sports Complex.

EXIT 65 (MARKED OSCEOLA PARKWAY) is the best exit for westbound travelers to access Animal Kingdom, Animal Kingdom Lodge, Pop Century Resort, Art of Animation Resort, All-Star Resorts, and the ESPN Wide World of Sports Complex.

EXIT 64 (MARKED US 192/MAGIC KINGDOM) is the best route for eastbound travelers to all Disney destinations.

EXIT 62 (MARKED DISNEY WORLD/CELEBRATION) is the first Disney exit you'll encounter if you're headed eastbound. This four-lane, controlled-access highway connects to the so-called Maingate of Walt Disney World. Accessing Walt Disney World via the next exit, Exit 64, also routes you through the main entrance.

TRANSPORTATION TO WALT DISNEY WORLD FROM THE AIRPORT

IF YOU FLEW INTO MCO, you have four basic options for getting to Walt Disney World:

1. TAXI Taxis carry four to eight passengers (depending on vehicle type). Rates vary according to distance. If your hotel is in the World, your fare will be about $52–$68, plus tip. For the US 192 Maingate area, it will cost about $55. To International Drive or downtown Orlando, expect to pay in the neighborhood of $33–$40.

2. SHUTTLE SERVICE Mears Transportation Group (☎ 407-423-5566; **mearstransportation.com**) provides your transportation if your vacation package includes airport transfers. Nonpackage travelers can also use the service. The shuttles collect passengers until they fill a van (or bus). They're then dispatched. Mears charges *per-person* rates (children under age 3 ride free). One-way and round-trip services are available.

From your hotel to the airport, you're likely to ride in a van (unless you're part of a tour group, for which Mears might send a bus). Because shuttles make several pickups, they ask you to leave much earlier than you'd depart if you were taking a cab or returning a rental car.

FROM THE AIRPORT TO:	ONE-WAY ADULT/CHILD	ROUND-TRIP ADULT/CHILD
INTERNATIONAL DRIVE	$19/$15	$30/$24
DOWNTOWN ORLANDO	$18/$15	$29/$23
WALT DISNEY WORLD–LAKE BUENA VISTA	$21/$17	$34/$27
US 192 MAINGATE AREA	$21/$17	$34/$27

3. TOWN-CAR SERVICE Like a taxi, town-car service will transport you directly from the airport to your hotel. The driver will usually be waiting for you in your airline's baggage-claim area. If saving time and hassle is worth the money, book a town car.

Tiffany Towncar Service (☎ 888-838-2161 or 407-370-2196; **tiffanytowncars.com**) provides a prompt, clean ride. The round-trip fee to a Disney or non-Disney resort in a town car is $115–$150 plus tip; one-way is about $65–$80. Tiffany offers a free 30-minute stop at a Publix supermarket en route to your hotel.

Quicksilver Tours & Transportation (☎ 888-GO-TO-WDW [468-6939] or 407-299-1434; **quicksilver-tours.com**) offers eight-person limos and ten-person vans in addition to four-person town cars. Round-trip rates in a town car range from $110 to $120 depending on location; round-trip rates in a van range from $130 to $135; round-trip limo rate is $240.

Mears Transportation Group (see previous page) also offers town-car service for around $165 round-trip.

4. RENTAL CARS These are readily available at MCO, both short- and long-term. If you don't want a car for your entire stay, most rental companies allow you to drop it off at certain hotels or one of their subsidiary locations in the Walt Disney World area. Likewise, you can pick up a car at any time during your stay at the same hotels and locations without trekking back to the airport.

DISNEY'S MAGICAL EXPRESS

THIS FREE BUS SERVICE runs between MCO and most Walt Disney World hotels. Guests staying at Disney-owned and -operated resorts are eligible. (Guests staying at the Swan, the Dolphin, Shades of Green, and the hotels of the Downtown Disney Resort Area are not.) In addition to transportation, Magical Express provides free luggage-delivery service between your airline and your Disney hotel, except if your flight arrives between 10 p.m. and 5 a.m., in which case you'll need to pick up your stuff from baggage claim.

To use the service, register your flight information with your resort reservation, either at the time of booking or as soon as you've booked your flights, by calling ☎ 866-599-0951 or using **mydisneyexperience.com**.

U.S. and Canadian travelers will receive their Magical Express paperwork in the mail 20–40 days before they arrive at Walt Disney World. The packet contains detailed instructions for getting around the airport, bus vouchers, and tags for checked luggage (two per traveler). Just check your bags as you normally would and plan to see them again in your hotel room.

Except for Canadians, travelers from other countries will not receive vouchers or tags and will need to go through Customs with bags in hand. Disney will take the bags for transport at the Magical Express Welcome Center, where international guests will also get their bus vouchers.

The Magical Express Welcome Center is on the B side of MCO's lower level. Cast members are stationed throughout the area to help you find your way. You can pick them out by their nautical costumes, the signs they're holding, and the big white Mickey gloves they wear.

If you already have your bus vouchers, just head straight to the bus check-in. A cast member will scan your vouchers and direct you to a holding area for your resort's bus line. In the meantime, your checked bags will be picked up at the airport, sorted by destination, and sent directly on to your room—if it's ready.

The day before you check out, you'll get a notification with your return information on it. This will include a time for you to board your bus back to MCO.

RENTING A CAR

READERS PLANNING TO STAY IN THE WORLD frequently contact us asking if they will need to rent a car. If your plans don't include restaurants, attractions, or other destinations outside of Disney World, our answer to that question is a very qualified no. That said . . .

unofficial **TIP**
The website **Zalyn** (**zalyn.com**) knows virtually every discount and coupon available for every car-rental agency, and it will apply all of them to see which gives you the lowest overall cost. With a little effort, you can often get a great deal.

You Should Plan to Rent a Car:

1. If your hotel is outside Walt Disney World.

2. If your hotel is in Walt Disney World and you want to dine someplace other than the theme parks and your own hotel.

3. If you plan to return to your hotel for naps or swimming during the day.

4. If you plan to visit other area theme parks or water parks.

GETTING ORIENTED

A GOOD MAP

READERS FREQUENTLY COMPLAIN about the signs and maps provided by Disney. While it's easy to find the major theme parks, locating other destinations can be challenging: Many Disney-supplied maps are stylized and hard to read, while others provide incomplete information. Your best bet, in addition to the maps in this guide, is **Alamo Rent A Car**'s road map of Walt Disney World. Get it from the front desk or concierge at the resorts.

Another very good map of the Orlando–Kissimmee–Disney World area is available free at the **AAA Car Care Center** operated by Goodyear, near the Magic Kingdom parking lot.

HOW *to* TRAVEL *around the* WORLD

TRANSPORTATION TRADE-OFFS FOR GUESTS: LODGING OUTSIDE WALT DISNEY WORLD

DISNEY DAY GUESTS (those not staying inside Walt Disney World) can use the monorail system, the bus system, and the boat system. If, for example, you go to Disney's Hollywood Studios in the morning, then decide to go to Epcot for lunch, you can take a bus directly there. The most important advice we can give day guests is to park their cars in the lot of the theme park or other Disney destination where they plan to finish their day. This is critical if you stay at a park until closing time.

ALL YOU NEED TO KNOW ABOUT DRIVING TO THE THEME PARKS

1. POSITIONING OF THE PARKING LOTS Disney's Animal Kingdom, Disney's Hollywood Studios, and Epcot parking lots are adjacent to each park's entrance. The Magic Kingdom parking lot is adjacent to the Transportation and Ticket Center (TTC). From the TTC you take either a ferry or the monorail to the Magic Kingdom entrance.

2. PAYING TO PARK Disney resort guests and Annual Pass holders park free. All others pay $15 per day.

3. FINDING YOUR CAR WHEN IT'S TIME TO GO Jot down, text, or take a phone picture of the section and row where you've parked. If

 unofficial **TIP**
Once you've paid to park in any major theme park lot, show your receipt and you'll be admitted into another park's lot on the same day without further charge.

WALT DISNEY WORLD GPS ADDRESSES AND COORDINATES

MAGIC KINGDOM PARKING LOT
3111 World Dr., Lake Buena Vista, FL 32830
N28° 25.124', W81° 34.871'

EPCOT PARKING LOT
200 Epcot Center Dr., Lake Buena Vista, FL 32830
N28° 22.869', W81° 32.964

ANIMAL KINGDOM PARKING LOT
551 N. Rainforest Rd., Lake Buena Vista, FL 32380
N28° 21.480', W81° 35.426'

Disney's Hollywood Studios Parking Lot
351 S. Studio Dr., Lake Buena Vista, FL 32830
N28° 21.425', W81° 33.618'

BLIZZARD BEACH PARKING LOT
1534 Blizzard Beach Dr., Lake Buena Vista, FL 32830
N28° 21.338', W81° 34.384'

TYPHOON LAGOON PARKING LOT
1145 Buena Vista Dr., Lake Buena Vista, FL 32830
N28° 22.162', W81° 31.576'

DOWNTOWN DISNEY PARKING LOT
1490 E. Buena Vista Dr., Lake Buena Vista, FL 32830
N28° 22.064', W81° 31.167'

---

you're driving a rental car, note the license-plate number. (You wouldn't believe how many white rental cars there are.)

4. GETTING FROM YOUR CAR TO THE PARK ENTRANCE Each lot provides trams to the park entrance or, at the Magic Kingdom, to the TTC. If you arrive early in the morning, it may be faster to walk to the entrance (or TTC) than to take the tram. At the TTC, Disney has added digital wait-time boards, showing you how long the wait is to board the express monorail to the Magic Kingdom or board the ferry. Choose the shorter of the two lines.

5. GETTING TO ANIMAL KINGDOM FOR PARK OPENING If you're staying on-property and are planning to be at this theme park when it opens, take a Disney bus from your resort instead of driving. Animal Kingdom's parking lot frequently opens 15 minutes before the park itself—which doesn't leave enough time to park, hop on a tram, and pass through security before park opening.

6. HOW MUCH TIME TO ALLOT FOR PARKING AND GETTING TO THE PARK ENTRANCE For Epcot and Disney's Animal Kingdom, it takes 10–15 minutes to pay, park, and walk or ride to the park entrance. At Disney's Hollywood Studios, allow 8–12 minutes; at the Magic Kingdom, it's 10–15 minutes to get to the TTC and another 20–30 to reach the park entrance via the monorail or the ferry. Allot another 10–20 minutes if you didn't buy your park admission in advance.

7. COMMUTING FROM PARK TO PARK You can commute to the other theme parks via Disney bus, or to and from the Magic Kingdom and Epcot by monorail. You can also, of course, commute via your own car. Using Disney transportation or your own car, allow 45–60 minutes entrance-to-entrance one-way. Again, **leave your car in the lot of the park where you'll finish the day.**

8. LEAVING THE PARK AT THE END OF THE DAY If you stay at a park until closing, expect the parking-lot trams, monorails, and ferries to be mobbed. (The Magic Kingdom has wait-time displays showing the lines for the monorail and ferry.) If the wait for the tram is unacceptable, walk to your car, or walk to the first stop on the tram route and wait there for a tram. When someone gets off, you can get on.

9. DINNER AND A QUICK EXIT One way to beat closing crowds at the Magic Kingdom is to arrange an Advance Reservation for dinner at one of the restaurants at the Contemporary Resort. When you leave the Magic Kingdom to go to dinner, move your car from the TTC lot to the Contemporary Resort. After dinner, either walk (8–10 minutes) or take the monorail back to the Magic Kingdom. When the park closes and everyone else is fighting their way onto the monorail or ferry, you can stroll leisurely back to the Contemporary, pick up your car, and be on your way. You can pull the same trick at Epcot by arranging an Advance Reservation at one of the Epcot resorts. After *IllumiNations* when the park closes, simply exit the park by the International Gateway and walk back to the resort where your car is parked.

10. CAR TROUBLE All the parking lots have security patrols that circulate through the lots. If you have a dead battery or some other automotive problem, the security patrols will help get you going. If you have more-serious trouble, the **AAA Car Care Center** (☎ 407-824-0976), operated by Goodyear and located in Walt Disney World near the Magic Kingdom parking lot, will help you. Prices are comparable to what you'd pay at home for most services. The Car Center stays pretty busy, so expect to leave your car for a while unless the fix is simple. Hours are Monday–Friday, 7 a.m.–7 p.m., and Saturday, 7 a.m.–4 p.m.

11. SCORING A GREAT PARKING PLACE Anytime you arrive at a park after noon, there will be some empty spots up front vacated by early arriving guests who have already departed.

Taking a Shuttle Bus from Your Out-of-the-World Hotel

MANY INDEPENDENT HOTELS AND MOTELS in the Walt Disney World area provide trams and buses. They deposit you near the theme park entrances, saving you parking fees. The rub is that they might not get you there as early as you desire (a critical point if you take our touring advice) or be available when you wish to return to your lodging. Also, some shuttles go directly to Disney World, while others stop at additional area lodgings.

If you're depending on shuttles, you'll want to leave the park at least 45 minutes before closing. If you stay until closing and lack the energy to mess with the shuttle, take a cab. Cab stands are near the Bus Information buildings at Disney's Animal Kingdom, Epcot, Disney's Hollywood Studios, and the TTC. If no cabs are on hand, staff at Bus Information will call one for you.

THE DISNEY TRANSPORTATION SYSTEM

IN THE MOST BASIC TERMS, the Disney Transportation System is a "hub and spoke" system. Hubs include the TTC, Downtown Disney, and all four major theme parks (from 2 hours before official opening time to 1 hour after closing). Although there are some exceptions, there is direct service from Disney resorts to the major theme parks and to Downtown Disney, and from park to park. If you want to go from resort to resort or most anywhere else, you will have to transfer at one of the hubs.

If a hotel offers boat or monorail service, its bus service will be limited; you'll have to transfer at a hub for many destinations. If you're staying at a Magic Kingdom resort served by monorail (Polynesian, Contemporary–Bay Lake Tower, Grand Floridian), you'll be able to commute efficiently to the Magic Kingdom. If you want to visit Epcot, you must take the monorail to the TTC and transfer to the Epcot monorail. (Guests at the Polynesian can eliminate the transfer by walking 5–10 minutes to the TTC and catching the direct monorail to Epcot.)

Walt Disney World Bus Service

Disney buses have an illuminated panel above the windshield that flashes the bus's destination. Also, theme parks have designated waiting areas for each Disney destination. To catch the bus to the Caribbean Beach Resort from Disney's Hollywood Studios, for example, go to the bus stop and wait in the area marked TO THE CARIBBEAN BEACH RESORT. At the resorts, go to any bus stop and wait for the bus displaying your destination on the illuminated panel. Directions to Disney destinations are available when you check in or at your hotel's Guest Relations desk.

Service from resorts to major theme parks is fairly direct. You may have intermediate stops, but you won't have to transfer. Service to the water parks and other Disney World hotels sometimes requires transfers.

Buses begin service to the theme parks at about 7 a.m. on days when the parks' official opening time is 9 a.m. Generally, buses run every 20 minutes. Buses to all four parks deliver you to the park entrance.

To be on hand for actual opening time (when official opening is 9 a.m.), catch direct buses to Epcot, Disney's Animal Kingdom, and Disney's Hollywood Studios between 7:30 and 8 a.m. Catch direct buses to the Magic Kingdom between 8 and 8:15 a.m. If you must transfer to reach your park, leave 15–20 minutes earlier. On days when official opening is 7 or 8 a.m., move up your departure time accordingly.

For your return bus trip in the evening, leave the park 40 minutes to an hour before closing to avoid the rush. If you're caught in the exodus, you may be inconvenienced, but you won't be stranded. Buses and and boats continue to operate for 1 hour after the parks close.

Walt Disney World Monorail Service

Picture the monorail system as three loops. Loop A is an express route that runs counter-clockwise connecting the Magic Kingdom with the TTC. Loop B runs clockwise alongside Loop A, making all stops, with service to (in this order) the TTC, Polynesian Resort, Grand Floridian Resort & Spa, Magic Kingdom, Contemporary Resort and Bay Lake Tower, and back to the TTC. The long Loop C dips southeast, connecting the TTC with Epcot. The hub for all loops is the TTC (where you usually park to visit the Magic Kingdom).

unofficial **TIP**
Monorails run for 1 hour after the Magic Kingdom and Epcot close. If a train is too crowded or you need transportation after the monorails have stopped, catch a bus or boat.

The monorail serving Magic Kingdom resorts usually starts an hour and a half before official opening. If you're staying at a Magic Kingdom resort and wish to be among the first in the park when official opening is 9 a.m., board the monorail at these times:

From the Contemporary and Bay Lake Tower	7:45–8 a.m.
From the Polynesian	7:50–8:05 a.m.
From the Grand Floridian	8–8:10 a.m.

If you're a day guest, you'll be allowed on the monorail at the TTC between 8:15 and 8:30 a.m. when official opening is 9 a.m. If you want to board earlier, walk from the TTC to the Polynesian Resort and board there.

The monorail connecting Epcot and the TTC begins operating at 7:30 a.m. when Epcot's official opening is 9 a.m. To be at Epcot when it opens, catch the Epcot monorail at the TTC by 8:05 a.m.

BARE NECESSITIES

CREDIT CARDS *and* MONEY

CREDIT CARDS

AMERICAN EXPRESS, DINERS CLUB, DISCOVER, Japan Credit Bureau, MasterCard, and Visa are accepted throughout Walt Disney World.

BANKING SERVICES

BANK SERVICE AT THE THEME PARKS is limited to ATMs, which are marked on the park maps and are plentiful throughout Walt Disney World; most MasterCard and Visa cards are accepted. To use an American Express card, you must sign an agreement with Amex before your trip. If your credit card doesn't work in the ATMs, a teller at any **SunTrust Bank** full-service location will process your transaction. The SunTrust closest to Disney World is at 1675 E. Buena Vista Dr., across from Downtown Disney Marketplace; for other Orlando-area branches, visit **suntrust.com**.

A LICENSE TO PRINT MONEY

ONE OF DISNEY'S MORE SUBLIME PLOYS for separating you from your money is the printing and issuing of **Disney Dollars**. Available throughout Disney World or by phone (☎ 407-566-4985) in denominations of $1, $5, $10, and $50, each emblazoned with a Disney character, the colorful cash can be used for purchases in Disney World, Disneyland, and Disney Stores nationwide. Disney Dollars can also be exchanged one-for-one with U.S. currency, but only while you're in Disney World. Also, you need your sales receipt to exchange for U.S. dollars. Disney money is sometimes a perk (for which you're charged dollar-for-dollar) offered with Walt Disney World travel packages.

PROBLEMS *and* HOW *to* SOLVE THEM

ATTRACTIONS CLOSED FOR REPAIRS

FIND OUT IN ADVANCE what rides and attractions may be closed during your visit. For complete refurbishment schedules, check online at **touringplans.com** or use our mobile app, **Lines.**

CAR TROUBLE

SECURITY PATROLS WILL HELP if you lock the keys in your parked car or find the battery dead. For more serious problems, the closest repair facility is the **AAA Car Care Center** near the Magic Kingdom parking lot (☎ 407-824-0976).

The nearest off-World repair center is **Maingate Citgo** (US 192 west of Interstate 4; ☎ 407-396-2721). Disney security can help you find it. Farther away but highly recommended by one of our Orlando-area researchers is **Riker's Automotive & Tire** (5700 Central Florida Pkwy., near SeaWorld; ☎ 407-238-9800; **rikersauto .com**). Says our source, "They do great work, and they're the only car place that has never tried to get extra money out of me because I'm a woman and know nothing about cars."

CELL PHONE SNAFUS

READERS REPORT THAT MOBILE RECEPTION in Walt Disney World can be frustratingly spotty. The problem is compounded by crowd noise and the ambient music played throughout the parks. Even if you have a good signal, it's an exasperating challenge to find someplace quiet enough to have a conversation. When possible, opt for texting instead.

GASOLINE

THERE ARE THREE **Hess** gas stations on Disney property. One station is adjacent to the AAA Car Care Center, on the exit road from the Transportation and Ticket Center (Magic Kingdom) parking lot. It's also convenient to the Shades of Green, Grand Floridian, and Polynesian resorts. Most centrally located is the Hess station at the corner of Buena Vista Drive and Epcot Resorts Boulevard, near the BoardWalk Inn. A third station, also on Buena Vista Drive, is across from the area formerly known as Pleasure Island in Downtown Disney.

LOST AND FOUND

IF YOU LOSE (OR FIND) SOMETHING in the **Magic Kingdom,** go to **City Hall.** At **Epcot,** go to the **Entrance Plaza.** At **Disney's Hollywood Studios,** go to **Hollywood Boulevard Guest Relations;** at **Disney's Animal Kingdom,** go to **Guest Relations** at the main entrance. If you discover your loss after you've left the park(s), call ☎ 407-824-4245 (all parks). If you're still on-site, call and ask to be transferred to the specific park's Lost and Found.

MEDICAL MATTERS

HEADACHE RELIEF Aspirin and other sundries are sold at the Emporium on Main Street in the Magic Kingdom (behind the counter; you must ask); at most retail shops in Epcot's Future World and World Showcase, Disney's Hollywood Studios, and Disney's Animal Kingdom; and at each Disney resort's gift shop.

ILLNESSES REQUIRING MEDICAL ATTENTION A **Centra Care** walk-in clinic is at 12500 South Apopka–Vineland Rd. (☎ 407-934-CARE). It's open 8 a.m.–midnight weekdays and 8 a.m.–8 p.m. weekends. Centra Care also operates a 24-hour physician-house-call service and runs a free shuttle (☎ 407-938-0650). **Buena Vista Urgent Care** (8216 World Center Dr., Suite D; ☎ 407-465-1110) is highly recommended by *Unofficial Guide* readers.

The **Medical Concierge** (☎ 888-648-5252; **themedicalconcierge .com**) has board-certified physicians available 24-7 for house calls to your hotel room. They offer in-room X-rays and IV therapy service as well as same-day dental and specialist appointments. They also rent medical equipment. Insurance receipts, insurance billing, and foreign-language interpretation are provided. Walk-in clinics are also available.

DOCS (Doctors on Call Service; ☎ 407-399-DOCS; **doctors oncallservice.com**) offers 24-hour house-call service.

Physician Room Service (☎ 407-238-2000; **physicianroom service.com**) provides board-certified doctor house calls to Walt Disney World–area guest rooms for adults and children.

DENTAL EMERGENCIES Call **Celebration Dental Group** (☎ 407-566-2222).

PRESCRIPTION MEDICINE Two nearby pharmacies are **Walgreens Lake Buena Vista** (☎ 407-238-0600) and **Winn-Dixie Pharmacy Lake Buena Vista** (☎ 407-465-8606). **Turner Drugs** (☎ 407-828-8125) charges $5 to deliver a filled prescription to your hotel's front desk. The service is available to Disney and non-Disney hotels in Turner Drugs' area. The delivery fee will be charged to your hotel account.

RAIN

WEATHER BAD? Go to the parks anyway. The crowds are lighter on rainy days, and most of the attractions and waiting areas are under cover. Showers, especially during the warmer months, usually don't last very long.

Ponchos cost about $7, umbrellas about $10. Ponchos sold at Disney World are made of clear plastic, so picking out somebody in your party on a rainy day could get a little tricky.

unofficial **TIP**
Rain gear isn't always displayed in shops, so you'll have to ask for it.

Walmart sells an inexpensive green poncho that will make your family emerald beacons in a plastic-covered sea of humanity.

SERVICES

MESSAGES

MESSAGES LEFT AT CITY HALL IN THE Magic Kingdom, Guest Relations at Epcot, Hollywood Boulevard Guest Relations at Disney's Hollywood Studios, or Guest Relations at Disney's Animal Kingdom can be retrieved at any of the four.

PHONE CHARGING

YOU CAN DROP OFF YOUR PHONE to be charged at any Guest Relations desk in any park. While they have cords and plugs for most phones, it helps to bring yours along. You'll be issued a claim check to pick up your phone, and phones are usually done charging in 1–2 hours. Charging stations are also available near the *Tangled*-themed bathrooms in Fantasyland in the Magic Kingdom. Look for them built into the faux-wood posts near the seating area.

LOCKERS AND PACKAGE PICK-UP

LOCKERS ARE AVAILABLE ON THE GROUND FLOOR of the Main Street railroad station in the Magic Kingdom, to the right of Spaceship Earth in Epcot, and on the Transportation and Ticket Center's east and west ends. At Disney's Hollywood Studios, lockers are to the right of the entrance at Oscar's Classical Car Souvenirs. Disney's Animal Kingdom lockers are to the left inside the entrance. Cost is $7 a day for small lockers and $9 a day for large lockers; prices include a $5 refundable deposit. Lockers at Blizzard Beach and Typhoon Lagoon cost $13 (small) and $15 (large), also with a $5 refundable deposit.

Package Pick-Up is available at each of the major parks. Ask the salesperson to send your purchases to Package Pick-Up. When you leave the park, they'll be waiting for you. Epcot has two exits, thus two Package Pick-Ups; specify the main entrance or the International Gateway. If you're staying at a Disney resort, you can also have the packages delivered to your resort's gift shop for pickup the following day. If you're leaving within 24 hours, however, take them with you or use the in-park pickup location.

CAMERAS AND FILM

CAMERA CENTERS AT THE PARKS sell disposable cameras for about $12 ($19 with flash). Developing is available at most Disney hotel gift shops and at Camera Centers. You can also have images on a memory card burned to a CD while you're in the parks. The cost is around $13 for 120 images and around $6.50 for an additional 120 images. Prints cost around 75¢ apiece. You'll need to leave your digital media with Disney while they create the CD, typically around 2–5 hours, so make sure you've got extra storage on hand.

unofficial **TIP**
Disney no longer offers film developing at the theme parks.

GROCERY STORES

FOR DOWN-TO-EARTH PRICES, try the **Publix** at either the intersection of International Drive and Irlo Bronson or just north of the intersection of Reams Road and FL 535, or **Winn-Dixie** on Apopka–Vineland Road, about a mile north of the Crossroads Shopping Center. Avoid the **Gooding's** in the Crossroads Shopping Center, across FL 535 from the Disney World entrance. Its location makes it undeniably convenient, but its selection is poor and you'll find the prices higher and more frightening than the Tower of Terror.

If you don't have a car or you don't want to take the time to go to the supermarket, **GardenGrocer** (**gardengrocer.com**) will shop for you and deliver your groceries. The best way to compile your order is on GardenGrocer's website before you leave home. It's simple, and the selection is huge. If there's something you want that's not on their list of available items, they'll try to find it for you. Delivery arrangements are per your instructions. If you're staying at a hotel, you can arrange for your groceries to be left with bell services. For the sake of order-fulfillment accuracy and customer service, GardenGrocer is primarily set up for online ordering. If you can't get online, though, you can order by phone (☎ 866-855-4350). For orders of $200 or more, there's no delivery charge; for orders less than $200, the delivery charge is $12; a minimum order of $40 is required. Note that Garden Grocer's delivery schedule may fill completely around holidays, at which point they'll stop accepting orders for delivery on those dates.

Wine and beer are sold in grocery stores. The best range of adult beverages is sold at the **ABC Fine Wine & Spirits** store less than a mile north of the Crossroads shopping center (11951 S. Apopka–Vineland Rd.; ☎ 407-239-0775)

PART EIGHT

WALT DISNEY WORLD DINING

▌▐ DINING *outside the* WORLD

LIKE ALL VISITORS TO WALT DISNEY WORLD, short-stay and last-minute visitors have an economic incentive to find dining options outside the parks: The food inside ain't cheap, in case you haven't heard. But these visitors have a logistical incentive as well—unless they book well ahead of time, their chances of getting a seat at a full-service restaurant on-property can be a crap shoot. Our recommendations for tasty, reasonably priced fare outside Walt Disney World are summarized on the next two pages.

MEAL DEALS You'll find discounts and two-for-one coupons for many area restaurants in freebie visitor guides available at hotels outside of Walt Disney World. The **Orlando–Orange County Official Visitors Center** (8723 International Dr.; ☎ 407-363-5872; open daily, 8:30 a.m.–6:30 p.m., except Christmas) offers a treasure trove of coupons and free visitor magazines. Online, check out **coupons alacarte.com** and **orlandocoupons.com** for printable coupons.

▌▐ DISNEY DINING 101

MORE THAN 135 RESTAURANTS operate within Walt Disney World, including about 70 full-service establishments. The variety is exceptional: everything from Moroccan lamb to Texas barbecue. Most eateries are expensive, and many serve less-than-distinguished fare, but there are good choices in every area of the World.

ADVANCE RESERVATIONS

MOST DINING RESERVATIONS AT DISNEY WORLD don't guarantee you a table at a specific time as they would at your typical

Where to Eat Outside Walt Disney World

AMERICAN

JOHNNIE'S HIDEAWAY 12551 FL 535, Orlando; ☎ 407-827-1111; **talkofthetownrestaurants.com/johnnies.html;** moderate–expensive. Seafood and steaks, with an emphasis on Florida cuisine.

THE RAVENOUS PIG* 1234 N. Orange Ave., Winter Park; ☎ 407-628-2333; **theravenouspig.com;** moderate–expensive. New American cuisine with an award-winning menu that changes frequently, with seasonal ingredients.

BARBECUE

BUBBALOU'S BODACIOUS BAR-B-QUE 5818 Conroy Rd., Orlando (near Universal Orlando); ☎ 407-295-1212; **bubbalous.com;** inexpensive. Tender, smoky barbecue; tomato-based Killer Sauce.

4 RIVERS SMOKEHOUSE 1047 S. Dillard St., Winter Garden; ☎ 407-474-8377; **4rsmokehouse.com;** inexpensive. Award-winning beef brisket; fried pickles, cheese grits, fried okra, and collard greens.

CHINESE

MING'S BISTRO* 1212 Woodward St., Orlando; ☎ 407-898-9672; inexpensive. Authentic Chinese, including dim sum, crispy roast pork, and roast duck.

CUBAN/SPANISH

COLUMBIA 649 Front St., Celebration; ☎ 407-566-1505; **columbia restaurant.com;** moderate. Cuban/Spanish creations such as paella and the 1905 Salad.

FRENCH

LE COQ AU VIN* 4800 S. Orange Ave., Orlando; ☎ 407-851-6980; **lecoqauvinrestaurant.com;** moderate–expensive. Country French cuisine in a relaxed atmosphere. Reservations suggested.

INDIAN

MEMORIES OF INDIA 7625 Turkey Lake Rd., Orlando; ☎ 407-370-3277; **memoriesofindiacuisine.com;** inexpensive–moderate. Classic tandoori dishes, samosas, *tikka masala,* and Sunday Champagne brunch with buffet.

RAGA 7559 W. Sand Lake Rd., Orlando; ☎ 407-985-2900; **ragarestaurant .com;** moderate. Blend of Indian, Pakistani, and Middle Eastern cuisines prepared with locally sourced ingredients.

ITALIAN

BICE ORLANDO RISTORANTE Loews Portofino Bay, 5601 Universal Blvd., Orlando; ☎ 407-503-1415; **orlando.bicegroup.com;** expensive. Authentic Italian; great wines.

ANTHONY'S COAL-FIRED PIZZA 8031 Turkey Lake Rd., Orlando; ☎ 407-363-9466; **anthonyscoalfiredpizza.com;** inexpensive. Pizza, eggplant, pasta, beer and wine.

JAPANESE/SUSHI

AMURA 7786 W. Sand Lake Rd., Orlando; ☎ 407-370-0007; **amura.com;** moderate. A favorite sushi bar for locals. The tempura is popular too.

*20 minutes or more from Walt Disney World

JAPANESE/SUSHI (CONT'D.)

NAGOYA SUSHI   7600 Dr. Phillips Blvd., Ste. 66, in the very rear of The Marketplace at Dr. Phillips; ☎ 407-248-8558; **nagoyasushi.com;** moderate. A small, intimate restaurant with great sushi and an extensive menu.

HANAMIZUKI   8255 International Dr., Orlando; ☎ 407-363-7200; **hanamizuki.us;** moderate–expensive. Pricey but authentic.

MEXICAN

CANTINA LAREDO   800 Via Dellagio Way, Orlando; ☎ 407-345-0186; **cantinalaredo.com;** moderate–expensive. Authentic Mexican, upscale setting.

CHEVYS FRESH MEX   12547 FL 535, Lake Buena Vista; ☎ 407-827-1052; **chevys.com;** inexpensive–moderate. Across from the FL 535 entrance to WDW.

EL PATRON   12167 S. Apopka–Vineland Rd., Orlando; ☎ 407-238-5300; **elpatronrestaurantcantina.com;** inexpensive. Family-owned restaurant serving freshly prepared Mexican dishes. Full bar.

MOE'S SOUTHWEST GRILL   7541-D W. Sand Lake Rd., Orlando; ☎ 407-264-9903; **moes.com;** inexpensive. Dependable southwestern fare.

TAQUITOS JALISCO   1041 S. Dillard St., Winter Garden; ☎ 407-654-0363; inexpensive. Low-key. Flautas, chicken *mole,* fajitas, burritos, good vegetarian.

SEAFOOD

BONEFISH GRILL   7830 W. Sand Lake Rd., Orlando; ☎ 407-355-7707; **bonefishgrill.com;** moderate. Casual setting along busy Restaurant Row on Sand Lake Road. Choose your fish; then choose a sauce to accompany.

CELEBRATION TOWN TAVERN   721 Front St., Celebration; ☎ 407-566-2526; **thecelebrationtowntavern.com;** moderate. Popular hangout for locals, with New England–style seafood. Clam chowder is a big hit.

STEAK/PRIME RIB

BULL & BEAR   Waldorf Astoria Orlando, 14200 Bonnet Creek Resort Ln., Orlando; ☎ 407-597-5500; **waldorfastoriaorlando.com/dining/bullandbear;** expensive. Classic steakhouse with a clubby ambience.

TEXAS DE BRAZIL   5259 International Dr., Orlando; ☎ 407-355-0355; **texasdebrazil.com;** expensive. All-you-can-eat Brazilian-style *churrascaria.* Ribs, filet mignon, chicken, lamb, and salad bar.

VITO'S CHOP HOUSE   8633 International Dr., Orlando; ☎ 407-354-2467; **vitoschophouse.com;** moderate. Upscale meat house with a taste of Tuscany.

THAI

RED BAMBOO   6803 S. Kirkman Rd. at International Dr., Orlando; ☎ 407-226-8997; **redbamboothai.com;** moderate. Acclaimed by Orlando dining critics for its authentic Thai dishes. Delicious vegetarian options; impressive wine list.

hometown restaurant. Instead of scheduling Advance Reservations for actual tables, reservations fill time slots. The number of slots available is based on the average length of time that guests occupy a table at a particular restaurant, adjusted for seasonality. Disney tries to fill every time slot for every seat in the restaurant. No seats—repeat, none—are reserved for walk-ins.

Some Disney restaurants charge a hefty no-show fee and are booked every day according to their actual capacity. The no-show rate is as high as 33% at restaurants that don't charge a penalty, especially during slower times of year, meaning that walk-ins stand a decent shot of getting a seat. But if you walk in during busier seasons, expect to either wait 40–75 minutes or be told that no tables are available.

Dinner reservations are generally easy to get within 60 days at most full-service restaurants as long as you're not particular about the time you eat. For breakfast and lunch at such wildly popular venues such as Cinderella's Royal Table at the Magic Kingdom, you'll need to book anywhere from 7 weeks to 180 days ahead. To make Advance Reservations, call ☎ 407-WDW-DINE or go to **disneyworld.disney.go.com/dining**.

WALT DISNEY WORLD RESTAURANT CATEGORIES

IN GENERAL, FOOD AND BEVERAGE offerings at Walt Disney World are defined by service, price, and convenience:

FULL-SERVICE RESTAURANTS Full-service restaurants are in all Disney resorts (except the All-Star complex, Port Orleans French Quarter, Pop Century, and Art of Animation) and all major theme parks, Downtown Disney Marketplace, and Downtown Disney West Side. Advance Reservations are recommended for all full-service restaurants except those in the Downtown Disney Resort Area, which are operated independently of Disney. The restaurants accept American Express, Carte Blanche, Diners Club, Japan Credit Bureau, MasterCard, and Visa.

BUFFETS AND FAMILY-STYLE RESTAURANTS Many of these have Disney characters in attendance, and most have a separate children's menu featuring dishes such as hot dogs, burgers, chicken nuggets, pizza, macaroni and cheese, and spaghetti and meatballs. In addition to the buffets, several restaurants serve a family-style, all-you-can-eat, fixed-price meal.

Advance Reservations arrangements are required for character buffets and recommended for all other buffets and family-style restaurants. Most major credit cards are accepted.

If you want to eat a lot but don't feel like standing in yet another line, then consider one of the all-you-can-eat family-style restaurants. These feature platters of food brought to your table in courses by a server. You can sample everything on the menu and eat as much as you like. You can even go back to a favorite appetizer after you finish the main course.

Family-style all-you-can-eat service is available at **Cinderella's Royal Table** (breakfast only) and the **Liberty Tree Tavern** (dinner only) in the Magic Kingdom; **The Garden Grill Restaurant** in the Land Pavilion in Epcot; **'Ohana** at the Polynesian Resort; **Garden Grove** (breakfast and lunch only) at the Swan; and **Whispering Canyon Cafe** at the Wilderness Lodge.

FOOD COURTS Featuring a collection of counter-service eateries under one roof, food courts can be found at the Moderate resorts (Coronado Springs, Caribbean Beach, Port Orleans) and Value resorts (All-Star, Art of Animation, and Pop Century). (The closest thing to a food court you'll find at the theme parks is **Sunshine Seasons** at Epcot.) Advance Reservations are neither required nor available at these restaurants.

COUNTER SERVICE Counter-service fast food is available in all theme parks and at Downtown Disney Marketplace, the Board-Walk, and Downtown Disney West Side. The food compares in quality with Captain D's, McDonald's, or Taco Bell but is more expensive, though often served in larger portions.

FAST CASUAL Somewhere between burgers and formal dining are the establishments in Disney's "fast casual" category, including three in the theme parks: **Tomorrowland Terrace Restaurant** in the Magic Kingdom, **Sunshine Seasons** in Epcot, and **Studio Catering Co.** in Disney's Hollywood Studios. Fast-casual restaurants feature menu choices a cut above what you would normally find at a typical counter-service location. (At Sunshine Seasons, for example, you can choose from rotisserie chicken or pork, tasty noodle bowls, or large sandwiches made with artisanal breads.) Entrees cost about $2 more on average than traditional counter service, but the variety and food quality more than make up for the difference.

VENDOR FOOD Vendors abound at the theme parks, Downtown Disney Marketplace, Downtown Disney West Side, and Disney's BoardWalk. Offerings include popcorn, ice-cream bars, churros (Mexican pastries), soft drinks, bottled water, and (in theme parks) fresh fruit. Prices include tax, and payment must be in cash.

SAVE MONEY, SAVE TIME

EVERY TIME YOU BUY A SODA AT THE THEME PARKS, it's going to set you back about $3, and everything else is comparably high. What's more, you lose a lot of touring time getting food, even if you confine your meals to vendors and counter service.

You can say, "Oh well, I'm on vacation" and throw prudence out the window, or you can plan ahead and not only save big bucks

THE COST OF COUNTER-SERVICE FOOD

Bagel or muffin	$2.79
Brownie	$3.29
Burrito	$7.09–$8.99
Cake or pie	$3.79
Cereal with milk	$3.19–$3.99
Cheeseburger with fries	$9.39–$9.99
Chicken-breast sandwich (*grilled*)	$8.99–$10.95
Chicken nuggets with fries	$8.69
Children's meal	$5.99
Chips	$2.69
Cookies	$2.39
Fish (*fried*) **basket with fries**	$7.99–$10.95
French fries	$2.79
Fruit (*whole*)	$1.49
Fruit cup/fruit salad	$3.59
Hot dog	$6.99 (*basket*), $8.99 (*gourmet*)
Ice cream/frozen novelties	$3.49
Nachos with cheese	$3.99–$7.69
PB&J sandwich	$2.49 (*à la carte*), $5.99 (*kids' meal*)
Pizza (*personal*)	$6.79–$9.49
Popcorn	$3.50–$5.25
Pretzel	$3.99–$4.75
Salad (*entrée*)	$5.99–$10.99
Salad (*side*)	$3.99
Smoked turkey leg	$9.49
Soup/chili	$2.99–$8.49
Sub/deli sandwich	$5.99–$10.59
Taco salad	$7.89–$8.59
Veggie burger	$7.99

but minimize the time you spend hunting and gathering. Here's how to do it:

1. Eat breakfast before you arrive. Restaurants outside the World offer some outstanding breakfast specials. Plus, some hotels furnish small refrigerators in their guest rooms, or you can rent a fridge or bring a cooler. If you can get by on cold cereal, pastries, fruit, and juice, this will save you a ton of money as well as time.

2. Stuff some snacks in a fanny pack and take them with you to the parks. Carry water bottles, or rely on drinking fountains for water.

3. Make lunch your main meal. Entrées are similar to those on the dinner menu, but prices are significantly lower.

THE COST OF COUNTER-SERVICE DRINKS		
DRINKS	**SMALL**	**LARGE**
Beer	$5.50–$8.00	$7.99–$12.00
Bottled water	$1.50	$2.50
Latte *(one size)*	$3.99	$3.99
Coffee *(one size)*	$2.19	$2.19
Float/milkshake/sundae *(one size)*	$4.49–$6.95	$4.49–$6.95
Fruit juice	$2.59	$2.89
Hot tea and cocoa *(one size)*	$2.19	$2.19
Milk	$1.69	$2.39
Soft drinks, iced tea, and lemonade	$2.59	$2.99

Refillable souvenir mugs cost $15.49 (free refills) at Disney resorts and $10 at water parks. Each person on a Disney Dining Plan gets a free mug, refillable only at his/her Disney resort.

4. All theme park restaurants are busiest between 11:30 a.m. and 2:15 p.m. for lunch and 6 and 9 p.m. for dinner. For shorter lines and faster service, don't eat during these hours, especially 12:30–1:30 p.m.

5. Many counter-service restaurants sell cold sandwiches. Buy a cold lunch minus drinks before 11:30 a.m., and carry it in small plastic bags until you're ready to eat (within an hour or so of purchase). Ditto for dinner. Buy drinks at the appropriate time from any convenient vendor.

6. Most fast-food eateries have more than one service window. Regardless of the time of day, check the lines at all windows before queuing. Sometimes a window that's staffed but out of the way will have a much shorter line or none at all. Note, however, that some windows may offer only certain items.

7. If you're short on time and the park closes early, stay until closing and eat dinner outside Disney World before returning to your hotel. If the park stays open late, eat dinner about 4 or 4:30 p.m. at the restaurant of your choice. You should sneak in just ahead of the dinner crowd.

DRESS

DRESS IS INFORMAL at most theme park restaurants, but Disney has a "business casual" dress code for some of its resort restaurants: khakis, dress slacks, jeans, or dress shorts with a collared shirt for men and capris, skirts, dresses, jeans, and dress shorts for women. Restaurants with this dress code are **Jiko—The Cooking Place** at Animal Kingdom Lodge & Villas, the **Flying Fish Cafe** at the BoardWalk, the **California Grill** at the Contemporary Resort, **Monsieur Paul** at Epcot's France Pavilion, **Cítricos** and **Narcoossee's** at the Grand

Floridian, **Artist Point** at Wilderness Lodge & Villas, **Yachtsman Steakhouse** at the Yacht Club Resort, **Todd English's bluezoo** and **Shula's Steak House** at the Dolphin, and **Il Mulino New York Trattoria** at the Swan. **Victoria & Albert's** at the Grand Floridian is the only Disney restaurant that requires men to wear a jacket to dinner.

Also, be aware that smoking is banned at all restaurants and lounges on Walt Disney World property. Diners who puff must feed their nicotine fix outdoors—and in the theme parks, that might also mean going to a designated smoking area.

A FEW CAVEATS

BEFORE YOU BEGIN EATING your way through the World, you need to know:

1. Theme park restaurants rush their customers in order to make room for the next group of diners. Dining at high speed may appeal to a family with young, restless children, but for people wanting to relax, it's more like eating in a pressure chamber than fine dining.

2. Disney restaurants have comparatively few tables for parties of two, and servers are generally disinclined to seat two guests at larger tables. If you're a duo, you might have to wait longer to be seated.

3. At full-service Disney restaurants, an automatic gratuity of 18% is added to your tab—even at buffets where you get your own food.

4. Disney adds a surcharge of $4 per adult and $2 per child to certain popular restaurants during weeks of peak attendance, including Presidents Day, Spring Break, Easter, mid-December–New Year's Eve, and every day from early June to early August. The following restaurants participate in the gouging: **Akershus Royal Banquet Hall** (Princess Storybook Dining), **Biergarten, Boma—Flavors of Africa** (breakfast and dinner), **Cape May Cafe** (breakfast and dinner buffet), **Chef Mickey's** (breakfast and dinner), **Cinderella's Royal Table, The Crystal Palace, Garden Grill Restaurant, Hollywood & Vine** (Play 'n Dine character buffets), **Liberty Tree Tavern** (dinner), **1900 Park Fare** (Supercalifragilistic Breakfast and Cinderella's Happily Ever After Dinner), **'Ohana** (breakfast and dinner), the **Spirit of Aloha Dinner Show,** Trail's End Restaurant at Fort Wilderness (an exception: $2 extra for adults and $1 for kids), and **Tusker House Restaurant.**

DISNEY DINING SUGGESTIONS

FOLLOWING ARE SUGGESTIONS FOR DINING at each of the major theme parks. If you're interested in trying a theme park full-service restaurant, be aware that the restaurants continue to serve after the park's official closing time. For example, we showed up at The Hollywood Brown Derby just as Disney's Hollywood Studios closed at 8 p.m. We were seated almost immediately and enjoyed a leisurely dinner while the crowds cleared out. Incidentally, don't worry if you're depending on Disney transportation: Buses, boats, and monorails run 1–2 hours after closing.

THE MAGIC KINGDOM

OF THE PARK'S six full-service restaurants, **Be Our Guest** (dinner) in New Fantasyland is the best, followed by **Liberty Tree Tavern** in Liberty Square and **The Plaza Restaurant** on Main Street. **Cinderella's Royal Table** in the castle and **The Crystal Palace** on Main Street serve decent-but-expensive buffets chaperoned by Disney characters. Avoid **Tony's Town Square Restaurant** on Main Street. You'll need to make Advance Reservations before you leave home if you want to eat at Cinderella's Royal Table or Be Our Guest.

EPCOT

FOR THE MOST PART, Epcot's restaurants have always served decent food, although World Showcase restaurants have occasionally been timid about delivering an honest representation of the host nation's cuisine. While these eateries have struggled with authenticity and have sometimes shied away from challenging the meat-and-potatoes palate of the average

unofficial **TIP**
Many Epcot eateries are overpriced, most conspicuously **Monsieur Paul** (France) and **Coral Reef Restaurant** (The Seas).

tourist, they are bolder now, encouraged by America's expanding appreciation of ethnic dining. True, the less adventuresome can still find sanitized and homogenized meals, but the same kitchens will serve up the real thing for anyone with a spark of curiosity. Representing decent value with their combination of attractive ambience and well-prepared food are **Via Napoli** (Italy), **Biergarten** (Germany), and **La Hacienda de San Angel** (Mexico). Biergarten (along with **Restaurant Marrakesh** in Morocco) offers live entertainment.

DISNEY'S ANIMAL KINGDOM

ANIMAL KINGDOM OFFERS A LOT OF counter-service fast food, along with **Tusker House**, a buffet-style restaurant, and **Yak & Yeti**, a table-service restaurant, in Asia. You'll find plenty of traditional Disney-theme-park food—hot dogs, hamburgers, and the like— but even the fast food is superior to typical Disney fare. Our two counter-service favorites: **Flame Tree Barbecue** in Discovery Island, with its waterfront dining pavilions, and **Yak & Yeti**

unofficial **TIP**
Flame Tree Barbecue in Safari Village is our pick of the Animal Kingdom litter, both in terms of food quality and atmosphere.

Local Food Cafes (just outside the full-service Yak & Yeti) for casual Asian dishes from egg rolls to crispy honey chicken.

The third full-service restaurant in Animal Kingdom, the **Rainforest Cafe,** has entrances both inside and outside the park (you don't have to buy park admission to eat there). Both Rainforest Cafes (the other is at Downtown Disney Marketplace) accept Advance Reservations.

DISNEY'S HOLLYWOOD STUDIOS

DINING AT DHS is more interesting than at the Magic Kingdom and less international than at Epcot. The park has five restaurants where Advance Reservations are recommended: **The Hollywood Brown Derby, 50's Prime Time Cafe, Sci-Fi Dine-In Theater Restaurant, Mama Melrose's Ristorante Italiano,** and the **Hollywood & Vine** buffet. The upscale Brown Derby is by far the best restaurant at the Studios. For simple Italian food, including pizza, Mama Melrose's is fine. At the Sci-Fi Dine-In, you eat in little cars at a simulated drive-in movie from the 1950s. Though you won't find a more entertaining restaurant in Walt Disney World, the food is quite disappointing. Somewhat better is the 50's Prime Time Cafe, where you sit in Mom's fabulous midcentury kitchen and scarf down meat loaf while watching clips of classic TV sitcoms. Hollywood & Vine features Disney Channel characters during breakfast and lunch.

WALT DISNEY WORLD RESTAURANTS
At a Glance

TO HELP YOU MAKE YOUR DINING CHOICES, we've compiled a quick-reference list of full-service restaurants at Disney World. Here you can check the restaurant's cuisine, location, overall rating, cost range, quality rating, and value rating. Restaurants are grouped by cuisine and listed within each category from the highest overall star rating to the lowest.

OVERALL RATING The overall rating represents the entire dining experience: style, service, and ambience, in addition to taste, presentation, and quality of food. Five stars is the highest rating and indicates that the restaurant offers the best of everything. Four-star restaurants are above average, and three-star restaurants offer good, though not necessarily memorable, meals. Two-star restaurants serve mediocre fare, and one-star restaurants are below average. Our star ratings don't correspond to ratings awarded by AAA, Mobil, Zagat, or other restaurant reviewers.

COST RANGE The next rating tells how much a full-service entree will cost. Appetizers, sides, soups/salads, desserts,

Inexpensive	**$15 or less per person**
Moderate	**$15–$28 per person**
Expensive	**More than $28 per person**

drinks, and tips aren't included. We've classified costs as inexpensive, moderate, or expensive.

QUALITY RATING The food quality is rated on a scale of one to five stars, five being the best rating attainable. The quality rating is based expressly on the taste, freshness of ingredients, preparation, presentation, and creativity of food served. There is no consideration of price. If you are a person who wants the best food available and cost is not an issue, you need look no further than the quality ratings.

VALUE RATING If, on the other hand, you are looking for both quality and value, then you should check the value rating, also expressed as stars. The greater the stars, the more you get for your dining dollar.

WDW Restaurants by Cuisine

CUISINE	LOCATION	OVERALL RATING	COST	QUALITY RATING	VALUE RATING
AFRICAN					
Jiko— The Cooking Place	Animal Kingdom Lodge/Jambo House	★★★★½	EXP	★★★★½	★★★½
Boma— Flavors of Africa	Animal Kingdom Lodge/Jambo House	★★★★	EXP	★★★★	★★★★½
Tusker House Restaurant	Animal Kingdom	★½	MOD	★	★★
AMERICAN					
California Grill (reopens 2013)	Contemporary	★★★★½	EXP	★★★★½	★★★
The Hollywood Brown Derby	DHS	★★★★	EXP	★★★★	★★★
Artist Point	Wilderness Lodge	★★★½	EXP	★★★★	★★★
Cape May Café	Beach Club	★★★½	MOD	★★★½	★★★★
Whispering Canyon Café	Wilderness Lodge	★★★	MOD	★★★½	★★★★
Captain's Grille	Yacht Club	★★★	MOD	★★★½	★★★
The Crystal Palace	Magic Kingdom	★★★	MOD	★★★½	★★★
House of Blues	Downtown Disney	★★★	MOD	★★★½	★★★
50's Prime Time Café	DHS	★★★	MOD	★★★	★★★
Liberty Tree Tavern	Magic Kingdom	★★★	MOD	★★★	★★★

WDW Restaurants by Cuisine (cont'd.)

CUISINE	LOCATION	OVERALL RATING	COST	QUALITY RATING	VALUE RATING
AMERICAN *(continued)*					
Cinderella's Royal Table	Magic Kingdom	★★★	EXP	★★★	★★
Olivia's Cafe	Old Key West	★★★	MOD	★★★	★★
T-REX	Downtown Disney	★★★	MOD	★★	★★
The Wave . . . of American Flavors	Contemporary	★★★	MOD	★★	★★
ESPN Club	BoardWalk	★★½	MOD	★★★	★★★
ESPN Wide World of Sports Cafe	ESPN Wide World of Sports Complex	★★½	MOD	★★★	★★★
Hollywood & Vine	DHS	★★½	MOD	★★★	★★★
1900 Park Fare	Grand Floridian	★★½	MOD	★★★	★★★
Chef Mickey's	Contemporary	★★½	EXP	★★★	★★★
Boatwrights Dining Hall	Port Orleans	★★½	MOD	★★★	★★
Grand Floridian Cafe	Grand Floridian	★★½	MOD	★★★	★★
Beaches & Cream Soda Shop	Beach Club	★★½	INEXP	★★½	★★½
Splitsville	Downtown Disney	★★½	MOD	★★½	★★
Planet Hollywood	Downtown Disney	★★½	MOD	★★	★★
Rainforest Cafe	Animal Kingdom and Downtown Disney	★★½	MOD	★★	★★
Garden Grove	Swan	★★	MOD	★★★	★★
Sci-Fi Dine-In Theater Restaurant	DHS	★★	MOD	★★½	★★
Garden Grill Restaurant	Epcot	★★	EXP	★★	★★★
Big River Grille & Brewing Works	BoardWalk	★★	MOD	★★	★★
The Fountain	Dolphin	★★	MOD	★★	★★
The Plaza Restaurant	Magic Kingdom	★★	MOD	★★	★★
Turf Club Bar & Grill	Saratoga Springs	★★	MOD	★★	★★
Trail's End Restaurant	Fort Wilderness Resort	★★	MOD	★★	★★
Wolfgang Puck Grand Cafe	Downtown Disney	★★	EXP	★½	★½
LakeView Restaurant	Wyndham LBV	★★	MOD	★	★★★
Tusker House Restaurant	Animal Kingdom	★½	MOD	★	★★
Maya Grill	Coronado Springs	★	MOD	★	★

WDW Restaurants by Cuisine (cont'd.)

CUISINE	LOCATION	OVERALL RATING	COST	QUALITY RATING	VALUE RATING
BUFFET					
Boma—Flavors of Africa	Animal Kingdom Lodge	★★★★	EXP	★★★★	★★★★½
Cape May Café	Beach Club	★★★½	MOD	★★★½	★★★★
The Crystal Palace	Magic Kingdom	★★★	MOD	★★★½	★★★
Akershus Royal Banquet Hall	Epcot	★★★	EXP	★★★	★★★★
Hollywood & Vine	DHS	★★½	MOD	★★★	★★★
1900 Park Fare	Grand Floridian	★★½	MOD	★★★	★★★
Chef Mickey's	Contemporary	★★½	EXP	★★★	★★★
Garden Grove	Swan	★★	MOD	★★★	★★
Biergarten	Epcot	★★	EXP	★★	★★★★
Trail's End Restaurant	Fort Wilderness Resort	★★	MOD	★★	★★
Tusker House Restaurant	Animal Kingdom	★½	MOD	★	★★
CHINESE					
Nine Dragons Restaurant	Epcot	★★★	MOD	★★★	★★
CUBAN					
Bongos Cuban Cafe	Downtown Disney	★★	MOD	★★	★★
ENGLISH					
Rose & Crown Dining Room	Epcot	★★★	MOD	★★★½	★★
FRENCH					
Monsieur Paul	Epcot	★★★★	EXP	★★★★½	★★★
Be Our Guest Restaurant	Magic Kingdom	★★★★	EXP	★★★★	★★★★
Les Chefs de France	Epcot	★★★	EXP	★★★	★★★
GERMAN					
Biergarten	Epcot	★★	EXP	★★	★★★★
GLOBAL					
Paradiso 37	Downtown Disney	★★½	INEXP	★★★	★★★
GOURMET					
Victoria & Albert's	Grand Floridian	★★★★★	EXP	★★★★★	★★★★
INDIAN/AFRICAN					
Sanaa	Animal Kingdom Villas–Kidani Village	★★★★	EXP	★★★★	★★★★

WDW Restaurants by Cuisine (cont'd.)

CUISINE	LOCATION	OVERALL RATING	COST	QUALITY RATING	VALUE RATING
IRISH					
Raglan Road Irish Pub & Restaurant	Downtown Disney	★★★★	MOD	★★★½	★★★
ITALIAN					
Tutto Italia Ristorante	Epcot	★★★★	EXP	★★★★	★★★
Via Napoli	Epcot	★★★★	MOD	★★★½	★★★
Andiamo Italian Bistro & Grille	Hilton	★★★	EXP	★★★	★★★
Il Mulino New York Trattoria	Swan	★★★	EXP	★★★	★★
Mama Melrose's Ristorante Italiano	DHS	★★½	MOD	★★★	★★
Tony's Town Square Restaurant	Magic Kingdom	★★½	MOD	★★★	★★
JAPANESE/SUSHI					
Kimonos	Swan	★★★★	MOD	★★★★½	★★★
Kona Island Sushi Bar	Polynesian	★★★★	MOD	★★★★	★★★★
Teppan Edo	Epcot	★★★½	EXP	★★★★	★★★
Tokyo Dining	Epcot	★★★	MOD	★★★★	★★★
Benihana	Hilton	★★★	MOD	★★★½	★★★
MEDITERRANEAN					
Kouzzina by Cat Cora	BoardWalk Inn	★★★★	MOD	★★★★	★★★★
Cítricos	Grand Floridian	★★★½	EXP	★★★★½	★★★
Fresh Mediterranean Market	Dolphin	★★½	MOD	★★½	★★
MEXICAN					
La Hacienda de San Angel	Epcot	★★★	Exp	★★★½	★★½
San Angel Inn	Epcot	★★★	EXP	★★	★★
MOROCCAN					
Restaurant Marrakesh	Epcot	★★	MOD	★★½	★★
NORWEGIAN					
Akershus Royal Banquet Hall	Epcot	★★★	EXP	★★★	★★★★
POLYNESIAN/PAN-ASIAN					
Kona Island Sushi Bar	Polynesian	★★★★	MOD	★★★★	★★★★
'Ohana	Polynesian	★★★	MOD	★★★½	★★★

WDW Restaurants by Cuisine (cont'd.)

CUISINE	LOCATION	OVERALL RATING	COST	QUALITY RATING	VALUE RATING
POLYNESIAN/PAN-ASIAN					
Kona Cafe	Polynesian	★★★	MOD	★★★	★★★★
Yak & Yeti Restaurant	Animal Kingdom	★★	EXP	★★½	★★
Avu Avu	Buena Vista Palace	★★	MOD	★★	★★★
SEAFOOD					
Narcoossee's	Grand Floridian	★★★★½	EXP	★★★½	★★
Flying Fish Café	BoardWalk	★★★★	EXP	★★★★	★★★
Artist Point	Wilderness Lodge	★★★½	EXP	★★★★	★★★
Todd English's bluezoo	Dolphin	★★★	EXP	★★★	★★
Fulton's Crab House	Downtown Disney	★★½	EXP	★★★½	★★
Shutters at Old Port Royale	Caribbean Beach	★★	MOD	★★½	★★
STEAK					
Shula's Steak House	Dolphin	★★★★	EXP	★★★★	★★
Le Cellier Steakhouse	Epcot	★★★½	EXP	★★★½	★★★
Yachtsman Steakhouse	Yacht Club	★★★	EXP	★★★½	★★
Shutters at Old Port Royale	Caribbean Beach	★★	MOD	★★½	★★

PART NINE

The MAGIC KINGDOM

OPENED IN 1971, THE MAGIC KINGDOM was the first built of Walt Disney World's four theme parks. It is undoubtedly what most people think of when they think of Disney World.

ARRIVING

IF YOU DRIVE, THE MAGIC KINGDOM **Ticket and Transportation Center (TTC)** parking lot opens about 2 hours before the park does. After paying a fee, you are directed to a parking space, then transported by tram to the TTC, where you catch a monorail or ferry to the entrance.

If you're staying at the Bay Lake Tower, Contemporary, Grand Floridian, or Polynesian Resorts, you can commute to the Magic Kingdom by monorail (guests at the Contemporary and Bay Lake Tower can walk there more quickly). If you stay at Wilderness Lodge and Villas or Fort Wilderness Campground, you can take a boat or bus. Guests at other Disney resorts can reach the park by bus. Disney lodging guests are deposited at the park's entrance, bypassing the TTC.

GETTING ORIENTED

AT THE MAGIC KINGDOM, stroller, wheelchair, and ECV/ESV rentals are in the train station; you'll find lockers on the right, just inside the entrance. On your left as you enter **Main Street, U.S.A.** is **City Hall,** the theme park's center for information, lost and found, guided tours, and entertainment schedules.

unofficial **TIP**
If you don't already have a handout guide map of the park, get one at City Hall.

The guide map found there lists all attractions, shops, and eating places; provides information about first aid, baby care, and assistance for the disabled; and gives tips for good photos. It also lists times for the day's special events, live entertainment, Disney-character parades, and concerts, and it also tells when and where to find Disney characters. The guide map is supplemented by a daily entertainment schedule known as the *Times Guide.*

Main Street ends at the **Central Plaza,** a hub from which branch the entrances to five other sections of the Magic Kingdom: **Adventureland, Frontierland, Liberty Square, Fantasyland,** and **Tomorrowland.**

Cinderella Castle, at the entrance to Fantasyland, is the Magic Kingdom's architectural icon and visual center. If you start in Adventureland and go clockwise around the Magic Kingdom, the castle spires will always be roughly on your right; if you start in Tomorrowland and go counterclockwise through the park, the spires will always be roughly on your left.

FANTASYLAND EXPANSION

WITH THE OPENING OF the **Seven Dwarfs Mine Train** in 2014, the Magic Kingdom will complete the Fantasyland expansion begun in 2010. The first phase of "New Fantasyland" opened in 2012, with attractions and restaurants that quickly joined the Magic Kingdom's must-do list. Parents with small children race each morning to *Enchanted Tales with Belle*—an interactive stage show and character greeting—the way that teens head for Space Mountain. Families will line up for an hour or more to eat lunch at the new **Be Our Guest Restaurant,** which serves the best food in the Magic Kingdom (dinner requires Advance Reservations 180 days before your visit).

STARTING *the* TOUR

TAKE ADVANTAGE OF WHAT DISNEY does best: the fantasy adventures of Splash Mountain and The Haunted Mansion and the various Audio-Animatronic (talking-robot) attractions, including *The Hall of Presidents* and Pirates of the Caribbean. Don't burn through daylight hours browsing the shops unless you plan to spend a minimum of 2½ days at the Magic Kingdom, and even then wait until midday or later. Eat breakfast early, and avoid lines at eateries by snacking during the day on food from vendors or, better yet, from your fanny pack. Except for Be Our Guest, fare at most Magic Kingdom eateries is on par with McDonald's.

unofficial **TIP**
Minimize the time you spend on midway-type rides; you probably have something similar near your hometown.

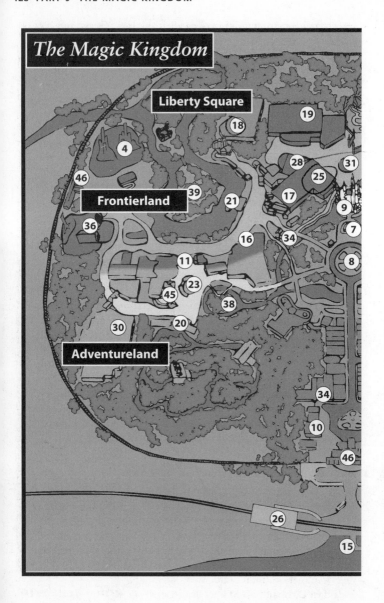

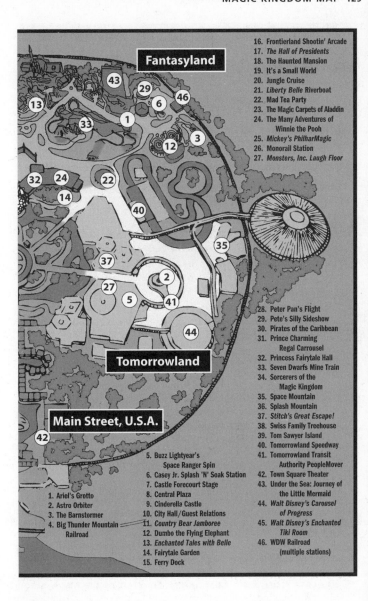

16. Frontierland Shootin' Arcade
17. *The Hall of Presidents*
18. The Haunted Mansion
19. *It's a Small World*
20. Jungle Cruise
21. *Liberty Belle* Riverboat
22. Mad Tea Party
23. The Magic Carpets of Aladdin
24. The Many Adventures of
    Winnie the Pooh
25. *Mickey's PhilharMagic*
26. Monorail Station
27. *Monsters, Inc. Laugh Floor*

28. Peter Pan's Flight
29. Pete's Silly Sideshow
30. Pirates of the Caribbean
31. Prince Charming
    Regal Carrousel
32. Princess Fairytale Hall
33. Seven Dwarfs Mine Train
34. Sorcerers of the
    Magic Kingdom
35. Space Mountain
36. Splash Mountain
37. *Stitch's Great Escape!*
38. Swiss Family Treehouse
39. Tom Sawyer Island
40. Tomorrowland Speedway
41. Tomorrowland Transit
    Authority PeopleMover
42. Town Square Theater
43. *Under the Sea: Journey of
    the Little Mermaid*
44. *Walt Disney's Carousel
    of Progress*
45. *Walt Disney's Enchanted
    Tiki Room*
46. WDW Railroad
    (multiple stations)

Fantasyland

Tomorrowland

Main Street, U.S.A.

5. Buzz Lightyear's
   Space Ranger Spin
6. Casey Jr. Splash 'N' Soak Station
7. Castle Forecourt Stage
8. Central Plaza
9. Cinderella Castle
10. City Hall/Guest Relations
11. *Country Bear Jamboree*
12. Dumbo the Flying Elephant
13. *Enchanted Tales with Belle*
14. Fairytale Garden
15. Ferry Dock

1. Ariel's Grotto
2. Astro Orbiter
3. The Barnstormer
4. Big Thunder Mountain
   Railroad

NOT TO BE MISSED AT THE MAGIC KINGDOM
ADVENTURELAND • Pirates of the Caribbean
FANTASYLAND • Peter Pan's Flight • *Mickey's PhilharMagic* • Seven Dwarfs Mine Train • The Many Adventures of Winnie the Pooh • Under the Sea: Journey of the Little Mermaid
FRONTIERLAND • Big Thunder Mountain Railroad • Splash Mountain
LIBERTY SQUARE • The Haunted Mansion
SPECIAL EVENTS • Evening Parade • *Celebrate the Magic* • *Wishes*
TOMORROWLAND • Space Mountain

■ MAIN STREET, *U.S.A.*

MAIN STREET IS A DISNEYFIED turn-of-the-19th-century small-town American street. Its buildings are real, not elaborate props. Attention to detail is exceptional: Furnishings and fixtures are true to the period. Along the street are shops, eating places, **City Hall,** and a fire station. Occasionally, horse-drawn trolleys, fire engines, and horseless carriages transport visitors along Main Street to the **Central Plaza.**

Character Greetings *(Fastpass)*

DESCRIPTION AND COMMENTS Meet Mickey, Minnie, and friends throughout the day at the **Town Square Theater** on Main Street, to your right as you enter the park. Check the *Times Guide* for details. The Disney princesses will also appear at the Town Square Theater until their permanent meet-and-greet headquarters, **Princess Fairytale Hall**, is ready in Fantasyland.

TOURING TIPS If the wait to meet Mickey or the princesses appears long, obtain Fastpasses to schedule your visit.

Sorcerers of the Magic Kingdom ★★★

Appeal by Age PRESCHOOL ★★★½ GRADE SCHOOL ★★★★½ TEENS ★★★★
YOUNG ADULTS ★★★★ OVER 30 ★★★★ SENIORS ★★★

What it is Interactive video game. **Scope and scale** Minor attraction. **When to go** Before 11 a.m. or after 8 p.m. **Special comments** Long lines to play. **Authors' rating** Great idea; ★★★. **Duration of presentation** About 2 minutes per step, 4 or 5 steps per game. **Probable waiting time per step** 10–15 minutes.

DESCRIPTION AND COMMENTS Sorcerers of the Magic Kingdom combines aspects of role-playing games such as Dungeons and Dragons with Disney characters and theme park attractions. Your objective: to help the wizard Merlin keep evildoers from taking over the Magic Kingdom. Merlin sends you on adventures in different parts of the park to fight these villains. Each land hosts a different adventure within the game.

Main Street Services

Most park services are centered on Main Street, U.S.A., including:

BABY CARE CENTER Next to The Crystal Palace, left around the Central Plaza (toward Adventureland)

BANKING SERVICES ATMs underneath the Main Street railroad station

FIRST AID Next to The Crystal Palace, left around the Central Plaza (toward Adventureland)

LIVE ENTERTAINMENT AND PARADE INFORMATION City Hall, at the railroad-station end of Main Street

LOST AND FOUND City Hall

LOST PERSONS City Hall

STORAGE LOCKERS Underneath the Main Street railroad station (all lockers cleaned out each night)

WALT DISNEY WORLD AND LOCAL ATTRACTION INFORMATION City Hall

WHEELCHAIR, ECV/ESV, AND STROLLER RENTALS Ground floor of the railroad station at the end of Main Street

The game is played with a set of trading cards—similar to baseball cards or Magic: The Gathering cards—with a different Disney character on each card. Each character possesses special properties that help it fight certain villains. Pick up the cards (free), plus a map showing where in the park you can play the game, at either the Fire Station on Main Street, U.S.A., or across from Sleepy Hollow Refreshments in Liberty Square.

You'll need your park ticket to pick up your first set of cards and start the game. One card, known as your "key," links you to your game. You'll need to present your key card when you pick up a set of cards to start your next adventure.

When you pick up your first set of cards, you'll view an instructional video explaining how to use them and the object of the game. Then you'll be sent to another location to start your first adventure. Each location in the park is associated with a unique symbol: an eye, a feather, a dragonfly, or something along those lines. Look for these symbols on the map to find the best route to your starting point.

Each adventure consists of four or five stops in a particular land. At each stop, another story will play on a computer screen, outlining what your villain is trying to do. Merlin will ask you to cast a spell, using your character cards, to stop the villain. Hold one or more of your cards up to the video display to cast your spell. Cameras in the display read your card, deploy the spell, and show you the results.

The game has three levels: easy, medium, and hard. The easy version is the default and is appropriate for small children;

holding up any one of your character cards is enough to defeat any villain. In more-advanced levels of the game, you need to display two or more character cards in specific combinations to defeat a particular villain. Different card combinations produce different spells, and only some spells work on certain characters in those advanced levels.

The audio at each step holds clues to which cards you should use against advanced villains. For example, if a villain says something like "Don't toy with me!" then you should look for cards with characters that are toys, such as the *Toy Story* characters; references to "being spotted" suggest using cards with characters from *101 Dalmatians;* and so on.

TOURING TIPS You'll probably encounter a line of 5–10 people ahead of you at each portal, especially if you play during the afternoon. One complete adventure should take about 30–60 minutes to play, depending on how crowded the park is. If the line to pick up cards is too long at the Main Street Fire Station, try the Liberty Square distribution point.

Walt Disney World Railroad ★★½

Appeal by Age	PRESCHOOL ★★★★	GRADE SCHOOL ★★★★	TEENS ★★★
YOUNG ADULTS ★★★★		OVER 30 ★★★★	SENIORS ★★★★

What it is Scenic railroad ride around perimeter of the Magic Kingdom, and transportation to Frontierland. **Scope and scale** Minor attraction. **When to go** Anytime. **Special comments** Main Street is usually the least congested station. **Authors' rating** Plenty to see; ★★½. **Duration of ride** About 20 minutes for a complete circuit. **Average wait in line per 100 people ahead of you** 8 minutes; assumes 2 or more trains operating. **Loading speed** Moderate.

DESCRIPTION AND COMMENTS A transportation ride blending an unusual variety of sights and experiences with an energy-saving way to get around the park. The train provides a glimpse of all lands except Adventureland.

TOURING TIPS Save the train until after you've seen the featured attractions, or use it when you need transportation. On busy days, lines form at the Frontierland Station but rarely at the Main Street Station. Wheelchair access is available at the Frontierland and Fantasyland Stations.

Only folded strollers are permitted on board, so you can't ride with your rented Disney stroller. You can, however, get a replacement stroller at your destination. Just take your personal belongings, stroller name card, and rental receipt with you on the train.

Finally, note that the railroad shuts down immediately before and during parades. Check your park map or *Times Guide* for parade times. Needless to say, this is not the time to queue up for the train.

Transportation Rides

DESCRIPTION AND COMMENTS Trolleys, buses, and the like that add color to Main Street.

TOURING TIPS Will save you a walk to the hub. Not worth a wait.

◘ ADVENTURELAND

ADVENTURELAND IS THE FIRST LAND to the left of Main Street. It combines an African-safari theme with elements of old New Orleans and the Caribbean.

Jungle Cruise (*Fastpass*) ★★★

Appeal by Age	PRESCHOOL ★★★★	GRADE SCHOOL ★★★★	TEENS ★★★½
YOUNG ADULTS ★★★½		OVER 30 ★★★★	SENIORS ★★★★

What it is Outdoor safari-themed boat-ride adventure. **Scope and scale** Major attraction. **When to go** Before 10 a.m. or 2 hours before closing, or use Fastpass. **Special comments** A lot of fun to ride at night! **Authors' rating** Among the oldest attractions in the park and a long-enduring Disney classic; ★★★. **Duration of ride** 8–9 minutes. **Average wait in line per 100 people ahead of you** 3½ minutes; assumes 10 boats operating. **Loading speed** Moderate.

DESCRIPTION AND COMMENTS An outdoor cruise through jungle waterways. Passengers encounter animatronic elephants, lions, hostile natives, and a menacing hippo. Boatman's spiel adds to the fun. The technology now seems dated and worn, but in the Jungle Cruise's defense, you can always depend on the robotic critters being present as you motor past.

TOURING TIPS A convoluted queuing area makes it difficult to estimate the length of your wait. Fortunately, the Jungle Cruise is a Fastpass attraction. Before you obtain a Fastpass, however, ask a cast member what the estimated wait in the standby line is.

The Magic Carpets of Aladdin ★★★

Appeal by Age	PRESCHOOL ★★★★½	GRADE SCHOOL ★★★★	TEENS ★★★
YOUNG ADULTS ★★★		OVER 30 ★★★	SENIORS ★★★

What it is Elaborate midway ride. **Scope and scale** Minor attraction. **When to go** Before 10 a.m. or in the hour before park closing. **Authors' rating** A visually appealing children's ride; ★★★. **Duration of ride** 1½ minutes. **Average wait in line per 100 people ahead of you** 16 minutes. **Loading speed** Slow.

DESCRIPTION AND COMMENTS A midway ride like Dumbo, except with magic carpets instead of elephants. Copying the innovation of One Fish, Two Fish at Universal's Islands of Adventure, the Aladdin ride has a spitting camel positioned to spray jets of water on carpet riders. Riders can maneuver their carpets up and down to spit back and side to side to avoid getting wet.

TOURING TIPS Like Dumbo, this ride has great eye appeal but extremely limited capacity (that is, it loads slowly). Try to get younger kids on during the first 30 minutes the park is open, or try just before park closing.

A Pirate's Adventure: Treasure of the Seven Seas ★★

Appeal by Age	TOO NEW TO RATE

What it is Interactive game. **Scope and scale** Diversion. **When to go** Anytime. **Authors' rating** Could be more challenging; ★★. **Duration of experience** About 20 minutes to play the entire game.

DESCRIPTION AND COMMENTS Similar to Agent P's World Showcase Adventure at Epcot (page 186), A Pirate's Adventure features interactive areas with physical props and narrations that lead guests through a quest to find lost treasure.

The journey begins at an old cartography shop near Golden Oak Outpost. Groups of up to six people are given a talisman (an RFID card) that will help them on their journey. Guests use the talisman to activate a TV screen, which will assign them one of five different missions. Your group is then given a map and sent off to find your first location. Once there, a member of your party touches the talisman to the symbol at the station, and the animation begins.

Each adventure has four or five stops throughout Adventureland, and each stop contains 30–45 seconds of activity. No strategy or action is required: You watch what unfolds on the screen, get your next destination, and head off.

TOURING TIPS Expendable. Even kids will find it too simple to stay interested. Try it during the middle of the day, if you must.

Pirates of the Caribbean ★★★★★

| Appeal by Age | PRESCHOOL ★★★½ | GRADE SCHOOL ★★★★ | TEENS ★★★★½ |
| YOUNG ADULTS ★★★★½ | OVER 30 ★★★★½ | SENIORS ★★★★½ |

What it is Indoor pirate-themed boat ride. **Scope and scale** Headliner. **When to go** Before noon or after 5 p.m. **Special comments** Frightens some children. **Authors' rating** Disney Audio-Animatronics at their best; not to be missed; ★★★★★. **Duration of ride** About 7½ minutes. **Average wait in line per 100 people ahead of you** 1½ minutes; assumes both waiting lines operating. **Loading speed** Fast.

DESCRIPTION AND COMMENTS An indoor cruise through a series of sets that depict a pirate raid on an island settlement, from bombardment of the fortress to debauchery after the victory. One of the most influential theme park attractions ever created, the Magic Kingdom's version retains the elaborate queuing area, grand scale, and detailed scenes that have awed audiences since its debut in Disneyland in 1967. The *Pirates of the Caribbean* movie series has boosted the ride's popularity, and guests' demands led to the addition of animatronic figures of the film's Captain Jack Sparrow and Captain Barbossa in scenes.

TOURING TIPS A timeless attraction. Engineered to move large crowds in a hurry, Pirates is a good attraction to see during late afternoon. It has two covered waiting lines.

Swiss Family Treehouse ★★★

| Appeal by Age | PRESCHOOL ★★★½ | GRADE SCHOOL ★★★½ | TEENS ★★★ |
| YOUNG ADULTS ★★★ | OVER 30 ★★★ | SENIORS ★★★ |

What it is Outdoor walk-through tree house. **Scope and scale** Minor attraction. **When to go** Before 11:30 a.m. or after 5 p.m. **Special comments** Requires climbing a lot of stairs. **Authors' rating** Incredible detail and execution; ★★★. **Duration of tour** 10–15 minutes. **Average wait in line per 100 people ahead of you** 7 minutes. **Loading speed** Doesn't apply.

DESCRIPTION AND COMMENTS An immense replica of the ship-wrecked family's tree house will turn your children into arboreal architects. It's the king of all tree houses, with its multiple stories and mechanical wizardry. Children enjoy the climbing and exercise; adults marvel at the ingenuity.

TOURING TIPS A self-guided walk-through tour involves a lot of stairs up and down, but no ropes, ladders, or anything fancy. People who stop for extra-long looks or to rest sometimes create bottlenecks that slow the crowd flow. Visit in late afternoon or early evening if you're on a one-day tour, or in the morning of your second day.

Walt Disney's Enchanted Tiki Room ★★★½

| Appeal by Age | PRESCHOOL ★★★½ | GRADE SCHOOL ★★★½ | TEENS ★★★ |
| YOUNG ADULTS ★★★½ | | OVER 30 ★★★½ | SENIORS ★★★½ |

What it is Audio-Animatronic Pacific-island musical-theater show. **Scope and scale** Minor attraction. **When to go** Before 11 a.m. or after 3:30 p.m. **Special comments** Frightens some preschoolers. **Authors' rating** Very, very . . . unusual; ★★★½. **Duration of presentation** 15½ minutes. **Preshow entertainment** Talking birds. **Probable waiting time** 15 minutes.

DESCRIPTION AND COMMENTS The current show here is a shortened version of the original attraction, which premiered at Disneyland in 1963. It stars four singing, wisecracking parrots (José, Fritz, Michael, and Pierre) and remains a favorite of many, including us. It can frighten younger kids, though.

TOURING TIPS Usually not too crowded. We go in the late afternoon, when we appreciate sitting in air-conditioned comfort with our brains in "park."

◧ FRONTIERLAND

FRONTIERLAND ADJOINS ADVENTURELAND as you move clockwise around the Magic Kingdom. The focus is on the Old West, with stockade-type structures and pioneer trappings.

Big Thunder Mountain Railroad (Fastpass) ★★★★

| Appeal by Age | PRESCHOOL ★★★★ | GRADE SCHOOL ★★★★½ | TEENS ★★★★½ |
| YOUNG ADULTS ★★★★½ | | OVER 30 ★★★★½ | SENIORS ★★★★ |

What it is Tame western-mining-themed coaster. **Scope and scale** Headliner. **When to go** Before 10 a.m., in the hour before closing, or use Fastpass. **Special comments** Must be 40" tall to ride; children younger than age 7 must ride with an adult. Switching-off option provided (see page 79). **Authors' rating** Great effects; relatively tame ride; not to be missed; ★★★★. **Duration of ride** About 3½ minutes. **Average wait in line per 100 people ahead of you** 2½ minutes; assumes 5 trains operating. **Loading speed** Moderate–fast.

DESCRIPTION AND COMMENTS Roller coaster through and around a Disney "mountain." The idea is that you're on a runaway mine train during the Gold Rush. This roller coaster is about 5 on a "scary scale" of 10. First-rate examples of Disney creativity are showcased: realistic mining town, falling rocks, and an earthquake, all humorously animated with swinging possums, petulant buzzards, and the like.

TOURING TIPS A superb Disney experience, but more mild than wild. Emphasis is more on the sights than on the thrill of the ride.

Nearby Splash Mountain affects traffic flow here—adventuresome guests ride Splash Mountain first, then go next door to ride Big Thunder. This means large crowds in Frontierland all day and long waits for the coaster. The best way to experience the Magic Kingdom's "mountains" is to ride Space Mountain one morning as soon as the park opens, then Splash Mountain and Big Thunder the next morning. If you only have one day, the order should be Space Mountain, (Buzz Lightyear (optional), Splash Mountain, and finally Big Thunder Mountain. If the wait exceeds 30 minutes when you arrive, use Fastpass.

Country Bear Jamboree ★★★

Appeal by Age	PRESCHOOL ★★★½	GRADE SCHOOL ★★★½	TEENS ★★★
YOUNG ADULTS ★★★	OVER 30 ★★★		SENIORS ★★★★

What it is Audio-Animatronic country hoedown. **Scope and scale** Major attraction. **When to go** Before 11:30 a.m., before a parade, or during the 2 hours before closing. **Special comments** Shows change at Christmas. **Authors' rating** Old and worn, but pure Disney; ★★★. **Duration of presentation** 15 minutes. **Preshow entertainment** None. **Probable waiting time** Not terribly popular but has a comparatively small capacity. Waiting time between noon and 5:30 p.m. on a busy day will average 11–23 minutes.

DESCRIPTION AND COMMENTS A charming cast of animatronic bears sing and stomp in a Western-style revue. Recent editing has cut a few minutes from the show, quickening its pace somewhat. However, most songs remain the same, and the geriatric bears seem a step away from assisted living.

TOURING TIPS During hot summer afternoons, rainy days, and busy times, the show draws large crowds from midmorning on.

Frontierland Shootin' Arcade ★½

Appeal by Age	PRESCHOOL ★★	GRADE SCHOOL ★★★★	TEENS ★★★½
YOUNG ADULTS ★★½	OVER 30 ★★★		SENIORS ★★★

What it is Electronic shooting gallery. **Scope and scale** Diversion. **When to go** Whenever convenient. **Special comments** Costs $1 per play. **Authors' rating** Very nifty shooting gallery; ★½.

DESCRIPTION AND COMMENTS Very elaborate. One of the few attractions not included in Magic Kingdom admission.

TOURING TIPS Not a place to waste time if you're on a tight schedule. If time allows, go on your second day. The fun is entirely in the target practice—no prizes can be won.

Splash Mountain (Fastpass) ★★★★★

Appeal by Age	PRESCHOOL ★★★★†	GRADE SCHOOL ★★★★½	TEENS ★★★★½
YOUNG ADULTS ★★★★★	OVER 30 ★★★★½		SENIORS ★★★★½

† *Many preschoolers are too short to meet the height requirement, and others are visually intimidated when they see the ride from the waiting line. Among preschoolers who actually ride, most give the attraction high marks.*

 What it is Indoor/outdoor water-flume adventure ride. **Scope and scale** Super-headliner. **When to go** As soon as the park opens, during afternoon or evening parades, just before closing, or use Fastpass. **Special comments** Must be 40" tall to ride; children younger than age 7 must ride with an adult. Switching-off option provided (see page 79). **Authors' rating** A soggy delight, and not to be missed; ★★★★★. **Duration of ride** About 10 minutes. **Average wait in line per 100 people ahead of you** 3½ minutes; assumes ride is operating at full capacity. **Loading speed** Moderate.

DESCRIPTION AND COMMENTS Splash Mountain combines steep chutes and animatronics with at least one special effect for each of the senses. The ride covers more than half a mile, splashing through swamps, caves, and backwoods bayous before climaxing in a five-story plunge and Br'er Rabbit's triumphant return home. More than a hundred Audio-Animatronic characters, including Br'er Rabbit, Br'er Bear, and Br'er Fox, regale riders with songs, including "Zip-a-Dee-Doo-Dah."

TOURING TIPS This happy, exciting, adventuresome ride vies with Space Mountain in Tomorrowland as the park's most popular attraction. Crowds build fast in the morning, and waits of more than 2 hours can be expected once the park fills. Get in line first thing, certainly no later than 45 minutes after the park opens. Long lines will persist all day.

If you have only one day to see the Magic Kingdom, ride Space Mountain first, then Buzz Lightyear (also in Tomorrowland), then hotfoot it over to Splash Mountain. If the wait is less than 30 minutes, go ahead and ride. Otherwise, obtain a Fastpass and return later to enjoy Splash Mountain. Fastpass strategies have been incorporated into the Magic Kingdom one-day touring plans (see pages 162–166). If you have two mornings to devote to the Magic Kingdom, experience Space Mountain one morning and Buzz Lightyear, Splash Mountain, and Big Thunder Mountain the next.

As occurs with Space Mountain, when the park opens, hundreds are poised to dash to Splash Mountain. The best strategy is to go to the end of Main Street and turn left to The Crystal Palace restaurant. In front of the restaurant is a bridge that provides a shortcut to Adventureland. Stake out a position at the barrier rope. When the park opens and the rope drops, move as fast as you comfortably can and cross the bridge to Adventureland.

Here's another shortcut: Just past the first group of buildings on your right, roughly across from the Swiss Family Treehouse, is a small passageway containing restrooms and phones. Easy to overlook, it connects Adventureland to Frontierland. Go through the passageway into Frontierland and take a hard left. As you emerge along the waterfront, Splash Mountain is straight ahead. If you miss the passageway, don't fool around looking for it. Continue straight through Adventureland to Splash Mountain.

Less exhausting in the morning is to commute to Splash Mountain via the Walt Disney World Railroad. Board at Main Street Station and wait for the park to open. The train will pull out of the station a few minutes after the rope drops at the Central Plaza end of Main Street. Ride to Frontierland Station (the first stop) and disembark. As you come down the stairs at the station, the entrance to Splash Mountain will be on your left. Because of the time required to unload at the station, train passengers will arrive at Splash Mountain about the same time as the lead element from the Central Plaza.

If you ride in front, you'll almost certainly get wet. Riders elsewhere get splashed, but usually not doused. Since you don't know which seat you'll be assigned, go prepared. On a cool day, carry a plastic garbage bag. Tear holes in the bottom and sides to make a water-resistant poncho (tuck the bag under your bottom). Leave your phone or camera with a nonriding member of your group, or wrap it in plastic. An alternative to the garbage-bag getup is to store a change of clothes and shoes in a rental locker. For any attraction where there's a distinct possibility of getting soaked, wear waterproof sandals, such as Tevas, and change back to regular shoes after the ride.

The steep chute you see when standing in line seems scary, but the drop looks worse than it is. Despite reassurances, however, many children wig out when they see it.

Tom Sawyer Island and Fort Langhorn ★★★

Appeal by Age PRESCHOOL ★★★½ GRADE SCHOOL ★★★★½ TEENS ★★★★ YOUNG ADULTS ★★★ OVER 30 ★★★½ SENIORS ★★★½

What it is Outdoor walk-through exhibit and rustic playground. **Scope and scale** Minor attraction. **When to go** Midmorning–late afternoon. **Special comments** Closes at dusk. **Authors' rating** Great for rambunctious kids; ★★★.

DESCRIPTION AND COMMENTS Tom Sawyer Island is a getaway within the park. It has hills to climb; a cave, windmill, and pioneer stockade (Fort Langhorn) to explore; a tipsy barrel bridge to cross; and paths to follow. You can watch riverboats chug past. It's a delight for adults and a godsend for children who have been in tow and closely supervised all day.

TOURING TIPS Tom Sawyer Island isn't one of the Magic Kingdom's more celebrated attractions, but it certainly is well conceived: Attention to detail is excellent, and kids love the frontier ambience. It's a must for families with children ages 5–15. If your group consist of adults, visit on your second day or on your first day after you've seen the attractions you most wanted to see.

Although children could spend a whole day on the island, plan on at least 20 minutes. Access is by raft from Frontierland; two operate simultaneously, and the trip is pretty efficient, although you may have to stand in line to board both ways.

Walt Disney World Railroad

DESCRIPTION AND COMMENTS Stops in Frontierland on its circle tour of the park. See page 132 for additional details.

TOURING TIPS Feet-saving link to Main Street and Fantasyland, but the Frontierland station is more congested than those stations.

◧ LIBERTY SQUARE

LIBERTY SQUARE re-creates America at the time of the American Revolution. The architecture is Federal or Colonial. The **Liberty Tree,** a live oak more than 130 years old, lends dignity and grace to the setting.

The Hall of Presidents ★★★

Appeal by Age	PRESCHOOL ★★½	GRADE SCHOOL ★★★	TEENS ★★★½
YOUNG ADULTS ★★★★		OVER 30 ★★★★	SENIORS ★★★★½

What it is Audio-Animatronic historical theater presentation. **Scope and scale** Major attraction. **When to go** Anytime. **Authors' rating** Impressive and moving; ★★★. **Duration of presentation** Almost 23 minutes. **Preshow entertainment** None. **Probable waiting time** The lines for this attraction look intimidating once you're inside the lobby, but they're swallowed up as the theater exchanges audiences. It would be exceptionally unusual not to be admitted to the next show.

DESCRIPTION AND COMMENTS George Washington joins Presidents Lincoln and Obama as the only chief executives with speaking parts; Morgan Freeman narrates. Revamped roughly every decade, the presentation remains inspirational and patriotic, highlighting milestones in American history. Very moving; one of Disney's best and most ambitious animatronic efforts.

TOURING TIPS Detail and costuming are masterly. This is one of the park's most popular attractions among older visitors. Don't be put off by long lines. The theater holds more than 700 people, thus swallowing large lines at a single gulp when visitors are admitted.

The Haunted Mansion ★★★★

Appeal by Age	PRESCHOOL ★★★½	GRADE SCHOOL ★★★★	TEENS ★★★★½
YOUNG ADULTS ★★★★½		OVER 30 ★★★★½	SENIORS ★★★★½

What it is Haunted-house dark ride. **Scope and scale** Major attraction. **When to go** Before 11:30 a.m. or after 8 p.m. **Special comments** Frightens some very young children. **Authors' rating** Some of Walt Disney World's best special effects; not to be missed; ★★★★. **Duration of ride** 7-minute ride plus a 1½-minute preshow. **Average wait in line per 100 people ahead of you** 2½ minutes; assumes both "stretch rooms" operating. **Loading speed** Fast.

DESCRIPTION AND COMMENTS Only slightly scarier than a whoopee cushion, The Haunted Mansion serves up some of the Magic Kingdom's best visual effects. "Doom Buggies" on a conveyor belt transport you through the house from parlor to attic, then through a graveyard. The ride's effects change tone with the setting: Those in the house are generally more spooky, while the graveyard effects, such as a ghostly opera singer wearing a Viking helmet, are there for laughs.

Some children become overly anxious about what they think they'll see. Almost nobody is scared by the actual sights.

TOURING TIPS Lines here ebb and flow more than those at most other Magic Kingdom hot spots because the Mansion is near *The Hall of Presidents* and the *Liberty Belle* Riverboat. These two attractions disgorge 700 and 450 people, respectively, when each show or ride ends, and many of these folks head straight for the Mansion. If you can't go before 11:30 a.m. or after 8 p.m., try to slip in between crowds.

Liberty Belle Riverboat ★★½

Appeal by Age	PRESCHOOL ★★★½	GRADE SCHOOL ★★★	TEENS ★★★
YOUNG ADULTS ★★★½	OVER 30 ★★★½		SENIORS ★★★★

What it is Outdoor scenic boat ride. **Scope and scale** Major attraction. **When to go** Anytime. **Authors' rating** Relaxing and scenic; ★★½. **Duration of ride** About 16 minutes. Average wait to board 10–14 minutes.

DESCRIPTION AND COMMENTS Large-capacity paddle-wheel riverboat navigates the waters around Tom Sawyer Island and Fort Langhorn, passing settler cabins, old mining paraphernalia, an Indian village, and a small menagerie of animatronic wildlife. A beautiful craft, the *Liberty Belle* provides a lofty perspective of Frontierland and Liberty Square.

TOURING TIPS A good attraction for the busy middle of the day. If you encounter huge crowds, chances are that the attraction has been inundated by a wave of guests coming from a just-concluded performance of *The Hall of Presidents.*

▌▐ FANTASYLAND

FANTASYLAND IS THE HEART OF THE MAGIC KINGDOM, an enchanting place spread gracefully like a miniature Alpine village beneath the steepled towers of **Cinderella Castle.**

An ambitious expansion of Fantasyland began in 2010 and will continue into 2014. While most of the remaining work will be occurring behind the scenes, you'll almost certainly see construction walls or exterior refurbishment all through Fantasyland until the expansion is complete. Check **touringplans.com** for updates.

Fantasyland is divided into three distinct sections. Directly behind Cinderella Castle and set upon a snowcapped mountain is **Beast's Castle,** part of a *Beauty and the Beast*–themed area. Most of this section holds dining and shopping, including **Be Our Guest Restaurant; Gaston's Tavern,** a small quick-service restaurant; and a gift shop. The far-right corner of Fantasyland—including **Dumbo, The Barnstormer** kiddie coaster, and the Fantasyland train station—is called **Storybook Circus** as a homage to Disney's *Dumbo.* The

middle of the new Fantasyland holds the headliners, including the
Little Mermaid and Seven Dwarfs attractions. Placing these in the
middle of the new land should allow for good traffic flow either to
the left (toward Beast's Castle) for dining, to the right for attractions
geared to smaller children, or back to the original Fantasyland for
classics such as **Peter Pan's Flight** and **The Many Adventures of Winnie the Pooh**. Completing the refurbishments are *Tangled*-themed
restrooms and an outdoor seating area (with phone-charging stations) near Peter Pan and It's a Small World.

Ariel's Grotto ★★★

Appeal by Age	PRESCHOOL ★★★★½	GRADE SCHOOL ★★★★	TEENS ★★★
YOUNG ADULTS ★★★½		OVER 30 ★★★½	SENIORS ★★★½

What it is Character-greeting venue. **Scope and scale** Minor attraction. **When to
go** Before 10:30 a.m. or during the last 2 hours before closing. **Authors' rating**
Not as themed as other character greetings; ★★★. **Duration of experience**
About 30–90 seconds. **Probable waiting time** 45 minutes. **Queue speed** Slow.

DESCRIPTION AND COMMENTS Ariel's elaborate home is next
to Under the Sea: Journey of the Little Mermaid, in the base of
the seaside cliffs under Prince Eric's Castle. Ariel (in mermaid
form) greets guests from a seashell throne.

TOURING TIPS May close an hour before the rest of the park. The
greeting area is set up almost as if to encourage guests to linger, which keeps the line long. The queue isn't air-conditioned—
surprising for a venue that's supposed to store fish.

The Barnstormer *(Fastpass)* ★★

Appeal by Age	PRESCHOOL ★★★★	GRADE SCHOOL ★★★★	TEENS ★★★
YOUNG ADULTS ★★★		OVER 30 ★★★	SENIORS ★★★

Lose Things

What it is Small roller coaster. **Scope and scale** Minor attraction.
When to go Before 10:30 a.m., during parades, or in the evening just
before the park closes. **Special comments** Must be 35" or taller to
ride. **Authors' rating** Great for little ones, but not worth the wait for
adults; ★★. **Duration of ride** About 53 seconds. **Average wait in line per
100 people ahead of you** 7 minutes. **Loading speed** Slow.

DESCRIPTION AND COMMENTS The Barnstormer is a very small
roller coaster. The ride is zippy but supershort. In fact, of the 53
seconds the ride is in motion, 32 seconds are consumed in leaving
the loading area, being ratcheted up the first hill, and braking
into the off-loading area. The actual time you spend careering
around the track is 21 seconds.

   The Barnstormer is a benign introduction to the roller-coaster
genre and a predictably positive way to help your children step
up to more-adventuresome rides. Simply put, a few circuits will
increase your little one's confidence and improve his or her
chances for enjoying Disney's more adult attractions.

TOURING TIPS The cars of this dinky coaster are too small for
most adults and tend to whiplash taller people. Parties without

children should skip this one. If you're touring with children, you have a problem: The ride is visually and aurally appealing to kids, and that translates to standing in slow-moving lines. If The Barnstormer is high on your children's hit parade, try to ride within the first hour that Fantasyland is open.

Casey Jr. Splash 'N' Soak Station

DESCRIPTION AND COMMENTS Casey Jr., the circus train from *Dumbo,* plays host to an absolutely drenching experience outside the Fantasyland Train Station in the Storybook Circus area. Expect a cadre of captive circus beasts to spray water on you in this elaborate water-play area. It's a marvel to watch.

TOURING TIPS Puts all other theme park splash areas to soaking shame. Bring a change of clothes and a big towel.

Dumbo the Flying Elephant *(Fastpass)* ★★★

**Appeal by Age   PRESCHOOL ★★★★½   GRADE SCHOOL ★★★★   TEENS ★★★
YOUNG   ADULTS   ★★★½   OVER   30   ★★★½   SENIORS   ★★★**

What it is Disneyfied midway ride. **Scope and scale** Minor attraction. **When to go** Before 10 a.m. or after 9 p.m. **Authors' rating** Disney's signature ride for children; ★★★. **Duration of ride** 1½ minutes. **Average wait in line per 100 people ahead of you** 20 minutes. **Loading speed** Slow.

DESCRIPTION AND COMMENTS A tame, happy ride based on the lovable flying pachyderm. Parents and children sit inside small fiberglass "elephants" mounted on long metal arms, which spin around a central axis. Controls inside each vehicle allow you to raise the arm, making you spin higher off the ground. Despite being little different from your average carnival ride, Dumbo is a favorite of many younger children.

As part of the Fantasyland expansion, Dumbo has moved to the upper-right corner of the land. The attraction's capacity has been doubled with the addition of a second ride—a clone of the first. These two changes, along with the addition of newer Fantasyland attractions, have drastically reduced the waits to ride. If you do find yourself with a wait, Dumbo also includes a covered queue featuring interactive elements (read: things your kids can play with to pass the time in line).

TOURING TIPS If Dumbo is essential to your child's happiness, make it your first stop, preferably within 15 minutes of park opening, or use Fastpass. An alternative is to try Dumbo during the last 2 hours the park is open. Besides lower crowds, the ride's lighting and effects make it much prettier at night.

Enchanted Tales with Belle   ★★★★

**Appeal by Age   PRESCHOOL ★★★★½   GRADE SCHOOL ★★★★½   TEENS ★★★½
YOUNG   ADULTS   ★★★★   OVER   30   ★★★★   SENIORS   ★★★★**

What it is Interactive character show. **Scope and scale** Minor attraction. **When to go** As soon as the park opens or during the last 2 hours before closing. **Authors' rating** The prettiest meet-and-greet in the park; ★★★★. **Duration of**

presentation About 20 minutes. **Preshow entertainment** As described below. **Probable waiting time** 10 minutes. **Queue speed** Slow.

DESCRIPTION AND COMMENTS A multiscene *Beauty and the Beast* experience that takes guests into Maurice's workshop, through a magic mirror, and into Beast's library, where the audience shares a story with Belle.

Enter the attraction by walking through Maurice's cottage, where you see mementos tracing Belle's childhood, including her favorite books, and lines drawn on one wall showing how fast Belle grew every year. From there you'll enter Maurice's workshop at the back of the cottage. An assortment of Maurice's odd wood gadgets covers every inch of the floor, walls, and ceiling. Take a moment to peruse the gadgets, then focus your attention on the mirror on the wall to the left of the entry door.

Soon enough, the room gets dark and the mirror begins to sparkle. Through magic and some really good carpentry skills, the mirror turns into a full-size doorway, through which guests enter into a wardrobe room. Once you're in the wardrobe room, the attraction's premise is explained: you're supposed to re-enact the story of *Beauty and the Beast* for Belle on her birthday, and guests are chosen to act out key parts in the play.

Once the parts are cast, everyone walks into the castle's library and takes a seat. Cast members explain how the play will take place and introduce Belle, who gives a short speech about how thrilled she is for everyone to be there. The play is acted out within a few minutes, and the actors get a chance to take photos with Belle and receive a small bookmark as a memento.

Enchanted Tales with Belle is the prettiest and most elaborate meet-and-greet station in Walt Disney World. For the lucky few who get to act in the play, it's also a chance to interact with Belle in a way that isn't possible in other character encounters. You may endure a 30-minute wait for a 3-minute show, but it's the best of its kind in Orlando. Your kids will love it.

TOURING TIPS *Enchanted Tales* is the new Dumbo, with long lines from the time the park opens. Since it's slow-loading and doesn't offer Fastpass, put it first on your touring plan, or try to visit during the last 2 hours the park is open.

It's a Small World ★★★

Appeal by Age	PRESCHOOL ★★★★½	GRADE SCHOOL ★★★★	TEENS ★★★
YOUNG ADULTS ★★★½	OVER 30 ★★★½		SENIORS ★★★★

What it is World-brotherhood-themed indoor boat ride. **Scope and scale** Major attraction. **When to go** Before 11 a.m., during parades, or after 7 p.m. **Authors' rating** Exponentially, um, cute; ★★★. **Duration of ride** About 11 minutes. **Average wait in line per 100 people ahead of you** 3½ minutes; assumes busy conditions with 30 or more boats operating. **Loading speed** Fast.

DESCRIPTION AND COMMENTS It's a Small World is a relentlessly upbeat indoor attraction with a mind-numbing tune that only a backhoe can dislodge from your brain. Small boats carry visitors on a tour around the world, with singing and dancing dolls showcasing the costumes and cultures of different nations. One of Disney's oldest entertainment offerings, Small World first unleashed its brainwashing song and lethally cute dolls on the real world at the 1964 New York World's Fair. We think it ranks with the *Enchanted Tiki Room* in the "What were they smokin'?" category.

TOURING TIPS Cool off here during the heat of the day. Lines are usually 30 minutes or less. If you wear a hearing aid, turn it off.

Mad Tea Party ★★

Appeal by Age	PRESCHOOL ★★★★½	GRADE SCHOOL ★★★★½	TEENS ★★★★
YOUNG ADULTS ★★★½	OVER 30 ★★★½		SENIORS ★★½

What it is Midway-type spinning ride. **Scope and scale** Minor attraction. **When to go** Before 11 a.m. or after 5 p.m. **Special comments** You can make the teacups spin faster by turning the wheel in the center of the cup. **Authors' rating** Fun but not worth the wait; ★★. **Duration of ride** 1½ minutes. **Average wait in line per 100 people ahead of you** 7½ minutes. **Loading speed** Slow.

DESCRIPTION AND COMMENTS Riders whirl feverishly in big teacups. *Alice in Wonderland*'s Mad Hatter provides the theme. Teens are fond of luring adults onto the teacups, then turning the wheel in the middle (making the cup spin faster), until the adults are plastered against the sides and on the verge of throwing up. Don't even *think* about getting on this ride with anyone younger than 21.

TOURING TIPS This ride, well done but not unique, is notoriously slow-loading. Skip it on a busy schedule—if the kids will let you. Ride the morning of your second day if your schedule permits.

The Many Adventures of Winnie the Pooh *(Fastpass)* ★★★½

Appeal by Age	PRESCHOOL ★★★★½	GRADE SCHOOL ★★★★	TEENS ★★★½
YOUNG ADULTS ★★★½	OVER 30 ★★★½		SENIORS ★★★★

What it is Indoor track ride. **Scope and scale** Minor attraction. **When to go** Before 10 a.m., in last hour park is open, or use Fastpass. **Authors' rating** Not to be missed; ★★★½. **Duration of ride** About 4 minutes. **Average wait in line per 100 people ahead of you** 4 minutes. **Loading speed** Moderate.

DESCRIPTION AND COMMENTS Pooh is sunny, upbeat, and fun. You ride a "Hunny Pot" through the pages of a huge picture book into the Hundred Acre Wood, where you encounter Pooh, Piglet, Eeyore, Owl, Rabbit, Tigger, Kanga, and Roo as they contend with a blustery day. There's even a dream sequence with Heffalumps and Woozles.

TOURING TIPS Pooh's Fastpass machines were relocated to *Mickey's PhilharMagic* during the Fantasyland construction. No word regarding whether they'll move back when construction is done in 2014.

Mickey's PhilharMagic *(Fastpass seasonally)* ★★★★

Appeal by Age	PRESCHOOL ★★★★	GRADE SCHOOL ★★★★½	TEENS ★★★★½
YOUNG ADULTS ★★★★½	OVER 30 ★★★★½		SENIORS ★★★★½

What it is 3-D movie. **Scope and scale** Major attraction. **When to go** Before 11 a.m. or during parades. **Special comments** Not to be missed. **Authors' rating** A zany masterpiece; ★★★★. **Duration of presentation** About 12 minutes. **Probable waiting time** 12–30 minutes.

DESCRIPTION AND COMMENTS *Mickey's PhilharMagic* features an odd collection of Disney characters, mixing Mickey and Donald with Simba and Ariel as well as Jasmine and Aladdin. Presented in a theater large enough to accommodate a 150-foot-wide screen—huge by 3-D movie standards—the 3-D movie is augmented by an arsenal of special effects built into the theater. The plot involves Mickey, as the conductor of the *PhilharMagic,* leaving the theater to solve a mystery. In his absence Donald appears and attempts to take charge, with disastrous results.

The attraction is one of Disney's best 3-D efforts. Brilliantly conceived, furiously paced, and laugh-out-loud funny, *Philhar-Magic* incorporates a hit parade of Disney's most beloved characters in a production that will leave you grinning.

TOURING TIPS Though the other 3-D movies are loud, in-your-face affairs, *Mickey's PhilharMagic* is much softer and cuddlier. Things still pop out of the screen, but they're really not scary. You should still proceed cautiously if you have kids under age 5 in your group, but it's the rare child who is frightened. The theater is large, so don't be alarmed to see a gaggle of people in the lobby.

Peter Pan's Flight *(Fastpass)* ★★★★

Appeal by Age	PRESCHOOL ★★★★½	GRADE SCHOOL ★★★★½	TEENS ★★★½
YOUNG ADULTS ★★★★	OVER 30 ★★★★		SENIORS ★★★★

What it is Indoor track ride. **Scope and scale** Minor attraction. **When to go** First or last 30 minutes the park is open, or use Fastpass. **Authors' rating** Nostalgic, mellow, and well done; not to be missed; ★★★★. **Duration of ride** A little over 3 minutes. **Average wait in line per 100 people ahead of you** 5½ minutes. **Loading speed** Moderate–slow.

DESCRIPTION AND COMMENTS Though not a major attraction, Peter Pan's Flight is an absolutely delight, its happy theme uniting some favorite Disney characters, beautiful effects, and charming music. An indoor attraction, Peter Pan's Flight offers a relaxing ride in a "flying pirate ship" over old London and thence to Never-Never Land, where Peter saves Wendy from walking the plank and Captain Hook rehearses for *Dancing with the Stars* on the snout of the ubiquitous crocodile. Unlike some dark rides, this won't frighten young children.

TOURING TIPS Count on long lines all day. Fortunately, much of the queue runs under the roof of the building, out of direct sun and rain. Ride before 10 a.m., during a parade, or just before the park closes, or use Fastpass.

If you use Fastpass, pick up your pass as early in the day as possible. Sometimes Peter Pan exhausts its whole day's supply of Fastpasses by 2 p.m.

Pete's Silly Sideshow ★★★½

Appeal by Age PRESCHOOL ★★★★½ GRADE SCHOOL ★★★★½ TEENS ★★★★ YOUNG ADULTS ★★★★ OVER 30 ★★★★ SENIORS ★★★

What it is Character-greeting venue. **Scope and scale** Minor attraction. **When to go** Before 11 a.m. or during the last 2 hours before closing. **Authors' rating** Well themed, with unique character costumes; ★★★½. **Duration of experience** 7 minutes per character. **Probable waiting time** 25 minutes. **Queue speed** Slow.

DESCRIPTION AND COMMENTS Pete's Silly Sideshow is a circus-themed character-greeting area in the Storybook Circus area. The characters' costumes are distinct from the ones normally seen around the parks. Characters include Goofy as The Great Goofini, Donald Duck as The Astounding Donaldo, Daisy Duck as Madame Daisy Fortuna, and Minnie Mouse as Minnie Magnifique.

TOURING TIPS On non–Extra Magic Hour days, Pete's opens 45 minutes later than the rest of the park and closes an hour before. The queue is indoors and air-conditioned. There is one queue for Goofy and Donald and a second queue for Minnie and Daisy. You can meet two characters at once, but you have to line up twice to meet all four.

Prince Charming Regal Carrousel ★★★

Appeal by Age PRESCHOOL ★★★★½ GRADE SCHOOL ★★★★ TEENS ★★★ YOUNG ADULTS ★★★ OVER 30 ★★★½ SENIORS ★★★½

What it is Merry-go-round. **Scope and scale** Minor attraction. **When to go** Anytime. **Special comments** Adults enjoy the beauty and nostalgia of this ride. **Authors' rating** A beautiful ride for children; ★★★. **Duration of ride** About 2 minutes. **Average wait in line per 100 people ahead of you** 5 minutes. **Loading speed** Slow.

DESCRIPTION AND COMMENTS One of the most elaborate and beautiful merry-go-rounds you'll ever see, especially when its lights are on.

TOURING TIPS While lovely to look at, the carousel loads and unloads very slowly.

Princess Fairytale Hall (opens 2013) ★★

Appeal by Age NOT OPEN AT PRESS TIME

What it is Character-greeting venue. **Scope and scale** Minor attraction. **When to go** Before 10:30 a.m. or after 4 p.m. **Authors' rating** You want princesses? We got 'em! ★★. **Duration of ride** 7–10 minutes (estimated). **Average wait in line per 100 people ahead of you** 35 minutes (estimated). **Loading speed** Slow.

DESCRIPTION AND COMMENTS Scheduled to open on the site of Snow White's Scary Adventures, Princess Fairytale Hall will be the central location for meeting Disney princesses in the Magic Kingdom. While Disney has not yet released details, we think the meet-and-greet process will work similarly to those of other Magic Kingdom character convos: The princesses will occupy a greeting room where 15–20 guests at a time are admitted. They'll be allowed to visit 7–10 minutes—long enough for a photo, an autograph, and a hug from each princess.

TOURING TIPS With all the new attractions in Fantasyland, it's possible that this one will be overlooked in the morning as guests head for the new rides. Check the line on your way out of Fantasyland to see if it's worth a quick stop.

Seven Dwarfs Mine Train (opens 2014) ★★

Appeal by Age	NOT YET OPEN

What it is Indoor/outdoor roller coaster. **Scope and scale** Major attraction. **When to go** Before 10 a.m., during parades, or in the evening. **Special comments** Height requirement (not yet available). **Authors' rating** N/A. **Duration of ride** N/A. **Average wait in line per 100 people ahead of you** N/A. **Loading speed** N/A.

DESCRIPTION AND COMMENTS In the pantheon of Disney coasters, Seven Dwarfs Mine Train is supposed to fit somewhere between The Barnstormer and Big Thunder Mountain Railroad. That is, it's geared to older grade-school kids who've been on amusement park rides before. There are no loops, inversions, or rolls in the track, and no massive hills or steep drops; rather, your ride vehicle's seats swing side-to-side as you go through turns. And—what a coincidence!—Disney has designed a curvy track with steep turns. There's also supposed to be an elaborate indoor section showing the dwarfs' underground operation.

The exterior design, including waterfalls, forests, and landscaping, is meant to join together all of the surrounding Fantasyland's various locations, including France and Germany. Forget hidden Mickeys—Seven Dwarfs needs a hidden Charlemagne.

TOURING TIPS We expect Mine Train to have long lines throughout the day. If your vacation won't be complete without a comprehensive tour of Fantasyland, see Mine Train first, then The Barnstormer, Dumbo, and Under the Sea. Mine Train should have Fastpass; use it if the line exceeds a 30-minute wait.

Under the Sea: Journey of the Little Mermaid (Fastpass) ★★★½

Appeal by Age	PRESCHOOL ★★★★½	GRADE SCHOOL ★★★★	TEENS ★★★½
YOUNG ADULTS ★★★★		OVER 30 ★★★★	SENIORS ★★★½

What it is Dark ride retelling the film's story. **Scope and scale** Major attraction. **When to go** Before 10:30 a.m., during the last 2 hours before closing, or use Fastpass. **Authors' rating** Colorful, but most effects are too simple for an attraction this big; ★★★½. **Duration of ride** About 5½ minutes. **Average wait in line per 100 people ahead of you** 3 minutes. **Loading speed** Fast.

DESCRIPTION AND COMMENTS Under the Sea takes riders through almost a dozen scenes retelling the story of *The Little Mermaid,* this time with Audio-Animatronics, video effects, and a vibrant 3-D set the size of a small theater.

Guests board a clamshell-shaped ride vehicle running along a continuously moving track (similar to The Haunted Mansion's). Then the ride "descends" under water, past Ariel's grotto and on to King Triton's undersea kingdom. The most detailed animatronic is of Ursula the Sea Witch, and she's a beauty. Other scenes hit the film's highlights, including Ariel meeting Prince Eric, her deal with Ursula to become human, and, of course, the couple's happy ending.

The attraction's exterior is attractive, with detailed rock work, water, and story elements. That said, most of the effects are unimaginative, such as starfish that do nothing but spin on a central axis or lobsters that simply turn left and right, and virtually the entire second half of the story is condensed into a handful of small scenes crammed together at the end of the ride.

TOURING TIPS Expect long waits throughout most of the day. If you can, ride early in the morning, late at night, or use Fastpass.

Walt Disney World Railroad

DESCRIPTION AND COMMENTS Stops in Fantasyland on its circuit of the park. See page 132 for additional details.

TOURING TIPS Pleasant link to Main Street and Frontierland . . . but so crowded in the afternoon that you'll almost certainly find it faster to walk anywhere in the park.

▌▊ TOMORROWLAND

TOMORROWLAND'S THEMES are technology and the future. Sounds like Epcot, you say? Well, Tomorrowland was a breeding ground for the ideas that spawned it. Yet Tomorrowland and Epcot are very different in more than scale. Epcot is educational, while Tomorrowland is for fun, depicting the future as envisioned in science fiction. Its design is meant to be ageless, presenting the future as imagined by dreamers and scientists in the 1920s and '30s— think Buck Rogers, fanciful mechanical rockets, and metallic cities spread beneath towering obelisks. *Newsweek* dubbed it "retro-future" when it debuted.

Astro Orbiter ★★

| Appeal by Age | PRESCHOOL ★★★★ | GRADE SCHOOL ★★★½ | TEENS ★★★½ |
| YOUNG ADULTS ★★★ | OVER 30 ★★★ | | SENIORS ★★½ |

What it is Buck Rogers–style rockets revolving around a central axis. **Scope and scale** Minor attraction. **When to go** Before 11 a.m. or after 5 p.m. **Special comments** This attraction is not as innocuous as it appears. **Authors' rating** Not worth the wait; ★★. **Duration of ride** 1½ minutes. **Average wait in line per 100 people ahead of you** 13½ minutes. **Loading speed** Slow.

DESCRIPTION AND COMMENTS Though visually appealing, the Astro Orbiter is still a slow-loading carnival ride. The fat little rocket ships simply fly in circles. The best thing about the Astro Orbiter is the nice view when you're aloft.

TOURING TIPS Expendable on any schedule. If you ride with preschoolers, seat them first, then board. The Astro Orbiter flies higher and faster than Dumbo and frightens some young children. It also apparently messes with some adults.

Buzz Lightyear's Space Ranger Spin
(Fastpass) ★★★★

Appeal by Age	PRESCHOOL ★★★★½	GRADE SCHOOL ★★★★½	TEENS ★★★★
YOUNG ADULTS ★★★★		OVER 30 ★★★★	SENIORS ★★★★

What it is Whimsical space-travel-themed indoor ride. **Scope and scale** Minor attraction. **When to go** First or last hour the park is open, or use Fastpass. **Authors' rating** Surreal shooting gallery; ★★★★. **Duration of ride** About 4½ minutes. **Average wait in line per 100 people ahead of you** 3 minutes. **Loading speed** Fast.

DESCRIPTION AND COMMENTS This attraction is based on the space-commando character of Buzz Lightyear from the film *Toy Story.* The marginal storyline has you and Buzz Lightyear trying to save the universe from the evil Emperor Zurg. You can spin your car and shoot simulated "laser cannons" at Zurg and his minions. The first room's mechanical claw and red robot contain high-value targets, so aim for these.

TOURING TIPS Each car is equipped with two laser cannons and a scorekeeping display. Each display is independent, so you can compete with your riding partner. A joystick allows you to spin the car to line up the various targets. Each time you pull the trigger, you'll release a red laser beam that you can see hitting or missing the target. Most folks' first ride is occupied with learning how to use the equipment and figuring out how the targets work. The next ride (like certain potato chips, one is not enough), you'll surprise yourself by how much better you do. *Unofficial* readers are unanimous in their praise of Buzz Lightyear. Some, in fact, spend hours riding it again and again.

Experience Buzz Lightyear after riding Space Mountain first thing in the morning, or use Fastpass.

Monsters, Inc. Laugh Floor ★★★½

Appeal by Age	PRESCHOOL ★★★½	GRADE SCHOOL ★★★★½	TEENS ★★★★
YOUNG ADULTS ★★★★		OVER 30 ★★★★	SENIORS ★★★★

What it is Interactive animated comedy routines. **Scope and scale** Major attraction. **When to go** Before 11 a.m. or after 4 p.m. **Special comments** You may be asked to participate in skits. **Authors' rating** Good concept, but the jokes are hit-and-miss; ★★★½. **Duration of presentation** About 15 minutes.

DESCRIPTION AND COMMENTS We learned in Disney/Pixar's *Monsters, Inc.* that children's screams could be converted into electricity, which was used to power a town inhabited by monsters. During the film, the monsters discovered that children's laughter was an even better source of energy. In this attraction, the monsters have set up a comedy club to capture as many laughs as possible. Mike Wazowski, the one-eyed character from the film, emcees the club's three comedy acts. Each consists of an animated monster (most not seen in the film) trying out various bad puns, corny jokes, and Abbott and Costello–like routines. Using the same cutting-edge technology as Epcot's popular *Turtle Talk with Crush,* behind-the-scenes Disney cast members voice the characters and often interact with audience members during the skits. As with any comedy club, some performers are funny and some are not. Disney has shown a willingness to try new material, though, so the show should remain fresh to repeat visitors.

TOURING TIPS The theater holds several hundred people, so there's no need to rush here first thing in the morning. Try to arrive late in the morning after you've visited other Tomorrowland attractions, or after the afternoon parade when guests start leaving the park.

Space Mountain *(Fastpass)* ★★★★

Appeal by Age	PRESCHOOL ★★½†	GRADE SCHOOL ★★★★	TEENS ★★★★★
YOUNG ADULTS ★★★★½		OVER 30 ★★★★½	SENIORS ★★★½

†*Some preschoolers love Space Mountain; others are frightened by it.*

What it is Roller coaster in the dark. **Scope and scale** Super-headliner. **When to go** When the park opens or use Fastpass. **Special comments** Great fun and action; much wilder than Big Thunder Mountain Railroad. 44" minimum height requirement; children younger than age 7 must be accompanied by an adult. Switching-off option provided (see page 79). **Authors' rating** Not to be missed; ★★★★. **Duration of ride** Almost 3 minutes. **Average wait in line per 100 people ahead of you** 3 minutes; assumes 2 tracks, with 1 dedicated to Fastpass riders, dispatching at 21-second intervals. **Loading speed** Moderate–fast.

DESCRIPTION AND COMMENTS Totally enclosed in a mammoth futuristic structure, Space Mountain has always been the Magic Kingdom's most popular attraction. The theme is a space flight through dark recesses of the galaxy. Effects are superb, and the ride is the fastest and wildest in the Magic Kingdom. As a coaster, Space Mountain is much zippier than Big Thunder Mountain Railroad, but much tamer than the Rock 'n' Roller Coaster at Disney's Hollywood Studios or Expedition Everest at Disney's Animal Kingdom.

As a headliner attraction, Space Mountain goes through regular refurbishments to add effects and maintain ride quality. Past improvements have included new lighting and effects, an improved sound system and soundtrack, and interactive games in the queue to help pass the time in line. Roller-coaster aficionados will tell you (correctly) that Space Mountain is a designer version of the Wild Mouse, a midway ride that's been around for almost 60 years. There are no long drops or swooping hills as there are on a traditional roller coaster—only quick, unexpected turns and small drops. Disney's contribution essentially was to add a space theme to the Wild Mouse and put it in the dark. And this does indeed make the Mouse seem wilder.

TOURING TIPS People who can handle a fairly wild roller-coaster ride will take Space Mountain in stride. What sets Space Mountain apart is that cars plummet through darkness, with only occasional lighting. Half the fun of Space Mountain is not knowing where the car will go next.

Space Mountain is a favorite of many Magic Kingdom visitors ages 7–60. Each morning before opening, particularly during summer and holiday periods, several hundred Space Mountain junkies crowd the rope barriers at the Central Plaza, awaiting the signal to head to the ride's entrance. To get ahead of the competition, be one of the first in the park. Proceed to the end of Main Street and wait at the entrance to Tomorrowland.

Couples touring with children too small to ride Space Mountain can both ride without waiting twice in line by taking advantage of "switching off." When you enter the Space Mountain line, tell the first cast member, Greeter One, that you want to switch off. The attendant will allow you, your spouse, and your small child (or children) to continue together, phoning ahead to tell Greeter Two to expect you. When you reach Greeter Two at the turnstile near the boarding area, you'll be given specific directions. One of you will proceed to ride while the other stays with the kids. Whoever rides will be admitted by the unloading attendant to stairs leading back up to the boarding area. Here you switch off. The second parent rides, and the first parent takes the kids down the stairs to the unloading area, where everybody is reunited and exits together.

Seats are one behind another, as opposed to side-by-side. Parents whose children meet the height and age requirements for Space Mountain can't sit next to their kids.

If you don't catch Space Mountain first in the morning, use Fastpass or try again during the 30 minutes before closing. To avoid overwhelming Space Mountain's air-conditioning system on hot days, would-be riders are sometimes held in line outside the entrance until the lines have subsided. The appearance from the outside is that the line is enormous when, in fact, most of the people waiting are those visible. This crowd-control technique, known as "stacking," discourages visitors from getting in line. Despite the apparently long line, the wait is usually no longer than if you had been allowed to queue inside.

Stitch's Great Escape!   ★★

| Appeal by Age PRESCHOOL ★★½ | GRADE SCHOOL ★★½ | TEENS ★★½ |
| YOUNG ADULTS ★★½ | OVER 30 ★★ | SENIORS ★★½ |

What it is Theater-in-the-round sci-fi show. **Scope and scale** Major attraction. **When to go** Before 11 a.m. or after 6 p.m.; try during parades. **Special comments** Frightens kids of all ages; 40" minimum height requirement. Switching-off option provided (see page 79). **Authors' rating** A cheap coat of paint on a broken car; ★★. **Duration of presentation** About 12 minutes. **Preshow entertainment** About 6 minutes. **Probable waiting time** 12–35 minutes.

DESCRIPTION AND COMMENTS *Stitch's Great Escape!* stars the havoc-wreaking little alien from the feature film *Lilo & Stitch*. In this show, Stitch is a prisoner of the galactic authorities and is being transferred to a processing facility en route to his final place of incarceration. He manages to escape by employing an efficient though gross trick, knocking out power to the facility in the process. One wonders why an alien civilization smart enough to master teleportation hasn't yet invented a backup power source. The rest of the attraction consists of Stitch lumbering around in the dark while cheap sound and odor effects are put upon the audience.

Unofficial Guide readers usually rate *Stitch's Great Escape!* as their least favorite of all Walt Disney World attractions. Guest response to this attraction is so overwhelmingly negative, in fact, that Disney has stopped trying to improve it.

TOURING TIPS *Stitch* is more than enough to scare the pants off many kids ages 6 and younger. Its height requirement is 40 inches—the same as Big Thunder Mountain Railroad—in an attempt to keep out easily frightened younger children. The fact that Big Thunder is a roller coaster and that this ride doesn't move should be a warning to parents about its fright potential.

Parents, take note: You're held in your seat by overhead restraints that will will prevent you from leaving your seat to comfort your child if the need arises.

Tomorrowland Speedway ★★

What it is Drive-'em-yourself miniature cars. **Scope and scale** Major attraction. **When to go** Before 10 a.m. or during the last 2 hours before closing. **Special comments** Kids must be 54" tall to drive unassisted. **Authors' rating** Boring for adults (★★); great for preschoolers. **Duration of ride** About 4¼ minutes. **Average wait in line per 100 people ahead of you** 4½ minutes; assumes 285-car turnover every 20 minutes. **Loading speed** Slow.

Queasy

DESCRIPTION AND COMMENTS An elaborate miniature raceway with gasoline-powered cars that travel up to 7 mph. The cars poke along on a guide rail, leaving the driver with little to do, but teenagers and many adults still enjoy it.

TOURING TIPS This ride is visually appealing but definitely one adults can skip. The 9-and-under crowd, however, love it. If your child is too short to drive, ride along and allow the child to steer the car while you work the foot pedal.

The line snakes across a pedestrian bridge to the loading areas. For a shorter wait, turn right off the bridge to the first loading area (rather than continuing to the second).

Tomorrowland Transit Authority PeopleMover ★★★

What it is Scenic tour of Tomorrowland. **Scope and scale** Minor attraction. **When to go** Anytime, but especially during hot, crowded times of day

(11:30 a.m.–4:30 p.m.). **Special comments** A good way to check out the line at Space Mountain and the Speedway. **Authors' rating** Scenic and relaxing; ★★★. **Duration of ride** 10 minutes. **Average wait in line per 100 people ahead of you** 1½ minutes; assumes 39 trains operating. **Loading speed** Fast.

DESCRIPTION AND COMMENTS The PeopleMover is a once-unique prototype of a linear-induction-powered mass-transit system. Its tramlike cars carry riders on a leisurely tour of Tomorrowland, including a peek inside Space Mountain. In ancient times, the attraction was called the WEDway PeopleMover ("WED" being the initials of one Walter Elias Disney).

TOURING TIPS Lines move quickly and you seldom have to wait. A relaxing choice during busier times of day.

Walt Disney's Carousel of Progress ★★★

Appeal by Age	PRESCHOOL ★★★½	GRADE SCHOOL ★★★½	TEENS ★★★½
YOUNG ADULTS ★★★★	OVER 30 ★★★★		SENIORS ★★★★

What it is Audio-animatronic theater production. **Scope and scale** Major attraction. **When to go** Anytime. **Authors' rating** Nostalgic, warm, and happy; ★★★. **Duration of presentation** 21 minutes. **Preshow entertainment** Documentary on the attraction's long history. **Probable waiting time** Less than 10 minutes.

DESCRIPTION AND COMMENTS *Walt Disney's Carousel of Progress* offers a nostalgic look at how technology and electricity have changed the lives of an audio-animatronic family over several generations. The family is easy to identify with, and a cheerful, sentimental tune bridges the generations.

TOURING TIPS The *Carousel* handles big crowds effectively and is a good choice during busier times of day. Because of its age, Carousel seems to have more minor operational glitches than most attractions, so you may be subjected to the same dialog and songs several times. Hey, look at it as extra air-conditioning.

LIVE ENTERTAINMENT *in* the MAGIC KINGDOM

FOR SPECIFIC EVENTS THE DAY YOU VISIT, check the live-entertainment schedule in your Disney guide map (free as you enter the park or at City Hall) or the *Times Guide*, available along with the guide map.

Our one-day touring plans exclude live performances in favor of seeing as much of the park as time permits (parades and shows siphon crowds away from popular rides). Nonetheless, the color and pageantry of live events are integral to the Magic Kingdom—and a persuasive argument for a second day of touring. Here's a list of regular performances and events that don't require reservations:

BAY LAKE AND SEVEN SEAS LAGOON FLOATING ELECTRICAL PAGEANT Usually performed at nightfall (9 p.m. at the Polynesian

Resort, 9:15 at the Grand Floridian, and 10:15 at the Contemporary Resort) on Seven Seas Lagoon and Bay Lake, this is a stunning electric-light show aboard small barges and set to electronic music. Take the monorail to the Contemporary, Grand Floridian, or Polynesian.

CAPTAIN JACK SPARROW'S PIRATE TUTORIAL Meet the legendary pirate and his crew in Adventureland. Check the *Times Guide* for schedules.

CASTLE FORECOURT STAGE The 20-minute *Dream-Along with Mickey* live show features Mickey, Minnie, Donald, Goofy, and a peck of princesses and other secondary characters, plus human backup dancers, in a show built around the premise that—*quelle horreur!*—Donald doesn't believe in the power of dreams. Crisis is averted via a frenetic whirlwind of song and dance.

 CELEBRATE THE MAGIC Videos and special effects are set to music and projected nightly on Cinderella Castle. The effects are tremendous: In one vignette, the entire castle becomes a kaleidoscope of brightly colored Mickeys and Donalds; in another, flames appear throughout the castle's windows to emulate a scene from the Pirates of the Caribbean ride. Best of all, Disney regularly updates the show's content to keep it fresh. We rate this as not to be missed.

DISNEY CHARACTER SHOWS AND APPEARANCES Most days, a character is on duty for photos and autographs from 9 a.m. to 10 p.m. next to City Hall. Mickey and Minnie (and, for a time, the Disney princesses) can be found in the Town Square Theater, to the right as you enter the park. Check your *Times Guide* for character-greeting locations and times. Shows at the Castle Forecourt Stage feature Disney characters several times a day; again, check the schedule.

FLAG RETREAT At 5 p.m. daily at Town Square (Walt Disney World Railroad end of Main Street). Sometimes performed with large college marching bands, sometimes with a smaller Disney band.

MAGIC KINGDOM BANDS Banjo, Dixieland, steel drum, marching, and fife-and-drum bands roam the park.

MOVE IT! SHAKE IT! CELEBRATE IT! PARADE Starting at the train-station end of Main Street, U.S.A. and working toward the Central Plaza, this short walk incorporates around a dozen guests with a handful of floats, characters, and entertainers. Music is provided by one of Disney's latest artists (Miley Cyrus currently—mercifully, no twerking is involved).

TINKER BELL'S FLIGHT This nice special effect in the sky above Cinderella Castle heralds the beginning of the *Wishes* fireworks show (when the park is open late).

TOMORROWLAND FORECOURT STAGE This two-story space behind the Astro Orbiter occasionally hosts DJ-led dance parties. Not worth a special trip, but a nice diversion if you're passing by.

***WISHES* FIREWORKS SHOW** Memorable vignettes and music from beloved Disney films combine with a stellar fireworks display while Jiminy Cricket narrates a lump-in-your-throat story about making wishes come true. For an uncluttered view and lighter crowds, watch from the end of Main Street between The Plaza Restaurant and Tomorrowland Terrace. Another good fireworks-viewing area is the second story of the Main Street railroad station. The spot we used to recommend, in the Tomorrowland Terrace area, was apparently so good that Disney decided they could charge for it. To view *Wishes* from this location now costs around $24 per adult and around $13 per child; the price includes a dessert buffet and non-alcoholic beverages. Make reservations 60 days in advance by calling ☎ 407-WDW-DINE (939-3463).

***WISHES* FIREWORKS CRUISE** For a different view, you can watch the fireworks from Seven Seas Lagoon aboard a chartered pontoon boat. The charter costs $293 for up to 8 people and just under $350 for 10 (tax included). Chips, soda, and water are provided; more-substantial food items may be arranged through reservations. Your Disney captain will take you for a little cruise and then position the boat in a perfect place to watch the fireworks. Because this is a private charter rather than a tour, only your group will be aboard. Life jackets are provided, but wearing them is at your discretion. To reserve a charter, call ☎ 407-WDW-PLAY (939-7529) at exactly 7 a.m. Eastern time about 180 days before the day you want to cruise. We recommend phoning about 185 days out to have a Disney agent specify the exact morning to call for reservations.

◼ PARADES

PARADES AT THE MAGIC KINGDOM ARE full-fledged spectaculars with dozens of Disney characters and amazing special effects. We rate the afternoon parade as outstanding and the evening parade as not to be missed.

unofficial TIP
Be advised that the Walt Disney World Railroad shuts down during parades, making it impossible to access other lands by train.

In addition to providing great entertainment, parades lure guests away from the attractions. If getting on rides appeals to you more than watching a parade, you'll find substantially shorter lines just before and during parades. Because the parade route doesn't pass through Adventureland, Tomorrowland, or Fantasyland, attractions in these lands are particularly good bets. Be forewarned: Parades disrupt traffic in the Magic

Kingdom. It's nearly impossible, for example, to get to Adventureland from Tomorrowland, or vice versa, during one.

AFTERNOON PARADE

USUALLY STAGED AT 3 P.M., this parade features bands, floats, and marching characters. A new afternoon parade, **Festival of Fantasy,** is supposed to debut in 2014, with an original score and new floats paying tribute to *The Little Mermaid, Tangled, Brave,* and other Disney films. Some elements—such as Disney characters—remain constant. Seasonal theming is added during major holidays.

EVENING PARADE(S)

THE EVENING PARADE IS A HIGH-TECH AFFAIR employing electroluminescent and fiber-optic technologies, light-spreading thermoplastics (don't try this at home!), and clouds of underlit liquid-nitrogen smoke. Don't worry, you won't need a gas mask or lead underwear to watch. The parade also offers music, Mickey Mouse, and twinkling lights. The evening parade is staged once or twice each evening, depending on the time of year. During less busy times of year, the evening parade is held only on weekends, and sometimes not even then. We rate it as not to be missed.

The **Main Street Electrical Parade** (MSEP) is the current nightly cavalcade at the Magic Kingdom. Its soundtrack—"Baroque Hoedown"—is a synthesizer-heavy testament to what prog rock might have been like with access to modern technology and Prozac. In our opinion, the Magic Kingdom's nighttime parade is always the best in Walt Disney World, and the Electrical Parade is the standard against which everything else is judged. Disney is known to swap out parades and may do so at any time. If you're at Disney World while MSEP is running, make a special trip to see it.

PARADE ROUTE AND VANTAGE POINTS

MAGIC KINGDOM PARADES CIRCLE TOWN SQUARE, head down Main Street, go around the Central Plaza, and cross the bridge to Liberty Square. In Liberty Square, they follow the waterfront and end in Frontierland. Sometimes they begin in Frontierland and run the route in the opposite direction. Most guests watch from the Central Plaza, or from Main Street. One of the best and most popular vantage points is the upper platform of the Walt Disney World Railroad station at the Town Square end of Main Street. Problem is, you have to stake out your position 30–45 minutes before the events begin.

Because most spectators pack Main Street and the Central Plaza, we recommend watching the parade from Liberty Square or Frontierland. Great vantage points frequently overlooked are as follows:

1. Sleepy Hollow snack-and-beverage shop, immediately to your right as you cross the bridge into Liberty Square. You'll have a perfect view of the parade as it crosses Liberty Square Bridge, but only when the parade begins on Main Street.

2. The pathway on the Liberty Square side of the moat from Sleepy Hollow snack-and-beverage shop to Cinderella Castle. Any point along this path offers a clear and unobstructed view as the parade crosses Liberty Square Bridge. Once again, this spot works only for parades coming from Main Street.

3. The covered walkway between Liberty Tree Tavern and The Diamond Horseshoe Saloon. This elevated vantage point is perfect (particularly on rainy days).

4. Elevated wooden platforms in front of the Frontierland Shootin' Arcade, Frontier Trading Post, and the building with the sign reading FRONTIER MERCANTILE. These spots usually get picked off 10–12 minutes before parade time.

5. Benches on the perimeter of the Central Plaza, between the entrances to Liberty Square and Adventureland. Usually unoccupied until after the parade begins, they offer a comfortable resting place and unobstructed (though somewhat distant) view of the parade as it crosses Liberty Square Bridge.

6. Liberty Square and Frontierland dockside areas.

7. The elevated porch of Tony's Town Square Restaurant on Main Street provides an elevated viewing platform and an easy path to the park exit when the fireworks are over.

Assuming it starts on Main Street (evening parades normally do), the parade takes 16–20 minutes to reach Liberty Square or Frontierland. On evenings when the parade runs twice, the first parade draws a huge crowd, siphoning guests from attractions. Many folks leave the park after the early parade, with many more departing following the fireworks (which are scheduled on the hour between the two parades).

Continue to tour after the fireworks. This is a particularly good time to ride Space Mountain and enjoy attractions in Adventureland. If you're touring Adventureland and the parade begins on Main Street, you won't have to assume your viewing position in Frontierland until 15 minutes after the parade kicks off. If you watch from the Splash Mountain side of the street and head for the attraction as the last float passes, you'll be able to ride with only a couple minutes' wait.

MAGIC KINGDOM
TOURING PLANS

OUR STEP-BY-STEP TOURING PLANS ARE field-tested for seeing *as much as possible* in one day with a minimum of time wasted in lines. They're designed to help you avoid crowds and bottlenecks on days of moderate-to-heavy attendance. Understand, however, that there's more to see in the Magic Kingdom than can be experienced in one day. Since we first began covering the Magic Kingdom, four headliner attractions and an entire new land have been added. Today, even if you could experience every attraction without any wait, it would still be virtually impossible to see all of the park in a single day.

On days of lighter attendance (see "Selecting the Time of Year for Your Visit," page 13), our plans will save you time, but they won't be as critical to successful touring as on busier days. Don't worry that other people will be following the plans and render them useless. Fewer than 1 in every 350 people in the park will have been exposed to this information.

In anticipation of Disney introducing Fastpass+ (see page 26), we've listed the approximate Fastpass+ return times for which you should attempt to make reservations. (The touring plan should work with anything close to the times shown.) In case Disney limits how many Fastpass+ reservations you can get, we've listed in the plans the attractions most likely to need Fastpass+ too. No matter what Disney does, we'll have the latest Fastpass+ and touring plan tools on **touringplans.com.**

CHOOSING THE APPROPRIATE TOURING PLAN

WE PRESENT FIVE MAGIC KINGDOM TOURING PLANS:

- Magic Kingdom One-Day Touring Plan for Adults
- Authors' Selective Magic Kingdom One-Day Touring Plan for Adults
- Magic Kingdom One-Day Touring Plan for Parents with Young Children
- Magic Kingdom Dumbo-or-Die-in-a-Day Touring Plan for Parents with Young Children
- Magic Kingdom Two-Day Touring Plan

If you have two days (or two mornings) at the Magic Kingdom, the Two-Day Touring Plan is *by far* the most relaxed and efficient. The two-day plan takes advantage of early morning, when lines are short and the park hasn't filled with guests. This plan works well year-round and eliminates much of the extra walking required by the one-day plans. The plan is perfect for guests who wish to sample both the attractions and the atmosphere of the Magic Kingdom.

unofficial **TIP**
No matter when the park closes, our two-day plan guarantees you the most efficient touring and the least time in lines.

If you only have one day but wish to see as much as possible, use the One-Day Touring Plan for Adults. It's exhausting, but it packs in the maximum. If you prefer a more relaxed visit, use the Authors' Selective One-Day Touring Plan. It includes the best the park has to offer (in the authors' opinion), eliminating some less impressive attractions.

If you have children younger than age 8, adopt the One-Day Touring Plan for Parents with Young Children. It's a compromise, blending the preferences of younger children with those of older siblings and adults. The plan includes many children's rides in Fantasyland but omits roller coaster rides and other attractions that frighten young children or are off-limits because of height requirements. Or use the One-Day Touring Plan for Adults or the Authors' Selective One-Day Touring Plan and take advantage of switching off, a technique where children accompany adults to the loading area of a ride with age and height requirements but don't board (see page 79).

The Dumbo-or-Die-in-a-Day Touring Plan for Parents with Young Children is designed for parents who will withhold no sacrifice for the children. On the Dumbo-or-Die plan, adults generally stand around, sweat, wipe noses, pay for stuff, and watch the children enjoy themselves. It's great!

Two-Day Touring Plan for Families with Young Children

If you have young children and are looking for a two-day itinerary, combine the Magic Kingdom One-Day Touring Plan for Parents with Young Children with the second day of the Magic Kingdom Two-Day Touring Plan.

Two-Day Touring Plan for Early Morning Touring on Day One and Afternoon–Evening Touring on Day Two

Many of you enjoy an early start at the Magic Kingdom on one day, followed by a second day with a lazy, sleep-in morning, resuming your touring in the afternoon and/or evening. If this appeals to you, use the Magic Kingdom One-Day Touring Plan for Adults or the Magic Kingdom One-Day Touring Plan for Parents with Small Children on your early day. Adhere to the touring plan for as long as it feels comfortable (many folks leave after the afternoon parade). On the second day, pick up where you left off. If you intend to use Fastpass on your second day, try to arrive at the park by 1 p.m. or the Fastpasses may be gone. (If Fastpass+ is available, make reservations in advance if possible.) Customize the remaining part of the touring plan to incorporate parades, fireworks, and other live performances according to your preferences.

"NOT A TOURING PLAN" TOURING PLANS

FOR THE TYPE-B READER, these touring plans avoid detailed step-by-step strategies for saving every last minute in line—they're more guidelines than actual rules. Use these to avoid the longest waits in line while having maximum flexibility to see whatever interests you in a particular part of the park.

FOR PARENTS OF SMALL CHILDREN WITH ONE DAY TO TOUR, ARRIVING AT PARK OPENING See Fantasyland first. See Frontierland and some of Adventureland, then take a midday break. Return to the park and complete your tour of Adventureland. Next see Liberty Square and Tomorrowland. End on Main Street for parades and fireworks.

FOR ADULTS WITH ONE DAY TO TOUR, ARRIVING AT PARK OPENING See Seven Dwarfs Mine Train and Peter Pan's Flight in Fantasyland, then Space Mountain and Buzz Lightyear. Tour Frontierland, Adventureland, and Liberty Square next, followed by the remaining attractions in Fantasyland and Tomorrowland. End on Main Street for parades and fireworks.

FOR PARENTS AND ADULTS WITH TWO DAYS TO TOUR *Note:* Either day works great for Disney resort guests on Extra Magic Hour mornings. Start Day One in Fantasyland (save Seven Dwarfs Mine Train for Day Two), then tour Frontierland and Pirates of the Caribbean in Adventureland. Take a midday break and return to Adventureland. Next see Liberty Square and the evening parade. See fireworks from Main Street. Begin Day Two in Tomorrowland. See any missed Adventureland or Frontierland attractions before leaving the park around midday.

FOR PARENTS AND ADULTS WITH AN AFTERNOON AND A FULL DAY For the afternoon, get Fastpasses, if possible, for any Frontierland and Adventureland headliners you can; save other headliners for later in the evening. Tour Liberty Square, Adventureland, and Frontierland, then see the evening parade and fireworks. On your full day of touring, see Fantasyland, and Tomorrowland (use Fastpass for Space Mountain), then catch any missed attractions from the previous afternoon.

THE SINGLE-DAY TOURING CONUNDRUM

TOURING THE MAGIC KINGDOM IN A DAY is complicated by the fact that the premier attractions are at almost opposite ends of the park: Splash Mountain and Big Thunder Mountain Railroad in Frontierland, Space Mountain and Buzz Lightyear in Tomorrowland, and Under the Sea: Journey of the Little Mermaid and Seven Dwarfs Mine Train in the top center. It's virtually impossible to ride all six without encountering lines at one or another. If you ride Space Mountain and see Buzz Lightyear immediately after the park opens, for example, you won't have much of a wait, if any. By the time you leave Tomorrowland and hurry to Fantasyland, however, the line for Seven Dwarfs will be substantial. The same situation prevails if you ride the Fantasyland duo first: Seven Dwarfs Mine Train and Under the Sea, no problem; Space Mountain and Buzz Lightyear, however, have fair-sized lines. From 10 minutes after opening until just before closing, lines are long at these headliners.

The best way to experience all six without long waits is to tour the Magic Kingdom over two mornings: Ride Space Mountain first thing one morning, then ride Buzz Lightyear; then ride Seven Dwarfs Mine Train, Under the Sea, Splash Mountain, and Big Thunder Mountain first thing on the other. If you have only one day, be present at opening time. Speed immediately to Space Mountain, then take in Buzz Lightyear. After Buzz Lightyear, rush to Fantasyland to scope out the situation at Seven Dwarfs Mine Train. If the posted wait time is 30 minutes or less, go ahead and hop in line. If the wait exceeds 30 minutes, get a Fastpass for Seven Dwarfs (or make advance Fastpass+ reservations if they're available), then ride Under the Sea. Save Frontierland for last.

PRELIMINARY INSTRUCTIONS FOR ALL MAGIC KINGDOM TOURING PLANS

ON DAYS OF MODERATE-TO-HEAVY ATTENDANCE, follow your chosen touring plan exactly, deviating only as follows:

1. When you aren't interested in an attraction it lists. For example, if the plan tells you to ride Space Mountain and you don't like roller coasters, just skip this step and proceed to the next.

2. When you encounter a very long line at an attraction the touring plan calls for. For example, let's say you arrive at The Haunted Mansion and find extremely long lines. It's possible that this is a temporary situation caused by several hundred people arriving en masse from a recently concluded performance of *The Hall of Presidents* nearby. If this is the case, skip The Haunted Mansion and go to the next step, returning later to retry The Haunted Mansion.

PARK-OPENING PROCEDURES

YOUR SUCCESS DURING your first hour of touring will be affected somewhat by the opening procedure Disney uses that day:

A. Guests are held at the turnstiles until the park opens. Hustle past Main Street and head for the first attraction on your touring plan.

B. Guests are admitted to Main Street a half-hour to an hour before the remaining lands open. Access to other lands will be blocked by a rope barrier at the Central Plaza end of Main Street. Once admitted, stake out a position at the rope barrier as follows:

If you're going to Frontierland or Adventureland first, stand in front of The Crystal Palace restaurant, on the left at the Central Plaza end of Main Street. Wait next to the rope barrier blocking the walkway to Adventureland. When the rope is dropped, move quickly to Frontierland by way of Adventureland.

If you're going to Tomorrowland first, wait at the entrance of the Tomorrowland bridge. When the rope drops, cross quickly.

If you're going to Fantasyland or Liberty Square first, go to the end of Main Street and line up left of center at the rope.

BEFORE YOU GO

1. Call ☎ 407-824-4321 the day before to confirm opening time.

2. Purchase admission before you arrive.

3. Familiarize yourself with park-opening procedures (above) and reread the touring plan you've chosen.

THE TOURING PLANS
Magic Kingdom One-Day Touring Plan for Adults

FOR Adults without young children.

ASSUMES Willingness to experience all major rides (including roller coasters) and shows.

START TIMES FOR FASTPASS+ Space Mountain, 10:25 a.m.; Big Thunder Mountain Railroad, 11:35 a.m.; Splash Mountain, 1:15 p.m.; Jungle Cruise, 2:05 p.m.; Under the Sea, 4:30 p.m.; Winnie the Pooh, 6:05 p.m.

1. Arrive at the park entrance 50 minutes (Disney resort guests) to 70 minutes (non-Disney resort guests) before opening. Rent strollers before opening. Get guide maps and the *Times Guide*.

2. As soon as the park opens, ride the Seven Dwarfs Mine Train in Fantasyland (opens 2014).

3. Take Peter Pan's Flight.

4. Obtain Fastpasses for Space Mountain in Tomorrowland.

5. Ride Buzz Lightyear's Space Ranger Spin.

6. .See *Monsters, Inc. Laugh Floor.*

7. Ride Space Mountain using the Fastpasses obtained earlier.

✓ 8. Get Fastpasses for Big Thunder Mountain Railroad in Frontierland.

9. Ride Pirates of the Caribbean in Adventureland.

10. Eat lunch. *Be our Guest*

11. Get Fastpasses for Splash Mountain in Frontierland.

12. Ride Big Thunder using the Fastpasses obtained earlier.

13. See *Walt Disney's Enchanted Tiki Room* in Adventureland.

14. Explore the Swiss Family Treehouse.

15. Obtain Fastpasses for Jungle Cruise.

16. See *Country Bear Jamboree* in Frontierland.

17. Ride Splash Mountain using the Fastpasses obtained earlier.

18. Take the Jungle Cruise using the Fastpasses obtained earlier.

19. In Liberty Square, see *The Hall of Presidents* and the *Liberty Belle* Riverboat (order doesn't matter).

20. See The Haunted Mansion.

21. In Fantasyland, get Fastpasses for Under the Sea.

22. Ride It's a Small World.

23. See *Mickey's PhilharMagic.*

24. Ride Under the Sea using the Fastpasses obtained earlier.

25. Obtain Fastpasses for The Many Adventures of Winnie the Pooh.

26. Ride round-trip on the WDW Railroad from Fantasyland.

27. Eat dinner.

28. Ride Pooh using the Fastpasses obtained earlier.

29. If time permits, see *Walt Disney's Carousel of Progress* and ride the Tomorrowland Transit Authority PeopleMover.

30. See the evening parade on Main Street.

31. See the evening castle light show and fireworks on Main Street. A good viewing spot is to the right of the Central Plaza, on the walkway toward Tomorrowland.

Authors' Selective Magic Kingdom One-Day Touring Plan for Adults

FOR Adults touring without young children.

ASSUMES Willingness to experience all major rides (including roller coasters) and shows.

START TIMES FOR FASTPASS+ Space Mountain, 10:25 a.m.; Big Thunder Mountain Railroad, 11:35 a.m.; Splash Mountain, 1:15 p.m.; Jungle Cruise, 1:55 p.m.; Under the Sea, 4:20 p.m.; Winnie the Pooh, 5:40 p.m.

1. Arrive at the park entrance 50 minutes (Disney resort guests) to 70 minutes (non-Disney resort guests) before opening. Rent strollers before opening. Get guide maps and the *Times Guide*.

2. As soon as the park opens, ride the Seven Dwarfs Mine Train in Fantasyland (opens 2014).

3. Take Peter Pan's Flight. *ambulatory*

4. Obtain Fastpasses for Space Mountain in Tomorrowland.

5. Ride Buzz Lightyear's Space Ranger Spin.

6. .See *Monsters, Inc. Laugh Floor.*

7. Ride Space Mountain using the Fastpasses obtained earlier.

8. Get Fastpasses for Big Thunder Mountain Railroad in Frontierland.

9. Ride Pirates of the Caribbean in Adventureland.

10. Eat lunch.

11. Get Fastpasses for Splash Mountain in Frontierland.

12. Ride Big Thunder using the Fastpasses obtained earlier.

13. See *Walt Disney's Enchanted Tiki Room* in Adventureland.

14. Explore the Swiss Family Treehouse.

15. Obtain Fastpasses for the Jungle Cruise.

16. Ride Splash Mountain using the Fastpasses obtained earlier.

17. Take the Jungle Cruise using the Fastpasses obtained earlier.

18. In Liberty Square, see *The Hall of Presidents* and the *Liberty Belle* Riverboat (order doesn't matter).

19. See The Haunted Mansion.

20. In Fantasyland, get Fastpasses for Under the Sea.

21. Ride It's a Small World.

22. See *Mickey's PhilharMagic.*

23. Obtain Fastpasses for The Many Adventures of Winnie the Pooh.

24. Ride Under the Sea using the Fastpasses obtained earlier.

25. Ride round-trip on the WDW Railroad from Fantasyland.

26. Eat dinner.

27. Ride Pooh using the Fastpasses obtained earlier.

28. Revisit any favorite attractions, try an interactive game, or see any missed attractions.

29. See the evening parade on Main Street.

30. See the evening castle light show and fireworks on Main Street. A good viewing spot is to the right of the Central Plaza, on the walkway toward Tomorrowland.

Magic Kingdom One-Day Touring Plan for Parents with Young Children

FOR Parents with children younger than age 8.

ASSUMES Periodic stops for rest, restrooms, and refreshments.

START TIMES FOR FASTPASS+ Peter Pan's Flight, 10:15 a.m.; Buzz Lightyear's Space Ranger Spin, 3:50 p.m.; Jungle Cruise, 5 p.m.; Winnie the Pooh, 7:35 p.m.; The Barnstormer and Dumbo, 7:25 p.m.; Under the Sea, 8:10 p.m.

1. Arrive at the park entrance 50 minutes (Disney resort guests) to 70 minutes (non-Disney resort guests) before opening. Rent strollers before opening. Get guide maps and the *Times Guide*.

2. As soon as the park opens, ride the Seven Dwarfs Mine Train in Fantasyland (opens 2014).

3. Obtain Fastpasses for Peter Pan's Flight.

4. See The Haunted Mansion in Liberty Square.

5. Ride It's a Small World in Fantasyland.

6. Take Peter Pan's Flight using the Fastpasses obtained earlier.

7. Ride Splash Mountain in Frontierland.

8. In Frontierland, take the raft over to Tom Sawyer Island. Allow at least 30 minutes to explore the island.

9. Eat lunch; leave the park for a midday break of at least 3 hours.

10. Return to the park and send one member of your family to obtain Fastpasses for Buzz Lightyear.

11. Meet Mickey Mouse on Main Street.

12. In Tomorrowland, see *Monsters, Inc. Laugh Floor*.

13. Ride Buzz Lightyear using the Fastpasses obtained earlier.

14. Obtain Fastpasses for the Jungle Cruise in Adventureland.

15. Ride Pirates of the Caribbean.

16. Eat dinner.

17. Take the Jungle Cruise using the Fastpasses obtained earlier.

18. In Fantasyland, obtain Fastpasses for Dumbo, The Barnstormer, and The Many Adventures of Winnie the Pooh.

19. See *Mickey's PhilharMagic*.

20. Meet the Disney princesses at Princess Fairytale Hall (opens 2013).

21. Get Fastpasses for Under the Sea.

22. Ride The Barnstormer using the Fastpasses obtained earlier.

23. Ride Dumbo using the Fastpasses obtained earlier.

24. Ride Pooh using the Fastpasses obtained earlier.

25. Ride Under the Sea using the Fastpasses obtained earlier.

26. See the evening parade on Main Street.

27. See the evening castle light show and fireworks on Main Street. A good viewing spot is to the right of the Central Plaza, on the walkway toward Tomorrowland.

TO CONVERT THIS ONE-DAY TOURING PLAN TO A TWO-DAY TOURING PLAN Follow Steps 1–12 on Day One. Begin Day Two by riding Buzz Lightyear. Skip steps 15–17, then follow steps 18–21. Save Step 12 for after lunch and end the day with fireworks. Day One works great when morning Extra Magic Hours are offered at the Magic Kingdom.

Magic Kingdom Dumbo-or-Die-in-a-Day Touring Plan for Parents with Young Children

FOR Parents with a martyr complex, or rich folks who are paying someone else to squire their kids around. The plan is designed for days when the park doesn't close until 9 p.m. or later.

ASSUMES Frequent stops for rest, restrooms, and refreshments.

START TIMES FOR FASTPASS+ Jungle Cruise, 11:10 a.m.; Under the Sea, 3:40 p.m.; Dumbo, 5:05 p.m.; The Barnstormer, 5:10 p.m.; Winnie the Pooh, 5:40 p.m.; Buzz Lightyear, 6:25 p.m. Prioritize Under the Sea, Pooh, and The Barnstormer.

1. Arrive at the park entrance 50 minutes (Disney resort guests) to 70 minutes (non-Disney resort guests) before opening. Rent strollers before opening. Get guide maps and the *Times Guide*.

2. As soon as the park opens, ride the Seven Dwarfs Mine Train in Fantasyland (opens 2014).

3. Take Peter Pan's Flight.

4. Ride Winnie the Pooh.

5. See The Haunted Mansion in Liberty Square.

6. Ride The Magic Carpets of Aladdin in Adventureland.

7. Obtain Fastpasses for the Jungle Cruise.

8. Ride Pirates of the Caribbean.

9. Take the raft to Tom Sawyer Island. Stay at least 30 minutes.

10. Take the Jungle Cruise using the Fastpasses obtained earlier.

11. Eat lunch; leave the park for a midday break of at least 3 hours.

12. Return to the park and get Fastpasses for Under the Sea in Fantasyland.

13. Ride the Prince Charming Regal Carrousel.

14. See *Mickey's PhilharMagic*.

15. Ride It's a Small World.

16. Ride Under the Sea using the Fastpasses obtained earlier.

17. Obtain Fastpasses for Dumbo and The Barnstormer.

18. Meet Mickey Mouse on Main Street or the Disney princesses in Princess Fairytale Hall (opens late 2013).

19. Ride Dumbo and The Barnstormer using the Fastpasses obtained earlier.

20. Send one member of your family to obtain Fastpasses for Buzz Lightyear in Tomorrowland.

21. Eat dinner.

22. Ride Buzz Lightyear using the Fastpasses obtained earlier.

23. Take a spin on the Tomorrowland Speedway.

24. See *Enchanted Tales with Belle* in Fantasyland.

25. Check the *Times Guide* for performance times for the castle light show, evening parade, and fireworks. Good viewing spots are to the right of The Plaza Restaurant.

TO CONVERT THIS ONE-DAY TOURING PLAN TO A TWO-DAY TOURING PLAN The idea is to split the park in half so that Tomorrowland, Storybook Circus, and a few of the other Fantasyland attractions are on the second day—like so:

Day One (in order): Get Fastpasses for Under the Sea, and then ride Peter Pan, The Haunted Mansion, It's a Small World, *Mickey's PhilharMagic,* and the Prince Charming Regal Carrousel. Next, use your Fastpasses to ride Under the Sea. Eat lunch and take a 3-hour break. Return and see Tom Sawyer Island and then get Fastpasses for Jungle Cruise. Ride Aladdin, Pirates, and Jungle Cruise (using your Fastpasses), and then eat dinner and meet Mickey Mouse. See the evening castle light show, parade, and fireworks.

Day Two (in order): Experience Seven Dwarfs Mine Train, *Enchanted Tales with Belle,* and The Many Adventures of Winnie the Pooh. Then get Fastpasses for Dumbo and The Barnstormer. Ride Buzz Lightyear, Tomorrowland Speedway, and then The Barnstormer and Dumbo using your Fastpasses. You should be done in time for a late lunch.

Magic Kingdom Two-Day Touring Plan

FOR Anyone wishing to spread his or her Magic Kingdom visit over two days.

ASSUMES Willingness to experience all major rides (including roller coasters) and shows.

START TIMES FOR FASTPASS+ *Day One:* Big Thunder Mountain Railroad, 10:35 a.m. *Day Two:* Buzz Lightyear's Space Ranger Spin, 11:40 a.m.; Space Mountain, 1:10 p.m.

Day One

1. Arrive at the park entrance 50 minutes (Disney resort guests) to 70 minutes (non-Disney resort guests) before opening. Rent strollers before opening. Get guide maps and the *Times Guide*.

2. As soon as the park opens, ride Peter Pan's Flight in Fantasyland.

3. Ride Winnie the Pooh.

4. Ride Under the Sea. Take the Walt Disney Railroad from Fantasyland to Frontierland if you don't feel like walking to the next step.

5. In Frontierland, get Fastpasses for Big Thunder Mountain Railroad.

6. Ride Splash Mountain.

7. Ride Pirates of the Caribbean in Adventureland.

8. Ride Big Thunder using the Fastpasses obtained earlier.

9. See The Haunted Mansion in Liberty Square.

10. Eat lunch.

11. In Liberty Square, see *The Hall of Presidents* and the *Liberty Belle* Riverboat (order doesn't matter).

12. See *Country Bear Jamboree* in Frontierland.

13. In Frontierland, take the raft over to Tom Sawyer Island. Allow at least 30 minutes to explore the island.

14. In Fantasyland, see It's a Small World.

15. See *Mickey's PhilharMagic*.

16. Tour Main Street, U.S.A., and meet any characters that interest you. Check the daily entertainment schedule for greeting locations and times.

17. Shop, see live entertainment, or revisit favorite attractions.

18. See the evening parade on Main Street.

19. See the evening castle light show and fireworks on Main Street. A good viewing spot is to the right of the Central Plaza, on the walkway toward Tomorrowland.

Day Two

1. Arrive at the park entrance 50 minutes (Disney resort guests) to 70 minutes (non-Disney resort guests) before opening. Rent strollers before opening. Get guide maps and the *Times Guide*.

2. As soon as the park opens, ride the Seven Dwarfs Mine Train in Fantasyland (opens 2014).

3. Take the Walt Disney World Railroad from Fantasyland to Frontierland. Walk to Adventureland and take the Jungle Cruise.

4. See *Walt Disney's Enchanted Tiki Room*.

5. Explore the Swiss Family Treehouse.

6. in Tomorrowland, get Fastpasses for Buzz Lightyear.

7. Ride the Tomorrowland Transit Authority PeopleMover.

8. See *Walt Disney's Carousel of Progress*.

9. Ride Buzz Lightyear using the Fastpasses obtained earlier.

10. Get Fastpasses for Space Mountain.

11. Eat lunch.

12. See *Monsters, Inc. Laugh Floor*.

13. Ride Space Mountain using the Fastpasses obtained earlier.

14. Shop, play interactive games, or revisit favorite attractions.

PART TEN

EPCOT

EDUCATION, INSPIRATION, AND CORPORATE IMAGERY are the focus at Epcot, the most adult of the Disney theme parks. Some people find the attempts at education to be superficial, while others want more entertainment and less education. Most visitors, however, find plenty of both.

Epcot is more than twice as big as either the Magic Kingdom or Disney's Hollywood Studios and, though smaller than Disney's Animal Kingdom, has more territory to be covered on foot. Epcot rarely sees the congestion so common to the Magic Kingdom, but it has lines every bit as long as those at the Jungle Cruise or Space Mountain. Visitors must come prepared to do considerable walking among attractions and a comparable amount of standing in line.

Epcot's size means you can't see it all in one day without skipping an attraction or two and giving others a cursory glance. A major difference between Epcot and the other parks, however, is that some Epcot attractions can be savored slowly or skimmed, depending on personal interests. For example, the first section of General Motors' Test Track is a thrill ride, the second a collection of walk-through exhibits.

THE EPCOT ACRONYM

WHEN IT OPENED IN 1982, Epcot was EPCOT Center. Before that, Walt Disney envisioned a utopian working city of the future that he called EPCOT, an acronym for *Experimental Prototype Community of Tomorrow*. Corporate Disney ultimately altered Walt's vision, and the city became a theme park, with only the name remaining. Because EPCOT Center had virtually nothing in common with the original concept, *EPCOT* eventually became *Epcot*.

NOT TO BE MISSED AT EPCOT		
FUTURE WORLD		
• Living with the Land	• The Seas Main Tank and Exhibits	• Spaceship Earth
• Mission: SPACE	• Soarin'	• Test Track
WORLD SHOWCASE		
• *The American Adventure*	• *IllumiNations*	• *Impressions de France*

OPERATING HOURS

EPCOT HAS TWO THEMED AREAS: **Future World** and **World Showcase**. Each has its own operating hours. Future World always opens before World Showcase in the morning and usually closes before World Showcase in the evening. Most of the year, World Showcase opens 2 hours later than Future World. For exact hours during your visit, call ☎ 407-824-4321 or visit **disneyworld.com**.

ARRIVING

PLAN TO ARRIVE AT THE TURNSTILES 30–40 minutes prior to official opening time. Give yourself an extra 10 minutes or so to park and make your way to the entrance.

If you are a guest at one of the Epcot resorts, it will take you about 20–30 minutes to walk from your hotel to the Future World section of Epcot via the International Gateway (the back entrance of Epcot). Instead of walking, you can catch a boat from your resort to the International Gateway and walk about 8 minutes to the Future World section. To reach the front (Future World) entrance of Epcot from the resorts, take a boat from your hotel to Disney's Hollywood Studios and transfer to an Epcot bus, take a bus to Downtown Disney and transfer to an Epcot bus, or best of all, take a cab.

unofficial **TIP**
Epcot has its own parking lot and, unlike at the Magic Kingdom, there's no need to take a monorail or ferry to reach the entrance.

Arriving by car is easy. Walk or take a tram from the parking lot to the front gate. Monorail service connects Epcot with the Transportation and Ticket Center, the Magic Kingdom (transfer required), and Magic Kingdom resorts (transfer required).

GETTING ORIENTED

EPCOT'S THEMED AREAS ARE DISTINCTLY DIFFERENT. **Future World** combines Disney creativity and major corporations' technological resources to examine where mankind has come from and where it's going. **World Showcase** features landmarks,

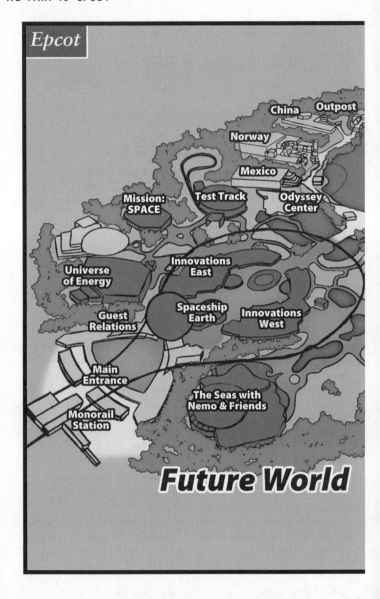

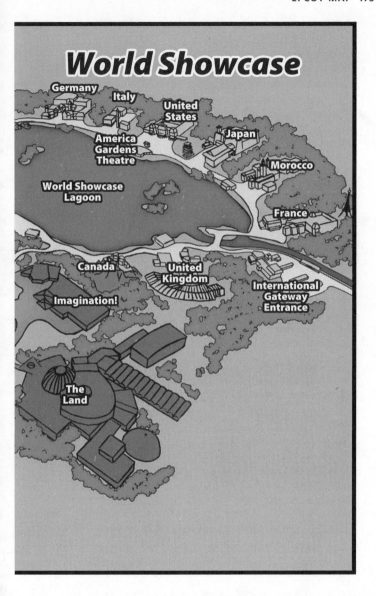

cuisine, and culture of almost a dozen nations and is meant to be a sort of permanent World's Fair.

At Epcot, the architectural symbol is **Spaceship Earth.** This 180-foot geosphere is visible from almost everywhere in the park. Like Cinderella Castle at the Magic Kingdom, Spaceship Earth can help you keep track of where you are in Epcot. But it's in a high-traffic area and isn't centrally located, so it isn't a good meeting place.

Any of the distinctive national pavilions in World Showcase makes a good meeting place, but be specific. "Hey, let's meet in Japan!" sounds fun, but each pavilion is a mini-town with buildings, monuments, gardens, and plazas. Pick a specific place in Japan—the sidewalk side of the pagoda, for example.

■ FUTURE WORLD

GLEAMING, FUTURISTIC STRUCTURES OF immense proportions define the first themed area you encounter at Epcot. Broad thoroughfares are punctuated with billowing fountains—all reflected in shining, space-age facades. Everything, including landscaping, is sparkling-clean and seems bigger than life. Pavilions dedicated to mankind's past, present, and future technological accomplishments form the perimeter of Future World. Front and center is **Spaceship Earth,** flanked by **Innoventions East and West.**

Future World Services

Epcot's service facilities in Future World include the following:

BABY CARE CENTER On the World Showcase side of the Odyssey Center

BANKING SERVICES ATMs outside the main entrance, on the Future World bridge, and in World Showcase at the Germany Pavilion

DINING RESERVATIONS At Guest Relations, to the left of Spaceship Earth

FIRST AID Next to the Baby Care Center on the World Showcase side of the Odyssey Center

LIVE ENTERTAINMENT INFORMATION At Guest Relations

LOST AND FOUND At the main entrance at the gift shop

LOST PERSONS At Guest Relations and the Baby Care Center on the World Showcase side of the Odyssey Center

WALT DISNEY WORLD AND LOCAL ATTRACTION INFORMATION At Guest Relations

WHEELCHAIR, ECV, ESV, AND STROLLER RENTALS Inside the main entrance and to the left, toward the rear of the Entrance Plaza

Most Epcot services are concentrated in Future World's Entrance Plaza, near the main gate.

GUEST RELATIONS

GUEST RELATIONS, left of the geosphere, is Epcot's equivalent of the Magic Kingdom's City Hall, serving as park headquarters and the primary information center. If you wish to eat in one of Epcot's sit-down restaurants and haven't made a reservation by calling ☎ 407-WDW-DINE (939-3463) or visiting **m.disneyworld.com** on your smartphone, you can make a reservation at Guest Relations or at any other sit-down restaurant in any of the parks. If you're near one of these locations, in-person is often faster than calling.

Spaceship Earth ★★★★

Appeal by Age	PRESCHOOL ★★★★	GRADE SCHOOL ★★★★	TEENS ★★★★
YOUNG ADULTS ★★★★½		OVER 30 ★★★★	SENIORS ★★★★½

What it is Educational dark ride through past, present, and future. **Scope and scale** Headliner. **When to go** Before 10 a.m. or after 4 p.m. **Special comments** If lines are long when you arrive, try again after 4 p.m. **Authors' rating** One of Epcot's best; not to be missed; ★★★★. **Duration of ride** About 16 minutes. **Average wait in line per 100 people ahead of you** 3 minutes. **Loading speed** Fast.

DESCRIPTION AND COMMENTS This ride spirals through the 18-story interior of Epcot's premier landmark, taking visitors past Audio-Animatronic scenes depicting mankind's developments in communications, from cave painting to printing to television to space communications and computer networks. The ride shows an amazing use of the geodesic sphere's interior.

Scenes are periodically redone to keep things fresh. Interactive video screens on the ride vehicles allow you to customize the ride's ending animated video. A postshow area with games and interactive exhibits rounds out the attraction.

TOURING TIPS Because it's near Epcot's main entrance, Spaceship Earth is inundated with arriving guests throughout the morning. If you're interested in riding Test Track, postpone Spaceship Earth until, say, after 4 p.m. Spaceship Earth loads continuously and quickly. If the line runs only along the right side of the sphere, you'll board in less than 15 minutes.

Innoventions East and West ★★★½

Appeal by Age	PRESCHOOL ★★★★	GRADE SCHOOL ★★★★	TEENS ★★★½
YOUNG ADULTS ★★★		OVER 30 ★★★½	SENIORS ★★★

What it is Static and hands-on exhibits relating to products and technologies of the near future. **Scope and scale** Major diversion. **When to go** On your second day at Epcot or after seeing all major attractions. **Special comments** Most exhibits demand time and participation to be rewarding; not much gained here by a quick walk-through. **Authors' rating** Something for everyone; ★★★½.

DESCRIPTION AND COMMENTS Innoventions, a huge, busy collection of hands-on walk-through exhibits sponsored by corporations, consists of two huge, crescent-shaped, glass-walled structures separated by a central plaza. Dynamic, interactive, and forward-looking, the area resembles a high-tech trade show.

Electronics and entertainment technology exhibits play a prominent role, as do ecology and "how things work" displays.

Our favorite attraction is Raytheon's **Sum of All Thrills,** a roller-coaster simulator in which you design the coaster track on a computer, then climb aboard a giant robotic arm to experience your creation. We've given it its own attraction review and added a step devoted to it in our Epcot touring plans.

TOURING TIPS Spend time at Innoventions on your second day at Epcot. If you have only one day, visit late if you have the time and endurance. (The one exception to this is Sum of All Thrills, which you should visit in the morning after Soarin', Test Track, and Mission: SPACE.)

Although many of these productions are worthwhile, the guest capacity of each theater is so small that long lines form. Skip exhibits with waits of more than 10 minutes, or experience them first thing in the morning on your second day.

CLUB COOL

DESCRIPTION AND COMMENTS Attached to the fountain side of Innoventions West is this combination retail space and soda fountain. It doesn't look like much, but inside, this Coca-Cola–sponsored exhibit provides free unlimited samples of soft drinks from around the world (some of them kind of strange). Because it's centrally located in Future World, it's a good meeting or break place; you can slake your thirst while waiting for your group.

Sum of All Thrills ★★★★

**Appeal by Age   PRESCHOOL ★★½   GRADE SCHOOL ★★★★★   TEENS ★★★★★
YOUNG ADULTS ★★★★½   OVER 30 ★★★★   SENIORS ★★★★**

What it is Combination hands-on exhibit and ride simulator. **Scope and scale** Minor attraction. **When to go** Before 10:30 a.m. or after 5 p.m. **Special comments** 48" minimum height requirement; 54" for track designs with inversions. **Authors' rating** Way cool; ★★★★. **Duration of attraction** 15 minutes. **Average wait in line per 100 people ahead of you** 40 minutes; assumes all simulators operating. **Loading speed** Slow.

DESCRIPTION AND COMMENTS Sum of All Thrills is a design-your-own-roller-coaster simulator in which you use a computer program to specify the drops, curves, and loops of a coaster track before boarding a robotic arm to experience your creation. Three vehicle options are available: bobsled, roller coaster, and jet aircraft. You can program actual loops into both the coaster and jet courses, and the robot arm will swing you upside down.

In addition to the vehicle, you also select the kinds of turns, loops, and hills in your track design. Using computer-design tools, you can further customize these components by changing the height and width of each piece as you go.

TOURING TIPS Not a high-capacity attraction, but also not on most guests' radar. Ride as early in the morning as possible.

Universe of Energy: *Ellen's Energy Adventure*
★★★★

What it is Combination ride and theater presentation about energy. **Scope and scale** Major attraction. **When to go** Before 11:15 a.m. or after 4:30 p.m. **Special comments** Don't be dismayed by long lines; 580 people enter the pavilion each time the theater changes audiences. **Authors' rating** The most unique theater in Walt Disney World; ★★★★. **Duration of presentation** About 26½ minutes. **Preshow entertainment** 8 minutes. **Probable waiting time** 20–40 minutes.

DESCRIPTION AND COMMENTS Audio-Animatronic dinosaurs and the unique traveling theater make this Exxon pavilion one of Future World's most popular. Because this is a theater with a ride component, the line doesn't move while the show is in progress. When the theater empties, however, a large chunk of the line disappears as people are admitted for the next show. Visitors are seated in what appears to be an ordinary theater while they watch a film about energy sources. Then the theater seats divide into six 97-passenger traveling cars that glide among the swamps and reptiles of a prehistoric forest. Special effects include the feel of warm, moist air from the swamp and the smell of sulfur from an erupting volcano.

   The accompanying film is a humorous and upbeat flick starring Ellen DeGeneres and Bill Nye that lightens the somewhat ponderous discussion of energy. Kids of all ages lose the thread during the educational segments, plus the dinosaurs frighten some preschoolers.

TOURING TIPS Because Universe of Energy can operate more than one show at a time, lines are generally tolerable.

Mission: SPACE *(Fastpass)* ★★★★

What it is Space-flight-simulation ride. **Scope and scale** Super-headliner. **When to go** First hour the park is open, or use Fastpass. **Special comments** Not recommended for pregnant women or people prone to motion sickness or claustrophobia; 44" minimum height requirement; a gentler nonspinning version is also available. **Authors' rating** Impressive; ★★★★. **Duration of ride** About 5 minutes plus preshow. **Average wait in line per 100 people ahead of you** 4 minutes.

Queasy

DESCRIPTION AND COMMENTS Mission: SPACE, among other things, is Disney's reply to all the cutting-edge attractions introduced over the past few years by crosstown rival Universal. The first truly groundbreaking Disney attraction since The Twilight Zone Tower of Terror, Mission: SPACE was one of the hottest tickets at Walt Disney World until two guests died after riding it in 2005 and 2006. While neither death was linked directly to the attraction, the negative publicity caused many guests to skip it entirely. In response, Disney added a tamer nonspinning version of Mission: SPACE in 2006.

Guests for both versions of the attraction enter the NASA Mission: SPACE Training Center, where they are introduced to the deep-space exploration program and then divided into groups for flight training. After orientation, they are strapped into space capsules for a simulated flight, where, of course, the unexpected happens. Each capsule accommodates a crew consisting of a group commander, pilot, navigator, and engineer, with a guest functioning in each role. The crew's skill and finesse (or, more often, lack thereof) in handling their respective responsibilities have no effect on the outcome of the flight. The capsules are small, and both ride versions are amazingly realistic. The nonspinning version does not subject your body to g-forces, but it does bounce and toss you around in a manner roughly comparable to other Disney motion simulators.

TOURING TIPS In minutes, Disney can reconfigure the ride's four centrifuges to either version of the attraction based on guest demand. In general, the kinder, gentler version has a wait time of about half that of its more harrowing counterpart.

Having experienced the industrial-strength version of Mission: SPACE under a variety of circumstances, we've always felt icky when riding it on an empty stomach, especially first thing in the morning. We came up with a number of potential explanations for this phenomenon, involving everything from low blood sugar and inner-ear disorders to some of us just not being astronaut material. Understandably disturbed by the latter possibility, we looked around for an expert opinion to explain what we were feeling. The number of organizations with experience studying the effects of high-g (high-gravity) forces on humans is limited to a select few: NASA, the Air Force, and Mad Tea Party cast members were the first to come to mind. As NASA is a codeveloper of Mission: SPACE, we called them. Amazingly, a spokesman told us that NASA no longer does much high-g training these days. And the agency was reluctant to pass along anything resembling medical advice to the general public.

Make a restroom stop before you get in line; you'll think your bladder has been to Mars and back for real before you get out of this attraction. Fastpass is generally needed only during times of peak attendance, and then only if you intend to ride during the middle of the day; mornings and dinnertimes should have shorter waits.

TEST TRACK PAVILION

DESCRIPTION AND COMMENTS Test Track, presented by General Motors, contains the Test Track ride and Inside Track, a collection of transportation-themed stationary exhibits and multimedia presentations. The pavilion is the last on the left before crossing into the World Showcase.

Many readers think that Test Track is "one big commercial" for General Motors. We agree that the promotional hype is more heavy-handed here than in most other business-sponsored attractions, but Test Track is nonetheless one of the most creatively conceived and executed attractions in Walt Disney World.

Test Track (Fastpass)   ★★★½

| Appeal by Age | PRESCHOOL ★★★½ | GRADE SCHOOL ★★★★½ | TEENS ★★★★ |
| YOUNG ADULTS ★★★★ | | OVER 30 ★★★★ | SENIORS ★★★½ |

What it is Automobile-test-track simulator ride. **Scope and scale** Super-headliner. **When to go** The first 30 minutes the park is open or just before closing, or use Fastpass. **Special comments** 40" minimum height requirement. **Authors' rating** Not to be missed; ★★★½. **Duration of ride** About 4 minutes. **Average wait in line per 100 people ahead of you** 4½ minutes. **Loading speed** Moderate–fast.

DESCRIPTION AND COMMENTS Test Track underwent a major refurbishment throughout most of 2012. Now sponsored by Chevrolet, Test Track's new presentation takes guests through the process of designing a new vehicle and then "testing" their car in a high-speed drive through and around the pavilion.

Guests entering the pavilion walk past displays of futuristic concept cars. Throughout the queue's walls are glossy video screens where engineers discuss the work of car design and consumers explain the characteristics of their perfect car.

After hearing about auto design, guests are admitted into the Chevrolet Design Studio to create their own concept car using a large touchscreen (like a giant iPad). Next, they board a six-seat ride vehicle, attached to a track on the ground, for an actual drive through Chevrolet's test track. The idea here is that guests are taking part in a computer simulation designed to test their vehicle's performance characteristics. Tests include braking, cornering, and acceleration, culminating in a spin around the outside of the pavilion at speeds of up to 65 miles per hour. The postshow area continues the creative process by allowing guests to craft commercials for their cars. Farther into the pavilion are displays of actual Chevys, many of which you can sit in.

TOURING TIPS Despite the sleek new look, it's still a challenge to keep Test Track running, especially in humid or wet conditions. When it works, it's one of the park's better attractions.

Be aware that the daily allocation of Fastpasses is often distributed by 4:30 p.m. If all Fastpasses are gone, another time-saving technique is to join the single-riders line, a separate line for people who don't object to riding alone. The objective is to fill the odd spaces left by groups that don't fill up the ride vehicle. Because most groups are unwilling to split up, single-rider lines are usually much shorter than the regular line.

IMAGINATION! PAVILION

DESCRIPTION AND COMMENTS Multiattraction pavilion on the west side of Innoventions West and down the walk from The

Land. Outside is an "upside-down waterfall" and one of our favorite Future World landmarks, the "jumping water," a fountain that hops over the heads of unsuspecting passersby.

TOURING TIPS We recommend early-morning or late-evening touring. See the individual attractions for specifics.

Captain EO ★★★

Appeal by Age	PRESCHOOL ★★½	GRADE SCHOOL ★★★	TEENS ★★★
YOUNG ADULTS ★★★		OVER 30 ★★★	SENIORS ★★★

What it is 3-D film with special effects. **Scope and scale** Headliners. **When to go** Before noon or after 4 p.m. **Special comments** Adults shouldn't be put off by the sci-fi theme or loud music. The high decibels frighten some children. **Authors' rating** ★★★. **Duration of presentation** About 17 minutes. **Preshow entertainment** 8 minutes. **Probable waiting time** 15 minutes

DESCRIPTION AND COMMENTS In response to Michael Jackson's death in 2009, Disney brought back his 3-D space-themed musical film presentation *Captain EO* for a "limited" engagement in its theme parks; at Epcot, that engagement is still ongoing, having supplanted *Honey, I Shrunk the Audience*. *Captain EO* originally ran here from 1986 to 1994.

Captain EO is the ultimate 1980s-era music video. Starring Jackson and directed by Francis Ford Coppola, this 3-D space fantasy is more than a film; it's a happening. Action on the screen is augmented by lasers, fiber optics, cannons, and a host of other special effects in the theater, as well as by some audience participation. There's not much of a story, but there's plenty of music and dancing performed by some of the most unlikely creatures ever to shake a tail feather.

TOURING TIPS Shows usually begin on the hour and half-hour. The sound level is earsplitting, frightening some young children. The venue is to the left of Journey into Imagination (see below); you don't have to ride to enter the theater. Avoid seats in the first several rows; if you sit too close to the screen, the 3-D images don't focus properly.

Journey into Imagination with Figment ★★½

Appeal by Age	PRESCHOOL ★★★★	GRADE SCHOOL ★★★½	TEENS ★★★
YOUNG ADULTS ★★★½		OVER 30 ★★★	SENIORS ★★★

What it is Dark fantasy-adventure ride. **Scope and scale** Major-attraction wannabe. **When to go** Anytime. **Authors' rating** ★★½. **Duration of ride** About 6 minutes. **Average wait in line per 100 people ahead of you** 2 minutes. **Loading speed** Fast.

DESCRIPTION AND COMMENTS Journey into Imagination takes you on a tour of the zany Imagination Institute. Sometimes you're a passive observer and sometimes you're a test subject as the ride provides a glimpse of the fictitious lab's inner workings. Stimulating all your senses and then some, it hits you with optical illusions, an experiment in which noise generates colors, a room that defies gravity, and other brain teasers. All along the way, Figment (a purple dragon) makes surprise appearances. After the ride, you can adjourn to an interactive exhibit area offering the latest in unique, hands-on imagery technology.

Pleasant rather than exciting, the ride falls short of the promise suggested by its name. Will you go to sleep? No. Will you find it amusing? Probably. Will you remember it tomorrow? Only Figment knows.

TOURING TIPS The standby wait for this attraction rarely exceeds 15 minutes. You can enjoy the interactive exhibit without taking the ride, so save it for later in the day.

THE LAND PAVILION

DESCRIPTION AND COMMENTS The Land is a huge pavilion that contains three attractions and several restaurants. Its emphasis has shifted from farming to environmental concerns.

TOURING TIPS This is a good place to grab a fast-food lunch. If you're here to see the attractions, however, don't go during mealtimes. Note that strollers aren't allowed inside.

The Circle of Life ★★★½

Appeal by Age	PRESCHOOL ★★★	GRADE SCHOOL ★★★½	TEENS ★★★
YOUNG ADULTS ★★★		OVER 30 ★★★	SENIORS ★★★½

What it is Film exploring humans' relationship with the environment. **Scope and scale** Minor attraction. **When to go** Anytime. **Authors' rating** Inspiring and enlightening; ★★★½. **Duration of presentation** About 20 minutes. **Preshow entertainment** Ecological slide show and trivia. **Probable waiting time** 10–15 minutes.

DESCRIPTION AND COMMENTS This playful yet educational film, starring Pumbaa, Simba, and Timon from *The Lion King*, spotlights the environmental interdependency of all creatures, demonstrating how easily the ecological balance can be upset. The message is sobering, but one that enlightens.

TOURING TIPS Every visitor should see this film. To stay ahead of the crowd, see it in late afternoon.

Living with the Land *(Fastpass seasonally)* ★★★★

Appeal by Age	PRESCHOOL ★★★½	GRADE SCHOOL ★★★★	TEENS ★★★★
YOUNG ADULTS ★★★★		OVER 30 ★★★★	SENIORS ★★★★

What it is Indoor boat-ride adventure chronicling the past, present, and future of farming and agriculture in the United States. **Scope and scale** Major attraction. **When to go** Before 11 a.m. or after 1 p.m. **Special comments** Go early in the morning and save other Land attractions (except for Soarin') for later in the day. The ride is on the pavilion's lower level. **Authors' rating** Informative without being dull; not to be missed; ★★★★. **Duration of ride** About 14 minutes. **Average wait in line per 100 people ahead of you** 3 minutes; assumes 15 boats operating. **Loading speed** Moderate.

DESCRIPTION AND COMMENTS This boat ride takes you through swamps, past inhospitable farm environments, and through a futuristic greenhouse where real crops are grown using the latest agricultural technologies.

TOURING TIPS See this attraction before the lunch crowd hits The Land restaurants, or use Fastpass. If you really enjoy Living with the Land or you have a special interest in the agricultural techniques demonstrated, take the **Behind the Seeds** tour. It's a 1-hour guided walk behind the scenes that examines advanced and experimental growing methods in-depth. The tour costs $19 for adults and $15 for children ages 3–9. Reservations are made on a space-available basis at the guided-tour waiting area near the entrance to Soarin'. This tour can also be reserved in advance by calling ☎ 407-WDW-TOUR.

Soarin' *(Fastpass)* ★★★★½

Appeal by Age PRESCHOOL ★★★★½ GRADE SCHOOL ★★★★★ TEENS ★★★★½
YOUNG ADULTS ★★★★½ OVER 30 ★★★★★ SENIORS ★★★★★

What it is Flight-simulation ride. **Scope and scale** Super-headliner. **When to go** First 30 minutes the park is open, or use Fastpass. **Special comments** Entrance on the lower level of the Land Pavilion. May induce motion sickness; 40" minimum height requirement; switching off available (see page 79). **Authors' rating** Exciting and mellow at the same time; ★★★★½. Not to be missed. **Duration of ride** 5½ minutes. **Average wait in line per 100 people ahead of you** 4 minutes; assumes 2 concourses operating. **Loading speed** Moderate.

DESCRIPTION AND COMMENTS Soarin' is a thrill ride for all ages, as exhilarating as a hawk on the wing yet as mellow as swinging in a hammock. If you've ever experienced flying dreams, you'll have some sense of how Soarin' feels.

Once you enter the main theater, you're secured in a seat not unlike those on inverted roller coasters. When everyone is in place, the rows of seats swing into position, making you feel as if the floor has dropped away, and you're suspended with your legs dangling. Thus hung out to dry, you embark on a simulated hang glider tour, with IMAX-quality images projected all around you and with the flight simulator moving in sync with the movie. The images are well chosen and drop-dead beautiful. Special effects include wind, sound, and even smell. The ride itself is thrilling but perfectly smooth. We think Soarin' is a must-experience for guests of any age who are tall enough to ride. And yes, senior citizens have told us they tried it and were crazy about it. On the other hand, a few readers who are afraid of heights have reported feeling anxious on Soarin'.

TOURING TIPS Having Soarin' opposite Test Track and Mission: SPACE in Future World takes some crowd pressure off both sides of the park. Keep in mind, however, that Test Track and Mission: SPACE serve up a little too much thrill for some guests. Soarin', conversely, is an almost platonic ride for any age. For that reason, it is at the top of our hit parade. Experience it before 9:30 a.m. or use Fastpass; expect all passes to be gone by 2 p.m. on days of moderate attendance or as early as noon on busier days.

THE SEAS WITH NEMO & FRIENDS PAVILION

THIS AREA ENCOMPASSES one of America's top marine aquariums, a ride that tunnels through the aquarium, an interactive animated film, and a number of first-class educational walk-through exhibits. It's a stunning package, one we rate as not to be missed. A comprehensive makeover featuring characters from Disney/Pixar's *Finding Nemo* has brought whimsy and much-needed levity to what theretofore was educationally brilliant but somewhat staid.

The Seas Main Tank and Exhibits ★★★½

Appeal by Age	PRESCHOOL ★★★★½	GRADE SCHOOL ★★★★½	TEENS ★★★★
YOUNG ADULTS ★★★★		OVER 30 ★★★★	SENIORS ★★★★

What it is A huge saltwater aquarium, plus exhibits on oceanography, ocean ecology, and sea life. **Scope and scale** Major attraction. **When to go** Before 11:30 a.m. or after 5 p.m. **Authors' rating** An excellent marine exhibit; ★★★½. **Average wait in line per 100 people ahead of you** 3½ minutes. **Loading speed** Fast.

DESCRIPTION AND COMMENTS The Seas is among Future World's most ambitious offerings. Scientists and divers conduct actual marine experiments in a 200-foot-diameter, 27-foot-deep main tank containing fish, mammals, and crustaceans in a simulation of an ocean ecosystem. Visitors can watch the activity through 8-inch-thick windows below the surface (including some in the Coral Reef Restaurant). On entering The Seas, you're directed to the loading area for The Seas with Nemo & Friends, an attraction that conveys you via a Plexiglas tunnel through The Seas' main tank. Following the ride, you disembark at Sea Base Alpha, where you can enjoy the attractions mentioned previously. (If the wait for the ride is too long, it's possible to head straight for the exhibits by going through the pavilion's exit, around back, and to the left of the main entrance.)

The Seas' fish population is substantial, but the strength of this attraction lies in the dozen or so exhibits offered after the ride. Visitors can view fish-breeding experiments, watch short films about sea life, and more. A delightful exhibit showcases clownfish (Nemo), regal blue tang (Dory), and other species featured in *Finding Nemo*. Other highlights include a haunting, hypnotic jellyfish tank; a sea horse aquarium; a stingray exhibit; and a manatee tank.

About two-thirds of the main aquarium is home to reef species, including sharks, rays, and a number of fish that you've seen in quiet repose on your dinner plate. The other third, separated by an inconspicuous divider, houses bottle-nosed dolphins and sea turtles. As you face the main aquarium, the most glare-free viewing windows for the dolphins are on the ground floor to the left by the escalators. For the reef species, it's the same floor on the right by the escalators. Stay as long as you wish.

TOURING TIPS With The Seas with Nemo & Friends and *Turtle Talk with Crush*, The Seas is one of Epcot's more popular venues. We recommend experiencing the ride and *Turtle Talk* in the morning before the park gets crowded, saving the excellent exhibits for later.

The Seas with Nemo & Friends ★★★

Appeal by Age PRESCHOOL ★★★★½ GRADE SCHOOL ★★★★ TEENS ★★★½ YOUNG ADULTS ★★★½ OVER 30 ★★★½ SENIORS ★★★★

What it is Ride through a tunnel in The Seas' main tank. **Scope and scale** Major attraction. **When to go** Before 10:30 a.m. or after 3 p.m. **Authors' rating** ★★★. **Duration of ride** 4 minutes. **Average wait in line per 100 people ahead of you** 3½ minutes. **Loading speed** Fast.

DESCRIPTION AND COMMENTS The Seas with Nemo & Friends is a high-tech ride featuring characters from the animated hit Finding Nemo. The ride likewise deposits you at the heart of The Seas, where the exhibits, Turtle Talk with Crush, and viewing platforms for the main aquarium are.

Upon entering The Seas, you're given the option of experiencing the ride or proceeding directly to the exhibit area. If you choose the ride, you'll be ushered to its loading area, where you'll be made comfortable in a "clamobile" for your journey through the aquarium. The attraction features technology that makes it seem as if the animated characters are swimming with live fish. Very cool.

Almost immediately you meet Mr. Ray and his class and learn that Nemo is missing. The remainder of the odyssey consists of finding Nemo with the help of Dory, Bruce, Marlin, Squirt, and Crush, all characters from the animated feature. Unlike the film, however, the ride ends with a musical finale.

TOURING TIPS The earlier you experience the ride the better; ditto for *Turtle Talk with Crush.* If waits are intolerable, come back after 3 p.m. or so.

Turtle Talk with Crush ★★★★

Appeal by Age PRESCHOOL ★★★★½ GRADE SCHOOL ★★★★½ TEENS ★★★★ YOUNG ADULTS ★★★★ OVER 30 ★★★★ SENIORS ★★★★

What it is An interactive animated film. **Scope and scale** Minor attraction. **When to go** Before 11 a.m. or after 3 p.m. **Authors' rating** A real spirit-lifter; ★★★★. **Duration of presentation** 17 minutes. **Preshow entertainment** None. **Probable waiting time** 10–20 minutes.

DESCRIPTION AND COMMENTS *Turtle Talk with Crush* is an interactive theater show starring the 153-year-old surfer-dude turtle from *Finding Nemo.* Although it starts like a typical Disney-theme-park movie, *Turtle Talk* quickly turns into a surprise interactive encounter as the on-screen Crush begins to have actual conversations with guests in the audience. Real-time computer graphics are used to accurately move Crush's mouth when forming words, and he's voiced by a guy who went to the Jeff Spicoli school of diction.

TOURING TIPS It's unusual to wait more than one or two shows to get in. If you find long lines in the morning, try coming back after 3 p.m., when more of the crowds have moved on to World Showcase.

The "Mom, I Can't Believe It's Disney!" Fountain ★★★★

Appeal by Age	PRESCHOOL ★★★★★	GRADE SCHOOL ★★★★★	TEENS ★★★★
YOUNG ADULTS ★★★★	OVER 30 ★★★★		SENIORS ★★★★★

What it is Combination fountain and shower. **When to go** When it's hot. **Scope and scale** Diversion. **Special comments** Secretly installed by Martians during *IllumiNations*. **Authors' rating** Yes! ★★★★. **Duration of experience** Indefinite. **Probable waiting time** None.

DESCRIPTION AND COMMENTS This simple fountain on the walkway linking Future World to World Showcase isn't much to look at, but it offers a truly spontaneous experience—rare in Walt Disney World, where everything is controlled, from the snow peas in your stir-fry to how frequently the crocodile yawns in the Jungle Cruise.

Spouts of water erupt randomly from the sidewalk. You can frolic in the water or let it cascade down on you or blow up your britches. On a broiling Florida day, when you think you might suddenly combust, fling yourself into the fountain and do decidedly un-Disney things. Dance, skip, sing, jump, splash, cavort, roll around, stick your toes down the spouts, or catch the water in your mouth as it descends. You can do all of this with your clothes on or, depending on your age, with your clothes off. It's hard to imagine so much personal freedom at Disney World and almost unthinkable to contemplate soggy people slogging and squishing around the park, but there you have it. Hurrah!

TOURING TIPS We don't know if the fountain's creator has been drummed out of the corps by the Disney Tribunal of People Who Sit on Sticks, but we're all grateful for his courage in introducing one thing that's not super-controlled. We do know your kids will be right in the middle of this thing before your brain sounds the alert. Our advice: pack a pair of dry shorts and turn the kids loose. You might even want to bring a spare pair for yourself. Or perhaps not.

▮ WORLD SHOWCASE

EPCOT'S SECOND THEMED AREA, World Showcase is an ongoing World's Fair encircling a picturesque 40-acre lagoon. The cuisine, culture, history, and architecture of almost a dozen countries are permanently displayed in individual national pavilions spaced along a 1.2-mile promenade. The pavilions replicate familiar landmarks and present representative street scenes from the host countries.

World Showcase features some of the loveliest gardens in the United States. In Germany, France, United Kingdom, Canada, and, to a lesser extent, China, they're sometimes tucked away and out of sight of pedestrian traffic on the World Showcase promenade.

Most adults enjoy World Showcase, but many children find it boring. To make it more interesting to children, most Epcot retail shops sell **Passport Kits** for about $10. Each kit contains a blank passport and stamps for every World Showcase country. As kids accompany their folks to each country, they tear out the appropriate stamp and stick it in the passport. The kit also contains basic information on the nations and a Mickey Mouse button. Disney has built a lot of profit into this little product, but we guess that isn't the issue. More important, parents tell us the Passport Kit helps get the kids through World Showcase with a minimum of impatience, whining, and tantrums.

unofficial **TIP**
To get your kids interested in World Showcase, buy them a Passport Kit and let them collect stamps from each Epcot country.

Children also enjoy **Kidcot Fun Stops**, designed to make World Showcase more interesting for the 5- to 12-year-old crowd. So simple and uncomplicated that you can't believe Disney people thought it up, the Fun Stops usually are nothing more than a large table on the sidewalk at each pavilion. Each table is staffed by a Disney cast member who stamps passports and supervises children in modest craft projects relating to the host country. Reports from parents about the Fun Stops have been uniformly positive.

Agent P's World Showcase Adventure ★★★★

| Appeal by Age | PRESCHOOL ★★★½ | GRADE SCHOOL ★★★★½ | TEENS ★★★★ |
| YOUNG ADULTS ★★★½ | | OVER 30 ★★★½ | SENIORS ★★★ |

What it is Interactive scavenger hunt in select World Showcase pavilions. **Scope and scale** Minor attraction. **When to go** Anytime. **Authors' rating** One of our favorite additions to the parks; ★★★★. **Duration of presentation** Allow 30 minutes per adventure. **Preshow entertainment** None. **Probable waiting time** None.

DESCRIPTION AND COMMENTS In their eponymous Disney Channel show, Phineas and Ferb have a pet platypus named Perry. In the presence of humans, Perry doesn't do a whole lot. (To be fair, we're not experts on typical platypus behavior, but read on.) When the kids aren't looking, though, Perry takes on the role of Agent P—a fedora-wearing, James Bond–esque secret agent who battles the evil Dr. Doofenshmirtz to prevent world domination (or at least domination of the tri-state area in which the show is based).

In Agent P's World Showcase Adventure, you're a secret agent helping Perry, and you receive a cell phone–like device before you're dispatched on a mission to your choice of seven World Showcase pavilions. Once you arrive at the pavilion, the device's video screen and audio provide various clues to help you solve a set of simple puzzles necessary for defeating Dr. Doofenshmirtz's plan. As you discover each clue, you'll find special effects such as talking statues and flaming lanterns, plus live "secret agents" stationed in the pavilions just for this attraction. For example, in a prior version of the game you were instructed to utter the phrase "Danger is my cup of tea" to someone working behind the counter at the United Kingdom's tea shop; he or she would respond by handing you a Twinings tea packet on which was printed a clue to solve a puzzle.

Agent P makes static World Showcase pavilions more interactive and kid-friendly. The adventures have simple clues, fast pacing, and neat rewards for solving the puzzles. *Unofficial* coauthor Len Testa's teenage daughter, Hannah, will happily spend an entire afternoon in World Showcase playing this game and drinking Japanese sodas. Don't be surprised if, having completed one pavilion's adventure, your child wants to do the same.

TOURING TIPS Playing the game is free, and no deposit is required for the device. You'll need a valid theme park ticket to sign up before you play, and you can choose both the time and location of your adventure. Register at Future World's Innoventions East or West building, or along the Odyssey Bridge connecting Future World to World Showcase. Before heading off to your chosen country, pick up your device at the Italy, Norway, or United Kingdom Pavilion or the east side of the main walkway from Future World to World Showcase.

Each group can have up to three devices for the same adventure. Because you're working with a device about the size of a mobile phone, it's best to have one device for every two people in your group.

NOW, MOVING CLOCKWISE around the World Showcase promenade, here are the nations represented and their attractions.

MEXICO PAVILION

DESCRIPTION AND COMMENTS Pre-Columbian pyramids dominate the architecture of this exhibit. One forms the pavilion's facade, and the other overlooks the restaurant and plaza alongside the boat ride—**Gran Fiesta Tour**—inside the pavilion.

TOURING TIPS A romantic and exciting testimony to Mexico's charms, the pyramids contain a large number of authentic and valuable artifacts. Many people zip past these treasures without stopping to look. The village scene inside the pavilion is beautiful and exquisitely detailed. A retail shop occupies most of the left half of the inner pavilion, while Mexico's Kidcot stop is in the first entryway inside the pyramid. On the opposite side of the main floor is **La Cava de Tequila**, a bar serving more than 70 varieties of tequila as well as margaritas and appetizers.

Gran Fiesta Tour Starring the Three Caballeros
★★½

| Appeal by Age | PRESCHOOL ★★★★ | GRADE SCHOOL ★★★★ | TEENS ★★★ |
| YOUNG ADULTS ★★★½ | OVER 30 ★★★ | | SENIORS ★★★½ |

What it is Indoor scenic boat ride. **Scope and scale** Minor attraction. **When to go** Before noon or after 5 p.m. **Authors' rating** Visually appealing, light, and relaxing; ★★½. **Duration of ride** About 7 minutes (plus 1½-minute wait to disembark). **Average wait in line per 100 people ahead of you** 4½ minutes; assumes 16 boats in operation. **Loading speed** Moderate.

DESCRIPTION AND COMMENTS The Gran Fiesta Tour incorporates animated versions of Donald Duck, José Carioca, and Panchito—an avian singing group called The Three Caballeros, from Disney's 1944 animated musical of the same name—to spice up what has been characterized as a slower-paced Mexican-style It's a Small World.

The ride's premise is that the Caballeros are scheduled to perform at a fiesta, but Donald has gone missing. Large video screens show Donald playing hooky, enjoying Mexico's pyramids, monuments, and watersports while José and Panchito search other Mexican points of interest. Everyone is reunited in time for a rousing concert near the end of the ride. Along the way, guests are treated to detailed scenes in eye-catching colors, and an impressive music system.

At the risk of sounding like the Disney geeks we are, we must point out that Panchito is technically the only Mexican Caballero; José Carioca is from Brazil, and Donald is from Burbank. In any case, more of the ride's visuals seem to be on the left side of the boat; have small children sit nearer the left to keep their attention, and listen for Donald's humorous monologue as you wait to disembark at the end of the ride.

TOURING TIPS If the line looks longer than 5 minutes, grab a margarita at La Cava del Tequila and come back in 15.

NORWAY PAVILION

DESCRIPTION AND COMMENTS The Norway Pavilion is complex, beautiful, and architecturally diverse. Surrounding a courtyard is an assortment of traditional Scandinavian buildings, including a replica of the 14th-century Akershus Castle, a wooden stave church (go inside—the doors open!), red-tiled cottages, and replicas of historic buildings representing the traditional designs of Bergen, Alesund, and Oslo. Attractions include an adventure boat ride in the mold of Pirates of the Caribbean, a movie about Norway, and a gallery of art and artifacts. The pavilion houses **Akershus Royal Banquet Hall,** a sit-down eatery that hosts princess character meals for breakfast, lunch, and dinner; breakfast here is one of the most popular character meals in the World. An open-air cafe attached to a bakery caters to those on the run. Shoppers will find abundant native handicrafts.

Maelstrom *(Fastpass)* ★★★

Appeal by Age	PRESCHOOL ★★★½	GRADE SCHOOL ★★★½	TEENS ★★★½
YOUNG ADULTS ★★★★		OVER 30 ★★★½	SENIORS ★★★½

What it is Indoor adventure boat ride. **Scope and scale** Major attraction. **When to go** Before 1 p.m., after 7 p.m., or use Fastpass. **Special comments** Animatronic polar bears may frighten a few small children. **Authors' rating** Too short but has its moments; ★★★. **Duration of ride** 4½ minutes, followed by a 5-minute film with a short wait in between; about 14 minutes for all. **Average wait in line per 100 people ahead of you** 4 minutes; assumes 12 or 13 boats operating. **Loading speed** Fast.

DESCRIPTION AND COMMENTS In one of Disney World's shorter water rides, guests board dragon-headed ships for a voyage through the fabled rivers and seas of Viking history and legend. They brave trolls, rocky gorges, waterfalls, and a storm at sea. A second-generation Disney water ride, the Viking voyage assembles an impressive array of special effects, combining visual, tactile, and auditory stimuli in a fast-paced and often humorous odyssey. Afterward, guests see a 5-minute film on Norway. We don't have any major problems with Maelstrom, but a vocal minority of our readers consider the ride too brief and resent having to sit through what they characterize as a travelogue.

TOURING TIPS Sometimes, several hundred guests from a recently concluded screening of *Reflections of China* arrive at Maelstrom en masse. Should you encounter this horde, postpone Maelstrom. If you don't want to see the Norway film, not to worry; you'll be given the opportunity to exit before the film begins.

CHINA PAVILION

DESCRIPTION AND COMMENTS A half-sized replica of the Temple of Heaven in Beijing identifies this pavilion. Gardens and reflecting ponds simulate those found in Suzhou, and an art gallery features a lotus-blossom gate and formal saddle roofline. The China Pavilion offers two restaurants: the quick-service **Lotus Blossom Cafe** and the full-service **Nine Dragons Restaurant,** (Advance Reservations recommended) which serves lamentably lackluster Chinese food in a lovely setting. **The Joy of Tea,** a tea stand and specialty-drink vendor, will feed your caffeine addiction until you can make it to Morocco's espresso bar.

The pavilion also hosts regularly updated exhibits on Chinese history, culture, or trendsetting developments. The current exhibit features a look at Chinese funeral sculptures, including miniature clay warriors who protect the tombs' occupants.

Reflections of China ★★★½

Appeal by Age	PRESCHOOL ★★	GRADE SCHOOL ★★★	TEENS ★★★½
YOUNG ADULTS ★★★½		OVER 30 ★★★★	SENIORS ★★★★

What it is Film about the Chinese people and country. **Scope and scale** Major attraction. **When to go** Anytime. **Special comments** Audience stands throughout the performance. **Authors' rating** A beautifully produced film; ★★★½.

Duration of presentation About 14 minutes. **Preshow entertainment** None. **Probable waiting time** 10 minutes.

DESCRIPTION AND COMMENTS Pass through the Hall of Prayer for Good Harvest to view the Circle-Vision 360 film *Reflections of China*. Warm and appealing, it's a brilliant (albeit politically sanitized) introduction to the people and the natural beauty of China.

TOURING TIPS The pavilion is truly beautiful—serene yet exciting. *Reflections of China* plays in a theater where guests must stand, but the film can usually be enjoyed anytime without much waiting. If you're touring World Showcase in a counterclockwise rotation and plan next to go to Norway and ride Maelstrom, position yourself on the far left of the theater (as you face the attendant's podium). After the show, be one of the first to exit. Hurry to Maelstrom as fast as you can to arrive ahead of the several hundred other *Reflections of China* patrons who will be right behind you.

GERMANY PAVILION

DESCRIPTION AND COMMENTS A clock tower, adorned with boy and girl figures, rises above the *platz* (plaza) marking the Germany Pavilion. Dominated by a fountain depicting St. George's victory over the dragon, the platz is encircled by buildings in the style of traditional German architecture. The main attraction is the **Biergarten,** a buffet that serves traditional German food and beer (Advance Reservations are required). Yodeling, folk dancing, and oompah-band music are part of the mealtime festivities.

The biggest draw in Germany may be **Karamell-Küche** ("Caramel Kitchen"), offering small caramel-covered sweets including apples, fudge, and cupcakes. We love coming here for a midday snack to tide us over before dinner. Also be sure to check out the large and elaborate model railroad just beyond the restrooms as you walk from Germany toward Italy.

TOURING TIPS The pavilion is pleasant and festive. Anytime is good for touring.

ITALY PAVILION

DESCRIPTION AND COMMENTS The entrance to Italy is marked by an 83-foot-tall campanile (bell tower) said to mirror the tower in St. Mark's Square in Venice. Left of the campanile is a replica of the 14th-century Doge's Palace, also in the famous square. The pavilion has a waterfront on the lagoon where gondolas are tied to striped moorings.

TOURING TIPS Streets and courtyards in the Italy Pavilion are among the most realistic in World Showcase. For a quick lunch, **Via Napoli** occasionally offers pizza by the slice; **Tutto Gusto Wine Cellar** serves appetizer plates along with libations. There's no film or ride, so you can tour the rest of the pavilion at any hour.

UNITED STATES PAVILION
The American Adventure ★★★★

| Appeal by Age | PRESCHOOL ★★★ | GRADE SCHOOL ★★★ | TEENS ★★★½ |
| YOUNG ADULTS ★★★★ | | OVER 30 ★★★★ | SENIORS ★★★★½ |

What it is Patriotic mixed-media and Audio-Animatronic theater presentation on U.S. history. **Scope and scale** Headliner. **When to go** Anytime. **Authors' rating** Disney's best historic/patriotic attraction; not to be missed; ★★★★. **Duration of presentation** About 29 minutes. **Preshow entertainment** Voices of Liberty chorale singing. **Probable waiting time** 16 minutes.

DESCRIPTION AND COMMENTS The United States Pavilion, generally referred to as The American Adventure, consists (not surprisingly) of a fast-food restaurant and a patriotic show, also called *The American Adventure*.

The presentation is a composite of everything Disney does best. Located in an imposing brick structure reminiscent of Colonial Philadelphia, the 29-minute production is a stirring, but sanitized, rendition of American history narrated by an animatronic Mark Twain (who carries a smoking cigar) and Ben Franklin (who climbs a set of stairs to visit Thomas Jefferson). Behind a stage (almost half the size of a football field) is a 28 x 155–foot rear-projection screen (the largest ever used) on which motion-picture images are interwoven with action on stage.

TOURING TIPS Architecturally, the U.S. Pavilion isn't as interesting as most others in World Showcase. But the presentation, our researchers believe, is the very best patriotic attraction in the Disney repertoire. It usually plays to capacity audiences from around 1:30 to 3:30 p.m., but it isn't hard to get into. Because of the theater's large capacity, it is highly unusual not to be admitted into the next performance. Because of its theme, the presentation is decidedly less compelling to non-Americans.

JAPAN PAVILION

DESCRIPTION AND COMMENTS The five-story, blue-roofed pagoda, inspired by a 17th-century shrine in Nara, sets this pavilion apart. A hill garden behind it features waterfalls, rocks, flowers, lanterns, paths, and rustic bridges. The building on the right (as one faces the entrance) was inspired by the ceremonial and coronation hall at the Imperial Palace at Kyoto. It contains restaurants and a U.S. outpost of Japan's **Mitsukoshi** department store. Through the center entrance and to the left is **Bijutsu-kan Gallery**, exhibiting colorful displays from Japanese pop culture.

TOURING TIPS Tasteful and elaborate, the pavilion creatively blends simplicity, architectural grandeur, and natural beauty. Tour anytime.

MOROCCO PAVILION

DESCRIPTION AND COMMENTS The bustling market, winding streets, lofty minarets, and stuccoed archways re-create the romance and intrigue of Marrakesh and Casablanca. Attention to detail makes Morocco one of the most exciting World Showcase pavilions. It also has a museum of Moorish art and **Restaurant Marrakesh,** which serves some unusual and difficult-to-find North African specialties.

TOURING TIPS Morocco has neither a ride nor theater, so tour it anytime.

FRANCE PAVILION

DESCRIPTION AND COMMENTS Naturally, a replica of the Eiffel Tower (a big one) is this pavilion's centerpiece. In the foreground, streets recall *la belle époque,* France's "beautiful time" between 1870 and 1910. The sidewalk cafe and restaurant are very popular, as is the pastry shop. You won't be the first visitor to buy a croissant to tide you over until your next real meal.

Impressions de France ★★★½

Appeal by Age PRESCHOOL ★★½	GRADE SCHOOL ★★★½	TEENS ★★★½	
YOUNG ADULTS ★★★★	OVER 30 ★★★★	SENIORS ★★★★½	

What it is Film essay on the French people and country. **Scope and scale** Major attraction. **When to go** Anytime. **Authors' rating** Exceedingly beautiful film; not to be missed; ★★★½. **Duration of presentation** About 18 minutes. **Preshow entertainment** None. **Probable waiting time** 15 minutes (at suggested times).

DESCRIPTION AND COMMENTS *Impressions de France* is an 18-minute movie projected over 200 degrees onto five screens. Unlike at China and Canada, you sit to view this well-made film introducing France's people, cities, and natural wonders.

TOURING TIPS The film usually begins on the hour and half-hour. Detail and the evocation of a bygone era enrich the atmosphere of this pavilion. Streets are small and become quite congested when visitors queue for the film.

UNITED KINGDOM PAVILION

DESCRIPTION AND COMMENTS A variety of period architecture attempts to capture Britain's city, town, and rural atmospheres. One street alone has a thatched-roof cottage, a four-story timber-and-plaster building, a pre-Georgian plaster building, a formal Palladian exterior of dressed stone, and a city square with a Hyde Park bandstand (whew!).

The pavilion is mostly shops. The **Rose & Crown Pub and Dining Room** is the only World Showcase full-service restaurant with dining on the water side of the promenade. For fast food, try the **Yorkshire County Fish Shop.**

TOURING TIPS TOURING TIPS There are no attractions here, hence minimal congestion, so tour anytime. Mary Poppins, Alice in Wonderland, and/or Pooh can occasionally be found in the character-greeting area; check the *Times Guide* for a schedule. Advance Reservations aren't required for the pub section of the Rose & Crown, making it a nice place to stop for a beer. (If you can't make up your mind, an "Imperial Sampler" of seven different brews—including Bass, Harp, Boddingtons, and Guinness—is available for about $11.)

CANADA PAVILION

DESCRIPTION AND COMMENTS Canada's cultural, natural, and architectural diversity are reflected in this large and impressive pavilion. Thirty-foot-tall totem poles embellish an American Indian village at the foot of a magnificent château-style hotel. Nearby is a rugged stone building said to be modeled after a famous landmark near Niagara Falls and that reflects Britain's influence on Canada. **Le Cellier,** a steakhouse on the pavilion's lower level, is one of Disney World's highest-rated restaurants. It almost always requires Advance Reservations; you'd have to be incredibly lucky to get a walk-in spot, but it doesn't hurt to ask.

O Canada!   ★★★½

| Appeal by Age | PRESCHOOL ★★★ | GRADE SCHOOL ★★★½ | TEENS ★★★½ |
| YOUNG ADULTS ★★★½ | | OVER 30 ★★★★ | SENIORS ★★★★ |

What it is Film essay on the Canadian people and their country. **Scope and scale** Major attraction. **When to go** Anytime. **Special comments** Audience stands during performance. **Authors' rating** Makes you want to catch the first plane to Canada; ★★★½. **Duration of presentation** About 15 minutes. **Preshow entertainment** None. **Probable waiting time** 9 minutes.

DESCRIPTION AND COMMENTS Starring Martin Short, *O Canada!* showcases Canada's natural beauty and population diversity and demonstrates the immense pride Canadians have in their country. Visitors leave the theater through **Victoria Gardens,** inspired by British Columbia's famed Butchart Gardens.

TOURING TIPS *O Canada!,* a large-capacity theater attraction (guests must stand), gets fairly heavy late-morning attendance because Canada is the first pavilion encountered as one travels counterclockwise around World Showcase Lagoon.

LIVE ENTERTAINMENT *in* EPCOT

LIVE ENTERTAINMENT IN EPCOT IS MORE diverse than it is in the Magic Kingdom. In World Showcase, it reflects the nations represented. Future World provides a perfect setting for new and experimental offerings. Information about live entertainment on the day you visit is contained in the Epcot guide map you obtain upon entry or at Guest Relations.

Here are some performers and performances you're apt to encounter:

AMERICA GARDENS THEATRE This large amphitheater, near the U.S. Pavilion, faces World Showcase Lagoon. It hosts pop (and oldies pop) musical acts throughout much of the year, as well as Epcot's popular Candlelight Processional for the Christmas holidays.

AROUND WORLD SHOWCASE Impromptu performances take place in and around the World Showcase pavilions. They include a strolling mariachi group in Mexico; street actors in Italy; a fife-and-drum corps or singing group (The Voices of Liberty) at the U.S. Pavilion; traditional songs, drums, and dances in Japan; white-faced mimes in France; street comedy and a rock band in the United Kingdom; and bagpipe rock in Canada, among other offerings. Street entertainment occurs about every half-hour.

DINNER AND LUNCH SHOWS Restaurants in World Showcase serve healthy portions of live entertainment to accompany the victuals. Find folk dancing and an oompah band in Germany, singing waiters in Italy, and belly dancers in Morocco. Shows are performed only at dinner in Italy, but at both lunch and dinner in Germany and Morocco. Advance Reservations are required.

DISNEY CHARACTERS Characters appear throughout Epcot (see pages 81 and 82 for a listing) and in live shows at the America Gardens Theatre and the Showcase Plaza between Mexico and Canada. Times are listed in the *Times Guide* available upon entry and at Guest Relations. Finally, **The Garden Grill Restaurant** in the Land Pavilion and **Akershus Royal Banquet Hall** in Norway offer character meals.

IN FUTURE WORLD A musical crew of drumming janitors works near the front entrance and at Innoventions Plaza (between the two Innoventions buildings and by the fountain) according to the daily entertainment schedule. They're occasionally complemented by an electric-keyboard band playing oldies tunes.

INNOVENTIONS FOUNTAIN SHOW Numerous times each day, the fountain situated between the two Innoventions buildings comes alive with pulsating, arching plumes of water synchronized to a musical score.

KIDCOT FUN STOPS World Showcase pavilions have areas called Kidcot Fun Stops, where younger children can hear a story or make some small craft representative of the host nation. The Fun Stops are informal, usually set up right on the walkway. During busy times of the year, you'll find Fun Stops at each country in World Showcase; at slower times, only a couple of zones operate. Many parents who thought Epcot would be a drag for their kids are pleasantly surprised by the Fun Stops experience.

ILLUMINATIONS

EPCOT'S GREAT OUTDOOR SPECTACLE integrates fireworks, laser lights, neon, and music in a stirring tribute to the nations of the world. It's the climax of every Epcot day.

IllumiNations has a plot and a theme, and it is loaded with symbolism. We'll provide the CliffsNotes version here, because it all sort of runs together in the show itself. The show kicks off with colliding stars that suggest the Big Bang, following which "chaos reigns in the universe." This display is soon replaced by twittering songbirds and various other manifestations signaling the nativity of the Earth. Next comes a brief history of time, from the dinosaurs to ancient Rome, all projected in images on a huge, floating globe. Man's art and inspiration then flash across the globe "in a collage of creativity." All this stimulates the globe to unfold "like a massive flower," bringing on the fireworks crescendo heralding the dawn of a new age. Although only the artistically sensitive will be able to differentiate all this from, say, the last 5 minutes of any *Transformers* movie, we thought you'd like to know what Disney says is happening.

Getting out of Epcot after IllumiNations (Read This Before Selecting a Viewing Spot)

Decide how quickly you want to leave the park after the show, then pick your vantage point. *IllumiNations* ends the day at Epcot. When it's over, only a couple of gift shops remain open. Because there's nothing to do, everyone leaves at once. This creates a great snarl at Package Pick-Up, the Epcot monorail station, and the Disney bus stop. It also pushes to the limit the tram system hauling guests to their cars in the parking lot. Stroller return, however, is extraordinarily efficient and doesn't cause any delay.

If you're staying at an Epcot resort (Swan, Dolphin, Yacht & Beach Club Resorts, and BoardWalk Inn & Villas), watch the show from somewhere on the southern (American Adventure) half of World Showcase Lagoon and then leave through the International Gateway between France and the United Kingdom. You can walk or take a boat back to your hotel from the International Gateway. If you have a car and you're visiting Epcot in the evening for dinner and *IllumiNations,* park at the Yacht or Beach Club. After the show, duck out the International Gateway and be on the road to your hotel in 15 minutes. We should warn you that there's a manned security gate at the entrances to most of the Epcot resorts, including the Yacht and Beach clubs. You will, of course, be admitted if you have legitimate business, such as dining at one of the hotel restaurants, or, if you park at the BoardWalk

Inn & Villas (requiring a slightly longer walk to Epcot), going to the clubs and restaurants at the BoardWalk. If you're staying at any other Disney hotel and you don't have a car, the fastest way home is to join the mass exodus through the main gate after *IllumiNations* and catch a bus or the monorail.

Those who have a car in the Epcot lot have a more problematic situation. To beat the crowd, find a viewing spot at the end of World Showcase Lagoon nearest Future World (and the exits). Leave as soon as *IllumiNations* concludes, trying to exit ahead of the crowd (note that thousands of people will be doing exactly the same thing). To get a good vantage point between Mexico and Canada on the northern end of the lagoon, stake out your spot 60–100 minutes before the show (45–90 minutes during less-busy periods). Conceivably, you may squander more time holding your spot before *IllumiNations* than you would if you watched from the less-congested southern end of the lagoon and took your chances with the crowd upon departure.

unofficial **TIP**
Everyone in your party should be told not to exit through the turnstiles until all noses have been counted.

More groups get separated and more children get lost after *IllumiNations* than at any other time. In summer, you will be walking in a throng of up to 30,000 people. If you're heading for the parking lot, anticipate this congestion and preselect a point in the Epcot entrance area where you can meet in the event that someone gets separated from the group. We recommend the fountain just inside the main entrance. It can be a nightmare if the group gets split up and you don't know whether the others are inside or outside the park.

For those with a car, the main problem is reaching it. Once there, traffic leaves the parking lot pretty well. If you paid close attention to where you parked, consider skipping the tram and walking. If you walk, watch your children closely and hang on to them for all you're worth. The parking lot is pretty wild at this time of night, with hundreds of moving cars.

Good Locations for Viewing IllumiNations and Other World Showcase Lagoon Performances

unofficial **TIP**
It's important not to position yourself under a tree, an awning, or anything else that blocks your overhead view.

The best place to be for any presentation on World Showcase Lagoon is in a seat on the lakeside veranda of **La Cantina de San Angel** in the Mexico Pavilion. Come early (at least 90 minutes before *IllumiNations* starts) and relax with a cold drink or snack while you wait for the show.

La Hacienda de San Angel in Mexico, the **Rose & Crown Pub** in the United Kingdom, and **Spice Road Table** in Morocco (opens late 2013) also have lagoonside seating. Because of a small wall at the Rose & Crown, however, the view isn't quite as good as from the Cantina. If you want to combine dinner at either location with *IllumiNations,* make a dinner reservation for about 1 hour and 15 minutes before showtime. Report a few minutes early for your seating and tell the host you want a table outside where you can view *IllumiNations* during or after dinner. In our experience, the staff will bend over backward to accommodate you. If you can't get a table outside, eat inside, then hang out until showtime. When the lights dim to indicate the start of *IllumiNations,* you'll be allowed to join the diners in watching it.

Because most guests run for the exits after a presentation, and because islands in the southern (U.S. Pavilion) half of the lagoon block the view from some places, the most popular spectator positions are along the northern waterfront from Norway and Mexico to Canada and the United Kingdom. It's usually necessary to claim a spot 60–100 minutes before *IllumiNations* begins. If you're late finishing dinner or you don't want to spend an hour-plus standing by a rail, here are some good viewing spots along the southern perimeter (moving counterclockwise from the U.K. to Germany) that often go unnoticed until 10–30 minutes before showtime:

unofficial **TIP** Although the northern end of the lagoon offers unquestionably excellent viewing, we advise that you claim a spot 40–60 minutes before *IllumiNations* begins.

1. **International Gateway Island** The pedestrian bridge across the canal near International Gateway spans an island that offers great viewing. This island normally fills 30 minutes or more before showtime.

2. **Second-floor (restaurant-level) deck of the Mitsukoshi building in Japan** An Asian arch slightly blocks your sightline, but this covered deck offers a great vantage point, especially if the weather is iffy. Only the Hacienda de San Angel in Mexico is more protected.

3. **Gondola landing at Italy** An elaborate waterfront promenade offers excellent viewing positions. Claim your spot at least 30 minutes before showtime.

4. **Boat dock opposite Germany** Another good vantage point, the dock generally fills 30 minutes before *IllumiNations.*

5. **Waterfront promenade by Germany** Views are good from the 90-foot-long lagoonside walkway between Germany and China.

None of the above viewing locations are reserved for *Unofficial Guide* readers, and on busier nights good spots go early. But we still won't hold down a slab of concrete for 2 hours before *IllumiNations* as some people do. Most nights, you can find an acceptable vantage point 15–30 minutes before the show. Because most of the action is significantly above ground level, you don't need to be right on the rail or have an unobstructed view of the water. If *IllumiNations* is a top priority for you and you want to be absolutely certain of getting a good viewing position, claim your place an hour or more before showtime.

IllumiNations *Cruise*

For a *really* good view, you can charter a pontoon boat for $346 with tax. Captained by a Disney cast member, the boat holds up to 10 guests. Your captain will take you for a little cruise and then position the boat in a perfect place to watch *IllumiNations*. Chips, soda, and water are provided; sandwiches and more-substantial food items may be arranged through Disney reservations or Yacht Club Private Dining (☎ 407-934-3160.) Cruises depart from Bayside Marina. A major indirect benefit of the charter is that you can enjoy *IllumiNations* without fighting the mob afterward. Because this is a private charter rather than a tour, only your group will be aboard. Life jackets are provided, but you can wear them at your discretion. Because there are few boats, charters sell out fast. To reserve, call ☎ 407-WDW-PLAY (939-7529) at exactly 7 a.m. 180 days before the day you want to charter. We recommend phoning about 185 days out to have a Disney agent specify the exact morning to call for reservations. Similar charters are available on the Seven Seas Lagoon to watch the Magic Kingdom fireworks.

◼❚ EPCOT TOURING PLANS

OUR EPCOT TOURING PLANS ARE FIELD-TESTED, step-by-step itineraries for seeing all major attractions at Epcot with a minimum of waiting in line. They're designed to keep you ahead of the crowds while the park is filling in the morning, and to place you at the less crowded attractions during Epcot's busier hours. They assume you would be happier doing a little extra walking rather than a lot of extra standing in line.

Touring Epcot is much more strenuous and demanding than touring the other theme parks, requiring about twice as much walking. Our plans will help you avoid crowds

*un**official*** **TIP**
Unlike the Magic Kingdom, Epcot has no effective in-park transportation; wherever you want to go, it's always quicker to walk.

and bottlenecks on days of moderate-to-heavy attendance, but they can't shorten the distance you have to walk. (Wear comfortable shoes.) On days of lighter attendance, when the crowd conditions aren't a critical factor, the plans will help you organize your tour.

In anticipation of Disney introducing Fastpass+ (see page 88), we've listed the approximate Fastpass+ return times for which you should attempt to make reservations. (The touring plan should work with anything close to the times shown.) In case Disney limits how many Fastpass+ reservations you can get, we've listed in the plans the attractions most likely to need Fastpass+ too. No matter what Disney does, we'll have the latest Fastpass+ and touring plan tools on **touringplans.com**.

We offer five touring plans:

EPCOT ONE-DAY TOURING PLAN This plan packs as much as possible into one long day and requires a lot of hustle and stamina. You'll be doing a lot of walking and some backtracking in order to avoid long waits in line. You might not complete the tour—how far you get depends on how quickly you move from attraction to attraction, how many times you rest and eat, how quickly the park fills, and what time it closes.

This plan is not recommended for families with very young children. If you're touring with young children and have only one day, use the Authors' Selective Epcot One-Day Touring Plan. Break after lunch and then relax at your hotel, returning to the park in late afternoon. If you can allocate two days to Epcot, use one of the Epcot two-day touring plans.

AUTHORS' SELECTIVE EPCOT ONE-DAY TOURING PLAN This plan eliminates what are, in the authors' opinion, some lesser attractions and offers a somewhat more relaxed tour if you have only one day. While the plan includes only what the authors believe is the best Epcot has to offer, exclusion of a particular attraction doesn't mean it isn't worthwhile.

Families with children younger than age 8 using this touring plan should review Epcot attractions in the Small-Child Fright-Potential Chart (pages 75–79). Rent a stroller for any child small enough to fit in one, and take your young children back to the hotel for a nap after lunch. If you can allocate two days to seeing Epcot, try one of the Epcot two-day touring plans.

EPCOT ONE-DAY TOURING PLAN FOR PARENTS WITH SMALL CHILDREN This touring plan is for parents and kids who want to experience Epcot's best attractions in a single day. It's the most popular Epcot touring plan at **touringplans.com**.

The plan includes a midday break of 3–4 hours. Make time for this break by skipping intense attractions such as Test Track and Mission: SPACE and by forgoing many World Showcase exhibits.

Families with children younger than age 8 using this touring plan should review Epcot attractions in our Small-Child Fright-Potential Chart in Part 6 (see pages 75–79), and rent a stroller for any child small enough to fit in one.

EPCOT TWO-DAY EARLY-RISER TOURING PLAN This is the most efficient Epcot touring plan, eliminating 90% of the back-tracking and extra walking required by the others while still providing a comprehensive tour. Most folks will complete each day of the plan by midafternoon. While the plan doesn't include *IllumiNations* or other evening festivities, these activities, along with dinner at an Epcot restaurant, can be added to the itinerary at your discretion.

As with the previous touring plans, families with children younger than age 8 using this plan should review Epcot attractions in the Small-Child Fright-Potential Chart (pages 75–790). Rent a stroller for any child small enough to fit.

"NOT A TOURING PLAN" TOURING PLANS

FOR PARENTS AND ADULTS WITH ONE DAY TO TOUR, ARRIVING AT PARK OPENING Obtain Fastpasses for Soarin' first, then see Test Track and Mission: SPACE. See remaining Future World West attractions, then tour Future World East. Tour World Showcase clockwise, starting in Mexico.

FOR PARENTS AND ADULTS WITH ONE DAY TO TOUR, ARRIVING LATE MORNING Try to obtain Fastpasses for Soarin', Test Track, or Mission: SPACE (in that order). See Future World East attractions, then Future World West. Tour World Showcase counterclockwise, starting in Canada.

FOR PARENTS AND ADULTS WITH TWO DAYS TO TOUR On Day One, see Future World East attractions and Mexico through the United States in World Showcase. On Day Two, tour Future World West and Canada through Japan.

PRELIMINARY INSTRUCTIONS FOR ALL EPCOT TOURING PLANS

1. Call ☎ 407-824-4321 in advance for the hours of operation on the day of your visit.

2. Make Advance Reservations at the Epcot full-service restaurant(s) of your choice before your visit.

THE TOURING PLANS
Epcot One-Day Touring Plan

FOR Adults and children ages 8 or older.

ASSUMES Willingness to experience all major rides and shows.

START TIME FOR FASTPASS+ Soarin', 10:25 a.m.

1. Arrive 40 minutes before official opening time. Get guide maps and the *Times Guide*.
2. As soon as the park opens, obtain Fastpasses for Soarin'.
3. In Future World East, ride Test Track.
4. Ride Mission: SPACE. Do not use Fastpass.
5. In Innoventions East, ride Sum of All Thrills.
6. Return to the Land Pavilion and ride Soarin' using the Fastpasses obtained earlier. Pick up extra passes if you want to ride again.
7. Ride Living with the Land.
8. See The Seas with Nemo & Friends and *Turtle Talk with Crush*.
9. Ride Journey into Imagination with Figment.
10. See *Captain EO*.
11. Eat lunch. We recommend Sunshine Seasons, in The Land.
12. Ride Spaceship Earth.
13. Ride *Ellen's Energy Adventure* in Future World East.
14. Tour the exhibits in Innoventions East.
15. If you have children, sign up for Agent P's World Showcase Adventure on the walk to World Showcase.
16. Take the Gran Fiesta Tour boat ride in Mexico.
17. Ride Maelstrom and tour the stave church in Norway.
18. See *Reflections of China*.
19. Tour Germany.
20. Visit Italy.
21. See *The American Adventure*.
22. Explore Japan.
23. Visit Morocco.
24. See *Impressions de France*.
25. Eat dinner.
26. Visit the United Kingdom.
27. Tour Canada and see *O Canada!*

La Cantana -Mexico

28. See *IllumiNations*. Prime viewing spots are along the lagoon between Canada and France.

Authors' Selective Epcot One-Day Touring Plan

FOR All parties.

ASSUMES Willingness to experience major rides and shows.

START TIME FOR FASTPASS+ Soarin', 10:25 a.m.

1. Arrive 40 minutes before official opening time. Get guide maps and the *Times Guide*.

2. As soon as the park opens, obtain Fastpasses for Soarin'.

3. In Future World East, ride Test Track.

4. Ride Mission: SPACE. Do not use Fastpass.

5. In Innoventions East, ride Sum of All Thrills.

6. Return to the Land Pavilion and ride Soarin' using the Fastpasses obtained earlier. Pick up extra passes if you want to ride again.

7. Ride Living with the Land.

8. See The Seas with Nemo & Friends and *Turtle Talk with Crush*.

9. See *Captain EO*.

10. Eat lunch. We recommend Sunshine Seasons, in The Land.

11. Ride Spaceship Earth.

12. Ride *Ellen's Energy Adventure* in Future World East.

13. Tour Canada and see *O Canada!*

14. See *Impressions de France*.

15. Visit Morocco.

16. Explore Japan.

17. See *The American Adventure*.

18. Visit Italy.

19. Tour Germany.

20. See *Reflections of China*.

21. Ride Maelstrom and tour the stave church in Norway.

22. Take the Gran Fiesta Tour boat ride in Mexico.

23. Eat dinner.

24. See *IllumiNations*. Prime viewing spots are along the lagoon between Canada and France.

Epcot One-Day Touring Plan for Parents with Small Children

FOR Parents with kids younger than age 8.

DAY ONE

1. Arrive 40 minutes before official opening time. Rent strollers before the park opens, if needed. Get guide maps and the *Times Guide*.

2. Ride Soarin' as soon as the park opens. If your kids aren't yet tall enough to ride, skip this step.

3. Ride Living with the Land.

4. See *The Circle of Life*.

5. Ride Journey into Imagination with Figment.

6. See *Captain EO*.

7. See The Seas with Nemo & Friends and *Turtle Talk with Crush*.

8. Eat lunch. We recommend Sunshine Seasons, in The Land.

9. Go back to your hotel for a midday break of 3–4 hours.

10. Return to the park and ride Spaceship Earth.

11. Ride *Ellen's Energy Adventure* in Future World East.

12. Sign up for Agent P's World Showcase Adventure on the walk to World Showcase.

13. See *O Canada!*

14. Eat dinner.

15. See *The American Adventure*.

16. Ride Maelstrom in Norway.

17. Take the Gran Fiesta Tour boat ride in Mexico.

18. See *The American Adventure*.

19. Visit Japan.

18. See *IllumiNations*. Prime viewing spots are along the lagoon between Canada and France.

Epcot Two-Day Early-Riser Touring Plan

FOR All parties.

DAY ONE

1. Arrive 40 minutes before official opening time. Get guide maps and the *Times Guide*.

2. At the Land Pavilion, ride Soarin'.

3. Ride Living with the Land. If you want to ride Soarin' again, get Fastpasses now.

4. See *The Circle of Life.*

5. Make dinner reservations at Guest Relations or by calling ☎ 407-WDW-DINE.

6. See The Seas with Nemo & Friends and *Turtle Talk with Crush.*

7. Ride Journey into Imagination with Figment.

8. See *Captain EO.*

9. If you have small children, sign up for Agent P's World Showcase Adventure on the way to World Showcase. Ask for a mission in either the United Kingdom or France.

10. Start a counterclockwise tour of World Showcase with the film *O Canada!* at Canada.

11. Explore the United Kingdom.

12. See *Impressions de France.*

13. Continue around the lagoon, or tour Innoventions West.

DAY TWO

1. Arrive 40 minutes before official opening time. Get guide maps and the *Times Guide.*

2. Ride Test Track. Use Fastpass if wait exceeds 30 minutes.

3. Ride Mission: SPACE.

4. Tour Innoventions East and ride Sum of All Thrills.

5. Ride *Ellen's Energy Adventure* in Future World East.

6. Ride Spaceship Earth.

7. Take the Gran Fiesta Tour boat ride at the Mexico Pavilion in World Showcase. This begins a counterclockwise tour of World Showcase.

8. Ride Maelstrom at Norway. Use Fastpass if wait exceeds 20 minutes.

9. See *Reflections of China*.

10. Visit Germany.

11. Visit Italy.

12. See *The American Adventure*.

13. Visit Japan.

14. Visit Morocco and tour the museum on the left side of the pavilion.

15. If you have kids, try Agent P's World Showcase Adventure in Japan.

16. Eat dinner and enjoy *IllumiNations*.

PART ELEVEN

DISNEY'S ANIMAL KINGDOM

AT 500 ACRES, DISNEY'S ANIMAL KINGDOM is five times the size of the Magic Kingdom and more than twice the size of Epcot, but most of its vast geography is accessible only on guided tours or as part of attractions. Animal Kingdom comprises six "lands": **The Oasis, Discovery Island, DinoLand U.S.A., Camp Minnie-Mickey, Africa,** and **Asia.** (A seventh section, **Rafiki's Planet Watch,** is touted as a land by Disney but doesn't really qualify as such in our eyes. Also, Camp Minnie-Mickey seems likely to close as of this writing. Its attractions are rumored to be relocating to make room for other projects.)

Its size notwithstanding, Disney's Animal Kingdom features a limited number of attractions: seven rides, several walk-through exhibits, an indoor theater, four amphitheaters, a conservation exhibit, and a children's playground.

With a decade and a half under its belt, Animal Kingdom has received mixed reviews. Guests complain loudly about the park layout and the necessity of backtracking through Discovery Island in order to access the various themed areas. However, most of the attractions (with one or two notable exceptions) have been well received. Also praised are the natural-habitat animal exhibits as well as the park architecture and landscaping.

■ ARRIVING

DISNEY'S ANIMAL KINGDOM IS OFF OSCEOLA PARKWAY in the southwest corner of Walt Disney World and is not too far from Blizzard Beach, the Coronado Springs Resort, and the All-Star Resorts. Animal Kingdom Lodge is about a mile away from the park on its northwest side. From Interstate 4, take Exit 64B, US 192, to the so-called Walt Disney World main entrance (World

Drive) and follow the signs to Animal Kingdom. The park has its own 6,000-car pay
parking lot with close-in parking for guests
with disabilities. Once parked, you can walk to
the entrance or catch a ride on one of Disney's
trademark trams.

unofficial TIP
Jot down the location
of your car, text yourself
a message, or snap
a picture of the row
you're parked in
with your phone or
digital camera.

Animal Kingdom is connected to other Walt
Disney World destinations by the Disney bus
system. If you're staying at a Disney resort and you plan to arrive at
Animal Kingdom entrance before park opening, use Disney transportation rather than taking your own car. The Animal Kingdom
parking lot often opens only 15 minutes before the park, causing
long lines and frustration for drivers.

OPERATING HOURS

ANIMAL KINGDOM, NOT UNEXPECTEDLY, hosted tremendous crowds during its early years. Consequently, Disney management has done a fair amount of fiddling and experimenting
with operating hours and opening procedures. Animal Kingdom's
opening time now roughly corresponds to that of the other parks.
Thus, you can expect a 9 a.m. opening during less busy times of
the year and an 8 a.m. opening during holidays and high season.
Animal Kingdom usually closes well before the other parks—
as early as 5 p.m., in fact, during off-season. More common is
a 6 or 7 p.m. closing.

Park-opening procedures at Animal Kingdom vary. Sometimes
guests arriving prior to the official opening time are admitted to
The Oasis and Discovery Island. The remainder of the park is
roped off until official opening time. The rest of the time, those
arriving early are held at the entrance turnstiles.

During slower or colder times of year, Disney may delay the
daily opening of Kali River Rapids in Asia, as well as the Boneyard
playground, the Wildlife Express Train, and Conservation Station.
These procedures may change, so check the *Times Guide* or our
mobile app, **Lines,** for the exact schedule when you arrive.

On holidays and other days of projected heavy attendance,
Disney will open the park 30–60 minutes early.

Many guests wrap up their touring and leave by 3:30 or 4 p.m.
Lines for the major rides and the 3-D movie in The Tree of Life
will usually thin appreciably between 4 p.m. and closing time. If
you arrive at 2 p.m. and take in a couple of stage shows (described
later), waits should be tolerable by the time you hit The Tree of
Life and the rides. As an added bonus for late-afternoon touring,
the animals tend to be more active.

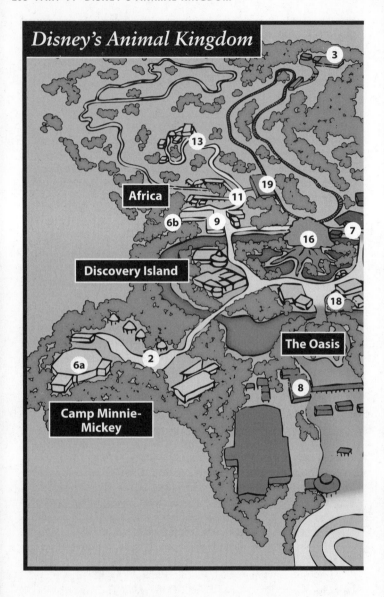

Disney's Animal Kingdom

Africa

Discovery Island

The Oasis

Camp Minnie-Mickey

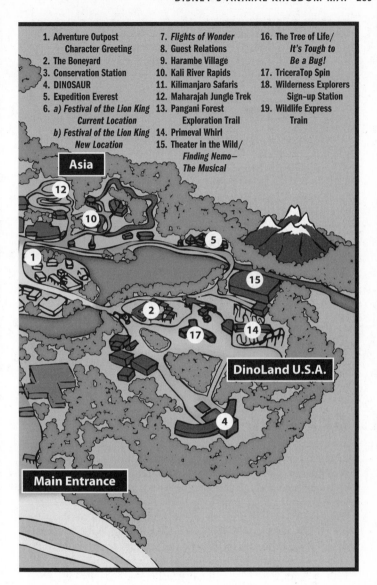

1. Adventure Outpost
   Character Greeting
2. The Boneyard
3. Conservation Station
4. DINOSAUR
5. Expedition Everest
6. *a) Festival of the Lion King*
   Current Location
   b) Festival of the Lion King
   New Location
7. *Flights of Wonder*
8. Guest Relations
9. Harambe Village
10. Kali River Rapids
11. Kilimanjaro Safaris
12. Maharajah Jungle Trek
13. Pangani Forest
    Exploration Trail
14. Primeval Whirl
15. Theater in the Wild/
    *Finding Nemo—
    The Musical*
16. The Tree of Life/
    *It's Tough to
    Be a Bug!*
17. TriceraTop Spin
18. Wilderness Explorers
    Sign-up Station
19. Wildlife Express
    Train

Asia

Main Entrance

DinoLand U.S.A.

NOT TO BE MISSED AT DISNEY'S ANIMAL KINGDOM	
AFRICA	• Kilimanjaro Safaris
ASIA	• Expedition Everest
CAMP MINNIE-MICKEY	• *Festival of the Lion King* (may relocate to Africa)
DINOLAND U.S.A.	• DINOSAUR • *Finding Nemo—The Musical*
DISCOVERY ISLAND	• *It's Tough to Be a Bug!*

Many guests wrap up their tour and leave by 3:30 or 4 p.m. Lines for the major rides and the 3-D movie in The Tree of Life will usually thin appreciably between 4 p.m. and closing time. If you arrive at 2 p.m. and take in a couple of stage shows (described later), waits should be tolerable by the time you hit The Tree of Life and the rides.

Animal Kingdom currently holds two morning Extra Magic Hours sessions per week. The extra morning session seems to be in response to the park eliminating evening Extra Magic Hours in 2011. As for the morning session, we don't think it saves you all that much time in line. Rather than be at the park before official opening, you're better off simply getting an extra hour of sleep and visiting when early entry is not in effect.

Kilimanjaro Safaris and the Pangani Forest Exploration Trail close around 30–60 minutes before sunset. Thus, as days get shorter with the change of seasons, the attractions close earlier in the day. In the fall, when the clocks are rolled back, Disney closes all animal exhibits as early as 4:45 p.m.

▮ GETTING ORIENTED

AT THE ENTRANCE PLAZA ARE TICKET KIOSKS fronting the main entrance. To your right, before the turnstiles, is an ATM. After you pass through the turnstiles, wheelchair and stroller rentals are to your right. Guest Relations—the park headquarters for information, handout park maps, entertainment schedules (*Times Guides*), missing persons, and lost and found—is to the left. Nearby are restrooms, public phones, and rental lockers. Beyond the entrance plaza, you enter **The Oasis,** a lushly vegetated network of converging pathways winding through a landscape punctuated with streams, waterfalls, and misty glades and inhabited by what Disney calls "colorful and unusual animals."

The park is arranged somewhat like the Magic Kingdom, in a hub-and-spoke configuration. The lush, tropical Oasis serves as Main Street, funneling visitors to **Discovery Island** at the center of the park. Dominated by the park's central icon, the 14-story hand-carved **Tree of Life,** Discovery Island is the park's retail and dining center. From Discovery Island, guests can access the respective themed areas of **Africa, Camp Minnie-Mickey** (while it's open), **Asia,** and **DinoLand U.S.A.** Discovery Island additionally hosts a theater attraction in The Tree of Life, and a number of short nature trails.

◼ *The* **OASIS**

THOUGH THE FUNCTIONAL PURPOSE of The Oasis is the same as that of Main Street in the Magic Kingdom (that is, to funnel guests to the center of the park), it also serves as what Disney calls a "transitional experience." In plain English, this means that it sets the stage and gets you into the right mood to enjoy Animal Kingdom. You will know the minute you pass through the turnstiles that this is not just another Main Street. Where Main Street, Hollywood Boulevard, and the Epcot entrance plaza direct you like an arrow straight into the heart of the respective parks, The Oasis immediately envelops you in an environment that is replete with choices. There is not one broad thoroughfare, but rather multiple paths. Each will deliver you to Discovery Island at the center of the park, but which path you choose and what you see along the way is up to you. There is nothing obvious about where

Disney's Animal Kingdom Services

Most of the park's service facilities are inside the main entrance and on Discovery Island as follows:

BABY CARE CENTER On Discovery Island, behind Creature Comforts

BANKING SERVICES ATMs at the main entrance, by the turnstiles, and near DINOSAUR in DinoLand U.S.A.

FILM AND CAMERAS Just inside the main entrance at Garden Gate Gifts, in Africa at Duka La Filimu and Mombasa Marketplace, and at other retail shops throughout the park

FIRST AID On Discovery Island, next to the Creature Comforts Shop

GUEST RELATIONS/INFORMATION Inside the main entrance to the left

LIVE ENTERTAINMENT AND PARADE INFORMATION Included in the park guide map, available free at Guest Relations

LOST AND FOUND Inside the main entrance to the left

LOST PERSONS Can be reported at Guest Relations and at the Baby Care Center on Discovery Island

STORAGE LOCKERS Inside the main entrance to the left

WHEELCHAIR, ECV/ESV, AND STROLLER RENTALS Inside the main entrance, to the right you are going, no Cinderella Castle or giant golf ball to beckon you. Instead there's a lush, green, canopied landscape with streams, grottoes, and waterfalls, an environment that promises adventure without revealing its nature.

The natural-habitat zoological exhibits in The Oasis are representative of the ones throughout the park. Although extraordinarily lush and beautiful, the exhibits are primarily designed for the comfort and well-being of the animals. A sign will identify the animal(s) in each exhibit, but there's no guarantee the animals will be immediately visible. Because most habitats are large and provide ample terrain for the occupants to hide, you must linger and concentrate, looking for small movements in the vegetation. When you do spot the animal, you may only make out a shadowy figure, or perhaps only a leg or a tail will be visible. In any event, don't expect the animals to stand out like a lump of coal in the snow. Animal watching Disney-style requires a sharp eye and a bit of effort.

unofficial **TIP**
The Oasis's exhibits are designed for the animals' comfort, so you need to be patient and look closely if you want to see these creatures.

TOURING TIPS The Oasis is a place at which to linger, a place to savor and appreciate. Although this is exactly what the designers intended, it will be largely lost on Disney-conditioned guests who blitz through at warp speed to queue up for the big attractions. If you're a blitzer in the morning, plan to spend some time in The Oasis on your way out of the park. The Oasis usually opens 30 minutes before and closes 30–60 minutes after the rest of the park.

DISCOVERY ISLAND

DISCOVERY ISLAND IS AN ISLAND OF tropical greenery and whimsical equatorial African architecture, executed in vibrant hues of teal, yellow, red, and blue. Connected to the other lands by bridges, the island is the hub from which guests can access the park's various themed areas. A village is arrayed in a crescent around the base of Animal Kingdom's signature landmark, **The Tree of Life.** Towering 14 stories above the village, The Tree of Life is this park's version of Cinderella Castle or Spaceship Earth. Flanked by pools, meadows, and exotic gardens populated by a diversity of birds and animals, The Tree of Life houses a theater attraction inspired by the Disney/Pixar film *A Bug's Life*.

unofficial **TIP**
It is here, in Discovery Island, that you will find **First Aid** and the **Baby Care Center.**

As you enter Discovery Island via the bridge from The Oasis and the main entrance, you will see The Tree of Life directly ahead at the 12 o'clock position, with the village at its base in a semi-circle. The bridge to Asia is to the right of the tree at the 2 o'clock position, with the bridge to DinoLand U.S.A. at roughly 4 o'clock. The bridge connecting The Oasis to Discovery Island is at the 6 o'clock position; the bridge to Camp Minnie-Mickey is at 8 o'clock; and the bridge to Africa is at 11 o'clock.

Discovery Island is the park's central shopping, dining, and services headquarters. **Island Mercantile** has the best selection of Disney-trademark merchandise. Counter-service food and snacks are available, but there are no full-service restaurants on Discovery Island (the three full-service restaurants in the park are the **Rainforest Cafe,** to the left of the main entrance; **Tusker House,** in Africa; and **Yak & Yeti Restaurant,** in Asia).

The Tree of Life: *It's Tough to Be a Bug!* ★★★★

Appeal by Age	PRESCHOOL ★★★½	GRADE SCHOOL ★★★★	TEENS ★★★★
YOUNG ADULTS ★★★★	OVER 30 ★★★★		SENIORS ★★★★½

What it is 3-D theater show. **Scope and scale** Major attraction. **When to go** Before 10:30 a.m., after 4 p.m., or use Fastpass. **Special comments** The theater is inside the tree. **Authors' rating** Zany and frenetic; ★★★★. **Duration of presentation** Approximately 7½ minutes. **Probable waiting time** 12–20 minutes.

DESCRIPTION AND COMMENTS The Tree of Life, apart from its size, is quite a work of art. Although from afar it is certainly magnificent and imposing, it is not until you examine the tree at close range that you truly appreciate its rich detail. What appears to be ancient gnarled bark is, in fact, hundreds of carvings that depict all manner of wildlife, each integrated seamlessly into the trunk, roots, and limbs of the tree. A stunning symbol of the interdependence of all living things, The Tree of Life is the most visually compelling structure to be found in any Disney park.

In sharp contrast to the grandeur of the tree is the subject of the attraction housed within its trunk. Called *It's Tough to Be a Bug!,* this humorous 3-D presentation is about the difficulties of being a very small creature. Contrasting with the relatively serious tone of Disney's Animal Kingdom in general, *It's Tough to Be a Bug!* stands virtually alone in providing some much-needed levity and whimsy. The show is similar to *Mickey's PhilharMagic* at the Magic Kingdom in that it combines a 3-D film with an arsenal of tactile and visual special effects. We rate *Bug* as not to be missed.

TOURING TIPS Although it's situated in the most eye-popping structure in the park, *It's Tough to Be a Bug!* is rarely crowded even on the busiest days, and Fastpass is almost never needed. We recommend going in the morning after you've experienced Kilimanjaro Safaris, Kali River Rapids, Expedition Everest, and DINOSAUR. If you miss the *Bug* in the morning, try again in the late afternoon.

Be advised that *It's Tough to Be a Bug!* is very intense and that the special effects will do a number on young children as well as anyone who is squeamish about insects.

◧ CAMP MINNIE-MICKEY

THIS LAND WAS DESIGNED to be the Disney characters' Animal Kingdom headquarters. Small compared with the other lands, it has a rustic, woodsy theme. As this guide was going to press in late 2013, Camp Minnie-Mickey's future was in limbo, but for the moment, in addition to hosting a character meeting-and-greeting area, it's home to a live stage show featuring Disney characters.

Situated in a cul-de-sac, Camp Minnie-Mickey has historically been a pedestrian nightmare. Lines for the stage show and from the character-greeting areas spill out into the congested walkways, making movement almost impossible. To compound the problem, hundreds of parked strollers clog the paths, squeezing the flow of traffic to a trickle. Meanwhile, hordes of guests trying to enter Camp Minnie-Mickey collide with guests trying to exit on the bridge connecting the camp to Discovery Island. It's a planning error of the first order, one that seems totally avoidable in a theme park with as much usable acreage as Animal Kingdom.

Word on the street is that most of Camp Minnie-Mickey's attractions will be relocated to other parts of the park in late 2013 or early 2014 to allow construction to begin on Animal Kingdom's new *Avatar*-themed land. Disney is mum on all of it, but we think Camp Minnie-Mickey's *Festival of the Lion King* will move to Africa, near Tusker House and the Dawa Bar.

Mickey and Minnie, for whom the camp is named, have already vacated, relocating their character meet-and-greet to the Adventurers Outpost on Discovery Island. Other characters are still on hand in Camp Minnie-Mickey, but we expect them to emigrate shortly. The as-yet-unnamed *Avatar* land is supposed to open sometime between 2016 and 2018.

Character Trails

DESCRIPTION AND COMMENTS Characters can be found at the end of each of several "character trails." Each trail has its own private reception area and, of course, its own queue. A sign in front of each queue tells you to which character the path leads. Mickey and Mickey, of course, were once constants, along with Goofy and Pluto. For the moment, the character lineup includes Donald, Chip 'n' Dale, Pocahontas, and Baloo. Disney has occasionally supplemented these with characters from its latest film, if the movie has anything to do with nature, animals, or the environment.

TOURING TIPS Characters usually appear an hour after the rest of the park opens. Waiting in line to see the characters can be extremely time-consuming. Assuming the trails haven't closed by the time you visit, we recommend going early in the morning or late in the afternoon. Because Animal Kingdom has fewer attractions than the other parks, expect to find a disproportionate number of guests in Camp Minnie-Mickey. If the place is really mobbed, you may want to consider meeting the characters in one of the other parks. Ditto for the stage show.

Festival of the Lion King ★★★★

Appeal by Age	PRESCHOOL ★★★★½	GRADE SCHOOL ★★★★½	TEENS ★★★★½
YOUNG ADULTS ★★★★½	OVER 30 ★★★★½		SENIORS ★★★★½

What it is Theater-in-the-round stage show. **Scope and scale** Major attraction. **When to go** Before 11 a.m. or after 4 p.m. **Special comments** Performance times are listed in the handout park map or *Times Guide*. **Authors' rating** Upbeat and spectacular, not to be missed; ★★★★. **Duration of presentation** 25 minutes. **Preshow entertainment** None. When to arrive 20–35 minutes before showtime.

DESCRIPTION AND COMMENTS This energetic production, inspired by Disney's *Lion King* feature, is part stage show, part parade, part circus. Guests are seated in four sets of bleachers surrounding the stage and organized into separate cheering sections, which are called on to make elephant, warthog, giraffe, and lion noises (you won't be alone if you don't know how to make a giraffe or warthog noise). There is a great deal of parading around, some acrobatics, and a lot of singing and dancing. By our count, every tune from *The Lion King* is belted out and reprised several times. No joke—if you don't know the words to all the songs by the end of the show, you must have been asleep.

TOURING TIPS *Festival of the Lion King* may be relocating to Africa, near Tusker House. Check your park map for its location when you visit. Your best bet is to go to the first show in the morning or to one of the last two performances in the evening. To see the show during the more crowded midday, you'll need to queue up at least 35–45 minutes before showtime. To minimize standing in the hot sun, refrain from hopping in line until the Disney people begin directing guests to the far-right queue. If you have small children or short adults in your party, sit higher up in the bleachers. The first five rows in particular have very little rise, making it difficult for those in rows two through five to see.

◨ AFRICA

AFRICA IS THE LARGEST of Animal Kingdom's lands, and guests enter through **Harambe,** a Disneyfied version of a modern rural African town. A market is equipped with modern cash registers; dining options consist of a sit-down buffet, limited counter service, and snack stands. What distinguishes Harambe is its understatement: Far from the stereotypical great-white-hunter image of an African town, Harambe is definitely (and realistically) not exotic. The buildings, while interesting, are architecturally simple. Though better maintained and more idealized than the real McCoy, Disney's Harambe would be a lot more at home in Kenya than the Magic Kingdom's Main Street would be in small-town Missouri.

Harambe serves as the gateway to the African veldt habitat, Animal Kingdom's largest and most ambitious zoological exhibit. Access to the veldt is via the **Kilimanjaro Safaris** attraction, at the end of Harambe's main drag near the fat-trunked baobab tree. Harambe is also the departure point for the train to **Rafiki's Planet Watch** and **Conservation Station**, the park's veterinary headquarters.

Kilimanjaro Safaris (Fastpass) ★★★★★

Appeal by Age PRESCHOOL ★★★★½ GRADE SCHOOL ★★★★½ TEENS ★★★★½ YOUNG ADULTS ★★★★½ OVER 30 ★★★★½ SENIORS ★★★★½

What it is Truck ride through an African wildlife reservation. **Scope and scale** Super-headliner. **When to go** As soon as the park opens or in the 2 hours before closing, or use Fastpass. **Authors' rating** Truly exceptional; not to be missed; ★★★★★. **Duration of ride** About 20 minutes. **Average wait in line per 100 people ahead of you** 4 minutes; assumes Full-capacity operation with 18-second dispatch interval. Loading speed Fast.

DESCRIPTION AND COMMENTS The park's premier zoological attraction, Kilimanjaro Safaris offers an exceptionally realistic, albeit brief, imitation of an actual African photo safari. Thirty-two guests at a time board tall, open safari vehicles and are dispatched into a simulated African veldt habitat. Animals such as zebras, wildebeests, impalas, Thomson's gazelles, giraffes, and even rhinos roam apparently free, while predators such as lions, as well as potentially dangerous large animals like hippos, are separated from both prey and guests by all-but-invisible, natural-appearing barriers. Although the animals have more than 100 acres of savanna, woodland, streams, and rocky hills to call home, careful placement of water holes, forage, and salt licks ensures that the critters are hanging out by the road when safari vehicles roll by.

A scripted narration provides a storyline about poachers in the area while an onboard guide points out and identifies the various animals encountered. Toward the end of the ride, the safari chases the poachers, who are after elephants.

Having traveled in Kenya and Tanzania, I (Bob) will tell you that Disney has done an amazing job of replicating the sub-Saharan east-African landscape. The main difference that an east African would notice is that Disney's version is greener and, generally speaking, less barren. As on a real African safari, what animals you see, and how many, is pretty much a matter of luck. We've experienced Kilimanjaro Safaris more than 100 times and had a different experience on each trip.

Winding through the Safaris is Disney's **Wild Africa Trek,** a behind-the-scenes tour that takes you into several of the attraction's animal enclosures (3 hours, $201 per person, guests age 8 and older). As you drive past the hippo pool or over the crocodile pool, look up for a series of rope bridges towering far above the ground. You may see Trekkers on tour.

TOURING TIPS Kilimanjaro Safaris is Animal Kingdom's number-two draw behind Expedition Everest. This is good news: by distributing guests more evenly throughout the park, Expedition Everest makes it unnecessary to run to the Kilimanjaro Safaris first thing in the morning. Our Animal Kingdom touring plan has you obtain Fastpasses for the safaris just before lunch. While your Fastpass return window approaches, you'll have plenty of time to eat and tour the rest of Africa. Before Expedition Everest, seeing the Safaris early meant backtracking to Africa later in the day to see exhibits and attractions that were not open first thing in the morning; our touring plan eliminates all of that extra walking, too.

Waits for Kilimanjaro Safaris diminish in late afternoon, sometimes as early as 3:30 p.m., but more commonly somewhat later. If the wait exceeds 30 minutes when you arrive, by all means use Fastpass. The downside to Fastpass, and the reason we prefer that you ride around lunchtime, is that there aren't many other attractions in Africa to occupy your attention while you wait for your Fastpass return time. This means you will probably be touring somewhere far removed when it's time to backtrack to Safaris.

If you want to take photos, be advised that the vehicle isn't guaranteed to stop at any location, although the drivers try their best to do so when big animals are sighted. Be prepared to snap at any time. Also, don't worry about the ride itself: It really isn't very rough. Finally, the only thing that a young child might find intimidating is crossing an "old bridge" that seems to collapse under your truck.

Pangani Forest Exploration Trail ★★★

Appeal by Age	PRESCHOOL ★★★★	GRADE SCHOOL ★★★★	TEENS ★★★★
YOUNG ADULTS ★★★★	OVER 30 ★★★★		SENIORS ★★★★½

What it is Walk-through zoological exhibit. **Scope and scale** Major attraction. **When to go** Anytime. **Authors' rating** ★★★★. **Duration of tour** About 20–25 minutes.

DESCRIPTION AND COMMENTS Because guests disembark from the safari at the entrance to the Pangani Forest Exploration Trail, many guests try the trail immediately after the safari. Winding between the domain of two troops of lowland gorillas, it's hard to see what, if anything, separates you from the primates. Also on the trail are a hippo pool with an underwater-viewing area, and a naked-mole-rat exhibit (we promise we're not making this up). A highlight of the trail is an exotic bird aviary so craftily designed that you can barely tell you're in an enclosure.

TOURING TIPS The Pangani Forest Exploration Trail is lush, beautiful, and jammed to the gills with people much of the time. Guests exiting the safari can choose between returning to Harambe or walking the Pangani Forest Exploration Trail. Not unexpectedly, many opt for the trail. Thus, when the safari is operating at full tilt, it spews hundreds of guests every couple of minutes onto the Exploration Trail. The one-way trail in turn becomes so clogged that nobody can move or see much of anything. After a minute or two, however, you catch the feel of the mob moving forward in small lurches. From then on you shift, elbow, grunt, and wriggle your way along, every so often coming to an animal exhibit. Here you endeavor to work your way close to the rail but are opposed by people trapped against the rail who are trying to rejoin the surging crowd. The animals, as well as their natural-habitat enclosures, are pretty nifty if you can fight close enough to see them.

Clearly this attraction is either badly designed, misplaced, or both. Your only real chance for enjoying it is to walk through before 10 a.m. (i.e., before the safari hits full stride) or after 2:30 p.m.

Another strategy, especially if you're more into the wildlife than the thrill rides, is to head for Kilimanjaro Safaris as soon as the park opens and get a Fastpass instead of riding. Early in the morning, the return window will be short, just short enough, in fact, for an uncrowded, leisurely tour of the Pangani Forest Exploration Trail before you go on safari.

RAFIKI'S PLANET WATCH

THIS AREA ISN'T REALLY a "land" and not really an attraction either. Our best guess is that Disney uses the name as an umbrella for Conservation Station, the petting zoo, and the environmental exhibits accessible from Harambe via the Wildlife Express Train. Presumably, Disney hopes that invoking Rafiki (a beloved character from *The Lion King*) will stimulate guests to make the effort to check out things in this far-flung outpost of the park.

Conservation Station and Affection Section ★★★

Appeal by Age	PRESCHOOL ★★★½	GRADE SCHOOL ★★★★	TEENS ★★★½
YOUNG ADULTS ★★★	OVER 30 ★★★★½		SENIORS ★★★★½

What it is Behind-the-scenes walk-through educational exhibit and petting zoo. **Scope and scale** Minor attraction. **When to go** Anytime. **Special comments** Opens 30 minutes after the rest of the park. **Authors' rating** Evolving; ★★★. Probable waiting time None.

DESCRIPTION AND COMMENTS Conservation Station is Animal Kingdom's veterinary and conservation headquarters. Located on the perimeter of the African section of the park, Conservation Station is, strictly speaking, a backstage, working facility. Here guests can meet wildlife experts, observe some of the

Station's ongoing projects, and learn about the behind-the-scenes operations of the park. The Station includes, among other things, a rehabilitation area for injured animals and a nursery for recently born (or hatched) critters. Vets and other experts are on hand to answer questions.

While there are several permanent exhibits, including the Affection Section (an animal-petting area), what you see at Conservation Station will largely depend on what's going on when you arrive. On the days we visited, there wasn't enough happening to warrant waiting in line twice (coming and going) for the train.

You can access Conservation Station by taking the Wildlife Express train directly from Harambe. To return to the center of the park, continue the loop from Conservation Station back to Harambe.

TOURING TIPS Conservation Station is interesting, but you have to invest a little effort, and it helps to be inquisitive. Because it's so removed from the rest of the park, you'll never bump into Conservation Station unless you take the train.

Habitat Habit!

DESCRIPTION AND COMMENTS Listed on park maps as an attraction is Habitat Habit!, on the pedestrian path between the train station and Conservation Station. It consists of a tiny collection of signs about wildlife and a few cotton-top tamarins. To call it an attraction is absurd.

Wildlife Express Train ★★

Appeal by Age	PRESCHOOL ★★★½	GRADE SCHOOL ★★★½	TEENS ★★★½
YOUNG ADULTS ★★★		OVER 30 ★★★½	SENIORS ★★★½

What it is Scenic railroad ride to Rafiki's Planet Watch and Conservation Station. **Scope and scale** Minor attraction. **When to go** Anytime. **Special comments** Opens 30 minutes after the rest of the park. **Authors' rating** Ho-hum; ★★. **Duration of ride** About 5–7 minutes one-way. **Average wait in line per 100 people ahead of you** 9 minutes. Loading speed Moderate.

DESCRIPTION AND COMMENTS A transportation ride that snakes behind the African wildlife reserve as it makes its loop connecting Harambe to Rafiki's Planet Watch and Conservation Station. En route, you see the nighttime enclosures for the animals that populate the Kilimanjaro Safaris. Similarly, returning to Harambe, you see the backstage areas of Asia. Regardless of the direction in which you're heading, the sights are not especially interesting.

TOURING TIPS Most guests will embark for Rafiki's Planet Watch and Conservation Station after experiencing the Kilimanjaro Safaris and the Pangani Forest Exploration Trail. Thus, the train begins to get crowded between 10 and 11 a.m. Though you may catch a glimpse of several species from the train, it can't compare to Kilimanjaro Safaris for seeing the animals.

ASIA

CROSSING THE ASIA BRIDGE from Discovery Island, you enter Asia through the village of Anandapur, a veritable collage of Asian themes inspired by the architecture and ruins of India, Thailand, Indonesia, and Nepal. Situated near the bank of the Chakranadi River (translation: "the river that runs in circles") and surrounded by lush vegetation, Anandapur provides access to a gibbon exhibit and to Asia's two feature attractions, the **Kali River Rapids** whitewater-raft ride and **Expedition Everest**. Also in Asia is **Flights of Wonder,** an educational production about birds.

Expedition Everest—yep, another mountain, and at 200 feet, the tallest in Florida—is a super-headliner roller coaster. You board an old mountain railway destined for the foot of Mount Everest that ends up racing both forward and backward through caverns and frigid canyons en route to paying a social call on the Abominable Snowman. Expedition Everest is billed as a "family thrill ride," which means simply that it's more like Big Thunder Mountain Railroad than like the Rock 'n' Roller Coaster.

Expedition Everest *(Fastpass)* ★★★★½

Appeal by Age	PRESCHOOL ★★★	GRADE SCHOOL ★★★★½	TEENS ★★★★★
YOUNG ADULTS ★★★★★		OVER 30 ★★★★★	SENIORS ★★★★

What it is High-speed outdoor roller coaster through Nepalese mountain village. **Scope and scale** Super-headliner. **When to go** Before 9:30 a.m. or after 3 p.m., or use Fastpass. **Special comments** 44" minimum height requirement. Switching-off option provided (see page 338). **Authors' rating** Contains some of the park's most stunning visual elements; not to be missed; ★★★★½. **Duration of ride** 3½ minutes. **Average wait in line per 100 people ahead of you** Just under 4 minutes; assumes 2 tracks operating. **Loading speed** Moderate–fast.

DESCRIPTION AND COMMENTS The first true roller coaster in Disney's Animal Kingdom, Expedition Everest has boasted the park's longest waits in line from the moment it opened—and for good reason. Your journey begins with an elaborate waiting area modeled after a Nepalese village. Then you board an old train headed for the top of Mount Everest and embark on a ride that results in a high-speed encounter with the Abominable Snowman himself.

The ride consists of tight turns (some while traveling backwards), hills, and dips, but no loops or inversions. From your departure at the loading station through your first high-speed descent, you'll see some of the most spectacular panoramas available in Walt Disney World. On a clear day you'll be able to view Coronado Springs Resort, Epcot's Spaceship Earth, and possibly downtown Orlando. But look quickly, because you'll immediately be propelled, projectile-like, through the inner and outer reaches of the mountain. The final drop and last few turns are among Disney's best-designed coaster effects. A few minor criticisms: At a couple of points, your vehicle is stopped while the ride's track is reconfigured, affecting the attraction's continuity. And while the Yeti Audio-Animatronic is undoubtedly impressive, he breaks down more than a 30-year old Fiat. But don't let these small shortcomings stop you from riding.

The coaster reaches a top speed of around 50 mph, just about twice that of Space Mountain, so expect to see the usual warnings for health and safety. The first few seats of these vehicles offer the best front-seat experience of any Disney coaster, indoor or out. If at all possible, ask to sit up front. Also, look for the animal droppings on display in the Fastpass return line—a deliberate attempt at verisimilitude, or did Disney run out of money for ride props and use whatever they could find? You decide.

TOURING TIPS Get Fastpasses for Everest first thing in the morning. Alternatively, ride immediately after the park opens or the last hour the park is open. If using Fastpass in the morning, try to tour DinoLand U.S.A. before you return; Kali River Rapids and *Flights of Wonder* may not open with the rest of Asia, so you'll backtrack less if you can get the must-see attractions in DinoLand covered early.

Flights of Wonder ★★★★

| Appeal by Age | PRESCHOOL ★★★★ | GRADE SCHOOL ★★★★½ | TEENS ★★★★ |
| YOUNG ADULTS ★★★★ | | OVER 30 ★★★★½ | SENIORS ★★★★½ |

What it is Stadium show about birds. **Scope and scale** Major attraction. **When to go** Anytime. **Special comments** Performance times listed in handout park map or *Times Guide*. **Authors' rating** Unique; ★★★★. **Duration of presentation** 30 minutes. **Preshow entertainment** None. **When to arrive** 20–30 minutes before showtime.

DESCRIPTION AND COMMENTS Both interesting and fun, *Flights of Wonder* is well paced and showcases a surprising number of different bird species. The show focuses on the natural talents and characteristics of the various species, so don't expect to see, say, parrots riding bicycles. The natural behaviors, however, far surpass any tricks learned from humans. Overall, the presentation is fascinating, and it exceeds most guests' expectations.

TOURING TIPS *Flights of Wonder* plays at the stadium located near the Asia Bridge on the walkway into Asia. Though the stadium is covered, it's not air-conditioned; thus, early-morning and late-afternoon performances are more comfortable.

Kali River Rapids *(Fastpass)* ★★★½

| Appeal by Age | PRESCHOOL ★★★★ | GRADE SCHOOL ★★★★½ | TEENS ★★★★ |
| YOUNG ADULTS ★★★★ | | OVER 30 ★★★★½ | SENIORS ★★★★½ |

What it is Whitewater-raft ride. **Scope and scale** Headliner. **When to go** First or last hour the park is open or use Fastpass. **Special comments** You're guaranteed to get wet. Opens 30 minutes after the rest of the park. 38" minimum height requirement. Switching-off option available (see page 79). **Authors' rating** Short but scenic; ★★★½. **Duration of ride** About 5 minutes. **Average wait in line per 100 people ahead of you** 5 minutes. **Loading speed** Moderate.

DESCRIPTION AND COMMENTS Whitewater-raft rides have been a hot-weather favorite of theme park patrons for more than 20 years. The ride itself consists of an un-guided trip down a man-made river in a circular rubber raft with a platform seating 12 people mounted on top. The raft essentially floats free in the current and is washed downstream through rapids and waves. Because the river is fairly wide, with numerous currents, eddies, and obstacles, there is no telling ex-actly where the raft will drift. Thus, each trip is different and exciting. At the end of the ride, a conveyor belt hauls the raft up to be unloaded and prepared for the next group of guests.

What distinguishes Kali River Rapids from other theme park raft rides is Disney's trademark attention to visual detail. Where many raft rides essentially plunge down a concrete ditch, Kali River Rapids flows through a dense rainforest, past waterfalls, temple ruins, and bamboo thickets, emerging into a cleared area where greedy loggers have ravaged the forest, and finally drifting back under the tropical canopy as the river cycles back to Anandapur. Along the way, your raft runs a gauntlet of rag-ing cataracts, logjams, and other dangers.

TOURING TIPS This attraction is hugely popular on hot summer days. Ride Kali River Rapids during the first or last hour the park is open or use Fastpass. Again, you'll probably get drenched on this ride—we recommend wearing shorts to the park and bringing along a jumbo-sized trash bag or bin liner, as well as a smaller plastic bag. Before boarding the raft, take off your socks and punch a hole in your jumbo bag for your head. Though you can also cut holes for your arms, you'll probably stay drier with your arms inside the bag. Use the smaller plastic bag to wrap around your shoes. If you're worried about mussing your 'do, bring a third bag for your head.

Other tips for staying dry (make that drier) include wearing as little as the law and Disney allow and storing a change of clothes in a park rental locker. Sandals are the perfect foot-wear for water rides. If you don't have sandals, try to prop your feet up above the bottom of the raft.

Maharajah Jungle Trek ★★★★

Appeal by Age PRESCHOOL ★★★★ GRADE SCHOOL ★★★★ TEENS ★★★★
YOUNG ADULTS ★★★★ OVER 30 ★★★★ SENIORS ★★★★½

What it is Walk-through zoological exhibit. **Scope and scale** Headliner. **When to go** Anytime. **Special comments** Opens 30 minutes after the rest of the park. **Authors' rating** A standard-setter for natural habitat design; ★★★★. Duration of tour About 20–30 minutes.

DESCRIPTION AND COMMENTS The Maharajah Jungle Trek is a zoological nature walk similar to the Pangani Forest Explora-tion Trail, but with an Asian setting and Asian animals. You start with Komodo dragons and then work up to Malayan tapirs. Next is a cave with fruit bats. Ruins of the maharaja's palace provide the setting for Bengal tigers. From the top of a parapet in the palace you can view a herd of blackbuck antelope and Asian deer. The trek concludes with an aviary.

Labyrinthine, overgrown, and elaborately detailed, the temple ruin would be a compelling attraction even without the animals. Throw in a few bats, bucks, and Bengals and you're in for a treat.

TOURING TIPS The Jungle Trek does not get as jammed up as the Pangani Forest Exploration Trail and is a good choice for midday touring when most of the other attractions are crowded. The downside, of course, is that the exhibit showcases tigers, tapirs, and other creatures that might not be as active in the heat of the day as mad dogs and Englishmen.

DINOLAND U.S.A.

THIS MOST TYPICALLY DISNEY OF ANIMAL KINGDOM'S lands is a cross between an anthropological dig and a quirky roadside attraction. Accessible via the bridge from Discovery Island, DinoLand U.S.A. is home to a children's play area, a nature trail, a 1,500-seat amphitheater, and **DINOSAUR,** one of Animal Kingdom's two thrill rides.

The Boneyard ★★★½

Appeal by Age	PRESCHOOL ★★★★½	GRADE SCHOOL ★★★★½	TEENS ★★★½
YOUNG ADULTS ★★½	OVER 30 ★★★		SENIORS ★★★

What it is Elaborate playground. **Scope and scale** Diversion. **When to go** Anytime. **Special comments** Opens 30 minutes after the rest of the park. **Authors' rating** Stimulating fun for children; ★★★½. **Duration of visit** Varies. **Probable waiting time** None.

DESCRIPTION AND COMMENTS This attraction is an elaborate playground, particularly appealing to kids age 12 and younger, but visually appealing to all ages. Arranged in the form of a rambling open-air dig site, The Boneyard offers plenty of opportunity for exploration and letting off steam. Playground equipment consists of the "skeletons" of *Triceratops, T. rex, Brachiosaurus,* and the like, on which children can swing, slide, and climb. In addition, there are sandpits for little ones to rummage through for bones and fossils.

TOURING TIPS Not the cleanest Disney attraction, but certainly one where younger children will want to spend some time. Aside from getting dirty, or at least sandy, be aware that The Boneyard gets mighty hot in the Florida sun. Keep your kids well hydrated and drag them into the shade from time to time. If your children will let you, save the playground until after you have experienced the main attractions. Because The Boneyard is so close to the center of the park, it's easy to stop in whenever your kids get itchy. While the little ones clamber around on giant femurs and ribs, you can sip a tall cool one in the shade (still keeping an eye on them, of course).

Be aware that The Boneyard rambles over about a half-acre and is multistoried. It's pretty easy to lose sight of a small child in the playground. Fortunately, there's only one entrance and exit.

DINOSAUR *(Fastpass)* ★★★★½

Appeal by Age	PRESCHOOL ★★½	GRADE SCHOOL ★★★½	TEENS ★★★★½
YOUNG ADULTS ★★★★	OVER 30 ★★★★		SENIORS ★★★½

What it is Motion-simulator dark ride. **Scope and scale** Super-headliner. **When to go** Before 10:30 a.m., after 4:30 p.m., or use Fastpass. **Special comments** 40" minimum height requirement. Switching-off option provided (see page 79). **Authors' rating** Not to be missed; ★★★★½. **Duration of ride** 3½ minutes. **Average wait in line per 100 people ahead of you** 3 minutes; assumes full-capacity operation with 18-second dispatch interval. **Loading speed** Fast.

DESCRIPTION AND COMMENTS DINOSAUR is a combination track ride and motion simulator. In addition to moving along a cleverly hidden track, the ride vehicle also bucks and pitches (the simulator part) in sync with the visuals and special effects. The plot has you traveling back in time on a mission of rescue and conservation. Your objective: to haul back a living dinosaur before the species becomes extinct. Whoever is operating the clock, however, cuts it a little close, and you arrive on the prehistoric scene just as a giant asteroid is hurtling toward Earth. General mayhem ensues as you evade carnivorous predators, catch Barney, and get the heck out of Dodge before the asteroid hits.

Elaborate even by Disney standards, the attraction provides a tense, frenetic ride embellished by the entire Imagineering arsenal of high-tech gimmickry. Although the ride is jerky, it's not too rough for seniors. The menacing dinosaurs, however, make DINOSAUR a no-go for younger kids.

TOURING TIPS Disney situated DINOSAUR in such a remote corner of the park that guests have to poke around to find it. This, in conjunction with the overwhelming popularity of Kilimanjaro Safaris and Expedition Everest, makes DINOSAUR the easiest super-headliner attraction at Disney World to get on. We recommend, nonetheless, that you ride early after obtaining Fastpasses for Expedition Everest.

Primeval Whirl *(Fastpass)* ★★★

Appeal by Age	PRESCHOOL ★★★½	GRADE SCHOOL ★★★★	TEENS ★★★★
YOUNG ADULTS ★★★½	OVER 30 ★★★½		SENIORS ★★★

What it is Small coaster. **Scope and scale** Minor attraction. **When to go** First or last hour the park is open, or use Fastpass. **Special comments** 48" minimum height requirement. Switching-off option provided (see page 79). **Authors' rating** "Wild mouse" on steroids; ★★★. **Duration of ride** Almost 2½ minutes. **Average wait in line per 100 people ahead of you** 4½ minutes. **Loading speed** Slow.

DESCRIPTION AND COMMENTS Primeval Whirl is a small coaster with short drops and curves, and it runs through the jaws of a dinosaur, among other things. What makes this coaster different is that the cars also spin. You can't control the spinning—it starts and stops according to how the ride is programmed. Sometimes the spin is braked to a jarring halt after half a revolution, and sometimes it's allowed to make one or two complete turns. The complete spins are fun, but the screeching-stop half-spins are almost painful. If you subtract the time it takes to ratchet up the first hill, the actual ride time is about 90 seconds.

TOURING TIPS As for Space Mountain, the ride is duplicated side-by-side, but with only one queue. When it runs smoothly, about 700 people per side can whirl in an hour—a goodly number for this type of attraction, but not enough to preclude long waits on busy-to-moderate days. If you want to ride, try to get on before 10 a.m.

Theater in the Wild: *Finding Nemo—The Musical* ★★★★

Appeal by Age	PRESCHOOL ★★★★½	GRADE SCHOOL ★★★★½	TEENS ★★★★
YOUNG ADULTS ★★★★½		OVER 30 ★★★★½	SENIORS ★★★★½

What it is Enclosed venue for live stage shows. **Scope and scale** Major attraction. **When to go** Anytime. **Special comments** Performance times are listed in the handout park map or *Times Guide*. **Authors' rating** Not to be missed; ★★★★. **Duration of presentation** About 35 minutes. **When to arrive** 30 minutes before showtime.

DESCRIPTION AND COMMENTS Another chapter in the Pixarization of Disney theme parks, *Finding Nemo* is arguably the most elaborate live show in any Disney World theme park. Incorporating dancing, special effects, and sophisticated digital backdrops of the undersea world, it features on-stage human performers retelling Nemo's story with colorful, larger-than-life puppets. To be fair, "puppets" doesn't adequately convey the size or detail of these props, many of which are as big as a car and require two people to manipulate. An original musical score was written for the show, which is a must-see for most Animal Kingdom guests. A few scenes, such as one in which Nemo's mom is eaten, may be too intense for some very small children. Some of the midshow musical numbers slow the pace, so the main concern for parents is whether the kids can sit still for an entire show. With that in mind, we advise parents to catch an afternoon performance—around 3 p.m. would be great—after seeing the rest of Animal Kingdom. If the kids get restless, you can either leave the show and catch the afternoon parade, or end your day at the park.

TOURING TIPS To get a seat, show up 20–25 minutes in advance for morning and late-afternoon shows, and 30–35 minutes in advance for shows scheduled between noon and 4:30 p.m. Access to the theater is via a relatively narrow pedestrian path—if you arrive as the previous show is letting out, you'll feel like a salmon swimming upstream.

TriceraTop Spin ★★

Appeal by Age	PRESCHOOL ★★★★½	GRADE SCHOOL ★★★★	TEENS ★★★
YOUNG ADULTS ★★½		OVER 30 ★★★	SENIORS ★★★½

What it is Hub-and-spoke midway ride. **Scope and scale** Minor attraction. **When to go** Before noon or after 3 p.m. **Authors' rating** Dumbo's prehistoric forebear; ★★. **Duration of ride** 1½ minutes. **Average wait in line per 100 people ahead of you** 10 minutes. **Loading speed** Slow.

DESCRIPTION AND COMMENTS Another Dumbo-like ride. Here you spin around a Central Plaza until a dinosaur pops out of the top of the hub. You'd think with the collective imagination of the Walt Disney Company, they'd come up with something a little more creative.

TOURING TIPS An attraction for the children. Come back later if the wait exceeds 20 minutes.

LIVE ENTERTAINMENT *in* DISNEY'S ANIMAL KINGDOM

AFTERNOON PARADE Mickey's Jammin' Jungle Parade is comparable to the parades at the other parks, complete with floats, Disney characters (especially those from *The Lion King*, *The Jungle Book*, and *Song of the South*), skaters, acrobats, and stilt walkers.

Though subject to change, the parade starts in Africa, crosses the bridge to Discovery Island, proceeds counterclockwise around the island, and then crosses the bridge to Asia. In Asia, the parade turns left and follows the walkway paralleling the river back to Africa. The walking path between Africa and Asia has several small cutouts that offer good views of the parade and excellent sun protection. As it's used mainly as a walkway, the path is also relatively uncrowded. (*Note:* The paths on Discovery Island get very crowded, making it easy to lose members of your party.)

ANIMAL ENCOUNTERS Throughout the day, knowledgeable Disney staff conduct impromptu short lectures on specific animals at the park. Look for a cast member in safari garb holding a bird, reptile, or small mammal.

GOODWILL AMBASSADORS A number of Asian and African natives are on-hand throughout the park. Both gracious and knowledgeable, they are delighted to discuss their country and its wildlife. Look for them in Harambe and along the Pangani Forest Exploration Trail in Africa, and in Anandapur and along the Maharajah Jungle Trek in Asia. They can also be found near the main entrance and at The Oasis.

KIDS' DISCOVERY CLUB Informal, creative activity stations offer kids ages 4–8 a structured learning experience as they tour Animal Kingdom. Set up along walkways in six themed areas, Discovery Club stations are manned by cast members who supervise a different activity at each station. A souvenir logbook, available free, is stamped at each station when the child completes the craft or exercise. Children enjoy collecting the stamps and noodling the puzzles in the logbook while in attraction lines.

STAGE SHOWS These are performed daily at the Lion King Theater in Camp Minnie-Mickey, at the Theater in the Wild in DinoLand U.S.A., and at the stadium in Asia. Shows at Camp Minnie-Mickey and DinoLand U.S.A. feature the Disney/Pixar characters.

STREET PERFORMERS These can be found most of the time at Discovery Island, at Harambe in Africa, at Anandapur in Asia, and in DinoLand U.S.A.

Far and away the most intriguing of these performers is the one you can't see—at least not at first. Totally bedecked in foliage and luxuriant vines is a stilt walker named **DiVine,** who blends so completely with Animal Kingdom's dense flora that you never notice her until she moves. We've seen guests standing less than a foot away gasp in amazement as DiVine brushes them with a leafy tendril. Usually found on the path between Asia and Africa, DiVine is a must-see. If you don't encounter her, ask a cast member when and where she can be found. Video of her is available at **YouTube** (go to **youtube.com** and search for "DiVine Disney's Animal Kingdom"), and excellent photographs of her are featured at **arondaparks.com/DeVine.htm.**

DISNEY'S ANIMAL KINGDOM TOURING PLANS

TOURING ANIMAL KINGDOM is not as complicated as touring the other parks because it has fewer attractions. Also, most Animal Kingdom rides, shows, and zoological exhibits are oriented to the entire family, thus eliminating differences of opinion regarding how to spend the day. At Animal Kingdom, the whole family can pretty much see and enjoy everything together.

Because there are fewer attractions than at the other parks, expect the crowds at Animal Kingdom to be more concentrated. If a line seems unusually long, ask an Animal Kingdom cast member what the estimated wait is. If the wait exceeds your tolerance, try the same attraction again after

unofficial **TIP**
For the time being, the limited number of attractions in Disney's Animal Kingdom can work to your advantage.

3 p.m., while a show is in progress at the Theater in the Wild in DinoLand U.S.A., or while some special event is going on.

In anticipation of Disney introducing Fastpass+ (see page 26), we've listed the approximate Fastpass+ return times for which you should attempt to make reservations. (The touring plan should work with anything close to the times shown.) In case Disney limits how many Fastpass+ reservations you can get, we've listed in the plans the attractions most likely to need Fastpass+ too. No matter what Disney does, we'll have the latest Fastpass+ and touring plan tools on **touringplans.com**.

"NOT A TOURING PLAN" TOURING PLANS

FOR THE TYPE-B READER, these touring plans avoid detailed, step-by-step strategies for saving every last minute in line. Use these guidelines to avoid the longest waits in line while having maximum flexibility to see whatever interests you in a particular part of the park.

FOR PARENTS AND ADULTS ARRIVING AT PARK OPENING Obtain Fastpasses for Expedition Everest in Asia, then begin a land-by-land counterclockwise tour of the park, starting in DinoLand U.S.A. Work in shows as you near them, but leave *Finding Nemo— The Musical* for last.

FOR PARENTS AND ADULTS ARRIVING LATE MORNING Obtain Fastpasses for Kilimanjaro Safaris, then begin a counterclockwise tour of the park starting in Africa, saving Kali River Rapids and Expedition Everest for last.

BEFORE YOU GO

1. Call ☎ 407-824-4321 before you go to check the park's hours of operation.
2. Purchase your admission prior to arrival.

Disney's Animal Kingdom One-Day Touring Plan

The Animal Kingdom One-Day Touring Plan assumes a willingness to experience all major rides and shows. Be forewarned that DINOSAUR, Primeval Whirl, and Kali River Rapids are sometimes frightening to children under age 8. Similarly, the theater attraction at The Tree of Life might be too intense for some preschoolers. When following the touring plan, simply skip any attraction you do not wish to experience.

START TIMES FOR FASTPASS+ Expedition Everest, 10:10 a.m.; Kilimanjaro Safaris, 12:30 p.m.

1. Arrive 40 minutes prior to opening.

2. Send one member of your party to get Fastpasses for Expedition Everest in Asia. The group should meet up at TriceraTop Spin in DinoLand U.S.A.

3. If you have small children, ride TriceraTop Spin.

4. Ride Primeval Whirl.

5. Follow the signs to DINOSAUR and ride.

6. In Asia, ride Kali River Rapids.

7. Ride Expedition Everest using the Fastpasses obtained earlier.

8. See *Flights of Wonder*. If wait exceeds 20 minutes, walk the Maharajah Jungle Trek first, then see the show.

9. Walk the Maharajah Jungle Trek if you haven't already done so.

10. Visit Africa and send one member of your party to obtain Fastpasses for Kilimanjaro Safaris.

11. Eat lunch. *Flame Tree BBQ*

12. Take the Wildlife Express Train from Africa to Conservation Station and Rafiki's Planet Watch. Tour the exhibits and take the train back to Africa.

13. Experience Kilimanjaro Safaris using the Fastpasses obtained earlier.

15. See *Festival of the Lion King,* currently in Camp Minnie-Mickey (likely relocating to Africa in late 2013 or early 2014).

14. Walk the Pangani Forest Exploration Trail.

16. See *Finding Nemo—The Musical* at Theater in the Wild in DinoLand U.S.A. if the next show is within 30 minutes. Otherwise, see *It's Tough to Be a Bug!* on Discovery Island and (if time permits) the exhibits at The Tree of Life.

17. If you have the time and interest (and small children), check out The Boneyard in DinoLand.

18. If you've not already done so, see *It's Tough to Be a Bug!* and the exhibits at The Tree of Life on Discovery Island.

19. Shop, snack, or repeat any attractions you especially enjoyed.

20. Visit the zoological exhibits throughout the park.

PART TWELVE

DISNEY'S HOLLYWOOD STUDIOS

◖◗ DHS: *An* OVERVIEW

FORMERLY KNOWN AS DISNEY-MGM STUDIOS, Disney's Hollywood Studios was hatched from a corporate rivalry and a wild, twisted plot. At a time when The Walt Disney Company was weak and fighting off "greenmail"—hostile-takeover bids—Universal's parent company at the time, MCA, announced that it was going to build an Orlando clone of its wildly successful Universal Studios Hollywood theme park. Behind the scenes, MCA was courting the real estate–rich Bass brothers of Texas, in hopes of securing their investment in the project. The Basses, however, defected to the Disney camp and were front and center when Michael Eisner suddenly announced that Disney, too, would build a movie theme park in Florida. A construction race ensued, but Universal, in the middle of developing new attraction technologies, was no match for Disney, which could import proven concepts and attractions from its other parks. In the end, Disney's Hollywood Studios opened May 1, 1989, more than a year before Universal Studios Florida.

THE END OF THE MGM CONNECTION

SO WHAT HAPPENED TO "DISNEY-MGM STUDIOS"? Disney purchased Pixar Animation Studios after partnering with the company on a series of highly successful films, including *Toy Story; A Bug's Life; Monsters, Inc.; Finding Nemo;* and *The Incredibles.* The cost of continuing an association with MGM, coupled with Pixar's arguably greater popularity, probably convinced Disney to rename the theme park. But rather than replace *MGM* with *Pixar,* Disney decided that *Hollywood* represented a more generic reference to moviemaking. In practice, however, many folks drop the *Holly-wood* entirely, referring to the park simply as "Disney Studios" or "The Studios."

WHAT'S OFFERED AT THE STUDIOS TODAY

DHS'S SOUNDSTAGES and facilities produced many television shows and films, both live-action and animated, in the park's early years. The 2003 Disney film *Brother Bear* was largely drawn—by hand!—in the Magic of Disney Animation attraction, and movie buffs will recognize DHS's landscape in the background of Jim Varney's magnum opus, *Ernest Saves Christmas*. TV series filmed here span everything from the ABC hit *Who Wants to Be a Million-aire?* to the Hulk Hogan fiasco *Thunder in Paradise*.

In addition, DHS once hosted a variety of attractions that explained how TV shows and movies are made. The *Monster Sound Show,* which ran during the Studios' first decade, used audience vol-unteers to show how sound effects were added to films; the contem-poraneous *SuperStar Television* reenacted famous TV scenes using "green screen" technology and theme park guests as actors.

Today, the *Studios* in "Disney's Hollywood Studios" is of little significance. Movie production left here long ago; it's been more than a decade since any television production of note has taken place; and only a handful of attractions remain that offer a peek behind the scenes, such as the Studio Backlot Tour and the *Indi-ana Jones Epic Stunt Spectacular!* Unfortunately—for those who loved its creative aspects, that is—DHS is now simply an amuse-ment park whose theme is movies and TV.

While many of the current attractions are entertaining, Disney's self-promotion is often blatant, inescapable, and distracting. The primary goal of any new DHS development, it seems, is to market an upcoming Disney film, TV franchise, or musical act. Most visi-tors are willing to forgive Disney its excesses, but hardcore devo-tees lament these changes and remember how good the Studios used to be when education was the goal instead of the medium.

Alas, what DHS does best these days is promote. Whereas self-promotion of Disney films and products was once subtle and in context, it is now blatant, inescapable, and detracting. Although most visitors are willing to forgive Disney its excesses, Studios veterans will lament the changes and remember how good it was when education was the goal instead of the medium.

TOURING CONSIDERATIONS

WHEREAS IT'S IMPOSSIBLE to see all of Epcot or the Magic Kingdom in one day, DHS is doable: There's far less ground to cover

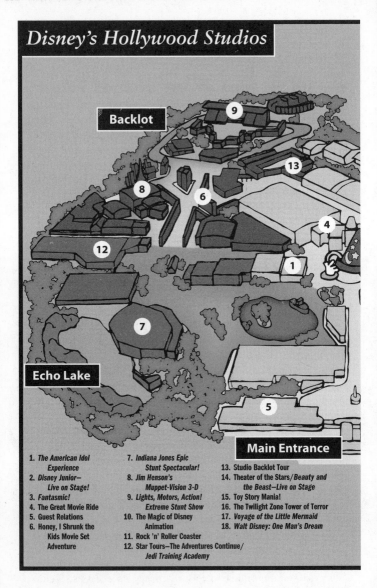

Disney's Hollywood Studios

Backlot

Echo Lake

Main Entrance

1. *The American Idol Experience*
2. *Disney Junior—Live on Stage!*
3. *Fantasmic!*
4. *The Great Movie Ride*
5. *Guest Relations*
6. *Honey, I Shrunk the Kids Movie Set Adventure*
7. *Indiana Jones Epic Stunt Spectacular!*
8. *Jim Henson's Muppet-Vision 3-D*
9. *Lights, Motors, Action! Extreme Stunt Show*
10. *The Magic of Disney Animation*
11. *Rock 'n' Roller Coaster*
12. *Star Tours—The Adventures Continue/ Jedi Training Academy*
13. *Studio Backlot Tour*
14. *Theater of the Stars/Beauty and the Beast—Live on Stage*
15. *Toy Story Mania!*
16. *The Twilight Zone Tower of Terror*
17. *Voyage of the Little Mermaid*
18. *Walt Disney: One Man's Dream*

NOT TO BE MISSED AT DISNEY'S HOLLYWOOD STUDIOS	
• *Fantasmic!*	• Studio Backlot Tour
• *Jim Henson's Muppet-Vision 3-D*	• Toy Story Mania!
• Rock 'n' Roller Coaster	• *Voyage of the Little Mermaid*
• Star Tours—The Adventures Continue	• The Twilight Zone Tower of Terror

by foot, trams carry guests through much of the backlot, and attractions are concentrated in an area about the size of Main Street, Tomorrowland, and Frontierland combined.

Because DHS is smaller, it's more affected by large crowds. Our touring plan will help you stay a step ahead of the mob and minimize waiting in line. It'll also help with the show-schedule problem, but even when the park is crowded, you can see almost everything in a day.

Because Disney's Hollywood Studios can be seen in as few as 8 hours, many guests who arrive early in the morning run out of things to do by late afternoon and leave the park. Their departure greatly thins the crowd and makes the Studios ideal for evening touring. The *Indiana Jones Epic Stunt Spectacular!* and productions at other outdoor theaters are infinitely more enjoyable during the evening than in the sweltering heat of the day.

unofficial **TIP**
After 5 p.m. or so, the lines for most attractions are manageable, and the park is cooler and more comfortable.

DHS is the home of ***Fantasmic!*** (profiled on page 237), the most dazzling nighttime-entertainment event in the Disney repertoire. Staged at least twice weekly, weather permitting, in its own theater behind The Twilight Zone Tower of Terror, *Fantasmic!* is not to be missed. Unfortunately, *Fantasmic!* draws crowds; some guests stay longer at DHS, and others arrive after dinner from other parks expressly to see the show. Although the crowds thin in the late afternoon, they build again as performance time approaches, making *Fantasmic!* a challenge to get into. Also adversely affected are Rock 'n' Roller Coaster and, to a lesser extent, The Twilight Zone Tower of Terror, both near the entrance to *Fantasmic!* Crowd levels throughout the remainder of the park, excluding at Toy Story Mania!, remain generally light.

ARRIVING

DISNEY'S HOLLYWOOD STUDIOS has its own pay parking lot and is served by the Disney transportation system. Most larger hotels outside the World shuttle guests to the Studios. If you

Hollywood Boulevard Services

Most of DHS's services are on Hollywood Boulevard, including:

BABY CARE CENTER At Guest Relations; baby food and other necessities available at Oscar's Super Service

BANKING SERVICES ATM outside the park to the right of the turnstiles and on Streets of America near Pizza Planet restaurant

FILM At The Darkroom on the right side of Hollywood Boulevard as you enter the park, just past Oscar's Super Service

FIRST AID At Guest Relations

LIVE ENTERTAINMENT AND CHARACTER INFORMATION Available free at Guest Relations and elsewhere in the park

LOST AND FOUND At Package Pick-Up, to the right of the entrance

LOST PERSONS Report lost persons at Guest Relations

STORAGE LOCKERS Rental lockers to the right of the main entrance, on the left of Oscar's Classic Car Souvenirs

WALT DISNEY WORLD AND LOCAL ATTRACTION INFORMATION At Guest Relations

WHEELCHAIR, ECV/ESV, AND STROLLER RENTALS To the right of the entrance, at Oscar's Super Service

drive, Disney's ubiquitous trams will transport you to the ticketing area and entrance gate.

GETTING ORIENTED

ON YOUR LEFT AS YOU ENTER, **Guest Relations** serves as the park headquarters and information center, similar to City Hall in the Magic Kingdom and Guest Relations at Epcot and Disney's Animal Kingdom. Go there for a map of the Studios, a schedule of live performances (*Times Guide*), lost persons, Package Pick-Up, lost and found (on the right side of the entrance), baby-care facilities, and general information, or in an emergency. To the right of the entrance are locker, stroller, and wheelchair rentals.

As at the Magic Kingdom, you enter the park and pass down a main street. In this case, it's the **Hollywood Boulevard** of the 1930s and '40s. At the end of Hollywood Boulevard is a replica of the famed **Chinese Theater.** Lording over the plaza in front of the theater is a 122-foot-tall replica of the sorcerer hat Mickey Mouse wore in the animated classic *Fantasia*. Besides providing photo ops, the hat is the park's most central landmark, making it a good meeting place if your group gets separated. (*Fun fact:* Mickey would have to be 350 feet tall to wear the hat.)

Though modest in size, the open-access areas of the Studios are confusingly arranged (a product of the park's hurried expansion in the early 1990s). As you face the hat, two guest areas—**Sunset Boulevard** and the **Animation Courtyard**—branch off Hollywood Boulevard to the right. Branching left off Hollywood Boulevard is the **Echo Lake** area. **Streets of America** wraps around the back of **Echo Lake**, while **Pixar Place**'s attractions are behind the Chinese Theater and to the left of the Animation Courtyard. Between Pixar Place and the Animation Courtyard is **Mickey Avenue** with its lone minor attraction.

Still farther to the rear is a limited-access area consisting of soundstages, technical facilities, wardrobe shops, administrative offices, and sets. These are accessible on a guided tour by tram and foot.

ATTRACTIONS

HOLLYWOOD BOULEVARD

THIS PALM-LINED THOROUGHFARE re-creates Tinseltown's main drag during the Golden Age of Hollywood. Most of DHS's service facilities are here, interspersed with eateries and shops. Merchandise includes Disney trademark items, movie-related souvenirs, and one-of-a-kind collectibles obtained from studio auctions and estate sales.

Hollywood characters and roving performers entertain on the boulevard, and other happenings pass this way.

The Great Movie Ride ★★★½

Appeal by Age	PRESCHOOL ★★★	GRADE SCHOOL ★★★½	TEENS ★★★½
YOUNG ADULTS ★★★½		OVER 30 ★★★★	SENIORS ★★★★

What it is Indoor movie-history ride. **Scope and scale** Headliner. **When to go** Before 11 a.m., during dinner, or after 8 p.m. **Special comments** Elaborate, with several surprises. **Authors' rating** Unique; ★★★½. **Duration of ride** About 19 minutes. **Average wait in line per 100 people ahead of you** 2 minutes; assumes all trains operating. **Loading speed** Fast.

DESCRIPTION AND COMMENTS Entering through a re-creation of Hollywood's Chinese Theater, guests board vehicles for a fast-paced tour of soundstage sets from classic films, including *Casablanca, Tarzan, The Wizard of Oz, Alien,* and *Raiders of the Lost Ark.* Each set is populated with Disney Audio-Animatronic characters, as well as the occasional human, all augmented by sound and lighting effects. One of Disney's larger and more ambitious dark rides, The Great Movie Ride encompasses 95,000 square feet and showcases some of the most famous scenes in filmmaking.

Life-size animatronic sculptures of stars, including Gene Kelly, John Wayne, James Cagney, and Julie Andrews, inhabit some of the largest sets ever constructed for a Disney ride.

TOURING TIPS It's rare to see a wait of more than 30 minutes at The Great Movie Ride except during Christmas. Part of the reason is that it's an interval-loading, high-capacity attraction, and part of the reason is that the films shown probably don't ring a bell with anyone under age 40. For what it's worth, actual wait times for the ride usually run about one-third shorter than the times posted.

SUNSET BOULEVARD

EVOKING THE 1940s, Sunset Boulevard is a major addition to Disney's Hollywood Studios. The first right off of Hollywood Boulevard, Sunset Boulevard provides another venue for dining, shopping, and street entertainment.

Fantasmic! ★★★★★

Appeal by Age PRESCHOOL ★★★½	**GRADE SCHOOL** ★★★★½	**TEENS** ★★★★½
YOUNG ADULTS ★★★★½	**OVER 30** ★★★★½	**SENIORS** ★★★★½

What it is Mixed-media nighttime spectacular. **Scope and scale** Super-headliner. **When to go** Check *Times Guide* for schedule; if 2 shows are offered, the second is less crowded. **Special comments** Disney's very best nighttime event. **Authors' rating** Not to be missed; ★★★★★. **Duration of presentation** 25 minutes. **Probable waiting time** 50–90 minutes for a seat, 35–40 minutes for standing room.

DESCRIPTION AND COMMENTS Off Sunset Boulevard behind the Tower of Terror, this mixed-media show is staged on an island opposite the 7,900-seat Hollywood Hills Amphitheater. By far the largest theater facility ever created by Disney, the amphitheater can accommodate an additional 2,000 standing guests for an audience of nearly 10,000.

Fantasmic! is the most innovative outdoor spectacle ever attempted at any theme park. Starring Mickey Mouse in his role as the Sorcerer's Apprentice from *Fantasia,* the production uses lasers, images projected on a shroud of mist, fireworks, lighting effects, and music in combinations so stunning you can scarcely believe what you're seeing. The plot is simple: good versus evil. The story gets lost in all the special effects at times, but no matter; it's the spectacle, not the storyline, that's powerful.

We don't receive many reports of young children being terrified by *Fantasmic!;* nonetheless, try to prepare your kids for what they'll see. You can mitigate the fright factor somewhat by sitting back a bit. Also, hang on to your kids after the show and give them instructions for regrouping should you get separated.

TOURING TIPS *Fantasmic!* is presented one or more times each evening, but Disney has been known to change the schedule, so check before you go. *Fantasmic!* is to Disney's Hollywood Studios what *IllumiNations* is to Epcot. While it's hard to imagine a 10,000-person stadium running out of space, that's just what happens almost every time the show is staged. On evenings when there are two performances, the second show will always be less crowded. If you attend the first (or only) scheduled performance, then show up at least an hour in advance. If you opt for the second show, arrive 50 minutes early. Disney has experimented with using Fastpass for reserved seating for *Fantasmic!*, and we expect this to become a regular offering. Check Disney's website or park map for availability.

Rainy and windy conditions sometimes cause *Fantasmic!* to be cancelled. Unfortunately, Disney officials usually don't make a final decision about whether to proceed or cancel until just before showtime. We've seen guests wait stoically for over an hour with no assurance that their patience and sacrifice will be rewarded. We don't recommend arriving more than 20 minutes before showtime on rainy or especially windy nights. On nights like these, pursue your own agenda until 10 minutes or so before showtime, then head to the stadium to see what happens.

***FANTASMIC!* DINING PACKAGE** If you eat lunch or dinner at **Hollywood & Vine, The Hollywood Brown Derby,** or **Mama Melrose's Ristorante Italiano,** you can obtain a voucher for the members of your dining party to enter *Fantasmic!* via a special entrance and sit in a reserved section of seats. In return for patronizing the restaurant, you can avoid 30–90 minutes waiting in the regular line.

You must call ☎ 407-WDW-DINE (939-3463) 180 days in advance and request the *Fantasmic!* Dining Package for the night you want to see the show. This is a real reservation, not an Advance Reservation, and must be guaranteed with a credit card at the time of booking. There's no additional charge for the package itself, but there is a $10 charge for canceling a reservation with less than 48 hours' notice.

Included in the package are fixed-price menus for all three restaurants as follows; respective prices are for adults and kids ages 3–9: *Hollywood & Vine:* buffet dinner, $29–$40/$13–$19; *The Hollywood Brown Derby:* lunch and dinner, $50–$57/$13–$19; *Mama Melrose's:* lunch and dinner, $35–$39/$13–$19. Non-alcoholic drinks and tax are included; park admission and gratuity are not. Prices fluctuate according to season, so call WDW-DINE if you want to know exactly what the dinner charge will be for a particular date.

Rock 'n' Roller Coaster (Fastpass) ★★★★

Appeal by Age	PRESCHOOL ★★	GRADE SCHOOL ★★★★½	TEENS ★★★★★
YOUNG ADULTS ★★★★★		OVER 30 ★★★★½	SENIORS ★★★½

What it is Rock-music-themed roller coaster. **Scope and scale** Headliner. **When to go** Before 10 a.m., in the hour before closing, or use Fastpass. **Special**

comments Must be 48" tall to ride; children younger than age 7 must ride with an adult. Switching-off option provided (see page 79). Note that there is a single-rider line for this attraction. **Authors' rating** Disney's wildest American coaster; not to be missed; ★★★★. **Duration of ride** Almost 1½ minutes. **Average wait in line per 100 people ahead of you** 2½ minutes; assumes all trains operating. **Loading speed** Moderate–fast.

Queasy

DESCRIPTION AND COMMENTS When it opened in 1999, Rock 'n' Roller Coaster was Disney's answer to the coaster proliferation at Universal's Islands of Adventure and Busch Gardens. Exponentially wilder than Space Mountain or Big Thunder Mountain in the Magic Kingdom, Rock 'n' Roller Coaster is an attraction for fans of high-speed thrill rides. Although the rock icons and synchronized music add measurably to the experience, the ride itself, as opposed to sights and sounds along the way, is the focus. Rock 'n' Roller Coaster's loops, corkscrews, and drops make Space Mountain seem like It's a Small World. What really makes this metal coaster unusual, however, is that first, it's in the dark (like Space Mountain, only with Southern California nighttime scenes instead of space), and second, you're launched up the first hill like a jet off a carrier deck. By the time you crest the hill, you'll have gone from 0 to 57 mph in less than three seconds. When you enter the first loop, you'll be pulling 5 g's—2 more than astronauts experience at liftoff on a space shuttle.

TOURING TIPS This ride is not for everyone. If Space Mountain or Big Thunder pushes your limits, stay away from Rock 'n' Roller Coaster.

Expect long lines except in the first 30 minutes after opening and during the late-evening performance of *Fantasmic!* Ride as soon as possible in the morning, or use Fastpass.

If you're on hand when the park opens, position yourself on the far left side of Sunset Boulevard as close to the rope barrier as possible. If there's already a crowd at the rope, you can usually work yourself forward by snaking along the wall of the Beverly Sunset Shop. Once you're in position, wait for the rope drop. When the park opens, cast members will walk the rope up the street toward Rock 'n' Roller Coaster and The Twilight Zone Tower of Terror. Stay on the far-left sidewalk and you'll be among the first to make the left turn to the entrance of the coaster. Usually the Disney people get out of the way and allow you to run the last 100 feet or so.

A good strategy for riding Rock 'n' Roller Coaster, Toy Story Mania!, and Tower of Terror with minimum waits is to rush first thing after opening to get Fastpasses for Toy Story Mania!, then line up for Rock 'n' Roller Coaster. Save Tower of Terror for last. If the standby line at Rock 'n' Roller Coaster is more than 30 minutes, consider using the Single Rider line. If the Single Rider line isn't an option, skip Rock 'n' Roller Coaster for now, ride Toy Story Mania!, and pick up Fastpasses for Rock 'n' Roller Coaster when you can.

Theater of the Stars: *Beauty and the Beast—Live on Stage* ★★★★

Appeal by Age	PRESCHOOL ★★★★½	GRADE SCHOOL ★★★★½	TEENS ★★★½
YOUNG ADULTS ★★★★	OVER 30 ★★★★½		SENIORS ★★★★½

What it is Live Hollywood-style musical, usually featuring Disney characters; performed in an open-air theater. **Scope and scale** Major attraction. **When to go** Anytime; evenings are cooler. **Special comments** Performances are listed in the daily *Times Guide*. **Authors' rating** Excellent; ★★★★. **Duration of presentation** 25 minutes. **Preshow entertainment** None. **When to arrive** 20–30 minutes before showtime.

DESCRIPTION AND COMMENTS Theater of the Stars combines Disney characters with singers and dancers in upbeat and humorous Hollywood musicals. The *Beauty and the Beast* show, in particular, is outstanding. The theater offers a clear field of vision from almost every seat. Best, a canopy protects the audience from the Florida sun (or rain), but the theater still gets mighty hot in the summer.

TOURING TIPS Unless you visit during the cooler months, see this show in the late afternoon or the evening. The production is so popular that you should show up 20–30 minutes early to get a seat.

The Twilight Zone Tower of Terror *(Fastpass)* ★★★★★

Appeal by Age	PRESCHOOL ★★½	GRADE SCHOOL ★★★★	TEENS ★★★★½
YOUNG ADULTS ★★★★★	OVER 30 ★★★★½		SENIORS ★★★★

What it is Sci-fi–themed indoor thrill ride. **Scope and scale** Super-headliner. **When to go** First or last 30 minutes the park is open or use Fastpass. **Special comments** 40" minimum height requirement. Switching-off option provided (see page 79). **Authors' rating** Walt Disney World's best attraction; not to be missed; ★★★★★. **Duration of ride** About 4 minutes plus preshow. **Average wait in line per 100 people ahead of you** 4 minutes; assumes all elevators operating. **Loading speed** Moderate.

DESCRIPTION AND COMMENTS The Tower of Terror is a different species of Disney thrill ride, though it borrows elements of The Haunted Mansion at the Magic Kingdom. The story is that you're touring a once-famous Hollywood hotel gone to ruin. As at Star Tours, the queuing area immerses guests in the adventure as they pass through the hotel's once-opulent public rooms. From the lobby, guests are escorted into the hotel's library, where Rod Serling, speaking from an old black-and-white television, greets the guests and introduces the plot.

The Tower of Terror is a whopper at 13-plus stories tall. Breaking tradition in terms of visually isolating themed areas, you can see the entire Studios from atop the tower . . . but you have to look quick.

The ride vehicle, one of the hotel's service elevators, takes guests to see the haunted hostelry. The tour begins innocuously, but at about the fifth floor things get pretty weird. Guests are subjected to a full range of eerie effects as they cross into the Twilight Zone. The climax of the adventure occurs when the elevator reaches the top floor—the 13th, of course—and the cable snaps.

The Tower has great potential for terrifying young children and rattling more-mature visitors. If you have teenagers in your party, use them as experimental probes. If they report back that they really, really liked the Tower of Terror, run like hell in the opposite direction.

TOURING TIPS The Tower is a veritable beacon, visible from outside the park and luring curious guests as soon as they enter. Because of its popularity with schoolkids, teens, and young adults, you can count on a footrace to the attraction, as well as to the nearby Rock 'n' Roller Coaster and Toy Story Mania!, when the park opens. Expect the Tower to be mobbed most of the day. Experience it as early as possible in the morning, in the evening before the park closes, or use Fastpass.

If you're on hand when the park opens and you want to ride Tower of Terror first, position yourself on the far right side of Sunset Boulevard as close to the rope barrier as possible. Once in position, wait for the rope to drop. When the park opens, cast members will walk the rope up the street toward Rock 'n' Roller Coaster and Tower of Terror. Just stay on the far right sidewalk and you'll be among the first to make the right turn to the entrance of the tower. Usually the Disney people get out of the way and allow you to run the last 100 feet or so. Also, be aware that about 65% of the folks waiting for the rope walk will head for Rock 'n' Roller Coaster. If you are not positioned on the far right, it will be almost impossible to move through the throng of coaster enthusiasts to make a right turn into Tower of Terror.

When you enter the library waiting area, stand in the far back corner across from the door where you entered and at the opposite end of the room from the TV. When the doors to the loading area open, you'll be one of the first admitted.

If you have young children (or anyone) who are apprehensive about this attraction, ask the attendant about switching off (page 79).

Our touring plan at the end of this chapter incorporates an optimal strategy for riding Tower of Terror, Rock 'n' Roller Coaster, and Toy Story Mania! with minimum waits.

ECHO LAKE

AN ACTUAL MINIATURE LAKE near the middle of the Studios, to the left of Hollywood Boulevard, Echo Lake pays homage to its real-life California counterpart, which served as the backdrop to many of Hollywood's early films. Echo Lake also serves as the architectural transition from Hollywood Boulevard's retro theming to Streets of America's film-set ambience.

The American Idol Experience ★★★★

Appeal by Age	PRESCHOOL ★★★½	GRADE SCHOOL ★★★★	TEENS ★★★★½
YOUNG ADULTS ★★★½		OVER 30 ★★★★	SENIORS ★★★★

What it is Theme park version of the TV show. **Scope and scale** Major attraction. **When to go** Anytime. **Special comments** Guests must be at least age 14 to perform. **Author's rating** Even if you don't watch the show, you'll find someone to cheer for; ★★★★. **Duration of presentation** 20 minutes for daytime preliminary shows, 40 minutes for the nighttime finale. **When to arrive** 20–30 minutes before showtime.

DESCRIPTION AND COMMENTS Based on the wildly popular TV talent search, *The American Idol Experience* has guests audition a cappella in front of a judge, just as in *American Idol*'s first shows of the season. Those who make the cut move on to a second audition and sing, karaoke-style, to a prerecorded track. The judges' picks from this round get to perform in one of the attraction's preliminary shows, held several times a day.

During the preliminaries, each contestant repeats his or her song from the second audition in front of a live audience of theme park guests. As with *Idol,* three judges—in this case, Disney cast members—provide feedback, some of it mildly snarky. Audience members decide the preliminary winners, who meet for one last showdown at night. The winner of the finale gets a "Dream Ticket"—a front-of-the-line pass to try out for *American Idol* in his or her hometown.

TOURING TIPS Usually scheduled around 7 p.m., the last show of the day offers (ostensibly) the best talent but runs twice as long as the daytime shows. If you have dinner reservations or are lining up early for *Fantasmic!* (see page 237), see one of the daytime shows. For complete details on auditioning and eligibility, go to **tinyurl.com/americanidolexperience.**

Indiana Jones Epic Stunt Spectacular! ★★★★

Appeal by Age	PRESCHOOL ★★★½	GRADE SCHOOL ★★★★	TEENS ★★★★½
YOUNG ADULTS ★★★★½		OVER 30 ★★★★	SENIORS ★★★★½

What it is Movie-stunt demonstration and action show. **Scope and scale** Headliner. **When to go** First 3 morning shows or last evening show. **Special comments** Performance times posted on a sign at the entrance to the theater; Fastpasses available seasonally. **Authors' rating** Done on a grand scale; ★★★★. **Duration of presentation** 30 minutes. **Preshow entertainment** Selection of "extras" from audience. **When to arrive** 20–30 minutes before showtime.

DESCRIPTION AND COMMENTS Coherent and educational, though somewhat unevenly paced, the popular production showcases professional stunt men and women who demonstrate dangerous stunts with a behind-the-scenes look at how it's done. Sets, props, and special effects are very elaborate.

TOURING TIPS The Stunt Theater holds 2,000 people; capacity audiences are common. The first performance is always the easiest to see. If the first show is at 10 a.m. or earlier, you can usually walk in, even if you arrive 5 minutes late. For the second performance, show up about 15–20 minutes ahead of time. For the third and subsequent shows, arrive 20–30 minutes early. If you plan to tour during late afternoon and evening, attend the last scheduled performance. If you want to beat the crowd out of the stadium, sit on the far right (as you face the staging area) and near the top.

Jedi Training Academy ★★★★

Appeal by Age	PRESCHOOL ★★★★½	GRADE SCHOOL ★★★★½	TEENS ★★★½
YOUNG ADULTS ★★★½		OVER 30 ★★★★	SENIORS ★★★½

What it is Outdoor stage show. **Scope and scale** Minor attraction. **When to go** First 2 shows of the day. **Special comments** To sign up your children to go on stage, visit the ABC Sound Studio building early in the morning; spots are first-come, first-served. **Authors' rating** A treat for young *Star Wars* lovers; ★★★★. **Duration of show** About 15 minutes. **When to arrive** 15 minutes before showtime.

DESCRIPTION AND COMMENTS *Jedi Training Academy* is staged several times daily to the left of the Star Tours building entrance, opposite Backlot Express. Young Skywalkers-in-training are selected from the audience to train in the ways of The Force and do battle against Darth Vader. If all this sounds too intense, it's not—Storm Troopers provide comic relief and, just as in the movies, the Jedi always win.

TOURING TIPS Surprisingly popular, given that Disney hasn't promoted it to the same level of hype as other shows. If you happen to have a brown robe similar to Obi-Wan's, bringing it along might boost your young one's chances of getting picked. If you plan to watch during summer afternoons, grab drinks at Backlot Express, right next door, about 20 minutes before the show starts.

Star Tours—The Adventures Continue *(Fastpass)* ★★★★

Appeal by Age	PRESCHOOL ★★★★	GRADE SCHOOL ★★★★½	TEENS ★★★★½
YOUNG ADULTS ★★★★½		OVER 30 ★★★★½	SENIORS ★★★★

What it is Indoor space-flight-simulation ride. **Scope and scale** Headliner. **When to go** Before 10 a.m., after 6 p.m., or use Fastpass. **Special comments** Expectant mothers and anyone prone to motion sickness are advised against riding. Too intense for many children younger than age 8; 40" minimum height requirement. **Authors' rating** A classic adventure; ★★★★. **Duration of ride** About 7 minutes. **Average wait in line per 100 people ahead of you** 5 minutes; assumes all simulators operating. **Loading speed** Moderate–fast.

DESCRIPTION AND COMMENTS Based on the *Star Wars* movie series, this was Disney's first modern simulator ride. Star Tours completed its first major overhaul in decades in 2011, with a new story based on the "pod racing" scene from *Star Wars Episode 1: The Phantom Menace*. The new version has lots of dips, turns, twists, and climbs as your vehicle goes through an intergalactic version of the chariot race in *Ben-Hur*. The new ride film is projected in high-definition 3-D and has more than 50 combinations of opening and ending scenes.

An interactive show, *Jedi Training Academy,* is staged several times daily to the left of the Star Tours building entrance, opposite Backlot Express. See previous page for details.

TOURING TIPS Try to ride before 10 a.m. or use Fastpass. If you have young children (or anyone) who are apprehensive about this attraction, ask the attendant about switching off (see page 79). Watch for throngs arriving from performances of the *Indiana Jones Epic Stunt Spectacular!* If you encounter a long line, try again later.

STREETS OF AMERICA

FORMERLY A WALK-THROUGH backlot movie set, Streets of America is now a designated themed area, or "land," that is home to four attractions. The back-lot street sets remain intact and serve as the primary pedestrian thoroughfare.

Honey, I Shrunk the Kids Movie Set Adventure ★★½

Appeal by Age PRESCHOOL ★★★★½ GRADE SCHOOL ★★★★½ TEENS ★★★½
YOUNG   ADULTS   ★★★   OVER   30   ★★★   SENIORS   ★★★

What it is Small but elaborate playground. **Scope and scale** Diversion. **When to go** Before 11 a.m. or after dark. **Special comments** Opens an hour later than the rest of the park. **Authors' rating** Great for young children, more of a curiosity for adults; ★★½. **Duration of presentation** Varies. **Average wait in line per 100 people ahead of you** 20 minutes.

DESCRIPTION AND COMMENTS This elaborate play space appeals to kids age 10 and younger. The story is that you've been "miniaturized" and must make your way through a yard full of 20-foot-tall blades of grass, giant ants, lawn sprinklers, and other oversize props. There are also tunnels, slides, and rope ladders to play on. All surface areas are padded, and Disney personnel are on hand to help keep children in some semblance of control.

TOURING TIPS The attraction has problems that are hard to "miniaturize." First, it isn't large enough to accommodate all the kids who would like to play. Only 240 people are allowed "on the set" at a time, and many of these are supervising parents or curious adults who hopped in line without knowing what they were waiting for. Frequently by 10:30 or 11 a.m., the playground is full, with dozens waiting outside.

Also, kids get to play as long as parents allow. This creates uneven traffic flow and unpredictable waits. If it weren't for the third flaw—that the attraction is poorly ventilated—there's no telling when anyone would leave.

If you visit during warmer months and want your children to experience the playground, get them in and out before 11 a.m.— by late morning, this attraction is way too hot and crowded for anyone to enjoy. Access the Movie Set Adventure via Streets of America or Pixar Place.

Jim Henson's Muppet-Vision 3-D ★★★★½

Appeal by Age   PRESCHOOL ★★★★   GRADE SCHOOL ★★★★½   TEENS ★★★★
YOUNG ADULTS ★★★★½   OVER 30 ★★★★   SENIORS ★★★★½

What it is 3-D movie starring the Muppets. **Scope and scale** Major attraction. **When to go** Before 11 a.m. or after 3 p.m. **Authors' rating** Uproarious; not to be missed; ★★★★½. **Duration of presentation** 17 minutes. **Preshow entertainment** Muppets on television. **Probable waiting time** 12 minutes.

DESCRIPTION AND COMMENTS *Muppet-Vision 3-D* provides a total sensory experience, with wild 3-D action augmented by auditory, visual, and tactile special effects. If you're tired and hot, this zany presentation will make you feel brand new. Arrive early and enjoy the hilarious video preshow.

TOURING TIPS This production is very popular. Before noon, waits peak at about 20 minutes. Also, watch for throngs arriving from just-concluded performances of the *Indiana Jones Epic Stunt Spectacular!* If you encounter a long line, try again later.

Lights, Motors, Action! Extreme Stunt Show ★★★½

Appeal by Age   PRESCHOOL ★★★★   GRADE SCHOOL ★★★★½   TEENS ★★★★½
YOUNG ADULTS ★★★★   OVER 30 ★★★★½   SENIORS ★★★★

What it is Auto stunt show. **Scope and scale** Headliner. **When to go** First show of the day or after 4 p.m. **Authors' rating** Good stunt work, slow pace; ★★★½. **Duration of presentation** 25–30 minutes. **Preshow entertainment** Selection of audience "volunteers." **When to arrive** 20–30 minutes before showtime.

DESCRIPTION AND COMMENTS This show, which originated at Disneyland Paris, features cars and motorcycles in a blur of chases, crashes, jumps, and explosions. The secrets behind the special effects are explained after each stunt sequence, with replays and different camera views shown on an enormous movie screen; the replays also serve to pass the time needed in placing the next stunt's props into position. While the stunt driving is excellent, the show plods along between tricks, and you will probably have had your fill by the time the last stunt ends. Expect about 6–8 minutes of real action in a show that runs 25–30 minutes.

TOURING TIPS The auto stunt show, at the end of the Streets of America, presents two to five performances daily. It's popular, but its remote location (the most distant attraction from the park entrance) helps distribute and moderate the crowds. Seating is in a 3,000-person stadium, so it's not difficult to find a seat except on the busiest days.

Studio Backlot Tour ★★★★

Appeal by Age   PRESCHOOL ★★★   GRADE SCHOOL ★★★½   TEENS ★★★
YOUNG ADULTS ★★★½   OVER 30 ★★★½   SENIORS ★★★½

What it is Combination tram and walking tour of modern film and video production. **Scope and scale** Headliner. **When to go** Before noon or after 5 p.m. **Special comments** Hit the restroom before getting in line. **Authors' rating** Educational and fun; not to be missed; ★★★★. **Duration of presentation** About 30 minutes. **Preshow entertainment** A video before the special-effects segment and another video in the tram boarding area.

DESCRIPTION AND COMMENTS Much of the Studios actually used to *be* studios, but little actual film or TV production takes place these days. Nonetheless, visitors can take a backstage tour to learn about production methods and technologies.

The tour begins on the edge of the backlot with the special-effects walking segment, then continues with the tram segment. To reach the tour, turn right off Hollywood Boulevard through the Studio Arch into the Animation Courtyard. Bear left at the corner where *Voyage of the Little Mermaid* is situated. Follow the street until you see a redbrick warehouse on your right. Go through the door and up the ramp.

The first stop is a special-effects water tank where technicians explain the mechanical and optical tricks that "turn the seemingly impossible into on-screen reality." Included are rain effects and a naval battle.

A prop room separates the special-effects tank and the tram tour. Trams depart about once every 4 minutes on busy days, winding among production and shop buildings. The tour continues through the backlot, where western desert canyons exist side-by-side with New York City brownstones. The tour's highlight is Catastrophe Canyon, an elaborate special-effects movie set where a thunderstorm, earthquake, oil-field fire, and flash flood are simulated.

TOURING TIPS Because the Backlot Tour is one of Disney's most efficient attractions, you will rarely wait more than 15 minutes (usually less than 10). Take the tour at your convenience.

PIXAR PLACE

THE WALKWAY BETWEEN *Voyage of the Little Mermaid* and the Studio Backlot Tour holds the popular Toy Story Mania! attraction. To emphasize the importance of the *Toy Story* franchise, this section of the park is called Pixar Place.

Toy Story Mania! (Fastpass) ★★★★½

Appeal by Age	PRESCHOOL ★★★★½	GRADE SCHOOL ★★★★★	TEENS ★★★★★
YOUNG ADULTS ★★★★★		OVER 30 ★★★★★	SENIORS ★★★★½

What it is 3-D ride through indoor shooting gallery. **Scope and scale** Headliner. **When to go** As soon as the park opens or use Fastpass. **Authors' rating** Not to be missed; ★★★★½. **Duration of ride** About 6½ minutes. **Average wait in line per 100 people ahead of you** 4½ minutes. **Loading speed** Fast.

DESCRIPTION AND COMMENTS Toy Story Mania! ushers in a whole new generation of Disney attraction: the "virtual dark ride." Since Disneyland opened in 1955, ride vehicles have moved past two- and three-dimensional sets often populated by Audio-Animatronic (AA) figures. These amazingly detailed sets and robotic figures defined the Disney Imagineering genius in attractions such as Pirates of the Caribbean, The Haunted Mansion, and Peter Pan's Flight. Now for Toy Story Mania!, the elaborate sets and endearing AA characters are gone. Imagine long corridors, totally empty, covered with reflective material. There's almost nothing there . . . until you put on your 3-D glasses. Instantly, the corridor is brimming with color and activity, thanks to projected computer-graphic (CG) images.

Conceptually, this is an interactive shooting gallery much like Buzz Lightyear's Space Ranger Spin (see page 528), but in Toy Story Mania!, your ride vehicle passes through a totally virtual midway, with booths offering such games as ring tossing and ball throwing. You use a cannon on your ride vehicle to play as you move along from booth to booth. Unlike the laser guns in Buzz Lightyear, however, the pull-string cannons in Toy Story Mania! take advantage of CG image technology to toss rings, shoot balls, even throw eggs and pies. Each game booth is manned by a *Toy Story* character who is right beside you in 3-D glory, cheering you on. In addition to 3-D imagery, you experience vehicle motion, wind, and water spray.

The ride begins with a training round to familiarize you with the games, then continues through a number of "real" games in which you compete against your riding mate. The technology has the ability to self-adjust the level of difficulty, and there are plenty of easy targets for small children to reach. *Tip:* Let the pull-string retract all the way back into the cannon before pulling it again.

Finally, and also of note, a new generation of "living character" AA figures has been introduced in the preshow queuing area. A 6-foot-tall Mr. Potato Head breaks new ground for an AA character by interacting with and talking to guests in real time (similar to *Turtle Talk with Crush*).

TOURING TIPS Because it's a ton of fun and it has a relatively low rider-per-hour capacity, Toy Story Mania! is the biggest bottleneck in Walt Disney World, surpassing even Test Track at Epcot. The only way to get aboard without a horrendous wait is to be one of the first through the turnstiles when the park opens and zoom to the attraction. Another alternative is to obtain Fastpasses for Toy Story Mania! as soon as the park opens and then backtrack to ride the Rock 'n' Roller Coaster and the Tower of Terror. Don't think you'll have all day to procure Fastpasses, though: even on days of moderate attendance, all Fastpasses for the day are usually gone by 11 a.m. Also, expect long queues at the Fastpass kiosks.

MICKEY AVENUE

MICKEY AVENUE HOSTS two minor attractions on the pedestrian promenade connecting Pixar Place and the Animation Courtyard.

The Legend of Captain Jack Sparrow ★★½

Appeal by Age	PRESCHOOL ★★★	GRADE SCHOOL ★★★½	TEENS ★★★½
YOUNG ADULTS ★★★½		OVER 30 ★★★	SENIORS ★★★

What it is Interactive film. **Scope and scale** Minor attraction. **When to go** After dinner. **Authors' rating** Promising technology, but not much story; ★★½. **Duration of presentation** Around 10 minutes. **Probable waiting time** 20–30 minutes.

DESCRIPTION AND COMMENTS This interactive walk-through attraction takes guests through pirate adventures, including a confrontation with skeleton pirates, singing mermaids, and a summoning of the squidlike Kraken. Virtually all of the presentation takes place in a room designed like a pirate's cave lair.

Animatronic figures and other props are placed around the room and used throughout the show. A talking skull, recognizable from Pirates of the Caribbean in the Magic Kingdom, serves as a narrator for each scene. Finally, an impressive holographic Jack Sparrow takes guests through a pirate oath, cementing their commitment to kidnapping, ransacking, and not-giving-a-hoot-ing.

That said, it's difficult to see who Disney thinks is the target audience for this attraction. For one thing, guests are instructed at various times to chant, roar, and stomp their feet in order to vanquish each threat, as if the entire audience were 3-year-olds. But the skeletons, monsters, and shooting are scary enough to frighten many small children, so it's not clear for whom the attraction is designed. If you can ignore the juvenile dialogue, the holographic Jack Sparrow and Johnny Depp's new scene are worth the few minutes you'll spend here.

TOURING TIPS May not open until late morning or noon; check the *Times Guide*. Because it's next to Toy Story Mania!, *Jack Sparrow* tends to draw guests who have either just finished riding or who have balked at getting in Toy Story's long line. If the wait for *Sparrow* is more than 20 minutes, try later in the day.

Walt Disney: One Man's Dream ★★★★

Appeal by Age	PRESCHOOL ★★½	GRADE SCHOOL ★★★½	TEENS ★★★★
YOUNG ADULTS ★★★★		OVER 30 ★★★★½	SENIORS ★★★★½

What it is Tribute to Walt Disney. **Scope and scale** Minor attraction. **When to go** Anytime. **Authors' rating** Excellent; ★★★. **Duration of presentation** 25 minutes. **Preshow entertainment** Disney memorabilia. **Probable waiting time** For the film, 10 minutes.

DESCRIPTION AND COMMENTS Launched in 2001 to celebrate the 100th anniversary of Walt Disney's birthday, *One Man's Dream* consists of an exhibit area showcasing Disney memorabilia and recordings, followed by a film documenting Disney's life. On display are a replica of Walt's California office, various innovations in animation developed by Disney, and early models and working plans for Walt Disney World and various Disney theme parks around the world. The film provides a personal glimpse of Disney and offers insights regarding both his successes and failures.

TOURING TIPS Give yourself some time here. Every minute spent among these extraordinary artifacts will enhance your visit, taking you back to a time when the creativity and vision that created Walt Disney World were personified by one struggling entrepreneur.

ANIMATION COURTYARD

THIS AREA IS TO THE RIGHT of the big blue sorcerer's hat in the middle of the park. It holds two large theaters used for live stage shows, plus a separate attraction focusing on Disney animation. Spend any time here, and you'll slowly realize it's just a big swath of asphalt, and in desperate need of some landscaping or a water feature.

Disney Junior—Live on Stage! ★★★★

Appeal by Age	PRESCHOOL ★★★★½	GRADE SCHOOL ★★★½	TEENS ★★★
YOUNG ADULTS ★★½		OVER 30 ★★★	SENIORS ★★★

What it is Live show for children. **Scope and scale** Minor attraction. **When to go** Per the daily entertainment schedule. **Authors' rating** A must for families with preschoolers; ★★★★. **Duration of presentation** 20 minutes. **Special comments** Audience sits on the floor. **When to arrive** 30+ minutes before showtime.

DESCRIPTION AND COMMENTS The show features characters from the Disney Channel's *Little Einsteins, Mickey Mouse Clubhouse, Jake and the Never Land Pirates,* and *Handy Manny,* plus other Disney Channel characters. *Disney Junior* uses elaborate puppets instead of live characters on stage. A simple plot serves as the platform for singing, dancing, some great puppetry, and a great deal of audience participation. The characters, who ooze love and goodness, rally throngs of tots and preschoolers to sing and dance along with them. All the jumping, squirming, and high-stepping is facilitated by having the audience sit on the floor so that kids can spontaneously erupt into motion when the mood strikes. Even for adults without children, it's a treat to watch the tykes rev up.

TOURING TIPS Staged in a huge building to the right of The Magic of Disney Animation. Get here at least 25 minutes before showtime, pick a spot on the floor, and take a breather until the action begins.

The Magic of Disney Animation ★★½

Appeal by Age	PRESCHOOL ★★★½	GRADE SCHOOL ★★★★	TEENS ★★★★
YOUNG ADULTS ★★★★		OVER 30 ★★★★	SENIORS ★★★★

What it is Overview of Disney animation process, with limited hands-on demonstrations. **Scope and scale** Minor attraction. **When to go** Anytime. **Special comments** Opens an hour later than the rest of the park. **Authors'**

rating Not as good as it used to be; ★★½. **Duration of presentation** 20 minutes. **Preshow entertainment** Gallery of animation art in waiting area. **Average wait in line per 100 people ahead of you** 7 minutes.

DESCRIPTION AND COMMENTS The consolidation of Disney Animation at the Burbank, California, studio has left this attraction without a story to tell. Park guests can still get a general overview of Disney's animation process, but they won't see the detailed work of actual artists as was possible in previous versions.

The revamped attraction starts in a small theater, where the audience is introduced to a cast-member host and Mushu, the dragon from Mulan. Between the host's speech, Mushu's constant interruptions, and a very brief taped segment with real Disney animators, guests are hard-pressed to learn anything about actual animation.

Next, the audience moves to another room with floor seating, where another cast member gives guests a verbal description of what used to be the walking tour of the actual animation studio. The cast member fields questions from the audience, but nothing truly enlightening is presented.

Afterwards, guests have the option of exiting the attraction or attending the Animation Academy (space is limited and is on a first-come, first-served basis). This is by far the most interesting segment of the attraction, but not designed for all guests. The animator works quickly, which seems to frustrate younger guests who need more time or assistance to get their drawing right.

TOURING TIPS Some days, the animation tour doesn't open until 10 or 11 a.m., by which time the park is pretty full. The tour is a relatively small-volume attraction, and lines can build on busy days by mid- to late morning.

Voyage of the Little Mermaid (Fastpass) ★★★★

**Appeal by Age   PRESCHOOL ★★★★½   GRADE SCHOOL ★★★★   TEENS ★★★½
YOUNG ADULTS ★★★★   OVER 30 ★★★★   SENIORS ★★★★**

What it is Musical stage show featuring characters from the Disney movie *The Little Mermaid.* **Scope and scale** Major attraction. **When to go** Before 9:45 a.m. or just before closing. **Authors' rating** Romantic, lovable, and humorous in the best Disney tradition; not to be missed; ★★★★. **Duration of presentation** 15 minutes. **Preshow entertainment** Taped ramblings about the decor in the preshow holding area. **Probable waiting time** Before 9:30 a.m., 10–30 minutes; after 9:30 a.m., 35–70 minutes.

DESCRIPTION AND COMMENTS *Voyage of the Little Mermaid* is a winner, appealing to every age. Cute without being silly or saccharine, and infinitely lovable, the *Little Mermaid* show is the most tender and romantic entertainment offered anywhere in Walt Disney World. The story is simple and engaging, the special effects impressive, and the Disney characters memorable.

TOURING TIPS Except during the busiest holiday periods, it's unusual for anyone in line not to be admitted to the next showing of *Mermaid.* Typical waits are usually under 25 minutes.

When you enter the preshow lobby, stand near the doors to the theater. When they open, go inside, pick a row of seats, and let 6–10 people enter the row ahead of you. The strategy is twofold: to obtain a good seat and be near the exit.

LIVE ENTERTAINMENT *at* DISNEY'S HOLLYWOOD STUDIOS

THE STUDIOS' LIVE-ENTERTAINMENT ROSTER includes theater shows, musical acts, roaming bands of street performers, and *Fantasmic!* (see page 237), the acclaimed nighttime water, fireworks, and laser show. Of all of these, the theater shows, musical acts, and street performers are generally as good as or better than comparable acts at the other Disney parks. You can read on for the details, but we'd be remiss if we didn't tell you to catch a show of **Mulch, Sweat, & Shears,** a group of landscaping "brothers" who make up a cover band that plays everything from AC/DC to Journey. Guests standing near the front may be invited into the act.

AFTERNOON PARADE Disney canceled the Studios' latest afternoon parade in 2013. No replacement had been named as we went to press.

DISNEY CHARACTERS Find characters in front of the Sorcerer's Hat, in front of the Magic of Disney Animation building, at the Phineas and Ferb/*Cars* Meet and Greet (near Mama Melrose's in Streets of America), in the Animation Courtyard, and along Pixar Place. Characters from *Monsters, Inc.* can sometimes be found near the Studio Backlot Tour. Check the *Times Guide* for times and locations of character appearances.

STREET ENTERTAINMENT The Studios has one of the best collections of roving street performers in all of Walt Disney World. Appearing primarily on Hollywood and Sunset boulevards, the cast of characters includes Hollywood stars and wannabes, their agents, directors, and gossip columnists. If you're looking for a spot to rest and a bit of entertainment, grab a drink and seek out these performers. Just keep in mind that the performers aren't shy about asking you to join in their antics.

DISNEY'S HOLLYWOOD STUDIOS TOURING PLANS

TOURING THE STUDIOS centers primarily around Toy Story Mania! and the fact that it simply cannot handle the number of guests who want to ride. A wonderful attraction for small children, it's therefore the first choice for families with young kids.

We've updated the Studios touring plan to include Fastpasses for Tower of Terror. This should eliminate the chance of encountering unexpected long lines in the evening on peak days.

In anticipation of Disney introducing Fastpass+ (see page 26), we've listed the approximate Fastpass+ return times for which you should attempt to make reservations. (The touring plan should work with anything close to the times shown.) Check for the latest Fastpass+ and touring plan tools on **touringplans.com**.

"NOT A TOURING PLAN" TOURING PLANS

FOR THE TYPE-B READER, these touring plans avoid detailed, step-by-step strategies for saving every last minute in line. Use these guidelines to avoid the longest waits in line while having maximum flexibility to see whatever interests you in a particular part of the park.

FOR PARENTS ARRIVING AT PARK OPENING Ride Toy Story Mania!, then head to Animation Courtyard to begin a counterclockwise tour of the park starting with *Voyage of the Little Mermaid*. Work in other shows as you near them. End the day on Sunset Boulevard for *Fantasmic!*

FOR ADULTS ARRIVING AT PARK OPENING Get Fastpasses for Toy Story Mania!, then begin a counterclockwise tour of the park with Rock 'n' Roller Coaster, Tower of Terror, and The Great Movie Ride. End the day in Animation Courtyard for Voyage of the Little Mermaid and The Magic of Disney Animation. Work in other shows as you near them. End the day on Sunset Boulevard for *Fantasmic!*

FOR PARENTS AND ADULTS ARRIVING LATE MORNING Try to get Fastpasses for Rock 'n' Roller Coaster or Tower of Terror (in that order). Start clockwise tour of park with Studio Backlot Tour, working in shows as you near them. Save Toy Story Mania! for last, grab a bite to eat, and see *Fantasmic!*

BEFORE YOU GO

1. Call ☎ 407-824-4321 to verify the park's hours.

2. Buy your admission before arriving.

3. Make lunch and dinner Advance Reservations, or reserve the *Fantasmic!* dinner package (if desired) before you arrive, by calling ☎ 407-WDW-DINE.

4. Review the daily *Times Guide* to get a fairly clear picture of your options.

Disney's Hollywood Studios One-Day Touring Plan

START TIMES FOR FASTPASS+ Star Tours, 1:45 p.m.; Rock 'n' Roller Coaster, 5:25 p.m.; Tower of Terror, 8:45 p.m.

1. Arrive at the park 30–40 minutes before official opening time. Obtain a park map and *Times Guide.*

2. As soon as the park opens, ride Toy Story Mania!

3. Ride The Great Movie Ride.

4. See *Voyage of the Little Mermaid.*

5. If you have small children, see *Disney Junior—Live on Stage!*

6. Take the Magic of Disney Animation tour.

7. Explore the Streets of America on the way to *Muppet-Vision 3-D.*

8. See *Muppet-Vision 3-D.*

9. Eat lunch.

10. Get Fastpasses for Star Tours—The Adventures Continue.

11. Work in the *Lights, Motors, Action! Extreme Stunt Show* and *The American Idol Experience.* Check the *Times Guide* for schedules.

12. Ride Star Tours in Echo Lake.

13. Send one member of your party to get Fastpasses for Rock 'n' Roller Coaster.

14. Take the Studio Backlot Tour.

15. See *Walt Disney: One Man's Dream.*

16. Work in *Beauty and the Beast—Live on Stage* and the *Indiana Jones Epic Stunt Spectacular!* Check the *Times Guide* for schedules.

17. Get Fastpasses for the Tower of Terror.

18. Ride Rock 'n' Roller Coaster using the Fastpasses obtained earlier.

19. Eat dinner and then tour Hollywood and Sunset Boulevards until your Fastpasses for Tower of Terror become valid.

20. Ride the Tower of Terror using the Fastpasses obtained earlier.

21. Enjoy *Fantasmic!* Plan on arriving 1 hour early to get good seats, 30 minutes early for standing-room-only.

PART THIRTEEN

The WATER PARKS

DISNEY HAS TWO SWIMMING THEME PARKS, and two independent water parks are in the area. At Disney World, **Typhoon Lagoon** is the most diverse Disney splash pad, while **Blizzard Beach** takes the prize for the most slides and most bizarre theme. Outside the World, find **Wet 'n Wild** on International Drive and **Aquatica by SeaWorld**.

At both Disney water parks, the following rules and prices apply: One cooler per family or group is allowed, but no glass and no alcoholic beverages; towels are $2; lockers are $13 small, $15 large (includes $5 refundable deposit); life jackets are available at no cost.

Guests can use automated ticket-vending machines to purchase admission at Blizzard Beach and Typhoon Lagoon. These machines use touch-screen technology and are intended to reduce the amount of time spent standing in line at ticket windows. Admission, including tax, runs $59 for adults and $50 for children ages 3–9. Parking is free. Children younger than age 3 are admitted free. For more information, call ☎ 407-939-6244.

◧ BLIZZARD BEACH

BLIZZARD BEACH IS DISNEY'S MOST EXOTIC water adventure park and, like Typhoon Lagoon, it arrived with its own legend. This time, the story goes, an entrepreneur tried to open a ski resort in Florida during a particularly savage winter. Alas, the snow melted; the palm trees grew back; and all that remained of the ski resort was its Alpine lodge, the ski lifts, and, of course, the mountain. Plunging off the mountain are ski slopes and bobsled runs transformed into waterslides. Visitors to Blizzard Beach catch the thaw: icicles drip and patches of snow remain. The melting snow has formed a lagoon (the wave pool), fed by gushing mountain streams.

In addition to the wave pool, there are 17 slides (2 of which are quite long), a children's swimming area, and a tranquil stream for tubing. Picnic areas and sunbathing beaches dot the park. **Summit Plummet,** one of the world's longest speed slides, begins with a steep 120-foot descent. The **Teamboat Springs** slide is 1,200 feet long.

TYPHOON LAGOON

TYPHOON LAGOON IS COMPARABLE in size to Blizzard Beach. Eleven waterslides and streams, some as long as 400 feet, drop from the top of a 100-foot-tall, man-made mountain. Landscaping and an "aftermath of a typhoon" theme add adventure to the wet rides.

Typhoon Lagoon provides water adventure for all ages. Activity pools for young children and families feature geysers, tame slides, bubble jets, and fountains. For the older and more adventurous are the enclosed **Humunga Kowabunga** speed slides, corkscrew storm slides, and three whitewater-raft rides (plus one children's rapids ride) plopping off **Mount Mayday.** Slower metabolisms will enjoy the scenic, meandering 2,100-foot-long stream that floats tubers through a hidden grotto and rain forest. And, of course, the sedentary will usually find plenty of sun to sleep in. Typhoon Lagoon's **surf pool** and **Shark Reef** are unique, and the wave pool is the world's largest inland surf facility, with waves up to 6 feet high. Shark Reef is a saltwater snorkeling pool where guests can swim among real fish.

WHEN *to* GO

THE BEST WAY TO AVOID STANDING IN LINES is to visit the Disney water parks when they're less crowded. Our research, conducted over many weeks in the parks, indicates that tourists, not locals, make up the majority of visitors on any given day. And because weekends are popular travel days, the water parks tend to be less crowded then. In fact, of the weekend days we evaluated, the parks never reached full capacity; during the week, conversely, one or both parks closed every Thursday we monitored, and both closed at least once every other weekday. If you're a Disney resort guest, by all means use your morning Extra Magic Hours privileges whenever they're

*un*official **TIP**
Fridays are good because people traveling by car commonly use this day to start home. Sunday morning also has lighter crowds.

offered; otherwise, we recommend that you go on a Monday or Friday.

If your schedule is flexible, a good time to visit the swimming parks is midafternoon to late in the day when the weather has cleared after a storm. The parks usually close during bad weather. If the storm is prolonged, most guests leave for their hotels. When Typhoon Lagoon or Blizzard Beach reopen after inclement weather has passed, you almost have a whole park to yourself.

PART FOURTEEN

BEYOND *the* PARKS

◪ DOWNTOWN DISNEY

THIS SHOPPING, DINING, AND ENTERTAINMENT development is strung along the banks of Village Lake.

COMING SOON: DISNEY SPRINGS

IN THE YEARS SINCE the nighttime-entertainment venues at the former Pleasure Island were closed, the powers-that-be have struggled to formulate an overall vision for Downtown Disney. After several fitful attempts, Disney has finally decided on an expansion themed to evoke a Florida waterfront town. Called Disney Springs, it will comprise the current three Downtown Disney areas and add a fourth. Pleasure Island will become **The Landing**. As the name implies, it's situated along the lake on one side and faces a new area, **Town Center,** on the opposite side of the development's namesake springs, the centerpiece of the expansion. Town Center will be built out toward the parking lot.

To the east of what will be Town Center and The Landing is **Downtown Disney Marketplace,** with an expanded World of Disney store. It's connected by bridge to Disney's Saratoga Springs Resort & Spa. Anchoring the opposite end of the complex is **Downtown Disney West Side,** featuring elevated observation platforms, restaurants, shops, a bowling venue, and a Cirque du Soleil show. In addition to pedestrian walkways, West Side, The Landing, and Marketplace will be connected by water taxi. Expansion construction began in April 2013 and will continue into 2016. Once complete, Disney Springs will expand from 75 to more than 150 shopping, dining, and entertainment venues.

DOWNTOWN DISNEY MARKETPLACE

ALTHOUGH THE MARKETPLACE OFFERS interactive fountains, a couple of playgrounds, a lakeside amphitheater, and watercraft rentals, it is primarily a shopping and dining venue. The centerpiece of shopping is the 50,000-square-foot **World of Disney,** the largest store in the world selling Disney-trademark merchandise.

At **Disney's Design-a-Tee** you can create customized T-shirts, and **Mickey's Pantry** offers Disney home and kitchen products, including the Donald Duck Press (joke!). Another noteworthy retailer is the **LEGO Imagination Center,** showcasing a number of huge and unbelievable sculptures made entirely of LEGO "bricks." Spaceships, sea serpents, sleeping tourists, and dinosaurs are just a few of the sculptures on display. **Once Upon a Toy** is a toys, games, and collectibles superstore. Rounding out the selection are stores specializing in resort wear, athletic attire and gear, Christmas decorations, Disney art and collectibles, and handmade craft items. Most retail establishments are open from 9:30 a.m. until 11:30 p.m.

Rainforest Cafe and **T-REX** are the headliner restaurants at the Marketplace. The others are **Pollo Campero,** a Latin chicken eatery; **Earl of Sandwich; Wolfgang Puck Express Cafe;** and **Ghirardelli Soda Fountain & Chocolate Shop.**

DOWNTOWN DISNEY WEST SIDE

WEST SIDE OFFERS A BROAD RANGE of entertainment, dining, and shopping. Restaurants include the **House of Blues,** which serves Cajun specialties; **Planet Hollywood,** offering movie memorabilia and basic American fare; **Bongos Cuban Cafe,** serving Cuban favorites; and **Wolfgang Puck Grand Cafe,** featuring California cuisine. West Side shopping is some of the most interesting in Disney World. For instance, there's **Pop Gallery,** selling high-end paintings and sculptures, and **D-Street,** offering "cutting edge" (that is, bizarre) apparel and Vinylmation figurines. Other shops include a **Harley-Davidson** showroom and a designer-sunglasses studio.

In the entertainment department are **DisneyQuest,** an interactive theme park contained in its own building; **House of Blues,** part of the chain of live-music-and-dining venues; and a 24-screen **AMC** movie theater. **Splitsville,** an upscale bowling, billiards, and dining venue, covers 45,000 square feet on two levels. Prices are astronomical at $15–$20 per person. If you feel like getting high, try **Characters in Flight,** where you ascend 400 feet over Downtown Disney in a tethered balloon (the characters are painted on the balloon—don't expect to float around up there with Br'er Fox). The weather-dependent ride operates 8:30 a.m.–midnight, lasts 8–10 minutes, and costs $18 for adults (age 10 and up) and $12 for kids (ages 3–9). It's also wheelchair-accessible.

The West Side is also home to **Cirque du Soleil** *La Nouba,* an amazing production show with a cast of more than 70 performers and musicians. House of Blues and *La Nouba* are described in Part 15, Nightlife in Walt Disney World.

DISNEYQUEST

IN CONCEPT AND ATTRACTION MIX, DisneyQuest is aimed at a youthful audience, say, 8–35 years of age, though younger and older patrons will enjoy much of what it offers. The feel is dynamic, bustling, and noisy. Those who haunt the video arcades at shopping malls will feel most at home at DisneyQuest. And like most malls, when late afternoon turns to evening, the median age at Disney-Quest rises with the arrival of adolescents and teens who have been released from parental supervision for a while.

You begin your experience in the **Departure Lobby,** adjacent to admission sales. From the Departure Lobby you enter a "Cyber-lator," a "transitional attraction" (read: elevator) hosted by the Genie from *Aladdin,* that delivers you to an entrance plaza called **Ventureport.** From here you can enter the four zones. As in the larger parks, each zone is distinctively themed. Some zones cover more than one floor, so, looking around, you can see things going on both above and below you. The four zones, in no particular order, are **Explore Zone, Score Zone, Create Zone,** and **Replay Zone.**

Though most kids and adolescents aren't going to care, the zone layout at DisneyQuest may confuse adults trying to orient themselves. Don't count on trapping certain kids in certain zones either, or planning a rendezvous inside one without designating a specific location. Each zone spreads out over multiple levels, with stairways, elevators, slides, and walkways linking them in a variety of ways. Still, as we said, the labyrinthine design of the place won't bother most youngsters, who are usually happy just to wander (or dash madly) between games and rides.

ESPN WIDE WORLD *of* SPORTS COMPLEX

THIS 220-ACRE, STATE-OF-THE-ART competition and train-ing center consists of a 9,500-seat ballpark, a fieldhouse, and dedi-cated venues for baseball, softball, tennis, track and field, beach volleyball, and 27 other sports. From Little League Baseball to rugby to beach volleyball, the complex hosts a mind-boggling calendar of professional and amateur competitions.

In late winter and early spring, the complex is the spring-training home of the Atlanta Braves. While Disney guests are welcome at the ESPN Wide World of Sports as paying spectators (prices vary according to event), none of the facilities are available for guests unless they're participants in a scheduled, organized competition. To learn which sporting events are scheduled during your visit, call ☎ 407-939-GAME (4263) or check the online calendar at **disney worldsports.com.**

Admission is $17 adults, $12 children ages 3–9 (prices include tax). Some events carry an extra charge. There's a restaurant, the **ESPN Wide World of Sports Grill,** but no on-site lodging.

The DISNEY WILDERNESS PRESERVE

ABOUT 40–60 MINUTES SOUTH of Walt Disney World is the Disney Wilderness Preserve, a wetlands-restoration area operated by The Nature Conservancy in partnership with Disney. At 12,000 acres, this is as real as Disney gets. There are hiking trails and an interpretive center. Trails wind through grassy savannas, beneath ancient cypress trees, and along the banks of pristine Lake Russell. More than 1,000 species of plants and animals call the preserve home. The preserve is open Monday–Friday, 9 a.m.–5 p.m., except for major holidays; admission is free, but donations are welcome. For more information and directions, call ☎ 407-935-0002 or visit **tinyurl.com/disneywildernesspreserve.**

WALT DISNEY WORLD SPEEDWAY

ADJACENT TO THE TRANSPORTATION and ticket center parking lot sits the Walt Disney World Speedway, a 1-mile tri-oval course. If you're a NASCAR fan, check out the **Richard Petty Driving Experience,** where you can ride in a two-seater stock car for $105 (3 laps) or learn to drive one for $478 (8 laps), $904 (18 laps), $1,383 (30 laps), or $2,235 (50 laps); prices include tax. There's also a teen (ages 14–19) ride-along for $31 when a parent purchases the full-price riding option. For information call ☎ 800-BE-PETTY (237-3889) or check out **drivepetty.com.**

Also at the speedway is the **Indy Racing Experience.** Usually starting in the afternoon when the Richard Petty folks have finished, this experience features sleeker, faster open-wheeled cars like those seen in the Indianapolis 500. You can ride in a modified two-seat Indy car or drive one of the single-seat cars. The cost is $425 (tax included) for eight laps. For information call ☎ 317-243-7171, ext. 106, or 888-357-5002, ext. 106, or visit **indyracingexperience.com.**

WALT DISNEY WORLD RECREATION

DISNEY RESORTS HANDLE boat, bike, and fishing-equipment rentals on an hourly basis. Just show up at the rental office during operating hours and they'll fix you up. The same goes for various fitness centers in the resort hotels. Golf, tennis, fishing expeditions, water-ski excursions, hayrides, trail rides, and most spa services must be scheduled in advance. Though every resort features an extensive selection of recreational options, those resorts situated on a navigable body of water offer the greatest variety. Also, the more upscale a resort, the more likely it is to have such amenities as a fitness center and spa. In addition, you can rent boats and other recreational equipment at Downtown Disney Marketplace.

WALT DISNEY WORLD GOLF

WALT DISNEY WORLD HAS FOUR GOLF COURSES, each expertly designed and meticulously maintained. The **Magnolia, Palm,** and **Oak Trail** courses, across Floridian Way from the Polynesian Resort, envelop the Shades of Green recreational complex; the pro shops and support facilities adjoin the Shades of Green hotel. **Lake Buena Vista Golf Course** is at Saratoga Springs Resort, near Walt Disney World Village and across the lake from the Disney Springs project. (**Osprey Ridge Golf Course,** adjacent to Fort Wilderness Campground, closed in 2013 and will be replaced by a course on a site shared by the new Four Seasons Resort and Golden Oak, a Disney-owned luxury residential development.)

Oak Trail is a nine-hole course for beginners. The other three courses are designed for the midhandicap player and, while interesting, are quite forgiving. All courses are popular, with morning tee times at a premium, especially January–April.

Peak season for all courses is January–May, and off-season is May–October; however, summer is peak season for the nongolf parts of Walt Disney World, including the hotels. Off-season and afternoon twilight rates are available. Carts are required (except at Oak Trail) and are included in the greens fee. Tee times may be reserved 90 days in advance by Disney resort guests and 60 days ahead by

unofficial **TIP**
To avoid the crowds, play on a Monday, Tuesday, or Wednesday and sign up for a late-afternoon tee time.

day guests with a credit card. Proper golf attire, including spike-less shoes, is required. A collared shirt and Bermuda-length shorts or slacks meet the requirements.

Besides the ability to book tee times further in advance, guests of Walt Disney World–owned resorts get other benefits that may sway a golfer's lodging decision. These include discounted greens fees, free club rental, and charge privileges. The single most important, and least known, benefit is the provision of free round-trip taxi transportation between the golf courses and your hotel, which lets you avoid moving your car or dragging your clubs on Disney buses. The cabs, which make access to the courses much simpler, are paid by vouchers happily supplied to hotel guests.

For more information, call ☎ 407-938-GOLF (4653); to book a tee time online, go to **golfwdw.com**.

MINIATURE GOLF

THE 11-ACRE **Fantasia Gardens** consists of two 18-hole dink-and-putt golf courses. One course is an "adventure" course, themed after Disney's animated film *Fantasia*. The other course, geared more toward older children and adults, is an innovative approach-and-putt course with sand traps and water hazards.

Fantasia Gardens is on Epcot Resorts Boulevard, across the street from the Walt Disney World Swan; it's open daily, 10 a.m.–11 p.m. To reach the course via Disney transportation, take a bus or boat to the Swan resort. The cost to putt, including tax, is $12.78 for adults and $10.65 for children ages 3–9. In case you arrive hungry or naked, Fantasia Gardens has a snack bar and gift shop. For more information, call ☎ 407-WDW-PLAY (939-7529).

In 1999, Disney opened **Winter Summerland,** a second minigolf facility, located next to Blizzard Beach water park. Winter Summerland offers two 18-hole courses—one has a blizzard-in-Florida theme, the other a tropical-holiday theme. It's open daily, 10 a.m.–11 p.m., and the cost is the same as for Fantasia Gardens.

unofficial **TIP**
The Winter Summerland courses are much easier than the Fantasia Gardens courses, making them a better choice for families with preteen children.

PART FIFTEEN

NIGHTLIFE *in* WALT DISNEY WORLD

▌ WALT DISNEY WORLD *at* NIGHT

DISNEY SO CLEVERLY CONSPIRES to exhaust you during the day that the thought of night activity sends most visitors into shock. Walt Disney World, however, offers much for the hearty and the nocturnal to do in the evenings.

IN THE THEME PARKS

EPCOT'S MAJOR EVENING EVENT is *IllumiNations,* a laser and fireworks show at World Showcase Lagoon. Showtime is listed in the daily entertainment schedule (*Times Guide*).

Magic Kingdom offerings include the popular evening parade(s); *Celebrate the Magic,* in which a high-tech light-and-video show is projected onto Cinderella Castle; and the *Wishes* fireworks show. Consult the *Times Guide* for performances.

On most nights of the year, Disney's Hollywood Studios presents *Fantasmic!,* a laser, special-effects, and water spectacular (see page 237). The *Times Guide* lists showtimes.

Disney's Animal Kingdom offers no nighttime entertainment.

AT THE HOTELS

A SORT OF MAIN STREET ELECTRICAL PARADE on barges, the **Floating Electrical Pageant** stars creatures of the sea. This nightly spectacle, with background music played on a doozy of a synthesizer, is one of our favorite Disney productions. The first performance of the short but captivating show is at 9 p.m. off the Polynesian Resort docks. From there, it circles around and repeats at the Grand

Floridian Resort & Spa at 9:15 p.m., heading afterward to Fort Wilderness Resort & Campground, Wilderness Lodge & Villas, and the Contemporary Resort and Bay Lake Tower.

For something more elaborate, consider a dinner theater. If you want to go honky-tonkin', the **Buena Vista Palace, Hilton,** and **Royal Plaza** hotels at the Downtown Disney Resort Area have lively (all right, all right, *relatively* lively) bars.

AT ANIMAL KINGDOM LODGE For children, there's African story-telling around a campfire each night, followed by a movie shown by the pool. In addition, kids can march around the lobby each evening at 8 p.m. during the **Zawadi Primal Parade.** Finally, guests can view animals after dark using night-vision goggles.

AT THE BOARDWALK **Jellyrolls** features dueling pianos and sing-alongs. **Big River Grille & Brewing Works** is Disney's first and only brewpub. Completing the BoardWalk's entertainment mix are the **ESPN Club,** a sports bar; the **Atlantic Dance Hall,** an upscale but largely deserted dance club; and several restaurants. Access is by foot from Epcot, by ferry from Disney's Hollywood Studios, and by bus from other Disney World locations. The *Unofficial Guide* research team rates Jellyrolls as its second favorite of all Disney nightspots (**Raglan Road Irish Pub & Restaurant** at Downtown Disney is our top pick). It's raucous, frequently hilarious, and positively rejuvenating. The piano players are outstanding. Best of all, it's strictly for adults.

AT CORONADO SPRINGS RESORT Perhaps Disney's hippest night-spot is the 5,000-square-foot **Rix Lounge,** a Vegas-ultralounge clone. DJs spin Top 40 tracks 9 p.m.–2 a.m.; a percussion band performs on select evenings. Few locals or resort guests have discovered Rix, so the place is frequently dead unless there's a big meeting or trade show at Coronado Springs. Also at this resort is the **Laguna Bar,** a romantic outdoor-terrace affair arrayed alongside the lake.

unofficial TIP
If you're into family films, all Disney resorts offer outdoor movies each evening. The largest screen is at **Fort Wilderness Resort & Campground.**

AT FORT WILDERNESS RESORT & CAMPGROUND The free nightly campfire program begins with a sing-along led by Chip 'n' Dale and progresses to cartoons and a Disney movie. For Disney lodging guests only.

AT DOWNTOWN DISNEY

PLEASURE ISLAND Disney World's nighttime-entertainment com-plex cashed in its chips in the fall of 2008. Gone are the BET Sound-stage Club, Mannequins Dance Palace, Motion, 8 TRAX, the Comedy Warehouse, and the much-loved Adventurers Club. This last so exemplified Disney whimsy that everyone thought it would surely escape the ax. No such luck. The Pleasure Island restaurants survived, though, as did a few shops. For now, the only live-music venue is **Raglan Road,** an Irish pub. The site is being redeveloped as part of the **Disney Springs** project (see page 257).

DOWNTOWN DISNEY MARKETPLACE It's flog-your-wallet each night at the Marketplace, with shops open until 11:30 p.m.

DOWNTOWN DISNEY WEST SIDE This is a 70-acre shopping, restaurant, and nightlife complex situated to the left of what once was Pleasure Island. The West Side features a 24-screen **AMC** movie complex, the **DisneyQuest** pay-for-play indoor theme park (see page 259), a permanent showplace for the extraordinary **Cirque du Soleil,** and a 2,000-capacity concert hall. The dining options include **Bongos Cuban Cafe,** a 450-seat Cajun restaurant at **House of Blues, Wolfgang Puck** (serving California fare), and **Bongos Cuban Cafe,** owned by Gloria and Emilio Estefan. The West Side can be accessed via Disney buses from most Disney World locations.

Cirque du Soleil *La Nouba*

Appeal by Age	UNDER 21 ★★★★	21–37 ★★★★	38–50 ★★★★	51 and up ★★★★½

Type of show Circus as theater. **Tickets and information** ☎ 407-939-7600; cirquedusoleil.com/lanouba. **Admission cost** *Category Front & Center:* $132.06 adults, $108.63 children ages 3–9; *Category 1:* $120.35 adults, $94.79 children; *Category 2:* $94.79 adults, $76.69 children; *Category 3:* $77.75 adults, $61.77 children. *Box Office Only:* $56.45 adults, $45.80 children (to buy tickets at this level, you must call or visit the box office directly). All prices include tax. **Cast size** 72. **Night of lowest attendance** Thursday. **Usual showtimes** Tuesday–Saturday, 6 p.m. and 9 p.m. **Authors' rating** ★★★★★. **Duration of presentation** 1 hour, 45 minutes (no intermission) plus preshow.

DESCRIPTION AND COMMENTS *La Nouba* is a far cry from a traditional circus, but it retains all the fun and excitement. It is whimsical, mystical, and sophisticated, yet pleasing to all ages. The action takes place on an elaborate stage that incorporates almost every part of the theater.

TOURING TIPS The audience is an integral part of *La Nouba*—at almost any time you might be plucked from your seat to participate. Our advice is to loosen up and roll with it. If you are too rigid, repressed, hung over, or whatever to get involved, politely but firmly decline to be conscripted. Then fix a death grip on the arms of your chair. Tickets for reserved seats can be purchased in advance at the Cirque box office or over the phone, using your credit card. Oh yeah, don't wait until the last minute; book well in advance from home.

House of Blues

Type of show Live concerts with an emphasis on rock and blues. **Tickets and information** ☎ 407-934-BLUE (2583); **hob.com. Admission cost with**

taxes About $8–$95, depending on who's performing. **Nights of lowest attendance** Monday and Tuesday. **Usual showtimes** Vary between 7 p.m. and 9:30 p.m., depending on who's performing.

DESCRIPTION AND COMMENTS House of Blues, developed by original Blues Brother Dan Aykroyd, features a restaurant and blues bar, as well as the concert hall. The restaurant serves Thursday–Saturday from 11 a.m. until 1:30 a.m., which makes it one of the few late-night-dining options in Walt Disney World. Live music cranks up every night at 10:30 p.m. in the restaurant–blues bar, but even before then, the joint is way beyond 110 decibels. The music hall next door features concerts by an eclectic array of musicians and groups. During one visit, the show bill listed gospel, blues, funk, ska, dance, salsa, rap, zydeco, hard rock, groove rock, and reggae groups over a two-week period.

TOURING TIPS Prices vary from night to night according to the fame and drawing power of the featured band. Tickets ranged from $8 to $62 during our visits but go higher when a really big name is scheduled.

The music hall is set up like a nightclub, with tables and bar stools for only about 150 people and standing room for a whopping 1,850 people. Folks dance when there's room and sometimes when there isn't. The tables and stools are first-come, first-served, with doors opening an hour before showtime on weekdays and 90 minutes before showtime on weekends. Acoustics are good, and the showroom is small enough to provide a relatively intimate concert experience. All shows are all ages unless otherwise indicated.

WALT DISNEY WORLD DINNER THEATERS

SEVERAL DINNER-THEATER SHOWS play each night at Walt Disney World, and unlike other Disney dining venues, they make hard reservations instead of Advance Reservations, meaning you must guarantee your reservation ahead of time with a credit card. You'll receive a confirmation number and be told to pick up your tickets at a Disney-hotel Guest Relations desk. Unless you cancel your tickets at least 48 hours before your reservation time, your credit card will still be charged the full amount. Dinner-show reservations can be made 180 days in advance; call ☎ 407-939-3463. While getting reservations for the *Spirit of Aloha Dinner Show* isn't terribly tough, booking the *Hoop-Dee-Doo Musical Revue* is a trick of the first order.

1. Call ☎ 407-939-3463 at 9 a.m. each morning while you're at Disney World to make a same-day reservation. There are three performances each night, and for all three combined, only 3–24 people total will be admitted with same-day reservations.

2. Arrive at the show of your choice 45 minutes before showtime (early and late shows are your best bets) and put your name on the standby list. If someone with reservations fails to show, you may be admitted.

Hoop-Dee-Doo Musical Revue

Pioneer Hall, Fort Wilderness Campground ☎ 407-939-3463. **Showtimes** 4, 6:15, and 8:30 p.m. nightly. **Cost** $55–$68 adults, $28–$35 children ages 3–9. Prices include tax and gratuity. **Discounts** Seasonal. **Type of seating** Tables of various sizes to fit the number in each party, set in an Old West–style dance hall. **Menu** All-you-can-eat barbecue ribs, fried chicken, corn, and strawberry shortcake. **Vegetarian alternative** On request (at least 24 hours in advance). **Beverages** Unlimited beer, wine, sangria, and soft drinks.

DESCRIPTION AND COMMENTS Six Wild West performers arrive by stagecoach (sound effects only) to entertain the crowd inside Pioneer Hall. There isn't much of a plot—just corny jokes interspersed with song or dance. The humor is of the *Hee Haw* ilk, but it's presented enthusiastically.

Audience participation includes sing-alongs, hand clapping, and a finale that uses volunteers to play parts on stage. Performers are accompanied by a banjo player and pianist who also play quietly while the food is being served. The fried chicken and corn on the cob are good, the ribs a bit tough though tasty. With the all-you-can-eat policy, at least you can get your money's worth by stuffing yourself silly.

Traveling to Fort Wilderness and absorbing the rustic atmosphere of Pioneer Hall augments the adventure. For repeat Disney World visitors, an annual visit to the revue is a tradition of sorts. Plus, warts and all, the revue is all Disney, and for some folks that's enough. The fact that performances sell out far in advance gives the experience a special aura.

Boat service may be suspended during thunderstorms, so if it's raining or it looks like it's about to rain, Disney will provide bus service from the parks.

Mickey's Backyard BBQ

Fort Wilderness Campground ☎ 407-939-3463. **Showtimes** Thursday and Saturday at 5, 6:30, and 7 p.m. **Cost** $51–$55 adults, $30–$32 children ages 3–9. Prices include tax and gratuity. **Type of seating** Picnic tables. **Menu** Baked chicken, barbecue pork ribs, burgers, hot dogs, corn, beans, mac-and-cheese, salads and slaw, bread, and watermelon and ice-cream bars for dessert. **Vegetarian alternatives** Available on request. **Beverages** Unlimited beer, wine, lemonade, and iced tea.

DESCRIPTION AND COMMENTS Situated along Bay Lake and held in a covered pavilion next to the site of the old River Country swimming park, *Mickey's Backyard BBQ* features Mickey, Minnie, Chip 'n' Dale, and Goofy, along with a country band and line dancing. Though the pavilion gets some breeze off Bay Lake, we recommend going during the spring or fall, if possible. The food is pretty good, as is, fortunately, the insect control.

The barbecue was previously offered only seasonally, from March through December, but is now year-round. Even so, dates are usually not entered into the WDW-DINE reservations system until about six months in advance. Once the dates are in the system, you can make an Advance Reservation for anytime during the dinner show's season.

The easiest way to get to the barbecue is to take a boat from the Magic Kingdom or from one of the Disney resorts on the Magic Kingdom monorail. Give yourself at least 45 minutes if you plan to arrive by boat. Ferry service may be suspended during thunderstorms, so if it's raining or it looks like it's about to rain, Disney will provide bus service from the parks.

Spirit of Aloha Dinner Show

Disney's Polynesian Resort ☎ 407-939-3463. **Showtimes** Tuesday–Saturday, 5:15 and 8 p.m. **Cost** $59–$72 adults, $30–$37 children ages 3–9. Prices include tax and gratuity. **Discounts** Seasonal. **Type of seating** Long rows of tables, with some separation between individual parties. The show is performed on an outdoor stage, but all seating is covered. Ceiling fans provide some air movement, but it can get warm, especially at the early show. **Menu** Tropical fruit, roasted chicken, island pork ribs, mixed vegetables, rice, and pineapple bread; chicken tenders, PB&J sandwiches, mac-and-cheese, and hot dogs for the kids. **Vegetarian alternatives** Available on request. **Beverages** Beer, wine, and soft drinks.

DESCRIPTION AND COMMENTS This show features South Seas–island native dancing followed by an all-you-can-eat "Polynesian-style" meal. The dancing is interesting and largely authentic, and the dancers are attractive though definitely PG-rated in the Disney tradition. We think the show has its moments and the meal is adequate, but neither is particularly special.

The show follows (tenuously) the common "girl leaves home for the big city, forgets her roots, and must rediscover them" theme. The performers are uniformly attractive ("Studmuffins!" said a female *Unofficial* researcher when asked about the men), and the dancing is very good. The story, however, never really makes sense as anything other than a thread with which to stitch together the musical numbers. Our show lasted for more than 2 hours and 15 minutes.

The food does little more than illustrate how difficult it must be to prepare the same meal for hundreds of people simultaneously. The roasted chicken is better than the ribs, but neither is anything special. We conditionally recommend *Spirit of Aloha* for special occasions, when the people celebrating get to go on stage. But go to the early show and get dessert somewhere else in the World.

APPENDIX

Disney-Speak Pocket Translator

Although it may come as a surprise to many, Walt Disney World has its own somewhat peculiar language. Here are some terms you are likely to bump into:

DISNEY-SPEAK	ENGLISH DEFINITION
ADVENTURE	Ride
ATTRACTION	Ride or theater show
ATTRACTION HOST	Ride operator
AUDIENCE	Crowd
BACKSTAGE	Behind the scenes, out of view of customers
CAST MEMBER	Employee
CHARACTER	Disney character impersonated by an employee
COSTUME	Work attire or uniform
DARK RIDE	Indoor ride
DAY GUEST	Any customer not staying at a Disney resort
FACE CHARACTER	A character who does not wear a head-covering costume (such as Snow White, Cinderella, and Jasmine)
GENERAL PUBLIC	Same as day guest
GREETER	Employee positioned at an attraction entrance
GUEST	Customer

Continued on next page

Disney-Speak Pocket Translator (cont'd.)

DISNEY-SPEAK	ENGLISH DEFINITION
HIDDEN MICKEYS	Frontal silhouette of Mickey's head worked subtly into the design of buildings, railings, vehicles, golf greens, attractions, and the like
ON STAGE	In full view of customers
PRESHOW	Entertainment at an attraction prior to the feature presentation
RESORT GUEST	A customer staying at a Disney resort
ROLE	An employee's job
SOFT OPENING	Opening a park or attraction before its stated opening date
TRANSITIONAL EXPERIENCE	An element of the queuing area and/or pre-show that provides a story line or information essential to understanding the attraction

ACCOMMODATIONS INDEX

Note: Page numbers of profiled hotels are in **boldface** type.

RESTAURANT INDEX

SUBJECT INDEX

2014 *Unofficial Guide* Reader Survey

If you'd like to express your opinion in writing about Walt Disney World or this guidebook, complete the following survey and mail it to:

> *Unofficial Guide* Reader Survey
> P.O. Box 43673
> Birmingham, AL 35243

Or fill out our online survey at **touringplans.com/walt-disney-world/survey**.

Inclusive dates of your visit: _____

Your hometown: _____

Your e-mail address: _____

Members of your party: Person 1   Person 2   Person 3   Person 4   Person 5

Gender: M F   M F   M F   M F   M F

Age: _____   _____   _____   _____   _____

How many times have you been to Walt Disney World? _____

CAR RENTALS Did you rent a car? _____ From what company? _____ Concerning your rental car, on a scale with 5 being best and 1 worst, how would you rate: Pickup-processing efficiency? _____ Return-processing efficiency? _____ Condition of the car? _____ Cleanliness of the car? _____ Airport-shuttle efficiency? _____

LODGING On your most recent WDW trip, where did you stay? _____

Have you stayed at any other hotels in the past 12 months? ❏ Yes ❏ No

Please indicate the hotels you have stayed at in the past year, or write in others.
❏ Ritz-Carlton ❏ Marriott Hyatt ❏ Super 8 ❏ Holiday Inn ❏ Fairfield Inn ❏ Embassy Suites ❏ Omni ❏ Ramada Inn ❏ Days Inn ❏ Hilton ❏ Drury Inn ❏ Millennium ❏ Four Seasons ❏ Radisson ❏ Best Western
Others _____

Please tell us how important the following amenities were in your selection of a Walt Disney World–area resort/hotel. Select up to five amenities, and rank them in order of importance using 1 for the most important and 5 for the least.

Cost____ Bar____ Distance to parks____ In-room dining/room service _____ Food court _____ Shuttle service to parks _____ Sit-down restaurant _____ Room size _____ Fine dining ___ Multiple-bedroom suites _____ Spa/fitness center _____ In-room kitchen _____ Pool _____ Shuttle service to/from airport _____ Architecture/ theme _____ Kids' activity center _____ Location inside WDW _____ On a scale with 5 being best and 1 being worst, please indicate how satisfied you were with your accommodations. Please add other items you feel are important. *When rating food services, please rate only meals eaten at your resort.*

Cleanliness of room _____ Size and layout of pool _____ Comfort of beds and pillows _____ Crowd level at the pool _____ Room size and layout _____ Cleanliness of pool area _____ Quietness of room _____ Shuttle to/from airport _____ Check-in/ out process_____ Shuttle to/from parks_____ Resort staff accessibility, friendliness, and knowledge _____ Recreational amenities (marina, bikes, fitness center, etc.) _____ Overall food-court experience _____ Ability to easily find your way around _____ Overall food-court value _____ Child-care services and facilities _____ Overall experience with the full-service restaurant _____ Overall layout of the resort _____ Overall value of full-service restaurant _____

Please check the number that best describes how satisfied you were with your total resort experience during this trip.

1 Very dissatisfied 2 Somewhat dissatisfied   3 Neither satisfied or dissatisfied
4 Somewhat satisfied   5 Very satisfied

Would you stay at this resort again? Yes ❑ No ❑

How likely are you to recommend this resort to a friend?
❑ Will definitely recommend   ❑ May recommend   ❑ Neutral
❑ Probably won't recommend   ❑ Definitely will not recommend

DINING Concerning your dining experiences:
How many restaurant meals (including fast food) did you average per day?
_____

How much (approximately) did your party spend on meals per day?
_____

Favorite restaurant outside Walt Disney World?
_____

PARK TOURING On a scale with 5 being best and 1 being worst, please rate how the touring plans worked:

PARK	NAME OF PLAN	RATING
Magic Kingdom	_____	
Epcot	_____	
Disney's Animal Kingdom	_____	
DHS	_____	

OTHER How did you hear about this guide? _____
_____

What other guidebooks or websites did you use on this trip?
On the 5-as-best, 1-as-worst scale, how would you rate them?

	NAME	RATING
Guidebooks	_____	
	_____	
websites	_____	
	_____	
	_____	

Using the same scale, how would you rate the *Unofficial Guide*?
Have you used other *Unofficial Guides*? Which ones?
_____

Additional comments you would like to share with us about your Walt Disney World vacation or about the *Unofficial Guide*:
_____
_____
_____
_____
_____
_____
_____
_____